"Scholar, professor, author, former newspaper reporter, maverick, and an advocate of First Amendment rights David Demers has written a ... highly readable and thought-provoking book." –*Lucy Heckman, St. John's University Library, Jamaica, NY*

[Sociologist] "C. Wright Mills defined sociology as the study of intersections between biography and history. By Mills's definition, this book is sociology *par excellence*. ... By tracing and reflecting on his personal initiatives and activities ... , Demers powerfully illuminates the direction of American society." –*Dr. Kenneth Westhues, professor emeritus of sociology, University of Waterloo, Canada, and expert on workplace mobbing*

"*Adventures of a Quixotic Professor* probes the systemic forces of bureaucracy and patterns of faculty co-optation and complicity that undermine, violate, and fail to defend the Enlightenment ideal of free speech. ... Ultimately ... the basic freedoms of us all hinge on the willingness of individuals ... to stand up and speak out. And Demers's tale is of how the freedoms of us all in the academy, and limits thereof, hinge on those who are 'crazy' enough to call colleges and universities, and ourselves, to our publicly expressed ideals." –*Dr. Gary D. Rhoades, former general secretary of the American Association of University Professors and professor of educational policy studies and practice at the University of Arizona*

"This book is ... incredibly well researched and a very interesting, relevant story. ... Demers has a great voice and manages to tell his narrative without sounding holier-than-thou or just someone with a grudge match." –*Amada Scott, librarian, Cambridge Springs Public Library, PA*

"With an approachable and easy style, Dr. Demers uses his life as a means to examine the history of the various sociological theories and trends that have shaped our culture to this day." –*Nancy Barthelemy, archivist, Peabody Institute Library, Peabody, MA*

[This book is] "part biographical study of his own fight for his First Amendment rights while working as a college professor and part background of social science and its application. ... it was very interesting."–*Princess of the Library,* http://princessofthelibrary.wordpress.com

[Law students' and attorneys'] "investigation of cases typically ends with the highest court's holding; here [Demers] provides compelling information about what is going on for the plaintiff during a trial and after. ... [This] book should make law students question whether, and to what extent, hourly rate should control the chance of prevailing on an issue as important as free speech." –*Miles DeCoster, third-year law student, Sandra Day O'Connor College of Law, Arizona State University*

[Demers's] "passionate commitment to being a proponent of change emanates off every page as well as his zest for upholding First Amendment issues." –*Anne M. Miskewitch, librarian, literature and world language department, Harold Washington Library Center, Chicago, IL*

"I loved every minute of this piece ... beautifully written and very interesting." –*Carolyn Walker, book reviewer, Writer's Digest*

"I admire [Demers's] ability to distill some difficult-to-grasp concepts without 'dumbing them down,' ... and [I] laugh at [his] jokes." –*Erin McKnight, senior editor, Kevin Anderson & Associates, New York*

"This was in some ways the most worthwhile manuscript I've ever read — the one that should be published as an expose on academic politics." – *Dr. Cherri Randall, book reviewer, Writer's Digest*

Adventures of a Quixotic Professor

Also by David Demers

*The Ivory Tower of Babel: Why the Social Sciences
    Are Failing to Live up to Their Promises*

The Luminar Papers: A Novel (in press)

History and Future of Mass Media: An Integrated Perspective

*The Rest of the Story: Life and Times of
    Arizona State Senate President Leo F. Corbet Jr.*

*How the Mass Media Really Work: An Introduction to
    Their Role as Institutions of Control and Change*
    With Taehyun Kim and Daniel Erickson

*Jelly Beans & Peanuts: Life and Times of Llewellyn Jenkins,
    an American Banker, Soldier and Family Man*

The Menace of the Corporate Newspaper: Fact or Fiction?

Global Media: Menace or Messiah?

Adventures of a Quixotic Professor

How One Man's Lifelong
Passion for Social Justice
Bristles Bureaucracies and
Sparks a Landmark
Free Speech Ruling

David Demers

Marquette Books LLC
Phoenix, Arizona

Copyright © 2021 MARQUETTE BOOKS LLC

All rights reserved. No part of this publication may be reproduced, stored in a retrieval system, or transmitted in any form or by any means, electronic, mechanical, photocopying, microfilming, recording, or otherwise, without permission of the publisher.

Printed in the United States of America | First Hardcover Edition September 2021

Library of Congress Cataloging-In-Publication Data

Names: Demers, David, 1953- author.
Title: Adventures of a quixotic professor : how one man's lifelong passion for social justice bristles bureaucracies and sparks a landmark free speech ruling / David Demers.
Description: First hardcover edition. | Phoenix, Arizona : Marquette Books LLC 2021. | Includes bibliographical references and indexes. | Summary: "Journalist-turned-media sociology professor David Demers grew up on a steady diet of social justice. His Lutheran elementary school teachers and college professors taught him the importance of democratic processes, speaking out against injustice, free speech, and the public's "right" to know. But when he creates a controversial plan to improve his academic unit, helps students publish some controversial stories, and writes some articles critical of powerful institutions, his organizations reprimand or try to fire him, and his journalism colleagues refuse to defend free speech rights. He is not alone. More than one million professors and K–12 faculty have been fired or reprimanded for things they've said on the job. Two-thirds of journalists also say they self-censor stories about their organizations because they fear the wrath of editors or publishers. Many targets of "workplace mobbing" quit their jobs and spend years in therapy. A few commit suicide. Some, like Demers, fight back with free speech lawsuits. Most lose. Demers wins, but the victories are bittersweet. If university administrators, journalism faculty and journalists fail to defend basic freedoms, he asks, how can society expect other organizations and citizens to defend them? Adventures of a Quixotic Professor will make you laugh, cry and scream for justice as it chronicles the personal costs and social and historical conditions of one man's lifelong fight for social justice – a journey that culminates in a federal appeals court decision [Demers v. Austin (Washington State University)], which, for the first time in history, extends constitutional protection to teachers for on-the-job speech outside of the classroom. Issues covered in this book: Demers v. Austin, workplace mobbing, bureaucratic bandwagon effect, anti-Enlightenment trends, adverse effect of bureaucracies on democratic processes, political impotence of social scientific research; and 40 tips for navigating bureaucratic politics"-- Provided by publisher.
Identifiers: LCCN 2020054449 | ISBN 9781732719798 (hardcover)
Subjects: LCSH: Teaching, Freedom of--United States. | Freedom of speech--United States. | Bullying in the workplace--United States. | Social justice--Study and teaching--United States.
Classification: LCC LC72.2 .D46 2021 | DDC 371.1--dc23
LC record available at https://lccn.loc.gov/2020054449

16421 North 31st Avenue
Phoenix, Arizona 85053
509-290-9240 (voice and text)
www.MarquetteBooks.com
books@marquettebooks.com
Celebrating 20 Years of Service

To my teachers,

Louis Armbrecht
Lee B. Becker
Donald Bird
Hazel Dicken-Garcia
Simon Dinitz
George A. Donohue
Sharon Dunwoody
Richard Lundman
Marco Marcet
Jeylan T. Mortimer
Suzanne Nichols
Edward Roth
Rudolph Schmidt
Henry Schulte
Joseph E. Scott
Phillip J. Tichenor
Margaret Y. Willis

"The reasonable man adapts himself to the world; the unreasonable one persists in trying to adapt the world to himself. Therefore, all progress depends on the unreasonable man."

—George Bernard Shaw

"A nation of sheep will beget a government of wolves."

—Edward R. Murrow

"There may come a time in the career of every sociologist when it is his solemn duty to raise hell."

—Edward A. Ross

Contents

Foreword by Gary Rhoades • xii
Author's Note • xix
Definitions • 2

PART I — FREE SPEECH DILEMMAS

1 — Grumpy Judges and Professors • 3
2 — The Long Drive Home • 9

PART II — FREE SPEECH BULLIES AT UW–RF

3 — A Flag Burning and Cockroaches • 15
4 — Damned Lies & Student Evaluations • 25
5 — 'You've Got No Case' • 37
6 — 'Nothin' But a Troublemaker' • 46

PART III — ANATOMY OF A FREE SPEECH ACTIVIST

7 — Lutherans and Bullies • 54
8 — Enlightenment for Everyone • 61
9 — The Sociological Imagination • 68
10 — The Lottery • 73
11 — Children of the Enlightenment • 76
12 — A Right Turn • 81
13 — A Journalistic Calling • 88
14 — Journalism Daze • 95
15 — The Descent of Journalism • 108
16 — 'More Truth Next Time' • 114
17 — Collective Manipulation • 123
18 — Noam Chomsky and Me • 134

19	–	Are Minneapolis Police Racist? • 140
20	–	Unfair Assessments • 147
21	–	The $64,000 Apology • 156

PART IV – CENSORED IN THE PALOUSE

22	–	Murder in the Palouse • 168
23	–	The Enlightened Journalist • 175
24	–	Censorship, Weak Ties and a Crisis • 187
25	–	Democracy Foiled Again • 192
26	–	An 'Enlightened' Research Program • 199
27	–	Family Matters • 212
28	–	Censored in Spokane • 220
29	–	Post-Tenure Affairs • 225

PART V – WSU'S IVORY TOWER OF BABEL

30	–	Purging the Palouse • 230
31	–	Workplace Mobbing • 240
32	–	Another Undemocratic Search • 246
33	–	My 7-Step Plan • 254
34	–	My Crummy Annual Review • 261
35	–	Murrow School Becomes a College • 265
36	–	More Censorship and Questions • 269
37	–	The Internal Audit Report • 276
38	–	What Happened to the Golden Rule? • 285
39	–	Bayly's Kangaroo Court • 288
40	–	Mediation Blues • 300
41	–	Time to Lawyer Up • 305
42	–	The Envy of Excellence • 312

PART VI – SECRET REPORTS, RULINGS & LESSONS

43	–	*Demers v. Austin* • 318
44	–	The State Auditor's 'Secret' Report • 324
45	–	The Damning Depositions • 328
46	–	A Motion to Dismiss • 339
47	–	An Appeal and Complicit Professors • 348

48 – The Enlightened Appeals Court • 358
49 – Impact of *Demers v. Austin* • 371
50 – Lessons of a Quixotic Professor • 383
Appendix – Essay: Future of the Enlightenment in America • 393
Acknowledgments • 420
Index • 423
Responses from Officials Mentioned in Book • 433
About the Author • 436

Foreword by Gary Rhoades

On September 30, 2010, I received an e-mail from Washington State University professor David Demers, who informed me that WSU administrators had forced as many as 10 tenured faculty to resign because they allegedly received unsatisfactory performance ratings in two or three post-tenure annual reviews.

The forced terminations came to light during a deposition conducted earlier that day as part of Demers's 2009 free speech lawsuit against WSU (*Demers v. Austin*).[1]

At the time, I was general secretary of the American Association of University Professors. I copied two AAUP staff members on the e-mail, who later examined the policy and informed Demers and me that the firings appeared to violate AAUP standards.

Using annual reviews to terminate tenured faculty makes it easier to fire faculty who oppose administrators' policies and actions (more details in Chapter 45). In fact, WSU administrators were using their termination policy to build a case to fire Demers, because, according to the lawsuit, they didn't like the 7-Step Plan he had created to improve the quality of his academic unit, the Edward R. Murrow School (now College) of Communication.

Demers's case illustrates that meaningful shared governance in colleges and

---

Dr. Gary D. Rhoades served as general secretary of the American Association of University Professors in Washington, D.C., from 2009 to 2011, when the free speech lawsuit *Demers v. Austin* (Washington State University) was filed in federal district court in Spokane, Washington. He is a professor of educational policy studies and practice at the University of Arizona and previously served as director of the Center for the Study of Higher Education and head of the Department of Educational Policy Studies and Analysis from July 2012 to July 2020. His books include *Managed Professionals* (SUNY Press, 1998) and *Academic Capitalism and the New Economy* (with Sheila Slaughter, Johns Hopkins University Press, 2004). His current book projects include *Organizing "Professionals": Academic Employees Negotiating a New Academy*.

universities depends upon the First Amendment right of free speech. That is a core analytical point of this compelling social memoir.

Adventures of a Quixotic Professor also probes the systemic forces of bureaucracy and patterns of faculty co-optation and complicity that undermine, violate, and fail to defend the Enlightenment ideal of free speech. Indeed, the *Demers v. Austin* Ninth Circuit Court of Appeals ruling offers a counterpoint to *Garcetti v. Ceballos* (2006), a U.S. Supreme Court decision that deprived public employees of free speech rights on the job. Some public universities in 41 states still invoke that decision to discipline and/or terminate faculty who have been critical of their administrations.

The *Demers* ruling established that faculty speech related to scholarship or teaching is covered by the First Amendment in public universities and colleges. The ruling also applies to K–12 faculty, but it covers only the nine Western states that make up the Ninth Circuit. The ruling does not protect faculty or teachers who work in private and proprietary educational institutions. The Ninth Circuit declared that professors as academic citizens may speak in the course of their duties about institutional matters openly and without fear of retaliation.

Remarkably, Washington State University invoked *Garcetti v Ceballos* — contrary to the university's own written policy embracing academic freedom and free speech rights — arguing that Demers's speech, articulated in the course of his duties, was not protected by the First Amendment. Even more remarkably, the WSU Faculty Senate did not come to Demers's defense.

Demers's book unabashedly offers an academic morality play embedded in the individualism of the Enlightenment Project, as he calls it, but embodied in the pre-Enlightenment character and idealism of Miguel Cervantes's heroic errant knight, Don Quixote. Demers offers a call to action for individuals to "do the right thing" (with a nod to Spike Lee). By that, he means that individuals should take on universities (and other powerful institutions) that deny them basic rights and thereby do them and academia harm. Throughout and in closing his book, Demers provides analysis and advice to individuals if they take on their universities. The tribulations and costs are high and are clearly laid out and detailed. Ultimately, though, Demers is a hopeful idealist, closing his book with this line: "I still believe one person can make a difference. Quixotic, I know."

As someone who has studied and has worked in various ways and venues to support meaningful shared governance and an independent voice for employees in academe, I, for one, am grateful to Demers for his hopeful idealism, and for his commitment and work culminating in the Court of Appeals decision. Indeed, all in academe should be as well, for his successful case defends a fundamental right that is at the core of higher education through meaningful shared governance: debate, challenge, and calling of higher education institutions to their publicly expressed values.

But this book is about more than this one legal case.

I appreciated and enjoyed Demers's stage-setting tale of his quixotic journey throughout his educational and professional careers leading up to that point. It provided a personal context and analytical grounding to more fully understand his lawsuit.

The *Demers v. Austin* case is briefly addressed in the first two chapters that foreshadow the later, fuller discussion of events that led up to the lawsuit and decision. These chapters serve as hook and tension-setter for what is to come. Four ensuing chapters further set the stage for Demers's academic activism, covering his time as an assistant professor of journalism at the University of Wisconsin, River Falls (UW–RF). That tale foreshadows Demers's commitment to and accomplishments on behalf of free speech and open public records. And it offers additional examples of management's resistance to those Enlightenment ideals, as well as to the failure of other faculty, individually and collectively, to support their colleague's principled battle.

In the third part of Demers's book, chapters take the reader through his educational experiences in (Lutheran) school and college. The story of this quixotic journey is fittingly grounded in Demers's coming to understand the value of free speech and civil liberties and of the power and importance of the individual as part of the "Enlightenment ideal." The journey is an interesting and varied one through Demers's work as a journalist, his times as an undergraduate and a master's student, a few years working in marketing, and then back to doctoral work in mass communication.

Throughout, the story centers on and is fittingly grounded in sociological and philosophical books and ideas that informed his development. One of those books included C. Wright Mills's *Sociological Imagination* (1959), which emphasizes the importance of intersecting personal biography with public history to fully understand the times.[2] That is precisely what Demers's book offers.

All of us in the academy (and beyond, perhaps especially in journalism) should be glad of the hopeful idealism and dogged persistence of Demers and of others like him. Why? Because one of the most common reasons underlying academic freedom cases investigated by the AAUP over the years has been that faculty were dismissed for criticizing administrators. Such a pattern undermines not just academic freedom, but also meaningful shared governance processes. The whole point of faculty involvement in such processes is for them to be able to express their ideas freely without fear of retaliation or retribution.

Sadly, though, far too often such fear of retaliation leads far too many faculty to remain silent, as was the case in Demers's situation, especially at WSU, as detailed in the remaining chapters of the book. That fear is all the more structurally embedded for adjunct and full-time contingent faculty (largely unaddressed in Demers's book), who frequently have little to no employment security and limited due process claims. So, too, with graduate student employees and postdocs, as well as staff of whom many are "at will" employees, which is to say that they are at the caprice, or whim, of their employers.

And perhaps at least as sadly, that fear and (worse) complicity define too many of the tenured professors (disproportionately white and male) who are part of formal shared governance processes. That is what I have witnessed and heard in my travels to campuses around the country as AAUP general secretary, in my research, and in several decades of involvement with organized academic labor nationally and with various local bargaining units and organizing campaigns. Fear of retaliation from managers is an all-too-common sentiment. And it is part of colleges' and universities' "disastrous path of disaster academic capitalism,"[3] undermining the academy's service to public responsibilities and public goods.

Yet, ironically, one of the most commonly invoked and least commonly exercised ideals in the academy is that of meaningful shared governance, even for tenure-stream faculty. In its classic 1966 "Statement on College and University Government," the AAUP established and has subsequently defended and advanced this ideal.[4] At the time, the statement was "commended" by the Association of Governing Boards (AGB) and by the American Council on Education. In a series of subsequent statements and reports, AGB has modified the idea to some extent, including emphasizing the need to incorporate contingent faculty in shared governance structures, but the basic idea and value of shared governance are still consistently invoked.[5] Moreover, in surveys of and statements by presidents, provosts, deans, and managerial associations, shared governance is consistently and positively invoked as an important value.

Unfortunately, that ideal of free speech, of academic freedom in speech about institutional matters and in shared governance, is honored more in the abstract than in practice. And the imminent, existential threat to that ideal identified by *Demers*, in the *Garcetti v Ceballos* Supreme Court case, is quite real.

When I became general secretary of the AAUP in January 2009, its Committee A had just appointed in November 2008 a subcommittee to address "academic freedom after *Garcetti v Ceballos.*" The title of the report, "Protecting an Independent Faculty Voice" (issued at the end of 2009), says it all. Indeed, the AAUP had filed an amicus brief in that case, speaking to the threat it posed for faculty if the ruling was to be applied to higher education settings (the case was about public sector officials). Indeed, as Demers details in his book (Chapter 46), not only the dissent by Justice David Souter but also the majority opinion by Justice Anthony M. Kennedy offered important wording excluding faculty: "We need not ... decide whether the analysis we conduct today would apply in the same manner to a case involving speech related to scholarship or teaching."

As Demers also details, the phrasing of "related to" would prove critical, because it extended First Amendment protections beyond classroom teaching and research to institutional matters. The AAUP report offered examples of language that could and should be included in faculty handbooks and collective bargaining agreements emphasizing that academic freedom extended to speech about institutional matters without fear of retaliation. As Demers notes, such language was adopted in the handbooks and collective bargaining agreements of some major universities such as Michigan, Minnesota, and Delaware. Indeed, the AAUP launched a national campaign after the release of the report, "Speak Up, Speak Out: Protect the Faculty Voice on Campus."[6]

The concerns and the AAUP campaign were well justified. Demers rightly indicates that in the four years after *Garcetti v. Ceballos*, courts on seven occasions invoked that case in denying free speech rights of faculty whose disciplining universities claimed their speech was uttered in the course of their official duties. As one of AAUP's national leaders, historian Larry Gerber, has written, we have been witnessing for some decades "the rise and decline of faculty governance."[7] Political scientist Benjamin Ginsberg placed part of the blame on the excessive hiring of administrators who have little or no teaching or scholarly research experience.[8]

Notably, and sadly, the Washington State University Faculty Senate was silent on Demers's case and offered no support. Certainly, threats to academic freedom from external groups and individuals are real and consequential. Just as true, though, is a variation on the classic phrase from the comic strip *Pogo*, "We have met the enemy and they are us."[9] In Demers's words, we should be attentive to "the enemy within." That is part of the value of his detailed rendering of the ways bureaucracy, academic mobbing, and complicity and passivity undermine our academic freedoms.

As Demers relates, amidst such patterns in the academy, those who speak out, like himself, tend to get labeled as "troublemakers," not just by some administrators, but also by some colleagues and by those who may be supportive of academic freedom in the abstract — even when the trouble being made is "good trouble," in the words of the famed civil rights leader John Lewis. The reference to groups like the AAUP and to broader structural patterns, campaigns and social movements is important. It is in their context that the idealism, commitment, and heroism of individuals can translate into making a difference.

Ultimately, though, basic freedoms hinge on the willingness of individuals to stand up and speak out. And Demers's tale shows how the freedoms of us all in the academy, and limits thereof, hinge on those who are "crazy" enough to call colleges and universities, and ourselves, to our publicly expressed ideals. What came to my mind in reading Demers's accessible and readable book was a famous scene in from Dale Wasserman's 1966 musical play, *Man of La Mancha*, when Cervantes, in prison, is responding to the Duke on "life as it should be."[10]

> *The Duke:* Why are you poets so fascinated with madmen?
>
> *Cervantes:* I suppose ... we have much in common.
>
> *The Duke:* You both turn your backs on life.
>
> *Cervantes:* We both select from life what pleases us.
>
> *The Duke:* A man must come to terms with life as it is!
>
> *Cervantes:* I have lived nearly 50 years, and I have seen life as it is. Pain, misery, hunger. ... cruelty beyond belief. I have heard the singing from taverns and the moans from the bundles of filth in the street. I have been a soldier and seen my comrades fall in battle ... or die more slowly under the lash in Africa. I have held them in my arms at the final moment. These were men who saw life as it is, yet they died despairing. No glory, no gallant last words ... only their eyes, filled with confusion, whimpering the question: "Why?" I do not think they asked why they were dying, but why they had lived. When life itself seems lunatic, who knows where madness lies? Perhaps to be too practical is madness. To surrender dreams — this may be madness; to seek treasure where there is only trash. Too much sanity may be madness — and maddest of all — to see life as it is, and not as it should be!

May we all recognize that the struggle for our freedoms, whether in academe or relatedly in broader society, lies in individually and collectively challenging and transforming structures that oppress those freedoms. Demers's book calls on us to take on that struggle in defense of what he calls the "Enlightenment ideal" of free speech in advancing meaningful shared governance. I echo that call now, as I did as AAUP general secretary in 2010, and encourage AAUP members and others to take up this struggle for academic freedom and meaningful shared governance, as part of AAUP's "Speak Up, Speak Out" campaign: "[I]t is time again for faculty not to submit to 'new realities' but to shape them, with our voices. If we act together, we have the opportunity to influence the future of higher education. If we do not exercise our voice, we lose it, and in the process, society loses."[11]

Academic freedoms, like all civil and human rights, are like muscles. If you don't exercise them, they atrophy. My thanks, then, to David Demers for exercising his academic freedom muscle.

Gary Rhoades
Professor of Higher Education
University of Arizona

Foreword Endnotes

1. *Demers v. Austin,* 746 F.3d 402 (9th Cir., January 29, 2014).
2. C. Wright Mills, *The Sociological Imagination* (New York: Oxford University Press, 1959).
3. Sheila Slaughter and Gary Rhoades, *Academic Capitalism and the New Economy: Markets, State, and Higher Education* (Baltimore: The Johns Hopkins University Press, 2004).
4. American Association of University Professors, *Policy Documents and Reports, Eleventh Edition* (Baltimore: The Johns Hopkins University Press, 2015).
5. Association of Governing Boards of Universities and Colleges, *AGB Statement on Institutional Governance* (Washington, D.C.: 1998); Association of Governing Boards of Universities and Colleges, *Statement on Board Responsibility for Institutional Governance* (Washington, D.C.: 2010); and Association of Governing Boards of Universities and Colleges, *Consequential Governance: Adding Value Where it Matters the Most* (Washington, D.C.: 2014).
6. American Association of University Professors, "Protecting an Independent Faculty Voice: Academic Freedom after *Garcetti v. Ceballos,*" AAUP Report (November/December 2009), retrieved February 3, 2021, from <https://www.aaup.org/NR/rdonlyres/B3991F98-98D5-4CC0-9102-ED26A7AA2892/0/Garcetti.pdf>.
7. Larry Gerber, *The Rise and Decline of Faculty Governance: Professionalization and the Modern American University* (Baltimore: The Johns Hopkins University Press, 2014).
8. Benjamin Ginsberg, *The Fall of the Faculty: The Rise of the All-Administrative University and Why It Matters* (New York: Oxford University Press, 2011).
9. In 1970, cartoonist Walt Kelly originally wrote, "We have met the enemy, and he is us" — an aphorism with a slight twist on United States Navy Commodore Oliver Hazard Perry's 1813 naval victory, which ended with the word "ours" instead of "us." Many writers also change the pronoun/verb "he is" to "they are."
10. Dale Wasserman (book), Joe Darion (lyrics), and Mitch Leigh (music), *Man of La Mancha: A Musical Play* (New York: Random House, 1966), pp. 60-61.
11. Gary Rhoades, "From the General Secretary: A Faculty Voice," *Academe, 96*(1): 55 (January-February 2010), p. 55.

Author's Note

When I presented in 2007 a controversial plan to improve my academic program at Washington State University, administrators tried to fire me.

I was not alone.

More than one million professors and K–12 schoolteachers at public institutions have been fired or reprimanded during the past century for saying things their administrators didn't like.[1] Among the recent list of victims were two engineering professors, one from Idaho who tried to save his department from an internal merger[2] and another from California who condemned the hiring of too many part-time faculty.[3]

Many faculty who are targets of administrative "workplace mobbing" quit their jobs and spend years in therapy.

A few commit suicide.[4]

Some, like me, fight back and file free speech lawsuits.

Most lose.[5]

I was fortunate.

In 2014, the Ninth Circuit Court of Appeals issued a landmark ruling in *Demers v. Austin* that extended constitutional protection to on-the-job service-related speech, sometimes called "shared governance" speech.[6] Federal courts have long held that private (off-the-job) speech and speech in the classroom and in scholarship at public universities deserve broad protection.[7] But this was the first time in history a court has protected faculty speech uttered outside of the classroom on issues of public concern related to scholarship or teaching, which includes comments about the structuring of academic programs. The two professors mentioned above likely would have won their cases had they been adjudicated after *Demers*.

The ruling, however, covers only nine states in the West.[8]

As of this writing, the other 41 states have no constitutional protection for service-related speech.[9] This means faculty in public university and K–12 school systems can be fired for simply raising concerns about administrative policies.[10]

Tenure cannot protect them, because the U.S. Supreme Court ruled in 2006 that public employees are not entitled to free speech while on the job.[11]

One of the goals of this book is to increase awareness of the lack of free speech protection for these 41 states.[12] My hope is that federal courts in those jurisdictions will follow the precedent set in *Demers*. A democracy cannot thrive if its teachers are muzzled, especially when it comes to issues of public concern related to scholarship or teaching.[13]

In addition to covering the legal issues surrounding *Demers v. Austin*, this book examines five more social problems: workplace mobbing, the bureaucratic bandwagon effect, anti-Enlightenment trends, the adverse effect of bureaucracies on democratic processes, and the political impotence of social scientific research. (See details in the table on next page.) Each of these problems could be a book unto itself, but all five are explored together here, because each played a role in the personal, social, and historical conditions that led up to the *Demers* ruling.

This social memoir draws its legitimacy in part from the late sociologist C. Wright Mills, who argued that "no social study that does not come back to the problems of biography, of history and of their intersections within a society has completed its intellectual journey."[14] He called this the "sociological imagination," which explores how culture and social and historical events and conditions influence the personal choices of social actors (individuals and organizations) and how those choices in turn influence (or not) other social actors.

My decision to file a free speech lawsuit against WSU stems in large part from the values, ideals and principles I acquired from teachers in my Lutheran elementary school and from my college professors, who also emphasized the ideals of free speech and the Age of Enlightenment.

I confess that I carried into adulthood a quixotic view of the world — one that shares some common ground with Cervantes's fictional character Don Quixote, who embarks on a mission to restore chivalry and goodness to Spain. Quixote's idealism (or madness) leads him into a number of misadventures, including battles with imagined rather than real adversaries (hence the phrase "tilting at windmills").

As a newspaper reporter and journalism and mass media sociology professor, I, too, embarked on a few missions to protect and advance ideals associated with free speech and civil liberties — ideals that I thought were widely shared among journalists and academics. I was surprised, though, to encounter a fair amount of backlash or indifference from editors, university administrators, professors, and journalists.

I attribute much of this resistance to two factors.

The first is rule-driven structural constraints of bureaucratic systems, which need compliant employees rather than those who raise concerns about the wisdom

Issues and Social Problems Examined in This Book

1. *Demers v. Austin*. This Ninth Circuit Court of Appeals case was the first in the nation to provide constitutional protection for faculty speech outside of the classroom. It protects shared governance on issues of public concern. In other words, faculty are allowed to criticize administrative policies and decisions without fear of reprisal, with the exception of criticism that severely disrupts the organization's ability to achieve its educational goals.

2. *Workplace Mobbing*. Public universities and school systems are highly susceptible to workplace mobbing, because tenured faculty have a right to due process and that makes it difficult to fire them.[15] But workplace mobbing is not unique to the field of education. Any organization — large or small, public or private — can engage in mobbing, which is characterized by attempts to harass workers or members until they quit or are forced out. Although I have no formal training in the study of workplace mobbing, I have a lot of personal experience, and I'll review some of the research in this growing field of study.[16]

3. *Bureaucratic Bandwagon*. I also have a lot of experience with what I call the "bureaucratic bandwagon effect." This condition appears when people with high moral standards suspend their beliefs to support an organizational goal or an elite position that contradicts those beliefs. The bandwagon effect is so strong that I've seen First Amendment scholars — people who have defended free speech ideals all of their lives — actively work to deny faculty and students free speech rights. Organizational rewards, such as pay increases and promotions, often play a role in co-opting such people. But an even stronger factor, I believe, is the need to be loved and accepted. People fear social isolation in the workplace.

4. *Anti-Enlightenment Trends*. Despite the *Demers* decision, there is a growing anti-Enlightenment trend in America that poses a major threat to the core values that defined this country, which include free speech, democracy, due process, and equality. This trend is driven in large part by anti-intellectual and reactionary political movements in America, which embrace social control over social tolerance and call for the infusion of dogma into politics. But university administrators also are partly responsible. They are monetizing their institutions, which means downsizing or eliminating non-profit-generating units that historically have played key roles in defending and promoting Enlightenment ideals. The most vulnerable disciplines are housed in the humanities, social sciences, and the library sciences. This includes journalism, English, philosophy, history, sociology and foreign languages. Enrollments, degrees, and number of faculty and programs have declined in either actual or relative terms or both over the past two or three decades.[17]

5. *Anti-Democratic Bureaucratic Problem*. The growth of the bureaucratic form of organization also is driving the anti-Enlightenment trend, because it discourages democratic processes and individual initiative. Bureaucracies can be democratized, but the leaders of such organizations — who include scholarly administrators who teach the value of democracy in their classes — have shown little interest in decentralizing power.

6. *Political Impotence of Social Science*. Although social scientists have been very effective in generating knowledge about society, they have had a very limited impact on the public policymaking process, according to a large body of research in public policy administration[18] as well as my personal experience. Policymakers routinely ignore such research unless it supports their policies or interests. I have characterized the political impotence problem as an "ivory tower of babel."[19] A major goal of universities is to produce knowledge that solves social problems, but ironically they usually do not reward faculty who produce scholarship that attempts to influence the public policymaking process. This hampers the Enlightenment project.

of administrative decisions and policies. The second is an administrative lack of commitment to free speech, civil liberties and democratic ideals.

In the end, Quixote regains his realism (or sanity) and dies without achieving his goal of reforming a corrupt world. The "jury" is still out on the question of whether any of my actions have produced any lasting social change and whether I am better characterized as quixotic nutcase or a progressive reformer (or perhaps a little of both). You, the reader, are free to judge.

In the final chapter of this book (Chapter 50), I provide a list of 40 lessons I learned from my experiences. These are meant to be generalities, not laws. Every situation has a different set of conditions that may or may not lend themselves to these expectations. What I'm trying to say is this: Be careful before you challenge a powerful bureaucracy or group. Although our culture embraces individualism in the ideal, our institutions operate as collectives that embrace social order.

The Appendix contains my "Essay on the Future of the Enlightenment in America." My position might be described as taking the middle ground between the highly optimistic view of Harvard University professor Steven Pinker (author of *Enlightenment Now*) and the semi-pessimistic anomie-driven concerns of cultural theorists. In my view, the deleterious effects of the Enlightenment would be eased substantially if public policy were driven more by knowledge than by the avaricious demands of political and economic elites and special interests.

Although various theories and scholarly ideas are explored in this book, my goal was to minimize the jargon in order to appeal to an audience larger than my scholarly colleagues. I have argued elsewhere that social scientists have spent too much time in the ivory tower, which has adversely affected their ability to influence citizens and the public policymaking process.[20]

Thus, the primary markets for this book include these eight groups: (1) faculty and administrators at public universities and K–12 school systems, (2) sociologists and their students, (3) journalists and mass communication scholars and their students, (4) lawyers and legal scholars, (5) free speech advocates and civil libertarian organizations, (6) political scientists and historians, (7) librarians, and (8) readers who are curious about what happens when one individual stands his ground against billion-dollar bureaucracies (the "individual v. collective problem").

ALL INDIVIDUALS named and associated with controversies identified in this book were provided with drafts of this manuscript and were invited to provide criticisms and comments. Their responses are printed verbatim at the end of this book and at <www.MarquetteBooks.com/response.html>. Pseudonyms are used for some individuals. Real names are used for public officials and public figures.

Author's Note Endnotes

1. No precise estimates are available, because faculty are often reprimanded behind closed doors and sometimes without their knowledge. But if each of the 1,600 public universities and 98,000 public schools in the United States had only one case during each decade in the twentieth century, the total number of cases would exceed one million. A list of prominent free speech cases in which professors were targeted for dismissal can be found under the "Academic Freedom" listing at Wikipedia <https://en.wikipedia.org/wiki/Academic_freedom#The_Lane_Rebels>. Communication Professor Steve Martin of Ripon University in Wisconsin has compiled a list of 36 cases involving university professors that, along with the two mentioned in this Preface, made news in their communities. For every case that makes news, there no doubt is another ten or hundred that never do.

2. *Sadid v. Idaho State Univ.*, Case No. 4:11-cv-00103-BLW (D. Idaho Dec. 10, 2013).

3. *Hong v. Grant*, 403 Fed. Appx. 236 (9th Cir. 2010). Juan Hong was a professor of chemical engineering at the University of California, Irvine.

4. Conservative criminology professor Mike Adams of the University of North Carolina in Wilmington committed suicide in 2020 after he was forced to retire over a controversial tweet. Adams had tweeted about the statewide COVID-19 crackdown on dining as he ate and drank with six men: "I almost felt like a free man who was not living in the slave state of North Carolina." He added, "Massa (Governor Roy) Cooper, let my people go!" More than 60,000 people signed a petition asking the university to fire him for his tweet. Adams previously had published two books criticizing political correctness on campus. The university tried to fire him once, but he sued and the courts ruled that his speech was private rather than job-related (see *Adams v. Trustees of the University of North Carolina–Wilmington*, 640 F.3d 550, 4th Cir. 2011). He was granted tenure and back pay. For details on his suicide, see Ian Miles Cheong, "Woke Media Celebrates Suicide of Professor Who Was Fired for Controversial Tweet," The Post Millenial (July 26, 2020), retrieved September 22, 2020, from <https://thepostmillennial.com/woke-media-celebrates-suicide-professor-fired-controversial-tweet>.

5. Popular culture extols the virtues of individualism in America, but the reality is that collectives, such as bureaucracies and corporations, have tremendous power over individuals. The courts historically have been very reluctant to second-guess public bureaucracies when it comes to employment matters. *Demers v. Austin* is the exception rather than rule.

6. *Demers v. Austin*, 746 F.3d 402 (9th Cir., January 29, 2014). This ruling replaced the original ruling of the panel, which was handed down on September 4, 2013. The major difference between the rulings is that the final one added a section title "'Speech Related to Scholarship or Teaching' Under Garcetti." The ruling cited 11 paragraphs verbatim from the 7-Step Plan to emphasize that the plan dealt with issues related to "scholarship or teaching."

7. Private universities, like private employers in general, are not constitutionally prohibited from terminating professors for their speech, but most do offer contractual protection (through faculty manuals) for speech related to scholarship or teaching. Some also protect speech that criticizes or challenges university administrators.

8. The states within the Ninth Circuit include Alaska, Arizona, California, Idaho, Hawaii, Nevada, Montana, Oregon, and Washington. Also included are the territories of Guam and Northern Mariana Islands.

9. The states not included in the Ninth Circuit are governed by *Garcetti v. Ceballos*, 547 U.S. 410 (2006), which held that public employees have no constitutional protection for on-the-job speech. To date, faculty in those areas have only won federal court cases when their speech was determined to be private, not on-the-job. A detailed analysis of *Garcetti* is provided later in this book.

10. Of course, most administrators tolerate dissent from faculty. Some even welcome such criticism. But there are many exceptions to the rule, and there are lots of ways for administrators to punish faculty without a formal accounting of their actions.

11. *Garcetti v. Ceballos*, 547 U.S. 410 (2006).

12. This book is a substantial revision and theoretical refinement of an earlier manuscript, titled *The Lonely Activist*, that had limited distribution. The major theme in the current volume is that America has abandoned its commitment to Age of Enlightenment ideals, especially with respect to political and economic power (democracy and economic equity). The essay at the end of this book expands upon this theme, using as evidence the anecdotes and social scientific evidence presented in the 50 chapters that precede it.

13. The third principle of the National Education Association is democracy. "We believe public education is the cornerstone of our republic. Public education provides individuals with the skills to be involved, informed, and engaged in our representative democracy." Retrieved from the NEA website October 5, 2020, at <https://www.nea.org/about-nea/mission-vision-values>.

14. C. Wright Mills, *The Sociological Imagination* (New York: Oxford University Press, 1959), p. 6.

15. Four states have abolished tenure for public schoolteachers: Florida, Indiana, North Carolina, and Kansas. But union contracts with school systems often provide due process for teachers.

16. I will examine the research of Dr. Kenneth Westhues, professor emeritus of sociology, University of Waterloo, Canada. See Chapters 31 and 42.

17. Alex Berezow, "Humanities Enrollment Is in Free Fall," *American Council on Science and Health* (July 31, 2018), retrieved October 21, 2020, from <https://www.acsh.org/news/2018/07/31/humanities-enrollment-free-fall-13243>; James S. House, "The Culminating Crisis of American Sociology and Its Role in Social Science and Public Policy: An Autobiographical, Multimethod, Reflexive Perspective," *The Annual Review of Sociology, 45*: 1-26 (2019), retrieved November 2, 2020, from <https://www.annualreviews.org/doi/pdf/10.1146/annurev-soc-073117-041052>; and Andrew Albanese, "Are Public Libraries in Decline? In The Freckle Report 2020, Tim Coates offers a sobering, data-driven view of the state of public libraries in the U.S. and the U.K.," *Publishers Weekly* (April 3, 2020), retrieved November 2, 2020, from <https://www.publishersweekly.com/pw/by-topic/industry-news/libraries/article/82925-are-public-libraries-in-decline.html>.

18. Much of this research is summarized in David Demers, *The Ivory Tower of Babel: Why the Social Sciences Are Failing to Live Up to Their Promises* (New York: Algora Publishing, 2011).

19. Ibid.

20. Ibid.

Part I

Free Speech Dilemmas

Definitions

Quixotic
Exceedingly idealistic, unrealistic and impractical

Academic freedom
A scholar's freedom to express ideas without interference

Civil liberties
Freedom from interference in one's pursuits, such as freedoms of expression, religion and assembly, and the legal right of due process

Enlightenment
A broad philosophy of thought that embraces freedom (over collectivism); reason (over dogma, superstition and traditionalism); civil liberties, including freedom of speech, the press, and religion; political equality; economic equity; progress; separation of church and state; democratic decision-making; decentralized power; due process; and governmental accountability

Workplace mobbing
Physical or emotional abuse to force someone out of the workplace through intimidation, humiliation, discrediting, and isolation

Chapter 1

Grumpy Judges and Professors

Wednesday, November 7, 2012
Seattle, Washington

The morning of my appeals court hearing has arrived, and I feel like barfing.

I've got that god-awful acidic taste in my throat, which means I'm one step away from the painful involuntary stomach convulsions and the surge of clumpy porridge that brings on the sense of asphyxiation.

Normally I can handle a lot of stress.

But this morning isn't normal.

The hearing in Seattle before a three-judge panel of the Ninth Circuit Court of Appeals will determine whether the First Amendment protects a 7-Step Plan I created to improve the quality of the Edward R. Murrow College of Communication at Washington State University, where I teach. If the court denies protection, then professors and schoolteachers in nine Western states will have no constitutional protection for speech that questions, among other things, the wisdom of administrators' policies and decisions.[1]

The hearing also will determine whether I, a tenured journalism professor and mass media sociologist in the Murrow College, will be forced out of my job and into bankruptcy. I have accumulated more than $350,000 in legal fees, which is five times greater than my annual salary.

How will I support my family if I lose?

I am so stressed that I pop a beta blocker to block the flow of adrenaline and the emotional state commonly called "stage fright." A colleague once told me that blood-pressure medications are more popular than sex among artists, musicians and actors. I find that hard to believe, because most of the performing artists I know are sex fiends, and a beta blocker is the foe of a good stiff one. I know these things, because I'm a social scientist with participant-observation experience.

I brush my teeth, shave, and shower.

The beta blocker is working.

My heart rate is down.

The butterflies are resting.

I'm more confident but not cocky enough to put on a multicolored progressive tie that could offend the three elderly white male judges presiding over this hearing. I play it safe and don a conservative navy-and-red-striped tie and match it with a light blue oxford shirt, tan slacks and a snappy dark blue sport coat.

Not too rich looking; not too poor.

J. C. Penney right.

It's raining and 43 degrees as I make the short drive from my hotel in downtown Seattle to a parking garage near the William K. Nakamura Courthouse. Court opens at nine, seventy-five minutes from now. I'm meeting my attorney, Judith Endejan of Graham & Dunn, for breakfast at Tulio, an upscale Italian restaurant located on Fifth Avenue, adjacent to the courthouse.

Judy arrives right on time in a dark blue pantsuit — garb that is sure to keep the judges' minds on the case and not her attire. We begin our conversation with complaints about the weather, because that's what people in Seattle do all winter long. Then she gives me a copy of her prepared notes, printed on a yellow legal pad.

"Is the organization of this presentation okay?" she asks, looking at me through radiant azure eyes that convey a gentle but sure-footed manner. Judy is about my age, 59, though I think she's smarter than me. I often feel that about other people, but it doesn't bother me. What bothers me are smart people who fail to use their intelligence. Judy's not one of them.

"You might want to reduce the background information a bit in case the judges cut you off," I suggest. Although I'm no expert on how to argue a case before an appeals court, I have watched a lot of courtroom TV dramas.

"Good suggestion," she says, adjusting her reading glasses. "Did we miss anything?"

"I don't think so. Nice job."

"You nervous?" she asks.

"Of course. And you?"

"No," she declares.

But I suspect she's a little nervous, too. After all, it's not every day that a First Amendment attorney has the privilege of appearing before the second-most powerful court system in the land, second only to the U.S. Supreme Court.

I can tell she's excited.

That calms me.

We walk half a block through the drizzle and enter the 10-story courthouse, which was built just before World War II. The floors are polished starburst-patterned terrazzo with shades of brown and beige. The walls are surfaced with turquoise, mustard and salmon terra cotta panels. Stepped coffers accent the ceilings. The architecture is art deco, a style that symbolically reflects an unwavering faith in social progress. My free speech lawsuit is a form of social progress, too — a call for decentralization of political power, because it asserts faculty have the right to criticize administrators' policies, a process commonly known as "shared governance."

Judy and I ride the elevator to the second floor, and shortly after entering the courtroom, the defendants' state-appointed assistant attorney general, Kathryn M. Battuello, greets us with a professional smile and handshake. I smile, too, but am disingenuous. It's hard for me to respect attorneys who argue against free speech rights, especially in the name of the state.

The legal brief she filed with the court maintains that I do not deserve First Amendment protection because my 7-Step Plan was penned in my role as a public employee, not as a citizen. The plan recommended, among other things,[2] that the Murrow College seek national accreditation for the print journalism and other mass media programs and remove the communication studies program from the college.

To back up the university's argument, the brief cited a 2006 U.S. Supreme Court decision in which the 5-4 conservative majority held that public employees have no free speech rights on the job, even when they find corruption among supervisors.[3] The plaintiff in the case was a prosecuting attorney who learned that police had fabricated information to obtain a search warrant. When his boss refused to correct the problem, the attorney filed a lawsuit. The high court basically said that it is better to control governmental employees than to root out government corruption. A bad decision.

Although Battuello's legal strategy casts the university and her four WSU administrative defendants as foes of free speech, a federal district court judge in Spokane followed precedent in June 2011 and threw my case out of court.[4] Today's hearing will determine whether that judge's decision was constitutional and whether I am entitled to collect damages and attorney fees if I win.

Promptly at nine the three black-robed judges enter the courtroom from a door that blends into the wall behind their seats. Three or four other court cases are scheduled before mine. Time drags, giving me another chance to perseverate on the wisdom of my decision to file the lawsuit three years ago.

"You're crazy," some colleagues and attorneys advised me at the time. "The university is too powerful. It will destroy you and your career."

"Even if you win, you may not even be able to recover your legal costs. How are you going to support your daughter?"

"Who really cares about your case? Twenty years from now, no one will care."

I console myself with advice offered by Izzy Stone, an investigative reporter and champion of civil liberties who uncovered corruption and abuse of power in American political and business institutions from the 1940s to the early 1970s: "The only kinds of fights worth fighting are those you are going to lose, because somebody has to fight them and lose and lose and lose until someday, somebody who believes as you do wins. ... You mustn't feel like a martyr. You've got to enjoy it."[5]

Very reassuring words except that, to be honest, I wasn't having much fun. I'd rather win now than become a de facto member of the Joan of Arc club.

When my case is called,[6] Judy leads me to the left side of the inner court area, where I sit in one of the chairs in front of a railing that separates the inner court area from the gallery. Battuello sits at a table on the right side. None of her four administrative-defendant clients show up. This surprises me. Did they feel confident they would win and thus their presence would do little to help their case? Or were they ashamed to show up at a hearing in which their lawyer takes a position opposed to free speech rights for faculty?

The three judges avoid any eye contact with me. I wonder if they are ever haunted by the eyes of those they rule against.

Judy speaks first, because I am appealing the lower-court ruling.

She gets off to a great start.[7]

"This case is not about a petty personality conflict instigated by a lazy disgruntled professor, as the administration would have you believe. Rather, this case is about a professor with a deeply felt view that the First Amendment should protect a professor's speech." She adds that I deserve protection because I submitted the 7-Step Plan as a citizen, on my personal business stationery,[8] not in my role as a government employee. But our legal brief argues that my speech is protected even if I submitted it as an employee.

Several minutes later, the lead judge, William A. Fletcher, interrupts Judy.

My heart skips a beat.

"I have trouble — speaking only for myself — treating that 7-Step Plan as clearly private speech," says Fletcher, who was appointed to the court by Bill Clinton in 1998. "[I]t originates when he is a member of a committee. It's clearly undertaken in tight relationship to his job and the things that he cares about in his job. He is suggesting an important restructuring of two departments. I mean, I have trouble seeing that as purely private speech."

Fletcher's demeanor is pleasant, somewhat out of step with what he just said.

"Your honor, might I address that?"

"Yes, please."

"Well, first of all, your honor, the question of whether it is part of his job duties, as this court has said in at least five cases, is a mixed question of fact and law that should be reserved for the trier of fact." She argues that only one part of my 7-Step Plan — removing the communication studies program from the Murrow College — was connected to my work on a college committee. The other six suggestions were unrelated to the committee's work and, therefore, are private speech.

"You know, I disagree with that," Fletcher strikes back. "The 7-Step Plan ... is a thoughtful proposition for restructuring how journalism is taught, how the faculty is organized, how money is raised. All of that has to do with running of the institution in a very important way."

My heart skips a couple more beats.

Battuello then presents the university's side of the case, asserting that my 7-Step Plan also does not deserve First Amendment protection because, among other things, it fails to address an issue of public concern. After all, she points out, I never accused the university of wrongdoing. She is correct.

Does anyone have a defibrillator?

"Obviously he [Demers] is not accusing the university of stealing money," Fletcher responds, knocking down her argument and restarting my heart. "We're not talking financial malfeasance. But it [7-Step Plan] is very clear that it [Murrow program] is managed in a way that it shouldn't be managed, and he has an important suggestion for improvement."

I appreciate Fletcher's comments, of course. But they don't cheer me up much, because he implies at one point that even if the First Amendment protects my speech, I may not be able to recover damages from the university because of "qualified immunity" — a doctrine that shields government officials from monetary damages if they did not violate "clearly established" law. In simple language, if the courts or the legislature do not clearly spell out what kinds of actions violate the Constitution, the offenders can't be punished.

"But if victims are denied compensation when offenders violate the Constitution, where's the fairness in that?" I want to add, but don't, because even plaintiffs like me don't have a free speech right to speak during such hearings.

After the hearing, Judy and I ride the elevator to the first level and sit on a bench in the hallway. I stare at the terrazzo floor for several seconds before revealing my thoughts: "I'm 99 percent certain we will lose the case, because Fletcher clearly thought my 7-Step Plan was job-related speech."

I was hoping Judy would dispute my prediction, but she doesn't. She simply says: "You never know until a court issues its ruling."

She is trying to cheer me up, of course.

That's part of her $345-an-hour job.

Chapter 1 Endnotes

1. Virtually all public universities have faculty manuals that purport to protect professors when they criticize administrators and their policies; however, these contract-based protections rarely stop administrators, or the courts, from firing or reprimanding faculty.

2. The plan urged administrators to (1) separate the mass communication program from the communication studies program (create two separate units); (2) hire a director of the Murrow School who has a strong professional background; (3) create a center for media research that conducts joint research projects with the professional community; (4) give outside professionals an active role in the development of the schools' curriculum; (5) give professional faculty a more active role in the development of the curriculum; (6) seek national accreditation for the mass communication programs; and (7) hire more professional faculty with substantial work experience. If the university adopted these changes, I agreed to donate $100,000 to the program. See Chapter 33 for more details about the plan.

3. *Garcetti v. Ceballos*, 547 U.S. 410 (2006). The decision in this case is controversial because it denies free speech protection to whistleblowers. In fact, the defendant in the case was an assistant district attorney who discovered that police has fabricated evidence to obtain a search warrant. More details on this case and others will be provided in later chapters.

4. *Demers v. Austin et al.* (2:09-cv-00334-RHW), U.S. District Court for the Eastern District of Washington (June 2, 2011).

5. Quote retrieved from <https://www.azquotes.com/author/14178- I_F_Stone>.

6. *Demers v. Austin*, 746 F.3d 402 (9th Cir., Jan. 29, 2014). This ruling replaced the original ruling of the panel, which was handed down on September 4, 2013. The major difference between the rulings is that the final one cited the 7-Step Plan in more depth. The panel apparently was trying to show university administrators that the content of the plan dealt with issues related to "scholarship or teaching," speech that it declared is protected by the First Amendment.

7. The hearing was tape-recorded. A copy of the recording can be obtained from the website for the Ninth Circuit Court <https://www.ca9.uscourts.gov/opinions>.

8. I founded Marquette Books, a book publishing company, in 2001. It has published more than 150 academic and trade books since then.

Chapter 2

The Long Drive Home

Wednesday, November 7, 2012
I-90, Between Seattle and Spokane

The drizzle feels colder as I lumber back to my seven-year-old Volvo XC-90 for the five-hour drive back to Spokane, where I live. Drivers heading east on I-90 who share the road with me are oblivious to my anxiety, as I am of theirs.

Psychiatrists and clinical psychologists often blame individuals for their stresses and usually prescribe solutions that require individuals to change their behaviors or thought patterns. But many individual problems, such as depression, stem from the demands or constraints created by social phenomena, such as laws and rules. Many salaried workers, for example, are expected or forced to work long hours, because 40 hours is simply not enough time to their jobs. Studies show that nearly two-thirds of Americans are ready to quit their jobs because of workplace stress, and job stress is a major cause of depression.[1]

Americans love to think of themselves as rugged individualists, but the reality is that organizations exert a lot of control over their lives. The "collective" is always there, like the hellhound in Robert Johnson's 1937 blues tune, which is now playing on my Sirius radio.[2]

> *I got to keep movin'... blues fallin' down like hail...*
> *Umm-mm-mm-mm, blues fallin' down like hail,*
> *... And the day keeps on worryin' me;*
> *there's a hellhound on my trail...*

My hellhounds don't have glowing red eyes or mangled fur or even a foul smell. But they, as administrators of a public university with a half-billion-dollar annual budget, are no less lethal. With the stroke of a pen or a tap on a keyboard, these administrative demons can take away raises, promotions, prestigious appointments, prized teaching assignments and careers.

I know these things, because this isn't the first time my passion for free speech and civil liberties has gotten me into trouble.

In the late 1970s, I interviewed a hockey coach who confessed that he had molested some of the boys on the team, but my editor, at the request of a county sheriff, deleted that quote from the story. Two years later, another editor killed a story I was researching about cancer rates in Midland, Michigan, after representatives of Dow Chemical Company, the largest employer in town, complained.

In 1989, the Minneapolis Police Department refused to give my journalism students access to routine reports about crimes committed by police officers, so I was forced to file an open records lawsuit. The case reached the Minnesota Supreme Court, which released some of the data — enough to show that evidence of racism existed in the police department nearly three decades before the death of George Floyd.[3]

In the mid-1990s, I helped journalism students publish some controversial stories and file an open records lawsuit to obtain access to student evaluations of faculty at the University of Wisconsin–River Falls. Administrators tried to fire me.

And, after I filed the lawsuit at Washington State University, not one faculty member on campus or four journalism deans who visited campus publicly condemned the university's attempt to squelch faculty speech. One of those deans, a First Amendment scholar, also actively opposed on his own campus an effort to provide free speech protection to all students and faculty.

I have many more stories, but my point is this: If university administrators, journalism faculty, journalists and governmental officials fail to defend and protect free speech and other civil liberties, how can society expect other organizations and citizens to embrace them?

America was the first nation in the world to create a federal constitutional republic — one that embraced not only free speech but democracy, due process, right to fair trial, political equality, rule of law, and freedom of religion, assembly and the press. But is America abandoning these ideals? Are they no longer relevant in a free-market system that critics say increasingly emphasizes wealth and technology as the only primary symbols of success?[4]

Or are my experiences simply aberrations — outliers, unrepresentative of the whole of experiences involving civil liberties on or off campus? Am I tilting at windmills? Is it even possible that I am the problem? After all, many administrators and colleagues saw it that way. They called me lots of names, including troublemaker, rabble-rouser, agitator, rebel, a professor with a hidden agenda, and, my favorite, sociopath.

Me? A sociopath?

Okay, I confess that when I was about seven years old I threw stones at a small window in the back of a semitrailer parked in a field. I had no guilt or remorse — until a sheriff's deputy yelled out, "We've got your bike."

I knew then that I had committed a crime, so I put my hands up and turned myself in. The deputy was eight feet tall, or so he seemed to me. He threatened to throw me in jail but decided he'd rather talk to my parents.

"They're working," I said, asserting a half-truth. My mother was at home.

Fortunately, I didn't have to go to jail. "I'll be keeping my eye on you, Dave," the peace officer said. "Now be careful on your ride home."

I learned an important lesson that day.

Never throw stones at trucks unless my bike is at my side.

But in hindsight perhaps the real lesson was "never throw stones at powerful institutions." No one understood this proposition better than Voltaire, the eighteenth-century French philosopher who spent much of his life on the run from the French authorities. He extolled the virtues of free speech but also warned of the folly of thinking that science and progress can eliminate injustice and wickedness. His timeless novel, *Candide*, chronicles the adventures of a young man whose optimism and idealism are swept away by the harsh realities of the real world.[5] At the end of the book, Candide concludes that the best course of action is to "tend one's own garden" — to stop trying to make the world a better place because humans are too flawed.

I may not have been a sociopath, but was I a Candide?

Should I have just kept my mouth shut when I perceived an injustice?

These questions and others swirl around my stress-weary mind as my SUV meanders through the Cascade Mountains east of Seattle, across the mighty Columbia River, and through central Washington's high and dry rolling plains just west of Spokane. When I arrive home, my wife, Theresa, and 12-year-old daughter, Lee Ann, tame my angst with hugs and kisses.

"I missed you, Dada," Lee Ann says.

"I missed you more, honey," I respond, giving her a big hug.

These simple words remind me again that family and relationships are the real wealth in life. This is my garden.

Yet even familial wealth is not untethered from the political, economic and social institutions that rule this land. When the government or corporations fire workers or deny opportunities or assistance to disadvantaged groups, familial relationships are often harmed and sometimes destroyed. In an interdependent world, we all depend upon each other to achieve our goals. Voltaire's book fails to acknowledge this, perhaps because he could not see the social and economic dependencies that French sociologist Émile Durkheim identified in his famous 1893 book, *The Division of Labor in Society*.[6] (Voltaire died a century before.)

That evening, after tucking my daughter into bed, I head to my office in the basement to write and distribute via e-mail a news release to several hundred colleagues and news organizations across the country. I've been distributing updates on the free speech battle at WSU since it began six years earlier.

Although local newspapers in Moscow and Lewiston, Idaho, and the *Chronicle of Higher Education* covered the story intermittently,[7] the two newspapers that I thought would have most thoroughly covered the story — the Spokane *Spokesman-Review* and the WSU campus student newspaper, the *Daily Evergreen* — devoted little space to the lawsuit, despite its obvious man-bites-dog newsworthiness: a journalism professor suing a journalism program for violations of the First Amendment.[8]

My objective in writing the news release is to soften what I perceive to be the coming disaster. In the world of politics, losing often leads to delegitimation of good principles and ideas — at least in the minds of outsiders or the public. And delegitimation, in turn, makes it more difficult to overcome injustices. Don't take my word for it, just ask any civil rights leader.

Although my news release cannot stop an adverse appeals court ruling, it might blunt delegitimation and prepare other free speech advocates for future battles, as Izzy Stone no doubt would have agreed.

J-PROFESSOR PREDICTS U.S. APPEALS COURT WILL DENY FACULTY RIGHT TO CRITICIZE ADMINISTRATORS

A journalism professor who filed a free speech lawsuit against four administrators at Washington State University is predicting the Ninth Circuit Court of Appeals will rule that university professors, as employees, do not have the right to criticize administrators and their policies.

"If I am right, it means the balance of power at universities in Washington State and eight other Western states will be radically altered," said David Demers, an associate professor of communication in The Edward R. Murrow College of Communication at WSU. "The decision will undermine shared governance, a centuries-old principle in which professors share power with administrators when it comes to making decisions that affect university budgets and programs. ... "

The Appeals Court panel didn't say when it would hand down its decision in my case. Judy estimates three months to two years. I wish for three months. It took 10.

By then, I was teaching a mass media law class in the Walter Cronkite School of Journalism and Mass Communication at Arizona State University.

Judy calls me 20 minutes before class.

"Dave," she says in a tone of voice that fails to give away the outcome, "I've got good news and bad."

Chapter 2 Endnotes

1. A list of studies is available at The American Institute of Stress, retrieved November 11, 2020, from <https://www.stress.org/42-worrying-workplace-stress-statistics>.

2. For a brief history of the song and its historical significance, see Ted Gioia, *Delta Blues* (New York: Norton Paperback, 2009 ed., originally published in 2008), pp. 181–182.

3. David Pearce Demers, Mark Engebretson, Jeane Fitzsimmons, and Darcy Dennison, "The Color of Justice: White People Are Almost Twice as Likely to Prevail in a Complaint Against a Minneapolis Police Officer — and Critics Claim Racism Is the Reason," *Twin Cities Reader* (March 25-31,1992), pp. 8-11. This study is discussed in Chapter 19.

4. Jacques Ellul, *The Technological Society* (New York: Vintage Books, 1964; translated from the French by John Wilkinson). Ellul argues that technology and the drive for efficiency are leading people to lose sight of the things that are truly important in life: family, freedom, and morality.

5. Voltaire, *Candide*, 2nd edition (New York: W. W. Norton, 1991; translated by Robert M. Adams; originally published 1759).

6. Émile Durkheim, *The Division of Labor in Society* (Glencoe, IL: Free Press, 1960), first published in 1893 as *De la Division du Travail Social,* and Ferdinand Tonnies, *Community and Society: Gemeinschaft und Gesellschaft*, translated and edited by Charles P. Loomis (Lansing, MI: The Michigan State University Press, 1957; first published in 1887).

7. Peter Schmidt, "Legal Dispute Pits Washington State U.'s Journalism School Against Free speech Groups," *The Chronicle of Higher Education* (March 1, 2012), retrieved September 2, 2020, from <http://chronicle.com/article/Legal-Dispute- Pits-Washington/130979>.

8. The snubs may have stemmed from a series of commentaries I wrote three years earlier that criticized the owners of the *Spokesman-Review* for refusing to publish commentaries and letters to the editor that were critical of the newspaper's controversial financial and political affairs in the community. See David Demers, *The Media Essays: From Local to Global* (Spokane, WA: Marquette Books, 2003). The WSU faculty adviser to the *Daily Evergreen* told me he thought the free speech lawsuit was newsworthy. I never approached the student editors because I did not want to interfere with their editorial independence.

Part II

Free Speech Bullies at UW-RF

Chapter 3

A Flag Burning and Cockroaches

Twenty Years Earlier
University of Wisconsin–River Falls

Political science professor Jeffrey Gerson had just told his students that flag burning was legal and now he was leading them outside to burn one.

It was March 11, 1991.

Forty-two degrees.

Chilly.

But Gerson's mind was on the day's lesson, not the weather.

He was hoping the demonstration would "put a fire under the students and get them thinking."[1] That was not an easy thing to do at the University of Wisconsin–River Falls. A survey of full-time students showed that half of them spent fewer than six hours studying per week.[2] That's about 24 hours less than professors usually recommend.[3]

Poor study habits bothered Gerson. This was his first year at UW–RF,[4] and he was determined to make education a meaningful experience for his students.

So, to set the stage for a vibrant class discussion, he divided the students into two groups. One would take a position in opposition to the Persian Gulf War and the other in support of it.

Gerson gave a short lecture on the U.S. Supreme Court decision in *Texas v. Johnson* (1989), which held that flag burning was speech protected by the First Amendment.[5] He escorted his class outside of South Hall, struck a match, and carefully ignited a four-by-six-inch American flag, which swiftly burned.[6]

"All of a sudden I hear banging," Gerson told me 18 years later.[7] "Two or three people in the basement of the building banged on the window. They were angry that I burned the flag, and they opened the window and yelled, 'You could have set the building on fire — we have chemicals down here.' Then one of them went to the telephone. When we got back to the classroom, campus security came to the door and said, 'Are you the one who burned the flag?' I told him I was, and then he went on to comment that 'you created a dangerous situation.'"

The accusations were absurd, of course.

"They were just angry about me burning a flag," Gerson said. "This was their way of expressing it."[8]

A short time after the flag burning, Gerson told a newspaper reporter at the *St. Paul Pioneer Dispatch*: "It was a good class. I think people really got into the discussion on both sides. I think it was an effective teaching tool."[9]

Some of his students agreed.

"Once he burned the flag, people started talking about it," one student told the reporter. "I think it was a very effective teaching method. It did spark discussion."[10]

Another said, "Most people thought he had a right to do it, and the others didn't seem to be able to convince him he shouldn't do it."[11]

At least one student thought the flag burning was wrong. She called her father, a county government official, who complained to UW–RF's top administrator, Chancellor Gary Thibodeau, who was aware of the controversy.

"If this guy wants to go burn a flag someplace, that's certainly his right," C. W. King, director of community programs for Chippewa County, told a reporter after contacting Thibodeau. "But, in his role as a professor, to force students to witness this kind of thing is an abuse of his position."[12]

Thibodeau, a biology professor with a flattop haircut, issued a written statement condemning Gerson for using "extraordinarily bad judgment in his choice of illustrations" and "offensive and insensitive" teaching methods.[13]

Gerson disagreed.

He said administrators "should be encouraging faculty to take chances and not try to stifle them."[14] A nonscientific telephone survey of 200 faculty by the UW–RF student newspaper seemed to agree: Six of ten supported Gerson's right to burn the flag.[15]

Gerson had planned to burn another flag in a separate class three days later, but he changed his mind after more than 200 students showed up to protest outside of his classroom. They recited the Pledge of Allegiance, sang the national anthem, and chanted "U-S-A."

"Everyone was just out showing their true colors," one student protestor said. "There was a lot of patriotism today."[16]

In a letter to UW System President Kenneth Shaw, state Senator Marvin Roshell (D-Chippewa Falls) said four of his constituents complained about the flag burning. Roshell suggested that "Gerson be returned to wherever he came from and not be invited back."[17] Roshell later questioned "whether academic freedom is the best thing we have" and described Gerson as "inept at his profession."

Gerson was stunned.

He — a presumed expert in politics — had misjudged the politics of some of his students and their parents. Many were from rural areas or small towns in Wisconsin and Minnesota, where conservative values run deep.

The law was on Gerson's side, of course.

But that didn't matter.

A month later, Gerson was informed that his one-year teaching contract would not be renewed and that he would not be a finalist for a permanent position in the department.

The head of the political science department later said the decision not to renew Gerson's contract was unrelated to the flag-burning incident. But he conceded that he could "probably not convince a lot of people of this."[18]

I would become one of them.

"HEY, DAVE, WHAT DO COCKROACHES and professors have in common?"

I was waiting to make copies of an exam when my new academic colleague and friend, Jimmy Whittier, a University of Wisconsin–River Falls business professor, asked me that question in October 1991.

"They are both disgusting?"

"No, but nice try," Jimmy replied as he collected copies from the machine's tray. "They are the only two species that consume their own kind."

I laughed, of course.

Self-deprecating jokes, whether applied to a person or profession, are almost always funny. They are a way of telling others that "we're not too big for our britches" even if we know we are.

I was thirty-eight years old and into my second month of teaching in the journalism department at UW–RF. I was ABD — All But Dissertation, which meant I had completed all of the requirements for a doctorate in mass communication at the University of Minnesota except the dissertation. I would finish that in a year.

Like most scholars starting their first jobs in academia, I was flush with energy, hope and pride. I was going to change the world, or at least part of it.

I also was scared to death.

To obtain tenure, I would have to publish refereed journal articles and get good teaching evaluations over the next six years. We new professors had heard stories of faculty who had been terminated before and at the end of that time period. We pitied them, of course. But not as much as we pitied ourselves. We were just starting the tenure gauntlet and had so much anxiety that even sex took a back seat.

"Would you like to make love tonight?" one of my recently graduated Ph.D. friends said his girlfriend asked him the evening before he was scheduled to teach.

"I'm sorry, honey," he told her. "I've got to review Karl Marx's conflict theory."

"I've got a conflict theory of my own," she retorted.

"What's that?"

"Your studies are going to ruin your sex life."

Two months later, she left him.

She was one helluva theorist.

My commute from Shoreview, a St. Paul suburb, to River Falls — a city of 10,000 residents located six miles east of the St. Croix River — took about forty-five minutes. During that time, I listened to rock n' roll, blues and jazz, especially Ray Charles, Queen, Stevie Ray Vaughan and Steely Dan. One of my favorite songs was Charles's "If It Wasn't for Bad Luck," which tells the story of a man who is left by his woman, kicked out of his house and wrongly accused of committing a crime.

That's why if it wasn't for bad luck, sugar
Oh, I tell everybody if it wasn't for bad luck now, now
I believe, I believe I would have no luck at all
I just wouldn't have no luck at all[19]

I loved that song even though I didn't believe in bad luck. Bad luck is a euphemism for "I screwed up, but I don't want to blame myself." I know there is no such thing as bad luck because there is no such thing as good luck. People always praise themselves, not luck, when they do something right.

When I started teaching at UW–RF, I was unaware of the Gerson flag-burning controversy, which had occurred about six months earlier.[20] I learned about it from Peter, another UW–RF professor, shortly after I heard the cockroach joke. He said no faculty publicly supported Gerson.

"That's a shame," I responded, shaking my head.

"So, you're saying Chancellor Thibodeau was wrong?"

"Depends. He certainly had the right as a citizen to disagree with Gerson's decision to burn the flag. But free speech advocates could point out that Thibodeau, as an administrator, should have defended Gerson's right to burn the flag. UW–RF even has a rule specifically protecting professors' rights to free speech. Why didn't more faculty criticize Thibodeau?"

"Don't know," Peter said, shrugging. "Fear, maybe. Why should faculty risk their careers and the well-being of their families for an abstract principle like free speech? It doesn't pay the bills, nor does it advance your career."

"But if all faculty felt like that, who would defend free speech rights on campus?"

"Hey, Dave, as a media sociologist, you know that there is no such thing as absolute free speech on campus or anywhere else. Information and knowledge are highly controlled in all societies. There's no protection for people who shout 'fire' in a theater that isn't burning. And what parent wants his or her children to cuss like a sailor?"

Peter had a good point. No constitutional right is absolute.

"But too much regulation can deny society access to new ideas," I passionately countered. "Gerson's teaching method might have been unorthodox, but it appears to have succeeded in stimulating a good intellectual discussion among his students. Isn't that a goal of education?"

Peter rolled his eyes.

"Should a criminologist shoot someone to teach students that murder needs to be outlawed? All faculty must make choices about what kind of content is appropriate in their classes. You know that." Peter paused and shook his head. "You sound like a hopeless idealist."

He was half right.

I was an idealist, but hopeful, not hopeless. A bit naive and temerarious, too.

I acquired some of these traits while working as a newspaper reporter in the late 1970s. Questioning and challenging government authorities was part of the job. I was never afraid to ask tough questions, because my sources had no power over me. My job was to get the news.

In fact, when I took the job at UW–RF, the thought never crossed my mind that it might have been inappropriate for professors to criticize university administrators. After all, the principle of shared governance required professors to speak up when administrators made bad decisions or violated rules or laws.[21] Administrators are supposed to share power with faculty. It's even in the Faculty Handbook, which I reviewed during my first week on the job.

Journalism professors like me also have an extra responsibility to safeguard free speech rights, both in and out of the university community. Most people have a poor understanding of the First Amendment. They say they support free speech, but many are not willing to defend the right of communists, fascists, and anarchists to speak out on issues in their communities. The corrective for evil or bad speech isn't censorship, as a U.S. Supreme Court justice once said, but more speech.[22]

Idealistic?

You bet I was.

As the weeks passed, though, I quickly forgot about the flag-burning incident. Like other professors, I came to see it — or perhaps wanted to see it — as an outlier, not as an indicator of a leadership or systemic problem.

My first three years at UW–RF were pleasant.

I taught courses in reporting, editing, media law, public opinion and media history — four per semester. This was a heavy teaching load for faculty who were also expected to conduct research. But I didn't mind. I loved both teaching and research.[23]

Although teaching was the No. 1 priority at UW–RF, as it is at most non-doctorate granting institutions, I was hired to help meet the scholarship and research criteria required for national accreditation of the journalism program. The other three faculty members in the journalism program did not have doctorates and, hence, were not expected to conduct research. Without a scholar in its ranks, the UW–RF journalism program would lose its national accreditation.[24] And if it lost accreditation, there would be two big consequences.

The first would be a loss of prestige and status for the program. The quality of a program affects its enrollments. Students are drawn to programs that are accredited, because there is the assurance that it is being managed properly and that they will graduate with a high-quality degree.

The second consequence of losing accreditation is loss of funding for the program. Accreditation keeps the funding flowing in, because to maintain accreditation the program must meet a number of quality checks, including offering courses that will achieve the goals of the program. Accreditation helps deter administrators from cutting funding to a program, because no administrator wants to be labeled as the one who caused a program to lose accreditation.

The UW–RF students were very likable.

But Gerson was right: Most were not very serious about their studies.

I attributed this problem mainly to the lax enrollment requirements at UW–RF. Although the admissions office looked at a variety of criteria when reviewing applications, for all practical purposes the only formal requirement was a high school grade-point average of C or better. In the early 1990s, this meant the university accepted more than 85 percent of the students who applied.[25]

UW–RF was not alone. Most of the 7,000 colleges and universities in the United States have easy entrance requirements. That's partly by design. In America, education is expected to be the great equalizer. If everyone is given access to an education, then everyone has an equal opportunity to climb the social and economic ladder.[26] Economic equality, in turn, is expected to produce a stable, democratic society.

That's the theory.

In practice, the higher education system in America does not operate on a level playing field. Students from privileged socioeconomic backgrounds still have a much higher probability of attending more elite educational institutions, such as Harvard, Princeton, Yale and Stanford, where admission standards are much tougher. In contrast, students from less privileged backgrounds have a much higher probability of attending community colleges and smaller public baccalaureate institutions like UW–RF.[27] Studies show over and over again that the highest paying jobs in society go to those who attend the elite institutions.[28]

Although UW–RF faculty often griped about students who failed to take their studies seriously, there were some bright, talented students among the 4,900 enrolled.

Nevertheless, like Gerson, I felt an obligation to make education meaningful to all my students, not just the brightest. My approach, to get them to study more, was to give challenging tests and quizzes.

I confess that I cannot say to this day whether this "stick" approach ever worked. But I can say with certainty that my pedagogy did not endear me to all my students.

"Your tests are unfair," some would complain. "They are too difficult."

"But even if they're unfair," I would respond, "everyone in class is subjected to the same level of unfairness. So, on a relative basis there is no bias. And that's how I distribute grades. I grade on a curve. I always give out some A grades in my classes."

Of course, my pedantic explanation did not mollify them.

In terms of teaching evaluations, my students rated me slightly above departmental and college-wide averages. I thought I deserved better. I attributed the ratings to my difficult tests, but I had no evidence to back this up and no one has ever told me that I am a charismatic teacher.

Although I had a heavy teaching load, I was a productive researcher. By my third year, I had published one scholarly book and eight refereed journal articles.

The director of our program, John Smith, was pleased. He gave me high ratings in my annual reviews during my first three years. At the beginning of my third year, he planned to support my request to go up early for promotion to associate professor, which would be effective in my fifth year. Normally faculty are promoted in their seventh year, at which time they also receive tenure.

I appreciated Smith's support.

Smith was an amiable man and well-liked by students and faculty, including me. He had worked in broadcasting for a short time before earning his master's degree and becoming a professor.

He wasn't a social scientist, but he was a good writer. He had written some books on paranormal phenomena that sold more than 200,000 copies.[29]

He had been at UW–RF for nearly two decades and played the lead role in securing national accreditation for the journalism program.[30] This was not easy to do. The standards for accreditation were, and continue to be, high. The UW–RF program had the distinction at that time of being the smallest accredited journalism program in the United States.[31]

The program served about 150 majors in print journalism and radio broadcasting. The other two full-time faculty included Casandra, who taught mostly print journalism courses, and Paul, who taught broadcasting courses.

Although my long-term goal was to get a job at a research university and work with graduate students, I was grateful to be teaching at UW–RF. My spouse at the time, Mona, had a good job as a market researcher at a major financial institution in Minneapolis.

Life was pretty good.

Chapter 3 Endnotes

1. Telephone interview with Jeffrey Gerson, November 29, 1999.

2. Students were asked to indicate how much time they spent "preparing for class (studying, reading, writing, rehearsing, and other activities related to your academic program)." A total of 1,368 students completed the College Student Experiences Questionnaire March 1-5, 1993. Source: Unpublished report prepared by Roger A. Ballou, Dean of Students, University of Wisconsin–River Falls (April 1993). With permission of Ballou, I shared the results of the survey with students in my classes.

3. Professors usually recommend two hours of study for every hour in class. The normal course load is 15 hours per week in a semester system, which equates to 30 hours of studying per week, or 4.3 hours per day. Since the 1990s, the amount of time college students in general spend studying has apparently declined even more. See Jeffrey R. Young, "Homework? What Homework? Students Seem to be Spending Less Time Studying than They Used to," *The Chronicle of Higher Education,* 49(15): A35 (December 6, 2002), and Daniel de Vise, "College Students Spending Less Time Studying," *The Washington Post* (May 23, 2012), available online at <http://bangordailynews.com/2012/05/22/news/nation/college-students-spending-less-time-studying>.

4. Gerson had a one-year appointment at UW–RF while the university searched for a permanent hire. He was one of the applicants for that permanent position.

5. Here is a summary of the facts of *Texas v. Johnson,* 491 U.S. 397 (1989): Gregory Lee Johnson was protesting Reagan Administration policies outside of the Republican National Convention in Dallas, Texas, in 1984. When Johnson and others reached Dallas City Hall, he doused a U.S. flag with kerosene and set it on fire while demonstrators shouted, "America, the red, white, and blue, we spit on you." Johnson was convicted of desecrating a venerated object, which was a crime under Texas state law. He was sentenced to one year in prison and fined $2,000. He appealed and the Texas Court of Criminal Appeals overturned his conviction, saying the state could not punish him because the burning of the flag was expressive conduct protected by the First Amendment. The state appealed the decision and in 1989 the U.S. Supreme Court, on a 5-4 vote, upheld the decision of the Texas court.

6. Gerson forgot to take a flag, so he went back to the political science office to get a small one. Some students brought their own flags, but only Gerson burned one.

7. Quote obtained during a telephone interview on January 6, 2009.

8. Ibid.

9. Bill Gardner, "Prof's Flag-burning Ignites Controversy," *St. Paul Pioneer Press Dispatch* (March 13, 1991), p. 1A.

10. Ibid.
11. Ibid.
12. Ibid.
13. Ibid.
14. Ibid.
15. Student journalists telephoned more than 200 faculty. They also surveyed students, who, by a 6-to-4 margin, said the flag burning was an inappropriate teaching tool. Source: Associated Press, "Faculty Back Professor Who Burned Flag," (March 24, 1991), p. 4C.
16. Ibid.
17. Ibid.
18. Bill Gardner, "UW-River Falls Professor Who Burned Flag Loses Job," *St. Paul Pioneer Press Dispatch* (April 27, 1991), p. 11A. For academic treatments of the flag-burning incident at UW–RF, see Robert Justin Goldstein, *Burning the Flag: The Great 1989-1990 American Flag Desecration Controversy* (Kent, OH: Kent State University Press, 1996), p. 356, and Michael Welch, *Flag Burning: Moral Panic and the Criminalization of Protest* (New York: Walter de Gruyter, 2000), p. 84. Gerson eventually earned tenure at the University of Massachusetts at Lowell.
19. Charles wrote the song with Jimmy Le in 1959. ABC records released it as a 45 single in 1969.
20. I conducted an archival search of the *Star Tribune* website on July 29, 2012, but could find no references to the 1991 flag-burning incident at the University of Wisconsin–River Falls.
21. Shared governance is the process by which the members of a university community, including administrators, faculty, students and staff, share responsibility for reaching collective decisions on matters of policy and procedure, including curriculum and budgeting.
22. The anti-censorship, more-speech argument was part of Justice Louis Brandeis' concurring opinion in *Whitney v. California*, 274 U.S. 357 (1927). The U.S. Supreme Court case examined whether an anti-communist California law was constitutional. Brandeis wrote: "Those who won our independence by revolution were not cowards. They did not fear political change. They did not exalt order at the cost of liberty. To courageous, self-reliant men, with confidence in the power of free and fearless reasoning applied through the processes of popular government, no danger flowing from speech can be deemed clear and present, unless the incidence of the evil apprehended is so imminent that it may befall before there is opportunity for full discussion. *If there be time to expose through discussion the falsehood and fallacies, to avert the evil by the processes of education, the remedy to be applied is more speech, not enforced silence.*" [emphasis added]
23. One common misconception about faculty is that they are lazy. I usually worked about 70 hours a week. Many of the younger faculty I knew did the same.
24. Journalism and mass communication programs are accredited through the Accrediting Council on Education in Journalism and Mass Communications. In 2012, only 109 of the 500-plus journalism programs in the United States were accredited. The UW–RF program gave up its accreditation status after UW–RF university officials decided not to seek re-accreditation.
25. The typical UW–RF student scored better than 59 percent of the students taking the SAT, a standardized entrance test. As a point of comparison, the average for students at the University of Michigan, which is rated the 23rd best national university, was 77 percent. Source: *America's Best Colleges 1998* (Washington, D.C.: U.S. News & World Report, 1997), p. 94. Prior to 1997, UW–RF officials refused to answer the magazine's annual survey of colleges.
26. About two-thirds of high school graduates in the United States attend college. But in 1992, students were far less prepared than they were in 1972. SAT verbal scores dropped about 60 points between those two decades. An increased emphasis on math may have caused part of

the decline.

27. Stacy Dickert-Conlin and Ross Rubenstein (editors), *Economic Inequality and Higher Education: Access, Persistence, and Success* (New York: Russell Sage Foundation, 2009).

28. Scott Jaschik, "College Selectivity and Income," *Inside Higher Education* (August 22, 2016), retrieved October 22, 2020, from <https://www.insidehighered.com/news/2016/08/22/study-finds-graduates-most-selective-colleges-enjoy-earnings-payoff>.

29. He wrote ghost stories, interviewing people who believed their homes were haunted.

30. Journalism programs are accredited through the Accrediting Council on Education in Journalism and Mass Communications. The purpose of the accreditation process is to enhance the quality of journalism and mass communication education.

31. In 2012, the program was no longer accredited.

Chapter 4

Damned Lies & Student Evaluations

September 1993
University of Wisconsin–River Falls

"Okay, what project would you like to take on this year?" I asked the dozen or so students attending the first meeting of the UW–RF chapter of the Society of Professional Journalists one day in September 1993.

For the past two years, I had been adviser to the group, which represents the interests of student and professional journalists and promotes First Amendment rights and open government and records. Most major journalism schools in the United States have a student chapter that sponsors educational activities, such as lectures and panels, and fundraising events.

The students stared at me and each other for a few seconds before one of them blurted out, "I'd like to see us go after student evaluations of faculty. There are a lot of terrible professors on campus. Why doesn't the university do something about that?"

Everyone in the room nodded.

At UW–RF, like most universities across the country, students evaluate their instructors at the end of a semester.[1] They rate their professors on a variety of criteria, including their overall effectiveness as teachers and their responsiveness to students' concerns.

The evaluation process is anonymous and most departments on campus treat the evaluations as confidential personnel records. The results are used to evaluate faculty for contract renewal, tenure and promotion.

"You know," I told the SPJ students, "university officials will argue that those records are confidential, because they are part of a faculty member's personnel file. They will fight attempts to release the records."

"We know that," the student who raised the issue said. "But we still feel they should be public. Students deserve to know how faculty are rated."

Although I was an advocate of government accountability, I hadn't formed an opinion on whether the teaching evaluations should be opened to the public. But my opinion was irrelevant. My role as adviser was to help students achieve their goals, not dictate their projects.

I agreed to help them, even though I was certain the university would reject the students' request. *But what a great learning experience for the students, especially if the case goes to court.*

To start the process, I advised the students to contact the office of Wisconsin Attorney General James Edward Doyle Jr., the highest-ranking legal adviser to the state and its agencies. They wrote a letter, and John Tallman, an assistant attorney general who represented the UW System, responded several weeks later, telling the students Doyle believed the student evaluation records should be available to the public. But Tallman said that Doyle, who would be elected governor of the state a decade later, did not have the authority to release them. Tallman did not elaborate.

On November 17, 1993, the students wrote a letter to Chancellor Thibodeau, requesting the records, citing Wisconsin's Open Records Law to justify the request.[2]

In the meantime, I informally canvassed faculty in our department and around campus.

"Those evaluations contain a lot of false statements and damned lies," one mathematics professor angrily told me. "Some are even defamatory. Students don't have to put their names on the evaluations, so they aren't accountable. The records should never be released to the public."

"Students are not competent to evaluate faculty," an English professor said. "Those ratings are biased. Faculty who give high grades get high evaluations."

All of the two dozen faculty and administrators I spoke with opposed release of the records, except one.

"Our department allows students to see those evaluations if they ask," said Bill Turnball, chair of the English department, during a college-level committee meeting I was attending.

"Really?" I asked.

"Yes," he said. "If a student wants to see the evaluations of a faculty member, we show them. We've never prohibited access to the evaluations when students request them."

"Do a lot of students ask for them?"

"Not many. We get a couple of requests every year."

Turnball pointed out that there was no formal university policy prohibiting the release of student evaluations, so the department wasn't violating any rules. But most departments, like journalism, treated them as confidential personnel records and refused to release them.

On December 2, Chancellor Thibodeau responded in writing to the SPJ students' request: "There is a need to protect the integrity of the evaluation process, both to ensure that evaluations are candid and thorough and to permit the university, as an employer, to use them as a basis for improving performance. Further, disclosure of this information could expose the reputations of individuals to possible damage."

SEVERAL DAYS AFTER Chancellor Thibodeau's response, John Smith appointed me adviser to the student newspaper on campus, the *Student Voice*.

The role of an adviser is to provide advice to students running the newspaper. The job was not too demanding. But it could be controversial.

For example, several months before I took the position, the newspaper published a display advertisement stating that the Holocaust never occurred. The ad came from a man who for many years would send the ad to college newspapers across the country, hoping some would publish it. Almost none did.

But the *Voice* advertising student staffers and the faculty adviser didn't read the content of the ad. The students just pasted it onto the page and accepted the $60 payment check from the man.

Of course, controversy erupted after it was published. Many administrators, faculty, and Jewish and Christian leaders around the area condemned the ad, its creator, and the student journalists.

Chancellor Thibodeau also criticized the *Voice* editors, saying they showed poor judgment. Everyone was demanding an apology.

"So what do you intend to do?" I asked one of the student editors.

"We're going to apologize."

"For what?" I said. "For not censoring someone? You know, a U.S. Supreme Court justice once said that prior restraint or censorship isn't the solution for evil or bad speech. More speech is. And this is exactly what happened. The local community responded with 'good speech,' and the 'hateful speech' has been drowned out. The system worked. You don't need to apologize. You actually helped remind the community that this is a society that respects free speech rights, even for those who hold controversial, false ideas."

A day later the student editors apologized.

I wasn't surprised. The students were scared. I probably would have done the same thing as an undergraduate. University administrators can be intimidating, because they yield a lot of power on campus.

Once again, it appeared to me that Thibodeau had failed in his role as administrator to support free speech rights on campus. He had the right to personally disagree, but free speech advocates say he should have defended the students' right to publish the ad.

No action was taken against the students or the faculty adviser, to the best of my knowledge. But nationwide, many advisers have lost their jobs over similar kinds of incidents.

To prevent such firings, conventional wisdom holds that the faculty adviser should be a tenured faculty member. Tenure, by the way, is not a "job for life," as many people assume. It is merely a guarantee that if a faculty member is fired, he or she is guaranteed administrative due process, which includes the right to a formal hearing of one's peers and the right to challenge accusers and the evidence. At most public and private universities, tenured faculty normally can be fired only for gross incompetence or for committing a felony. But small departments like the one at UW–RF often don't have enough tenured faculty to do the newspaper advising job, so the baton was passed to me, the new untenured guy with the lowest seniority.

My philosophy of advising was simple and shared by many other campus newspaper advisers across the country: Students control the editorial process, even to the degree that they be permitted to publish content that would be offensive or libelous.

Of course, as adviser, I would strongly advise against doing that. But the final decision rests with the students, not me.

IN JANUARY 1994, I began teaching an advanced reporting course in which I asked students to develop an investigative project. Several students were interested in looking at faculty salaries, so I helped them conduct a computer analysis of faculty salaries.

I had coauthored a book on the use of quantitative social science research methods in journalism,[3] and the project was perfect for illustrating what has come to be called "precision journalism." University officials gave us a file containing information on salaries. I ran the computer analyses and showed the students how to interpret them.

The findings revealed great disparity in faculty salaries between various departments on campus. Salaries at universities are not based on the principle of equal pay for equal work. For example, business professors who taught research methods were paid about 50 percent more than social science professors who taught similar courses. English professors and library scholars made less than journalism and social science professors.[4]

University officials attributed these differences to "market factors." Business professors are paid more, they argued, because comparable jobs in the real world pay more. English professors are paid less because the demand for those jobs is far greater than the number of positions available.

The study also found that female faculty at UW–RF earned slightly less than male faculty, about $1,700 a year less. This difference persisted even after statistically removing the effects for years of service, tenure, age, department, and other factors.[5]

In percentage terms, women were making about 4 percent less per year than men — a differential that I thought was quite small given the national pay differential for women for all jobs at that time was 21 percent after removing the effects of demographics.[6] If there was some gender discrimination built into the salary structure at UW–RF, it wasn't much.

In March, I helped the students write a three-part series for the *Student Voice*, the last of which published the salaries of all university faculty and administrators. I wrote up the results from the statistical analysis. The students conducted the interviews and wrote the rest of the series. The series was informative and, in my opinion, not very controversial.

But, unbeknownst to me at the time, Chancellor Thibodeau was upset over the finding that female faculty were paid slightly less than male faculty, presumably because it made his administration look biased. About a year later he told a reporter for the Student Press Law Center that the study was not "complex enough," but his administration never asked me to justify the data or methodology.[7]

Some faculty and administrators also were angry about their salaries being published in the newspaper. This surprised me, because they are public employees, and everyone knows salaries for public officials are public data.

"What's the big deal?" I said to one faculty member who was upset about the salary data being made public.

"This is a small town," she responded. "People are upset that others know what they make. Faculty are also angry because it shows who is and who is not being favored by the administration."

To me, the latter comment justified the very reason for publishing the salaries — to make government accountable for its decisions. Faculty have a right to know their colleagues' salaries, if for no other reason than to reduce cronyism. Taxpayers also have a right to know how their tax dollars are being spent.

My democratically driven journalistic philosophy was appreciated by some students but not by many faculty and administrators, as I would soon learn.

IN MID-JANUARY 1994, the SPJ students and I contacted SPJ regional director Terry Rindfleisch, a working journalist himself, who was delighted to help with the students' attempt to get access to the student evaluations. The regional chapter committed several hundred dollars to hire an attorney.

The freedom of information lawsuit was filed March 23, 1994.

"We're the reason professors are here," Tiffany Thibideau, one of the SPJ students, told the *Milwaukee Sentinel*, which published a news story about the lawsuit.[8] "We do the evaluating, and we should be able to see them. A student should be able to know what other students thought of a professor." Two other students, Kimberly Deane and Susan Morrison, also agreed to be named as plaintiffs in the case.[9]

One day after the story appeared, Peter Seguin, the attorney representing the SPJ students, called me.

"Dave, do you have any evidence that might help our case?" he asked.

"An English professor told me several months ago that his department gives the results of the evaluations to students when they ask for them," I said.

"Great. That shows capriciousness in the handling of the evaluations. Who is the professor?"

"Bill Turnball — chair of the English Department."

"I'll give him a call."

A day later Seguin called back.

"Turnball denies ever telling you that the English Department gave the evaluations to the students."

"That's false, Pete," I said emphatically. "We talked openly about it at a meeting, and several other faculty were there."

The next day, journalism chair John Smith came into my office. His face was flushed.

"Dave, Bill Turnball wants a written apology from you," he blurted. "He said Peter Seguin called him and asked him about the English Department's policy of giving students the evaluations of faculty. He denies telling you that. He wants an apology."

"John, Bill is lying," I said, feeling my pulse increase and my one-fourth Irish cheeks filling with blood. "He told me in front of other faculty at a meeting that his department gave the evaluations to students who asked for them. I cannot apologize, because that's what he told me."

Of course, I expected my boss to back me up, not only because I worked for him but also because journalism faculty are supposed to be devoted to openness and accountability in government.

He didn't.

He was getting angry.

"Bill is my friend, Dave," he shouted. "You will apologize, or he can destroy your career."

I couldn't believe what I was hearing. Like Gerson, I had failed to take into account the politics of a small university community. Loyalty often trumps principles.

This turned out to be the pivotal point in the dispute. If I apologized, the controversy would blow over. If I stood by my principles, I might lose my job. But I figured Smith's comment that Bill could destroy my career was exaggerated. So there was only one answer I could give.

"I cannot apologize, John. He lied to our attorney."[10]

My response sealed my fate.

ABOUT TWO WEEKS after the SPJ lawsuit was filed, the UW–RF Faculty Senate suspended the student evaluation process until the lawsuit was settled. The resolution also contained language supporting Chancellor Thibodeau's earlier decision not to release the records.

In contrast, UW–RF students, in a campus-wide referendum conducted just before the resolution, voted 7-to-1 in favor of the SPJ students' attempts to get access to the records. Student senators ignored the referendum, however, and passed a resolution supporting the Faculty Senate and Chancellor Thibodeau. Student senators identified with the university power structure, not with their own rank-and-file.

"Traitors," one journalism student complained to me in my office.

Yet ignoring the wishes of the governed is a very common feature of America's representative democracy. Polls show that a majority of citizens want more regulation of gun ownership, more efforts to combat pollution and global warming, and a single government program to provide health care.[11] But none of these desires has been turned into policy, as of this writing.

In early April 1994, after the Faculty Senate and student votes, a political science professor whom I had befriended confronted me in a stairwell.

"You've done a great disservice to this university, Dave," she said angrily, referring to the lawsuit to open up the student evaluations.

"I am just helping students achieve their goals," I said. "Besides, the courts will probably rule against the students. This is a good lesson in how politics works."

I thought she would understand, because she was a political scientist.

I was wrong.

I wondered whether she received poor evaluations from the students.

ON APRIL 13, 1994, I received a phone call from one of the SPJ students who was working at the student newspaper office.

"Dave, the attorney general's office has ruled that the student evaluations of faculty are public data," she said. "We won. Isn't that incredible?"

Wow.

I could hear students rejoicing and laughing in the background. What a great lesson this had been. They made government more accountable to people. They changed the world, just a little bit.

Several days later, the full story emerged. The Wisconsin Attorney General's Office had notified the University of Wisconsin System that the AG's office would not defend the university in the Society of Professional Journalists lawsuit. AG Doyle "ruled" the evaluation records were public data under state law. Unbeknownst to us, the AG's office had been telling UW System administrators for years that the student evaluations were public data, but UW officials at all campuses throughout the state ignored them.[12] The SPJ lawsuit forced the issue into public view.

"We have concluded that the public records law requires that the public have access to those student evaluations," Assistant Attorney General Alan Lee told Chancellor Thibodeau in a letter dated April 7, 1994. "We therefore advise that you make the records available as soon as possible."[13]

UW System President Katherine Lyall, who had authority over two dozen UW campuses in the state, said the system would comply with the AG's request. But she defended Thibodeau's decision to deny access to the records.

"Chancellor Gary Thibodeau made an appropriate response when he denied the students' request. Today's action in no way reflects on his decision, which has received strong support from the Faculty Senate, the Student Senate and members of the UW-River Falls faculty."[14]

"She conveniently forgot to mention that seven out of eight UW–RF students were not among the supporters," one of the SPJ students pointed out.

"She also forgot to mention that the AG's office had told her that the records were public data," I added.

UW–RF political science chair Jan Hillard told a reporter for the UW–RF *Student Voice* that "no one was against the evaluations. Faculty were upset that promises stated in department chair manuals about what was public or private were changed."[15]

SPJ Regional Director Terry Rindfleisch told the *Student Voice* that he was surprised and pleased the records were made public so quickly. He said he was proud of the students for pursuing their beliefs.[16]

Me too.

IN MAY 1994, the Midwest Region 7 Society of Professional Journalists Board of Directors named the UW–RF chapter the Top Regional Student Chapter because of their efforts forcing the release of the student evaluations.

At the awards banquet, I was surprised when Rindfleisch also announced that the regional chapter had given me a Director's Award for Outstanding Service as faculty adviser. As I got up from the table, my students were smiling and clapping. They all knew about the award but had kept it a secret. I blushed.

Later, the national SPJ Board of Directors presented the UW–RF student chapter with a national First Amendment Award, one of the most prestigious national awards that could be granted to a student chapter.

The student evaluations of faculty were eventually released. The *Student Voice* published them in one issue. It was probably the most-read issue in the history of the newspaper. I received a few stern looks from professors as I passed them in the halls and on the sidewalks. But the issue died down very quickly.

It was a glorious time for the students.

But the elation didn't last long for me.

IN LATE MAY, several faculty and staff told me privately that my role in helping students sue the university and publish the faculty salary stories might have an adverse impact on my chances of being retained or tenured. I dismissed the comments at first, because I believed academic freedom protected me. But I had trouble sleeping. I had to know for sure, because I had to come up with a plan to protect my career.

So I wrote to College of Liberal Arts and Sciences Dean *Cal Stricter*, John Smith's superior and friend, asking whether my involvement in the SPJ lawsuit and faculty salary project could "be used to deny me tenure, or are tenure decisions based solely on one's performance in teaching, research and community service?"[17]

Stricter didn't pull any punches.

"Yes," he said.[18]

Holy shit!

Meanwhile, tensions were high in the journalism office.

One of the two journalism professors was very loyal to Smith and quickly came to his defense. This professor could have defended my (the faculty's) right to free speech, even if the professor disagreed with aspects of my actions in helping the students. But the professor didn't, and the loyalty defense has many admirers. How many of us would stand up for principle if it meant our innocent friends or loved ones could be harmed?

The other journalism professor had good relations with both Smith and me. But bureaucracies, and all organizations for that matter, provide lots of rewards for members who remain loyal to them, and there are many disincentives for those who challenge the power structure. So why should any faculty member stick their neck out for another faculty member, especially if they have nothing substantial to gain?

The upshot is that I had no right to expect either of the two journalism faculty members to side with me in this dispute. They were acting in their own best interests, which is a fundamental assumption underlying many economic theories of human behavior.

AS THE DAYS PASSED, the complaints about me were coming from multiple sources. One faculty member told me that faculty from various departments across the campus complained frequently about me over lunch. I used to be invited to those lunches.

A number of professors also complained to Smith. One even asked: "What's Demers's hidden agenda?" Another faculty member told a student: "Demers is a sociopath."[19]

The whole thing was surreal.

It reminded me of the role Gary Cooper played in *High Noon* — in that classic scene where the camera pans back to show Cooper standing alone in the street as the bad guys arrive in town. No one in town would stand with Cooper.

"Colleagues, let's get the rope," I could hear the faculty saying at lunch.

Fortunately, the semester ended without a hanging.

But I was an emotional wreck. I was getting about five hours or less of sleep a night. I was short-tempered with people. I wasn't just worried about losing a job — I was worried about losing my career. *What university would hire a professor who has been fired from his job?*

Yet I was still in denial.

I kept telling myself that the university couldn't fire me. After all, SPJ, the nation's leading journalism organization, had just given the students and me awards for our work. I had better-than-average student evaluations and an outstanding publication record; in fact, I had more publications than most of the full professors on campus. Smith had even supported my decision to go up early for promotion to associate professor.

Surely the principle of academic freedom also protected me. The American Association of University Professors, which American philosopher John Dewey helped to create, defined academic freedom as encompassing "the right of faculty to full freedom in research and in the publication of results, freedom in the classroom in discussing their subject."

Yes, I am on solid ground, I tried to assure myself.

But as Johann Wolfgang von Goethe once said, "With wisdom grows doubt."[20]

I decided to contact an attorney.

Chapter 4 Endnotes

1. I say "usually" because UW–RF rules allowed tenured full professors to selectively administer the evaluations in only some of their classes.
2. Wisconsin Public Records Law, Wis. Stat. §§ 19.31 through 19.39. The law was enacted in 1981.
3. David Pearce Demers and Suzanne Nichols, *Precision Journalism: A Practical Guide* (Newbury Park, CA: Sage Publications, 1987).
4. These differences continue to this day at most universities.
5. The study employed multiple regression and other multivariate statistical techniques and controlled for a number of factors, including age, years of service, tenure status, department, rank and gender.
6. Joseph G. Altonji and Rebecca M. Blank, "Race and Gender in the Labor Market," pp. 3143-3259 in Orley Ashenfelter and David Card (editors)," *Handbook of Labor Economics*, Vol. 3 (Netherlands: Elsevier Science B.V., 1999).
7. "Professor Fights School for Job," *Student Press Law Center Report XVI*, 16(3): 36-37 (Washington, D.C., Fall 1995), p. 37. Available online at <http://issuu.com/splc/docs/v16n3-fall95>. My background in statistics and regression modeling was extensive. I worked for four years as a senior market research analyst before obtaining my Ph.D.
8. Joe Williams, "Access: Students Sue School to See Evaluations," *Milwaukee Sentinel* (April 8, 1994), p. 1A.
9. Some of the SPJ students were afraid to add their names as plaintiffs. The decision was voluntary.
10. During the heated exchange, my office door was open. The administrative assistant in our office — a sweet, kind elderly woman who would soon retire — was visibly shaking after Smith left my office. Betty would, for the next year, be torn over her friendship to both Smith and me. She and I sometimes would chat about the controversy before other faculty arrived. She was like a caring parent trying to solve a dispute between two sons she loved. But there was nothing she could do, nor did I expect help. She reported to Smith, and her loyalties must stay there, because she needed that job. As the years passed, Betty would send me an e-mail now and then, to see how I was doing. Once we chatted on the phone. And then, after several more years passed, I never heard from her. Betty — the sweet maternalistic woman who wanted everyone to get along — had died. I think of her often.
11. John Gramlich and Katherine Schaeffer, "7 Facts about Guns in the U.S.," Pew Research Center (October 22, 2019), retrieved October 23, 2020, from <https://www.pewresearch.org/fact-tank/2019/10/22/facts-about-guns-in-united-states>; Alec Tyson, "How Important Is Climate Change to Voters in the 2020 Election?" Pew Research Center (October 6, 2020), retrieved October 23, 2020, from <https://www.pewresearch.org/fact-tank/2020/10/06/how-important-is-climate-change-to-voters-in-the-2020-election>; and Bradley Jones, "Increasing Share of Americans favor a single government program to provide health care coverage," Pew Research Center (September 29, 2020), retrieved October 23, 2020, from <www.pewresearch.org/fact-tank/2020/09/29/increasing-share-of-americans-favor-a-single-government-program-to-provide-health-care-coverage>. For a general review of the decline of democratic politics, see Jonathan Rauch, "How American Politics Went Insane: It Happened Gradually—and until the U.S. Figures out how to Treat the Problem, It Will only get Worse," *The Atlantic* (July/August, 2016), retrieved October 23, 2020, from <www.theatlantic.com/magazine/archive/2016/07/how-american-politics-went-insane/485570>.
12. If the AG's office had not believed the records were public data, would the SPJ students have won in court? I doubt it. Most state laws treat student evaluations as nonpublic

personnel data.

13. "Student Lawsuit Forces UW-River Falls to Open Files," *The* (University of Wisconsin-Stevens Point) *Pointer* (April 21, 1994), p. 1.

14. Ibid.

15. David Anderson and Patrice Peterson, "Evaluations Are Opened," *Student Voice* (April 14, 1994), p. 1A, 5A.

16. Ibid.

17. I deliberately designed this question to distinguish the free speech component of my actions (helping the students) from the objective criteria that are supposed to be used to evaluate an employee's performance.

18. I wrote to the dean on June 27, 1994.

19. About twenty years would pass before I learned about this comment.

20. Quoted in Eric H. Kessler and James R. Bailey, "Introduction: Understanding, Applying and Developing Organizational and Managerial Wisdom," pp. xv-lxxiv in Eric H. Kessler and James R. Bailey (editors), *Handbook of Organizational and Managerial Wisdom* (Thousand Oaks, CA: Sage Publications), p. xxvii.

Chapter 5

'You've Got No Case'

July 1994
Attorney's Office, Madison

The attorney leaned forward and clasped his hands. "If they decide to fire you, you'll lose."

"You're kidding," I moaned. "What about academic freedom?"

My spouse Mona and I were sitting in the office of Jay Willardson, an employment attorney in Madison, Wisconsin, which was a five-hour drive from our home in Shoreview, Minnesota. I got Jay's name from a colleague.

It was the summer after I learned that I could be fired for my role in helping students obtain access to student evaluations of faculty. I gave Jay a 10-minute summary of my academic freedom case, and he didn't pull any punches.

"Listen, no one wins those cases. The only cases that win are those arising from the protected categories. If you're a woman, a minority, over age 50, or have a unique set of religious beliefs, you might have a chance. But none of those apply to you, and even if they did the university will create a host of other reasons to fire you."

I could feel the blood draining from my face.

"Right now, university officials are probably developing a long list of things to hang you on, and your boss and other faculty and administrators are actively helping to develop that list. Academic freedom and the First Amendment are noble ideals, but it is virtually impossible to win a lawsuit using them as a defense. I'm sorry. I wish I could be more positive, but the legal system doesn't really provide much protection for faculty who speak their minds."

Could Jay be right?

Although I taught courses in mass media law and knew a fair amount about the First Amendment, I was no expert on free speech in the academy. I knew that courts had generally held that the First Amendment protects controversial speech uttered in the classroom and in scholarship. But what about my service-related efforts to help SPJ students obtain access to student evaluations and publish the controversial stories? Did my actions go beyond the bounds of the Constitution? Or was the employment attorney speaking beyond his knowledge? After all, he was an employment attorney, not an expert on the First Amendment.

Yes, he could be wrong, but for the moment he was the only hope I had. I gave him a thousand-dollar retainer and he gave me some advice on navigating the bureaucratic backwaters.

"Do your job, keep copies of everything, keep communicating with your boss, and keep contributing to departmental goals."

I was crestfallen on the drive back home.

Mona could feel that. "I've got a book at home that I think you'll find inspirational, Dave. You've got a lot in common with the main character."

The book was Ayn Rand's *The Fountainhead*, which chronicles the adventures of an architect who refuses to compromise his principles. Of course, in the end, he defeats his enemies and gets the woman of his dreams.

Mona was right — the story lifted my spirits, even though I found Rand's extremist form of individualism difficult to swallow. Her theory provides no room for compassion, as this quote from Howard Roark, the book's protagonist, shows: "Independence is the only gauge of human virtue and value. What a man is and makes of himself; not what he has or hasn't done for others. There is no substitute for personal dignity."[1]

The fight for free speech isn't a fight for any one individual.

It's a fight for everyone, and its purpose is to check power.

I HAD HOPED summer break of 1994 would cool things down at the university.

It didn't.

When school resumed again in fall, Smith continued to shun me. I was excluded from some of the decisions affecting the department.

The stress was getting to me, but I didn't realize how much.

Kendra, one of my students who was about my age, around 40, came into my office and declared: "Dave, you're no fun anymore. What's happened to you?"

She was right.

I didn't laugh or joke anymore. I was always serious and obsessed with the details of the dispute. It was difficult to put it out of my mind.

I apologized and, after speaking with Mona, I scheduled an appointment with a psychiatrist to get something to help me sleep. After 10 minutes of discussion, the doc rendered his diagnosis: "You're suffering from clinical depression."

Me?

I was stunned and relieved at the same time. Stunned because I thought I was tough enough to survive this ordeal. Relieved because now there was some hope that I could get some sleep.

The doc put me on an antidepressant and a non-narcotic sleeping aid, and five weeks later I was a new man. I was amazed at the effectiveness of the medication.

AS THE WEEKS PASSED, things at the university didn't improve.

So I followed the advice of world heavyweight boxing champion Jack Dempsey, who is credited with saying, "The best defense is a good offense."[2]

I informed several colleagues that I had hired an attorney. My goal was to get administrators off my back — to let them know that I was prepared to fight this out.

But my plan backfired.

When Smith heard that, he reduced his interactions with me even more.

I became, in the lexicon of the scholar, persona non grata — an "unwelcomed person." In ancient Greece, the worst punishment that could befall someone was not death — it was banishment from the community, which denied the offender burial with his family and, thus, access to heaven.

Now I understood why my high school English teacher forced me and my fellow students to write a book report about the Titan Prometheus, who defied Zeus and gave humans fire, knowledge and culture. In response, Zeus chained him to a rock, and a buzzard (or eagle in some accounts) would pluck out his liver every day. Prometheus declared:

Behold me bound, a God to evil doomed,
The foe of Zeus, and held
In hatred by all Gods
Who tread the courts of Zeus:
And this for my great love,
Too great, for mortal men.[3]

In other words, Prometheus loved humans so much that he sacrificed himself.[4]

To be honest, I had no intention of sacrificing myself.

I love my liver and my career.

But I also had passion for protecting the principle of free speech. If university administrators can punish faculty who help student journalists cover controversial issues on campus, then what is to stop them from punishing faculty who question ill-conceived administrative policies or decisions? If I had to sacrifice my job to protect that principle, then so be it.

University administrators did not understand my passion. They viewed me as a non-team player, as a naive idealist and rule-breaker.

In fact, when I left my university office for the drive home one day, I found a black-and-white line drawing of Don Quixote and his sidekick Sancho Panza pinned beneath my windshield wiper. Quixote was the fictional character in Miguel de Cervantes's famous seventeenth-century novel[5] who goes insane after reading many chivalric romances and embarks on a ludicrous mission with Sancho to revive chivalry for the betterment of Spain. They endure many indignities and humiliations. In the end, Quixote regains his sanity and denounces chivalric truths. Then he dies from a fever, which brings an end to the knights errant.

Well, that flier pierced me like the dull tip of Quixote's spear.

Was I naive?

Maybe.

Was I idealistic?

Of course.

But even naive, idealistic people can achieve goals.

So I responded like any good follower of Quixote would: I tore the flier up and vowed to press on, which meant I needed to develop a plan if I were going to defeat my enemies, real or imagined.

I knew I would be denied early promotion and perhaps renewal of my contract. What I didn't know, though, was how the university would justify the decision.

My performance on all three criteria for tenure and promotion — teaching, research and service — was very good for three straight years. So how could they justify a firing?

The answer came several days later, in mid-September, when I was making copies of tests.

"Collegiality," said Jimmy, my business professor colleague. "They can fire you if they think you're not nice enough or if you don't play well with others on the playground."

"What?"

"I'm not kidding. Go look at university rules."

Sure enough, there it was, in Chapter 4 of the UW–RF Faculty Handbook, under "Promotional Criteria," under subsection "Contribution to the University," paragraph (b). I could feel the chains tightening on my wrists and ankles as I read the paragraph:

> Ability and willingness to maintain such working relations with colleagues as are essential to effective accomplishment of the mission of the academic unit, the college and the university.

In other words, if you aren't nice to your colleagues, the university can fire you.
My career is over. Send me to the underworld.

I didn't sleep well that night. I couldn't stop perseverating on the issue of collegiality. In the unwritten norms of academic life, there's an expectation that faculty and administrators respect each other and work together to solve social problems. Nothing wrong with that.

Yet collegiality has a dark side.

Sociologist Max Weber warned that elites (university administrators in this case) sometimes use collegiality as a mechanism to control individuals — to prevent experts and professionals from challenging their authority.[6] The American Association of University Professors and other organizations picked up on this theme in the twentieth century, arguing that punishing professors for not being nice tramples on their free speech rights. They urged universities to eliminate collegiality clauses from their handbooks, and many did. Could the University of Wisconsin system be one of them?

Later that morning I called the UW System office in Madison, where I was handed over to an attorney who dealt with university policies and rules.

"Several years ago," she said, "we informed all of the satellite campuses to strike collegiality clauses from their faculty handbooks and administrative rules. When it comes to evaluating an employee, the key criterion is job performance — not attitude or whether others like you."[7] The collegiality clause at UW–RF was probably still on the books, she said, because someone had failed to implement the strike order.[8]

Unchain me.

For the first time in months, I felt hopeful.

But how was I going to prove that collegiality would be the cause of my anticipated dismissal? No administrator would admit to it.

I needed to find someone who had inside knowledge.

Someone like an accreditation official.

THE JOURNALISM PROGRAM was up for re-accreditation this semester, and the site visit team for the Accrediting Council on Education in Journalism and Mass Communications would be here in a week or two.

So on September 21, 1994, I snail-mailed team chair Sue Talberson informing her about the controversy in the department. My hope was that she and the team might serve as independent moderators and help resolve the conflict.

Wishful thinking on my part.

A brief in-person meeting with Sue after she arrived revealed that she had been co-opted into the administrative point of view. She had spent much of her professional life managing newspapers, working as a publisher and executive editor. She identified with management, not rank-and-file.

So I returned to option A — obtain evidence of collegiality.

Sue would never openly declare that the university was violating the collegiality clause and the First Amendment. So, I had only one other viable option: to secretly tape-record her. I got the idea from the *Lexington Herald-Leader*.

In 1986, the newspaper won a Pulitzer Prize for publishing a series of stories that exposed cash payoffs to University of Kentucky basketball players in violation of NCAA regulations.[9] Early in the investigation, reporters and editors made a decision to secretly tape-record conversations with players and others from whom they were receiving incriminating evidence.

Second-party tape recording, as this is called in legal circles, was not illegal. At the time, Kentucky and 39 other states, including Wisconsin, permitted one party to a conversation to record conversations without the knowledge of the other party.

Attorneys and police are devotees of second-party tape recording. Some attorneys secretly record conversations with clients to protect themselves from malpractice lawsuits. Police use second-party tape recording to collect evidence against lawbreakers.

Although the practice is now legal in 38 states, some people and journalists still think it's unethical. In 1974, the American Bar Association ruled that it generally was unethical for attorneys but not for police. In 2001, the ABA reversed itself and said it was not unethical, at least in areas where it was not outlawed.[10]

Journalists have never reached consensus on the issue. But one thing is certain: The secret tape recording saved the *Herald-Leader* from libel lawsuits. After the stories were published, some of the sources who gave incriminating evidence tried to recant their statements.

My case was a bit different.

I wasn't acting as a journalist. I wasn't going to publish the results of the recording in a news story. I was an employee who was trying to save his job and possibly his career, and I was trying to prevent the university from violating the First Amendment. You might call me a "free speech cop." I would use the recording as evidence in a hearing or a lawsuit, much like police use evidence to convict the bad guys.

I purchased a small tape recorder and put it in my desk drawer just before my meeting with Sue and turned it on. I was nervous. I don't like the idea of deceiving people, but I had no other choice.

Sue and I chatted for a while about various issues, including the dispute over the controversial student newspaper articles and the SPJ lawsuit. She said university administrators were angry because I had hired an attorney.

"I know that you've hired an attorney. My one question is, Why did you hire the attorney? Or what is it the attorney has been hired to do?"[11]

I told her I hired the attorney to protect my due process rights.

"I can tell you the impact of hiring the attorney has basically been to shut the university out of process," she added. "You shut it down. In hiring that lawyer and making it a civil action, now there is a fear that everything that is said to you is going to wind up as documentation and so on. I know they have a great sense of respect for you as a teacher and I know they would not say this, but I picked up a strong sense of sorrow. And they really want to resolve this, but now that the lawyers are involved they feel that their hands are totally tied."

Wow!

I took a deep breath and sat back in my chair. She was suggesting that I was being punished for hiring an attorney. I wanted to ask more questions about that, but I was worried a digression could derail my goal of obtaining evidence about collegiality.

"Do you think I'll be fired?" I calmly asked.

She said she believed I would be fired if the university and I didn't sit down and talk.

I told her my attorney had tried to do that, but university officials thus far had refused to negotiate.

"For any teacher to get tenure there has to be a good productive working relationship," Sue said. "So that's the thing that has to be established. So that you can all move ahead together."

"A good working relationship certainly is a great asset," I said, preparing to bait her. "What you're suggesting to me is that they feel that collegiality is still an important part of being able to be part of the university community."

"Well, it always has been and probably always will be, and that's the nature of tenure."

BINGO.

Sue went on for a couple more minutes, talking about how much she disliked tenure and how she believed employers, including universities, should have the power to fire workers or faculty whenever they wish.

She talked about trust and good working relationships.

I didn't disagree that good working relationships are useful, but I said protecting free speech rights of faculty takes precedence. "The rules of the university say that faculty are evaluated for teaching, research and service. The UW System eliminated the collegiality clause several years ago."

"Oh, I didn't realize it was eliminated," she said. "But the thing is, you know, that hiring of legal counsel usually comes after you go through the process, not before."

In other words, she was saying that I could still be punished for hiring an attorney.

Her comments made me question whether she, a journalism professor, really understood the function of tenure and free speech in a university setting. She told me she was an absolutist in terms of the First Amendment, but she failed to see the contradictions in her statements.

I secretly recorded conversations with two other university employees, both of whom would become members of my promotion and retention committee. They, too, confirmed that university officials were upset with me because I helped students file the lawsuit and write stories about faculty salaries and because I hired the attorney.

Now I believed I had all the evidence I needed to defend myself.

My next step was to inform university officials to shut this down before it really turns ugly. My departmental promotion and retention hearing would be a good place to do that.

Chapter 5 Endnotes

1. Ayn Rand, *The Fountainhead* (New York: Signet, 1996; originally published in 1949), p. 681.

2. The idea behind Dempsey's aphorism can be traced further back in history. George Washington wrote in 1799: "Make them believe, that offensive operations, often times, are the surest, if not the only (in some cases) means of defense." Source: George Washington to John Trumbull, June 25, 1799, National Archives, Founders Online, retrieved October 24, 2020, from < http://founders.archives.gov/documents/Washington/ 06-04-02-0120>.

3. Aeschylus, *Prometheus Bound*, translated by E. H. Plumptre, Vol. VIII, Part 4, The Harvard Classics (New York: P. F. Collier & Son, 1909-14), Lines 132-137.

4. In some tales, Ulysses (or Hercules in Roman mythology) saves Prometheus.

5. Miguel de Cervantes Saavedra, *Don Quixote*, translated by Samuel Putman, edited by Peter Anthony Motteux and John Ozell (New York: The Modern Library, 1930).

6. Max Weber, *The Theory of Social and Economic Organization*, translated by A. M. Henderson and Talcott Parsons (New York: The Free Press, 1964; originally published in 1947), p. 402.

7. Despite the decision by UW System attorneys to strike the collegiality clause, courts across the country often have ruled that universities may take collegiality into account when assessing the performance of faculty. See Mary Ann Connell and Frederick G. Savage, "Does Collegiality Count? While Academics Debate the Importance of Collegiality in Faculty Personnel Decisions, the Courts Have Spoken. They Won't Protect Truculent Professors," *Academe*, 87(6) (November/December 2001), retrieved January 31, 2009, from <www.aaup.org/AAUP/pubsres/academe/2001/ND/Feat/Conn.htm>.

8. The collegiality clause was eliminated from the handbook sometime after my lawsuit,

as the 2011 UW–RF Faculty Handbook contains no mention of the word "collegiality" in its criterion for promotion and tenure. The 2011 language under Chapter 4, Subsection 3.2.1 reads: "Performance criteria: (c1) Effectiveness in teaching; (c2) Professional involvement and accomplishments ... in research/scholarly/creative activity; (c3) Contributions ... at the departmental, College, University, community, state, national, or international level in categories other than those identified above." Retrieved September 1, 2012, from <http://www.uwrf.edu/FacultySenate/Handbook/Chapter4/Handbook4s3.cfm>.

9. Jeffrey A. Marx and Michael M. York, "Playing Above the Rules: Boosters' Cash, Gifts Lined Pockets of UK Players," *Lexington Herald-Leader* (October 27, 1985), pp. A1, A11, A12. The lead of the story stated: "For years, ordinary fans have rewarded University of Kentucky basketball players with a loyalty that is nationally known. What is less known is that a small group of boosters has been giving the players something extra: a steady stream of cash." Thirty-one of the 33 players said they knew of improper activities when they were playing; 26 said they participated. The NCAA investigated but 32 of the 33 people said they were misquoted or quoted out of context in the series. The investigation was dropped. However, three years later, the program was involved in another scandal, and the NCAA penalized the university.

10. Charles Doyle, "Wiretapping, Tape Recorders, and Legal Ethics: An Overview of Questions Posed by Attorney Involvement in Secretly Recording Conversation," Congressional Research Service (7-5700, R42650), (August 9, 2012), retrieved September 1, 2012, from <www.fas.org/sgp/crs/misc/R42650.pdf>.

11. The conversation that follows was taken directly from the tape recorded meeting, which is still in my possession.

Chapter 6

'Nothin' But a Troublemaker'

Early November 1994
University of Wisconsin–River Falls

The professor's body was shaking and her voice crackled as she shouted, "I can't believe you secretly recorded Sue. That's offensive, Dave. Unethical. Did you ever secretly tape me? I feel violated. This is shameful. What you did was wrong. Wrong!"

I had just informed her and the other members of the journalism faculty that I had evidence the university was violating the First Amendment. The meeting was to consider my request for early promotion to associate professor and my yearly contract renewal.

I don't remember the exact date of the meeting, but I do remember what the professor and I said.

"I never tape-recorded conversations with you," I said calmly, looking at her. "I only taped conversations with Sue and two of the people on my promotion and annual review committee. It was the only way to show that the university was violating the First Amendment. If there was any other way to produce the evidence, I would have done it. But there was no other way."

Smith and other faculty at the meeting didn't address my allegations that the university was violating the First Amendment. They didn't care. For them, the controversy had become personal.

At this point, there was no question that my request for promotion and renewal of my annual contract would be rejected.

But the meeting was not a waste of time.

There was one very inspiring moment.

It came when Patrice Peterson, who was the top student in our program, offered testimony in support of my application. She informed me before the hearing that she was going to do this. I asked her to reconsider, because her testimony would have no effect other than to possibly hurt her standing with the other professors.

But she had good relations with all of the faculty.

She ignored my advice.

Did I mention that she was the number one student in our program and the entire university that year?[1]

I SLEPT WELL that evening.

But evenings like this would the exception rather than the rule for the next six months. I was getting about three to six hours a night. When I woke, I usually went to my office in the basement and worked on my research and book projects for the rest of the night. That took my mind off the controversy, at least temporarily, and it also increased my productivity as a scholar.

By this time — my fourth year at UW–RF — I had published 12 refereed journal articles and two peer-reviewed academic books. I was working on a third.

Meanwhile, Sue's accreditation team noted in its report that there was no evidence that the dispute was interfering with the education of students at the university. I was relieved, because some university officials were hinting that they would use that as another excuse to fire me.

Of course, one could have posed the opposite argument — that insulating students from such a dispute would actually conflict with educational goals. Disputes are, after all, a part of life. But I was just grateful that I didn't have to spend scores of more hours fighting another charge.

On November 29, 1994, Jay, my employment attorney, offered a compromise to resolve the conflict: expunge the records, including letters or materials that Smith and others had put together about the dispute, and then move on. I thought the university would accept it. It was inexpensive and easy.

But a week later, John Tallman, the same assistant attorney general who told my students that student evaluations were public data, notified Jay that the university would not accept the offer.

In that moment, my status on campus changed from pariah to demon.

ON DECEMBER 16, 1994, Smith and three faculty members from other departments met in closed session to consider my request for promotion to associate professor as well as to issue an advisory vote on progress toward tenure. As expected, this formal Journalism Department Retention Committee rejected my request and issued an adverse vote on progress toward tenure.

"Professor Demers' inability to maintain productive communication channels within his department has inhibited his ability to contribute to department goals," the committee said.

That comment surprised me. Sue pointed out that it was university officials, not I, who had stopped communicating, because they didn't like the fact that I had hired an attorney.

The retention committee vote also revealed the rationale that administrators would use to fire me: "failure to maintain productive communication channels."

That was nearly the same line that a prison guard used in the movie *Cool Hand Luke* before punishing Paul Newman, who played Luke. That movie was shown to my entire high school during my junior year.

One could easily argue that a failure to communicate is simply an element of collegiality. That's because faculty in general are notoriously famous for not getting along, with each other or with administrators. Hell, if a failure to communicate was used as a criterion to terminate faculty, half the faculty in America would have to be fired.

But I knew now that no matter how elaborate or careful I was in developing rational arguments to support my case, administrators would never listen. When you hold power, you don't have to listen.

Or respond.

Or be nice.

But I concede that the administration's failure-to-communicate allegation was clever strategy, because it meant I would have to prove that it was indicator of collegiality. More time and effort.

A better plan was to get administrators to say, in their own words, that they were using collegiality as the grounds for dismissal. I decided I would bait them during my appeals in spring.

THE NEXT THREE MONTHS were difficult.

I was the most hated faculty member on campus.

Faculty who knew me would avoid walking near me and avert their eyes when I looked at them. "But I'm fighting for your free speech rights," I wanted to tell them, but it was futile. They would never understand. The collective had framed me as a troublemaker, and there was little I could do to alter that reality.

The only friendly colleague I had left on campus was Jimmy, the business professor. He and I chatted on a number of occasions about my dilemma as the months passed. He was supportive, at least for a while. But I could tell he was uneasy with our meetings, so I stopped confiding in him.

I had plenty of colleagues at other universities who sympathized with my plight. But they didn't have much information about what was going on. E-mail was awkward to use in those days, and the telephone was too time-consuming.

The worst part of the controversy was the toll it was taking on my marriage. Mona was always supportive, but the dispute stole time away from our relationship. Time is not something you can recover. I still feel bad about that.

On March 6, 1995, the Journalism Department Retention Committee issued its final decision regarding my request for promotion and contract renewal. I lost again.

Two reasons were given this time.[2]

The first was that I allegedly had failed to establish a working relationship with faculty because I had closed off communication. The second reason given was my secret audio taping of Sue and two members of the retention committee.

"Tenure is based on some assurance that a good, productive working relationship over the long term is likely," the committee wrote. "Without evidence of that, an institution is playing loose with the best interests of students in the long run."

I responded in writing that this statement violates the prohibition against collegiality. I added that taping the officials did not violate university policy or the law, and that it was the only way to prove university officials were violating the First Amendment.

The committee and university officials never responded to my comments. Bureaucracies are like that. They only respond when they want to.

On March 15, I got a bit of good news.

The College of Arts and Sciences Promotion Committee voted in favor of my request for promotion. This committee was composed of faculty from other departments — faculty who were not personally involved in or affected by the dispute. The committee concluded that my teaching, service and research met or exceeded university standards.

But support from this committee didn't matter. In university systems, administrators hold final power when it comes to tenure and promotion decisions. The final decision rested with three administrators: the dean, vice chancellor, and chancellor. I would meet one-to-one with all three.

Dean Stricter told me he was going to vote against retention because a "faculty member must have good working relations with colleagues." To ensure collegiality was the basis of his decision, I baited him with the "outlawed" wording directly out of the UW–RF Faculty Handbook.

"Do you think 'ability and willingness to maintain good working relations with colleagues is essential to accomplishing the mission of the department and university' and should this policy be used to assess whether I should be granted tenure and promotion here?"

"Of course," he said.

He allowed me to openly tape-record our meeting.

The vice chancellor at the university, who was the next up the chain of command in terms of ruling on my request for retention, also allowed me to tape-record our meeting. He, too, confirmed that collegiality was the reason he would vote against me.

The chancellor of the university, Gary Thibodeau, refused to allow me to tape-record our conversation, so I left his office without an interview. But that meeting would not have affected the outcome. Thibodeau had already made up his mind.

My subsequent appeals were ignored as the school year came to a close. The university gave me one year to pack my bags.[3]

The extra year didn't give me much solace.

My thoughts were filled with anxiety that my academic career was coming to an end. But I can't say I didn't know this could happen. I knew the risks. Principles be a pain in the ass sometimes.

"DEMERS DESERVED THIS," I overheard one professor telling another as I was leaving North Hall, on the last day of class in spring 1995. "He's nothin' but a troublemaker."

Was I a troublemaker?

That question tormented me as I drove home that evening. It brought to mind the 1976 Willie Nelson song, "The Troublemaker."

I could tell the moment that I saw Him
He was nothing but the trouble-making kind
His hair was much too long and His motley group of friends
Had nothing but rebellion on their minds[4]

As the lyrics suggest, a troublemaker is often defined as a person who habitually causes difficulty or problems and incites others to defy those in authority.[5] Jesus was the troublemaker in Nelson's song.

Jesus and I never incited others to defy those in authority.

But he and I were very different in all other respects. He was the "son of God." I was the son of a printer. He could walk on water and convert it to wine. I was not a good swimmer but I was an excellent wine drinker.

"You're going to need a miracle to get out of this one," one of my graduate school colleagues told me. "You're an activist without a social movement — a lonely activist."

He was right.

I was an activist.

I learned this role decades earlier from my Lutheran elementary schoolteachers, from bullies in high school, and from my undergraduate journalism and social science professors.

Chapter 6 Endnotes

1. The journalism faculty did not punish her. In fact, she earned the department's top graduating student award that spring, and all of the faculty, including me, voted in favor. In addition, she earned the university's top graduating student award.

2. Recommendation of the Journalism Department Retention Committee for Retention of David Pearce Demers (March 15, 1995).

3. At most universities, when contracts are not renewed, faculty are allowed to teach for one more year. This gives them some time to find another job.

4. "The Troublemaker," from *The Troublemaker* album (Columbia Records, 1976).

5. This definition was provided by Google.

Part III

Anatomy of a Free Speech Activist

Chapter 7

Lutherans and Bullies

The 1960s
Frankenmuth, Michigan

I grew up in an apolitical family.

Both of my parents, who were high school graduates, worked hard to make ends meet. My dad was a printer and my mother an insurance underwriter. They didn't have time for politics or protest. They had four kids to support: me and my younger brother and two younger sisters.

Many years later, when I was a graduate student, I stumbled upon a book that provided a structural explanation for my parents' lack of political acumen. The authors, who were British sociologists, called it the "dull compulsion of economic relationships."[1] In plain English, my parents, like most people, didn't have time to get involved in politics that might make the world a better place because they were too busy trying to survive.

We lived in a small, conservative town in Michigan called Frankenmuth — population 2,500, located about 90 miles north of Detroit. Lutheran missionaries from Franconia (now part of Bavaria), Germany, founded the town in 1845.

"Franken what?" people would say when I told them where I was from. "Franken" represents the province and "mut" means "courage," so "courage of the Franconians," I would elaborate. "Franken—what?" they would respond.

The goal of the first settlers was pragmatic — to convert the Chippewa Indians living in the area. That mission didn't last long. The Indians left as more white people took over everything.

In the early years, Frankenmuth was a logging and farming community. One of the hotels in town developed a reputation for serving savory chicken dinners and homemade beer and wine. In the 1920s, William Zehnder Sr. purchased the hotel and renovated it, further cementing the town's reputation as a destination for good food and spirits.

During the Prohibition era, Zehnder's quietly continued to serve beer and wine. On July 30, 1930, federal agents from Detroit raided Zehnder's and the Fischer Hotel across the street. Zehnder was fined $3,800 and Herman Fischer, owner of the hotel, was fined $8,800. The latter fine was the highest paid during the Prohibition era.

Zehnder was a member of St. Lorenz Lutheran Church in Frankenmuth. He told the congregation that he would apologize if other members of the congregation who violated the law did the same thing. The pastor saved everyone the embarrassment, pointing out that the law was "crazy."[2]

Those Germans loved their beer and wine.

To the best of my knowledge, the decision to violate Prohibition laws was the most radical organized act of defiance mainstream Frankenmuthers ever committed against the U.S. political system.

During the 1950s, another Frankenmuther named Wallace "Wally" Bronner began making and painting Christmas bulbs in the basement of his house. Twenty years later his business was the largest Christmas store in the world, and Frankenmuth was now the third most popular tourist destination in Michigan, right behind Henry Ford Museum/Greenfield Village in Dearborn to the south and Mackinaw Island to the north.[3]

More than two million people were visiting Frankenmuth each year to eat chicken dinners at Zehnder's or the Bavarian Inn (the former Fischer Hotel) and to shop at Bronner's Christmas store or one of the scores of little specialty stores adorned in Bavarian architecture.

IN MY ELEMENTARY YEARS, I attended St. Lorenz Lutheran School, which served 650 students, making it the largest Lutheran elementary school in the United States.

The teachers taught us the importance of individual responsibility, hard work, frugality, honesty and deferred gratification. They also told us that we should "treat others as you would have them treat you"[4] and apologize when we wronged or hurt someone. Apologizing was particularly important, because it was a sign of humility — a sign that the person committing the wrong respected the dignity and worth of the person who was wronged. People or organizations that never apologize are arrogant, self-absorbed and disrespectful, according to our teachers.

Our Lutheran teachers also taught us to tell the truth, respect our parents and elders, help others whenever we could, practice thriftiness, work hard and confront social injustice. The latter did not mean Lutherans should challenge the military-industrial establishment. For the most part, Lutherans accepted the established political order.

But Lutherans did have at least one "enemy" in those days: The Catholics, who, we were told, distorted the Bible and had a history of persecuting Lutherans and other Protestants. The Catholics could be going to hell. I say "could be" because the

Lutheran teachers never told us outright that Catholics were destined for eternal damnation, but we kids were smart enough to connect the dots.[5]

Times have changed.

I don't think Lutheran teachers today are as judgmental as in the past. But you wouldn't be reading this book right now had one of my two parents been a Catholic.

"Are you Catholic or do you smoke?" my dad asked my mother when they met for the first time in 1949 at a roller-skating rink.

"No," my mother responded.

Thanks, Mom.

I was a well-behaved, quiet kid. Shy. Very religious. Honest to a fault. I would have ratted on my brother.

In my younger years, I spent more time watching television than reading or studying, which I regret to some extent. I loved Westerns and adventure movies and the stars who dominated them, including Jimmy Stewart, Gregory Peck, Henry Fonda, Glenn Ford, Robert Mitchum, John Wayne, Cary Grant and Gary Cooper. The story line in the movies was almost always the same: bad guys raise hell; good guys (often one individual) save the day.

I was particularly inspired by Cooper's role as Marshal Will Kane in *High Noon*. He stood alone against the bad guys when the townsfolk refused to help him. Kane defended democracy and the rule of law, even at great cost to himself, as he was shot by the bad guys (but lived).

From ages 14 to 16, I worked at the Bavarian Inn, as did hundreds of other kids through the years. The businesses kept growing because the families had nowhere else to invest the profits.

Lutherans didn't tolerate "conspicuous consumption," a term introduced by Norwegian American economist and sociologist Thorstein Veblen (1857–1929) in his 1899 book *The Theory of the Leisure Class*. Veblen applied the term to the nouveau riche, an economic class that emerged in the nineteenth century as a result of the accumulation of wealth in modern capitalism.[6] In F. Scott Fitzgerald's novel *The Great Gatsby*, the nouveau riche were those who lived in West Egg on Long Island Sound, including Gatsby himself.

The term "conspicuous consumption"— more popularly referred to in the 1960s as "keeping up with the Joneses" — is now broadly applied to people who spend money on goods and services to show off their status as opposed to just using them for their intrinsic value.

My Lutheran school education ended in eighth grade, at which time I joined the so-called heathens in high school. They didn't respect the Ten Commandments like we Lutheran kids did.

Take the Sixth Commandment, for example. "Thou shalt not kill."

We Lutheran kids interpreted that to mean you also should not hurt other people. But some football players at Frankenmuth High School disagreed. They enjoyed using their lineman-sized hands to lift and pin me — at 96 pounds, the third smallest boy in the entire school of 624 — by my neck against the hallway walls. Another senior bully preferred to slug me in the stomach or back during gym roll call, when the coach would turn his back.

When my parents complained about the bullying, the gym coach suggested I put on the boxing gloves and duke it out with Ted, the six-foot tall, 170-pound gut-slugger. Before I had a chance to decline this brattish offer, slugger-boy did me a favor: He dropped out of school.

I facetiously tell people today that "I coulda been a rich man" had I been born 40 years later, when parents decided the courts were better than boxing rings for taking down bullies and complicit school systems.

But, as we Lutherans like to say, there is always a silver lining.

Being bullied in high school nourished in me an empathy for the underdog, which is an essential trait for good journalists, professors and social activists. Although I never bullied anyone in high school, I would be lying if I said I never strayed from the path of the righteous.

I was a fringe member of the faux-hippie clique during my junior and senior years. We "hippies" had long hair and thought we were cool. We drove around in our muscle cars, listening to loud rock music while drinking beer and smoking cigarettes. Some of us were experimenting with marijuana and other drugs.

And some of us were experimenting with love.

I dated a cheerleader from another high school for nearly a year. It was wonderful until she asked me to marry her and have children. Hell, I was only 16. I had a hard time taking care of myself.

Of course, during these times my friends and I were in a desperate search for identity in an increasingly complex world — a world in which individuals, especially college students, were questioning the power of traditional paternalistic authorities to control their lives.

That antiestablishment theme got a boost from a number of 1960s-era Hollywood films,[7] including *Cool Hand Luke*, which starred Paul Newman as Lucas Jackson, a decorated war veteran who is sent to a southern chain-gang prison for cutting off the tops of parking meters in a drunken stupor.[8]

Luke tells the prisoners he cut them off to settle an "old score," but he doesn't explain what he means by that. Some viewers assumed stress from his war experiences in either World War II or the Korean War (not specified in the movie) played some role.

In prison, Luke refuses to submit not only the prison camp's repressive authority system, but to the inmates' authority system as well. He earns the respect of the prisoners after fighting a more powerful inmate, eating 50 boiled eggs, and trying to escape on several occasions. The escapes earn him severe beatings from prison guards, who throw him in the "box" in an attempt to break him.

The captain of the guards, while beating Luke with a stick, delivers the most famous line in the movie: "What we've got here is failure to communicate." At the end of the movie, Luke mocks the guards with that phrase (adding the article "a" before the word "failure"), just before a rifle shot rings out.

The movie was shown to the entire FHS student body in the school's gymnasium during my junior year.

One of my best high school friends, Scott, recalled years later that the purpose of the movie was "to help motivate us (students) to be good people."[9]

Another friend, Rod, concurred and jestingly added that "if we students failed to get a good education, we would end up talking like — chewing and spitting tobacco like — the people in the movie."

But if the purpose of the movie was to scare us into conforming, I'm not sure it was very effective. To me and others, Luke was not the bad guy. He was the hero. And he also was a victim — a victim of a corrupt correctional system and a naive military bureaucracy, which expected that young soldiers would be unaffected by combat and killing.

Of course, the film never said the stress of war made Luke cut off the parking meter heads. But the screenwriters could not have expected that viewers would fail to make the connection, given the many psychological and emotional problems suffered by soldiers returning from the Vietnam War during the 1960s.[10]

A good real-life example is Ted the bully — the senior who used to slug me in gym class. Shortly after he dropped out of school, he was arrested for stealing a car and armed robbery.

The judge gave him a choice: jail or Vietnam.

Ted chose the latter.

He chose poorly.

Through the years, Ted tried to suppress memories of the horrors he witnessed in Vietnam, according to one relative. His wife eventually kicked him out. Doctors tried to treat his mental illness. But in 2007, at the age of 57, he shot himself in the kitchen while his daughter was taking a shower in the bathroom.

"The storm is stilled and he is at rest," his obituary stated.[11]
Some might say just deserts, or bad Karma.
I had no love for Ted.
But no one, not even Ted the bully, deserves to suffer the mental torture that war unleashes upon people, or at least that was my state of mind in those days.

ALTHOUGH I STRONGLY IDENTIFIED with Cool Hand Luke's character, in real life I was more like the inmates in the movie, who didn't have enough courage to challenge the system like Luke did.

The biggest act of defiance I committed during high school was helping a fellow friend and classmate skip classes. I crossed out his name on attendance slips. The assistant principal punished me with several after-school detention hours. Fortunately, the school did not have a "box."

But Luke and I did share one thing in common: Neither of us had a clear vision of what we wanted to do with our lives.

My high school counselor, a middle-aged woman who I met on two occasions, discouraged me from attending a four-year college because my grades were mediocre (B-). I admit it. I was a lazy student. I hadn't learned the importance of getting a good education.

Like a good Lutheran, I complied with her advice and enrolled in a community college near my home. Thus, when I started college in fall of 1971, I was, without question, more of a conformist than an activist.

But the Vietnam War and my professors changed me.

I became more politically active after entering college, partly because my life depended upon it and partly because my professors were teaching me about the ideals that made America great.

Chapter 7 Endnotes

1. Nicholas Abercrombie, Steven Hill and Brian S. Turner, *The Dominant Ideology Thesis* (London: Allen & Unwin ,1980).

2. A brief history of Zehnder's is available at <http://www.zehnders.com/new-site/about-us/history.htm>.

3. Frankenmuth is now one of the three top tourist attractions in Michigan, drawing nearly 3 million visitors a year.

4. The Biblical citation is Matthew 7:12. "Do unto others as you would have others do unto you."

5. Tensions between Catholics and Lutherans began to wane in the 1950s and early 1960s. The irony today is that people today often comment about how similar Catholicism is to

Lutheranism.

6. Thorstein Veblen, *The Theory of the Leisure Class: An Economic Study of Institutions* (New York: The Macmillan Co., 1912).

7. Other movies that question traditional authority or offered counter-cultural views included *Dr. Strangelove* (1964), *The Graduate* (1967), *Bonnie and Clyde* (1967), *Easy Rider* (1969), *Alice's Restaurant* (1969), and *Five Easy Pieces* (1970).

8. *Cool Hand Luke* was released in 1967. It was directed by Stuart Rosenberg. The screenplay was adapted from Donn Pearce's 1965 novel of the same name. He and Frank Pierson wrote the script. The film was nominated for five Academy Awards. George Kennedy won an Oscar for Best Supporting Actor. The script does not specify the year in which the events take place, nor does it identify which war Luke fought in. However, based on the age of the vehicles shown in the movie, the events probably took place in the late 1940s or early 1950s. Luke probably fought in World War II, although some reviewers have suggested that it was the Korean War. The screen writers may have purposely left Luke's war service vague.

9. On June 3, 2013, I asked Scott, Rod and other classmates what they recalled about the movie event. Scott and Rod's quotations are taken from e-mails they sent me on June 4 and 5, 2013, respectively.

10. Donn Pearce, who wrote the novel upon which the film was based, drew heavily from his personal experiences in writing the book and screenplay.

11. His obituary was published in the Oct. 17, 2007, issue of the *Saginaw* (Michigan) *News*.

Chapter 8

Enlightenment for Everyone

Fall Semester 1971
Delta College, Saginaw, Michigan

Political science professor Roger Taggard leaned on the lectern and took a big drag from his Marlboro, blowing smoke into the air, moments before beginning the day's lecture.[1]

"Picture yourself in eighteenth-century England," he told his class of 50 students, which included me, "and you're watching a mob of Englishmen surround a Frenchman as he's walking back to the inn where he was staying. Then the mob shouts, 'Hang him! Hang the Frenchman!'"

For a brief moment, everyone in that room could hear a dropped cigarette butt hit the floor.[2]

"But the mob was no match for this man," Taggard added, taking another puff. "'Men of England,' the man said to the mob. 'You wish to kill me because I am a Frenchman. Am I not punished enough in not being born an Englishman?'"

I grinned.

"That clever remark quickly disarmed the mob," Taggard said. "In fact, the crowd even cheered and escorted the Frenchman safely to his lodge. The year was 1726. And the charmer was Voltaire, who would go down in history as one of the most important philosophers of the Age of Enlightenment. Some scholars also call him the father of the French Revolution."

Taggard dropping his lit cig onto the tiled floor and extinguished it with a twist of his leather-soled shoe.

In 1971, professors and students could smoke in class. I'm not kidding. It was up to the professor. Nearly 40 percent of college students smoked then. Cigarettes were cheap — 25 to 30 cents a pack, and the dangers of smoking were still being suppressed by the powerful tobacco lobby. Classrooms were often filled with a haze, especially during the winter, when the windows were closed. The floors were filled with butts at the end of the day.

Disgusting, I know.

But nonsmokers rarely complained. Smokers ruled back then.

It was my first semester in college. Delta College was located north of Saginaw near I-75. Most of the students were commuters who worked jobs. I was enrolled full time and worked as a short-order cook in a Frankenmuth restaurant.

TAGGARD WAS the kind of professor who liked to stimulate a class discussion. Today's session was no exception.

"What is the most central idea of the Enlightenment?" he asked.

Twenty seconds of awkward silence elapsed.

Some students withdrew eye contact from the professor, hoping this would diminish the chances of them being called upon to answer the question.

"To enlighten?" said a wisecracking male student in the back row.

Several students near him chuckled.

"That response is less than enlightening," the professor said, triggering a few more chuckles. "From what or from whom were they being enlightened?"

The students responded.

"From the church."

"From paternalism."

"Despotic rulers."

"Narrow-minded professors."

"Precisely — with present company excluded, of course," Taggard said, drawing more chuckles.

"The central idea of the Enlightenment," he said, "is that human reason — not supernatural forces, tradition, superstition or dogma — should guide human affairs.[3] This was a big deal. It legitimized the idea of separating the church from the state and reduced the political power of religious institutions in Europe and Great Britain."

Taggard added that Voltaire and other Enlightenment philosophers — including fellow French thinkers Jean-Jacques Rousseau and Baron de Montesquieu; Isaac Newton and John Locke of England; and Scots David Hume and Adam Smith — wrote books and articles that embraced reason, scientific knowledge and the worth of the individual.

Rousseau maintained that people were free in a "natural state" (like animals) but were subjected (or enslaved) by society and governments. To end this subordination, he argued that legitimate political authority comes only from a "social contract" agreed upon by all citizens.[4]

Locke agreed. The government's job was to protect "natural rights," and if it failed to do that, then people had the authority to replace that government, by force if necessary, and create a new social contract.

"They opposed tyranny and argued that ordinary people should play a bigger role in governing their communities and the state," Taggard said. "Most believed humans could, through scientific research and free-market economics, solve social problems and make the world a better place."[5]

"But," one student interjected, "haven't people always thought that science could help make the world a better place?"

"Good question, and the answer is no. In fact, prior to the sixteenth century, most university scholars subscribed to a philosophy called scholasticism. This was the idea that all knowledge came from church leaders and the works of Aristotle. In contrast, Voltaire and others argued that knowledge of the real world came through observation and reason. The world was one big lab experiment — out there to be discovered. Doubt everything, philosopher René Descartes declared. Then use logic and observation to rediscover and understand the world."

Although Taggard was clearly an advocate of the Age of Enlightenment, he did point out that there was a downside. Rousseau was worried about the moral degradation that came with reason, science and progress.[6] Industrialization and urbanization would, in fact, generate many social problems.

LECTURES LIKE THIS were changing the way I looked at the world.

I began to see that the anti-Vietnam War movement was not an isolated historical event but part of a larger social movement already several hundred years old — one that had introduced the world to the importance of individualism, democracy, free speech, due process, freedom of religion and self-governance.

Voltaire became my favorite Enlightenment philosopher. He criticized despotic authority and its penchant for suppressing free speech. In his *Treatise on Toleration*, he wrote, "We cannot cure the powerful of ambition, but we can cure the people of superstition. We can, by speech and pen, make men more enlightened and better."[7]

Voltaire wrote a number of other historical and theatrical works.

But his masterpiece was *Candide*,[8] a short book written in 1758 that attacked religious fanaticism and the injustices of war and class status. Candide is a young, innocent, naive disciple of Doctor Pangloss, who preaches that "in the best of possible worlds ... all is for the best." Pangloss means "windbag," and he symbolically represents the philosophy of established religion, which holds that people should accept all forms of suffering and evil without complaint and always look for the silver lining.

Candide suffers many indignities and becomes disillusioned with the world. In the end, he concludes that "we must cultivate our gardens" — in other words, one must reject idealistic dreams and live within one's limitations.[9]

I loved this book because its "best of possible worlds" maxim characterized the way many Lutherans and other Christians saw the world. No matter how bad things get, they always look for the silver lining.

Nothing wrong with this.

But, as Voltaire and, later, Karl Marx pointed out, embracing the silver lining often discourages people from trying to fix real-world problems.[10]

THE ENLIGHTENMENT had a tremendous impact on American history, but Taggard said most high school textbooks give it very little attention.[11] I vaguely recalled it being mentioned in a history class.

Thomas Paine drew on Enlightenment ideals when he wrote *Common Sense*, a pamphlet that sought to justify why the colonies should break away from Great Britain.

When Thomas Jefferson and Benjamin Franklin wrote the Declaration of Independence, they copied, almost verbatim, John Locke's famous phrase about life and liberty. Locke wrote that "no one ought to harm another in his right to life, health, liberty, or possessions" and that government exists only "with the consent of the governed."[12] Jefferson and Franklin wrote: "We hold these Truths to be self-evident, that all Men are created equal, that they are endowed by their Creator with certain unalienable Rights, that among these are *Life, Liberty and the pursuit of Happiness*."[13] [emphasis added]

James Madison borrowed heavily from Montesquieu, Locke and Rousseau when drafting the U.S. Constitution and creating the three branches of government. Montesquieu said that "government should be set up so that no man need be afraid of another." His prescription was to diffuse or decentralize power by creating separate branches of government (e.g., executive, legislative, judicial), each of which presumably would be a corrective to the abuses of the others.[14]

Enlightenment ideals permeate every mainstream institution in America, and the Bill of Rights draws heavily from them.

The legal system is not supposed to convict people without "due process of law," which includes the right of presumed innocence until proven guilty; the right to remain silent; the right to an attorney; the right to a public trial and impartial jury; the right to confront accusers and to cross-examine witnesses; the right to refuse to answer questions that might incriminate a person; and the right to equal protection of the law regardless of race, creed, color, religion, ethnic origin, age, handicaps or sex.[15]

The government is not supposed to punish people for their speech or religious preference, nor should it deny freedom of the press to journalists, who embrace the idea that their role is to make government accountable to the people.

The modern university has benefited more from the Enlightenment than perhaps any other social institution. The humanities became a "secular religion" whose mission became one of searching for meaning in life as well as providing a moral compass outside of organized religion. The social sciences focused on creating solutions to social problems, especially crime, poverty and discrimination, which themselves stemmed from increasing industrialization and urbanization.

The academy, Taggard said, inherited the responsibility of passing on Enlightenment ideals to the next generation of leaders. "That's why this course and many others in the social sciences and humanities extol the virtues of democratic decision-making, equality, free speech, and other civil liberties."

He also pointed out that the debate over the U.S. military draft is simply part of the larger debate over whether society should respect the rights of the individual. The Enlightenment philosophers argued that the most important power possessed by an individual was the individual's right to self-determination, to be the master of their own destiny, and to fight for social justice.

"You can see this ideal," Taggard said, "in Hollywood movies, which show the lone cowboy or sheriff standing up to the bad guys; the rogue cop who violates the rules but always beats lawbreakers; the falsely accused defendants who exonerate themselves; the superhero who defends society; and the individual who bucks the collective in a future dystopian world characterized by almost complete social control. Of course, these enlightened individuals almost always triumph in the end, and the message is clear: One individual can make a difference.

"But is this message realistic?" Taggard asked our class. "Can one individual really make a difference today?"

"I don't think so," said one long-haired bearded student. "The military-industrial complex is very powerful in America. Ordinary people and students have little power. Opinion polls show that nearly three-fourths of Americans are opposed to the Vietnam War, but the war goes on nevertheless. Power comes from the top down, not from the bottom up."

"I disagree," said a woman with short, blond hair. "People have the right to vote in America, and if they don't like the leadership, they can throw it out. The war goes on because the public has not demanded an end to it."

"That's not true," replied the bearded student. "We students and the public have been demanding an end to the war, but Nixon ignores the public. He's an ass."

"Actually, the ass is a symbol for the Democratic Party," a male student in the last row responded. "Nixon is a Republican, an elephant."

"You're an ass," the ass-accuser replied.

Several students gasped and private conversations broke out across the room.

"Okay, okay," Taggard said. "Let's get back to the question of making a difference. Let me ask it in another way. Are political, economic and judicial institutions in America as democratic as people are taught to believe? Are they egalitarian, tolerant of free speech, just and fair? Do those institutions encourage their members to practice and defend Enlightenment ideals?"

The discussion lasted another 15 minutes.

About two-thirds of the students were skeptical of the idea that America embraced Enlightenment ideals. They pointed out that society had failed to provide equal rights to women and minorities and that the public never had a voice in whether the United States should go to war in Vietnam. Bureaucrats made the decision.

I was in the skeptical camp, but I still believed that one individual could make a difference. The hopeful idealist, I was.

I LOVED COLLEGE. For the first time in my life, I felt a strong sense of purpose. I was becoming more interested in politics. I loved to study and was getting good grades.

The only problem was that I wanted to attend a university with more prestige and move away from home.

In January 1972, after one semester at Delta, I transferred to Central Michigan University, which one of my best friends from high school, Jerry, was attending.

I wanted to learn more about the Vietnam War and politics.

So I took my first class in sociology.[16]

Chapter 8 Endnotes

1. Taggard is a composite character from several different courses I took over six years. The story of Voltaire is taken from Clifton Fadiman and André Bernard (editors), *Bartlett's Book of Anecdotes* (Boston: Little, Brown and Company, 2000), p. 556.

2. In the early 1970s, there were no rules prohibiting smoking in classrooms. It was up to the instructor. About half of the faculty and students were smokers, including me. Oddly, nonsmokers rarely complained.

3. German philosopher Immanuel Kant defined Enlightenment (*die Aufklärung*) as emancipation from "man's self-incurred immaturity."

4. Jean-Jacques Rousseau, *The Social Contract*, translated by Maurice Cranston (Middlesex, England: Penguin Books, 1968; originally published in 1762).

5. For a sampling of the writings from these individuals and other philosophers associated with The Enlightenment, see Isaac Kramnick (ed.), *The Portable Enlightenment Reader* (New York: Penguin, 1995).

6. Aaron R. Hanlon, "Steven Pinker's New Book on the Enlightenment Is a Huge Hit. Too Bad It Gets the Enlightenment Wrong," Vox.com (May 17, 2018), retrieved November 17, 2020, from <www.vox.com/the-big-idea/2018/5/17/17362548/pinker-enlightenment-now-two-cultures-rationality-war-debate>.

7. Voltaire, *Toleration and Other Essays by Voltaire*, translated, with an Introduction, by Joseph McCabe (New York: G.P. Putnam's Sons, 1912), see chapter "On Superstition," retrieved November 17, 2012, from <http://oll.libertyfund.org/title/349/28217/1575812>.

8. Voltaire, *Candide*, 2nd ed., translated by Robert M. Adams (New York: W. W. Norton, 1991; originally published in 1759).

9. Voltaire settled in Ferney, France, in 1758 and lived there until 1778, when he moved to Paris and died there at the age of 83.

10. Karl Marx would later argue that religion was the "opium of the people," helping to prevent them from acquiring class consciousness and an understanding of how capitalists were exploiting their labor. Karl Marx, "A Contribution to the Critique of Hegel's Philosophy of Right," *Deutsch-Französische Jahrbücher* (February 7 and 10, 1844).

11. Some scholars characterize the American Revolutionary War as the beginning of "applied Enlightenment." See Ralf Dahrendorf, *Die Angewandte Aufklärung* (*The Enlightenment Applied*, Frankfurt: Fischer Verlag, 1968). Today the application of Enlightenment ideals to the real world is often called "modernity." Postmodernity is a critique of the Enlightenment, but many of its adherents ironically embrace ideals like truth, reason and democracy.

12. John Locke, *Two Treatises of Government*, edited by Peter Laslett (Cambridge: Cambridge University Press, 1988; originally published anonymously in 1689).

13. Jefferson and Franklin replaced the word "possessions" with the phrase "pursuit of happiness," because they wanted to downplay the role of the government in protecting property. The Fourth Amendment eventually would accommodate Locke's concern about private property.

14. Charles de Secondat (Baron de) Montesquieu, *The Spirit of the Laws* (2 Vols., originally published anonymously, 1748).

15. The concept of due process of law goes back to the *Magna Carta*, but it was the Fifth Amendment to the American Constitution, not English law, that gave due process of law the force of law: "No person shall ... be deprived of life, liberty, or property, without due process of law." In other words, the government must respect the legal rights of the individual when it seeks to punish him or her. If the government violates these rights, then it violates the rule of law, or the idea that law, as opposed to the prejudices of those with power, is the ultimate power of the society. The rule of law is often cited as the key factor that separates democracy from totalitarianism.

16. Sociologist George J. McCall points out that student unrest during the Vietnam War and President Lyndon B. Johnson's Great Society program provoked "an impelling demand to exhibit the 'social relevance' of all fields of learning. The political involvement of academic social scientists increased sharply during that period, in turn provoking the Stockman retaliatory measures against social science during the ... Reagan administration." George J. McCall, "Social Science and Social Problem Solving: An Analytic Introduction," pp. 3-18 in George J. McCall and George H. Weber, *Social Science and Public Policy: The Roles of Academic Disciplines in Policy Analysis* (Port Washington, NY: Associated Faculty Press, 1984), p. 4.

Chapter 9

The Sociological Imagination

January 10, 1972
Central Michigan University

My sociology professor was standing on a podium, looking over his notes that were strewn on the lectern.

James Roman had dark brown hair, parted in the middle, down to his shoulders. *This is going to be a cool class,* I thought, taking a seat in the fifth row. *He's one of us.*

Although the phrase "Get a damn haircut, hippie!" had passed into history by 1972, long-haired male professors were still the exception to the rule. The fact that I thought the class was going to be cool simply because the professor looked like us students was a "social fact" that itself was ripe for a sociological study,[1] although I didn't recognize it at the time.

Roman lived up to my expectations.

"The goal of sociology," he told our class of a hundred students, "is to solve social problems. As societies become more complex, so do their problems. Crime, economic and political inequality, bigotry, overpopulation, urban decay, divorce, unequal access to education, economic instability, and war are topics that sociologists study and hope to solve."

I was in paradise — well, what I mean to say is that these subjects were of great interest to me.

I had lots of company.

From 1966 to 1972, enrollments in sociology programs in the United States soared, going from 15,203 to 35,630.[2] No one doubted that the Vietnam War and the civil rights and women's movements were the prime causes.

Many students were less concerned with getting a good job than with finding a meaningful career that could help make the world a better place. I was one of them.

MY TRANSITION from Delta College to CMU was seamless. The Ph.D.-granting university was located in Mount Pleasant, a city of 20,000 in central lower Michigan about a three-hour drive northwest of Detroit and 80 minutes from Frankenmuth.

I was assigned to Merrill Hall, an all-male dormitory where I shared a room with three other young men. Jerry, my best friend from high school, lived in the room across the hall. A decade or so later Merrill would gain fame as the place where actor and director Jeff Daniels lived for a time before dropping out to pursue an acting career.

It was glorious to live away from home — to come and go as I pleased.

I liked to party, but my studies took precedence, especially sociology.

Our textbook, titled simply *Introduction to Sociology*,[3] pointed out that industrialization was threatening the environment, producing cycles of prosperity and depression, creating huge disparities in wealth and income between people, and breaking down traditional values and norms that previously had kept crime and vice in check. Sociologists must ask a number of questions, including "How do societies perpetuate themselves, teaching their children to believe most of what they are taught until they think of the attitudes as their own? ... What are the functions of nonconformity?"[4]

The founder of sociology, French philosopher Auguste Comte (1798–1857), believed sociology should pattern itself after the natural sciences, not only in its methods but also in terms of the role it would play for humankind.[5] He coined the term "positivism" to refer to his new theoretical approach,[6] which involved attacking the idea of speculative knowledge.[7] Comte didn't argue that scientific knowledge was absolute or that it was the only form of knowledge. He simply encouraged the use of research methods in the natural sciences to study and understand human behavior.

The founder of American sociology, Frank Lester Ward (1841–1913), also subscribed to this view. Ward "was convinced that man could help direct the course of social change," and he himself "devoted a great deal of energy to social reform."[8] He championed free public education and full social and political equality for women. What surprised me was that more than a half century had passed and women still were treated as second-class citizens in the 1970s.

Edward A. Ross (1866–1951), another early sociologist, also advocated an active role for sociology. In the third edition of his *Principles of Sociology*, he wrote, "Must we be content with such betterments of society as come of themselves? Or may we put in a hand to bring about desired changes? Surely the latter!" He added, "We suppress smallpox, typhus, diphtheria, the bubonic plague — why should we not endeavor to banish such social maladies as prostitution, juvenile delinquency, child exploitation, trampery, mob violence, family disintegration, religious rancor, and race antagonism?"[9]

Ross was a progressive and outspoken critic of the so-called robber barons, a derogatory term for nineteenth-century capitalists who built their fortunes by exploiting the masses. Ross advocated legislation to ban child labor, limit working hours, create a minimum wage for women, and install safety equipment in factories.

He was ahead of his time on most issues.

Except race.

He was a bigot.[10]

As a professor at Stanford University in the 1890s, Ross criticized the Stanford family for using Chinese immigrants to build the rail lines for Southern Pacific. In response, Jane Eliza Lathrop Stanford forced the university president to ask for Ross's resignation in 1900. The university also dismissed another professor who defended Ross, which in turn prompted a half-dozen other professors to resign in protest. These actions motivated John Dewey and other professors to develop the tenure system at American universities in order to protect the free speech rights of faculty.[11]

Ross also offered up a great quote. "There may come a time in the career of every sociologist when it is his solemn duty to raise hell." *What a great phrase to put on a T-shirt*, I thought.

Although most nineteenth-century sociologists believed social science should work to fix societal problems, not all were fully behind the idea. William Graham Sumner (1840–1910), who taught the first class in sociology in America, vigorously opposed the idea of "social planning."[12] Sumner promoted English sociologist Herbert Spencer's (1820–1903) idea of evolution, which emphasized that social change — increasing complexity in society — occurred naturally rather than through direct intervention from humans.

Spencer, a hard-core individualist, argued that society must be free from governmental or reformist intervention. The only role Spencer was prepared to give the state (government) was that of protecting individual rights and society against outside enemies. Everything else was to be left to the free market. Hence, Spencer — not Darwin or biologists, as is commonly believed — coined the phrase "survival of the fittest."[13]

Spencer's ideas were very popular in the late 1800s, but they were thoroughly trashed in the nineteenth century because they often were used to justify mistreatment of factory workers and to explain why the poor were poor (i.e., they were biologically inferior).[14]

Our textbook, curiously, didn't mention this.

But the authors did take what might be called a moderate position on the debate over whether social science should try to change the world: "Although the modern sociologist hopes his findings will help the human race, he sees his task as primarily the intellectual quest for knowledge and explanation. ... [T]he sociologist must study and learn; society, hopefully can put his knowledge to use."[15]

Hopefully? What a strange qualification. If this knowledge is not put to use, then of what use is it?

It didn't take me long to conclude that Comte, Ward and Ross had the best approach.[16] But in later years I would learn that even though most social scientists agree that knowledge gained in research should guide public policy, many are reluctant to become politically active. They believe that social scientists should create the knowledge, but policymakers, not scientists, should put that knowledge to use.[17]

In principle, I didn't have a problem with this.

But what if policymakers ignore or refuse to use that knowledge when making decisions?[18] Do social scientists have a moral obligation to prevent policymakers from making decisions that might harm people or society?

Chapter 9 Endnotes

1. A large body of research now exists that explores the impact of perceptions of others, self and trustworthiness. "Study Shows Trustworthy People Perceived to Look Similar to Ourselves," *Science News* (November 7, 2013), retrieved October 27, 2020, from <www.sciencedaily.com/releases/2013/11/131107094406.htm>. Original source: Harry Farmer, Ryan McKay and Manos Tsakiris, "Trust in Me: Trustworthy Others Are Seen as More Physically Similar to the Self," *Psychological Science* 25(1): 290-292 (October 28, 2013), retrieved June 2, 2015, from <https://doi.org/10.1177/ 0956797613494852>.

2. After the war ended in 1975, enrollments in sociology declined precipitously, dropping to a low of 12,165 in 1985 despite increasing college student populations. Today they are back up to about 28,000, partly because of the popularity of criminology, which prepares students for jobs as police, probation and parole officers, and prison guards. Source: Department of Education/National Center for Education Statistics: Integrated Postsecondary Education Data System Completion Survey, available online at <www.nsf.gov>.

3. Elbert W. Stewart and James A. Glynn, *Introduction to Sociology* (New York: McGraw-Hill Book Company, 1971), pp. 248-252.

4. Ibid., pp. 7-8.

5. Lewis Coser, *Masters of Sociological Thought: Ideas in Historical and Social Context* (New York: Harcourt Brace Jovanovich, Inc., 1971).

6. Since the 1960s, positivism has been the whipping boy of a large number of philosophers and social scientists, most of whom are educated in the humanities. Some of the criticism has merit, but some of it fails to understand the historical significance of positivism, which advanced science through its critique of religious dogma, scholasticism and speculation.

7. *Scholasticism* is the term that scholars often use to describe the dogmatic approach to knowledge that characterized thinking during Comte's time. Scholasticism essentially held that the Bible and the writings of Aristotle comprised all the knowledge that people needed to function in the world. Proponents of this view objected to the idea of a science that actively sought to understand the natural world and use that knowledge to help improve human conditions.

8. Stewart and Glynn, *Introduction to Sociology*, p.16. Ward also wrote a book promoting the role of social scientists as change agents: Lester F. Ward, *Applied Sociology: A Treatise on the*

Conscious Improvement of Society by Society (Boston: Ginn, 1906).

9. Edward Alsworth Ross, *Principles of Sociology*, 3rd edition (New York: Appleton Century Crofts, Inc., 1938), p. 642. By the way, Ross was dismissed from his post at Stanford University after the university's benefactor, Mrs. Stanford, demanded he be fired for criticizing the use of Chinese immigrant labor to build the rail lines for Southern Pacific, which was owned by the Stanford family. The firing helped promote the concept of academic freedom as well as the development of tenure in the American university system.

10. By the 1930s, Ross had recanted his racist views.

11. Warren J. Samuels, "The Firing of E. A. Ross from Stanford University: Injustice Compounded by Deception?" *The Journal of Economic Education*, 22(2): 183-190 (Spring 1991).

12. Stewart and Glynn, *Introduction to Sociology*, p. 16.

13. Biologists today do not normally use the term "survival of the fittest." They prefer "natural selection," which does not require that only the fittest survive, but that all organisms capable of reproducing are fit enough to survive.

14. Spencer was referred to as a Social Darwinist.

15. Stewart and Glynn, *Introduction to Sociology*, pp. 4, 8, 16 and 21, respectively.

16. For a more in-depth treatment of the ideas of Comte, Ward, Sumner, Spencer and other early sociologists, see Craig Calhoun, "Sociology in America: An Introduction," pp. 1-38 (Chapter 1) in Craig Calhoun (ed.), *Sociology in America: A History* (Chicago: University of Chicago Press, 2007).

17. David Demers, *The Ivory Tower of Babel: Why the Social Sciences Are Failing to Live Up to Their Promises* (New York: Algora Publishing, 2011).

18. Social science research on the impact of social science research shows that it has far less impact on policymaking than does ideology of the policymaker. See Demers, *Ivory Tower of Babel*.

Chapter 10

The Lottery

Wednesday, February 2, 1972
Central Michigan University

"Hey, Dave, how much money you got?" asked Johnny, who was holding a wad of cash in his left hand.

I pulled out my skinny wallet. "Two bucks. Why?"

"I'm takin' up a collection for the Selective Service draft lottery tomorrow. The unlucky bastard who comes closest to No. 1 wins the pot."

"Small consolation for getting sent to Vietnam, eh?" I sarcastically responded, handing Johnny the two bills.

"Yeah, man. This is one lottery I don't want to win."

Johnny was canvassing dorm rooms on the third floor of Merrill Hall on the Central Michigan University campus that evening, asking for donations from all those who were born in 1953.

By the end of the evening, he had collected $44.37 from about two dozen potential draftees. Not much money in absolute terms, but in those days a small fortune for a college freshman, who typically carried less than $5 in his wallet.

On the following day about a dozen of us 18-year-olds gathered in Bob's room down the hall to listen to the results of the lottery on the radio.

A week earlier President Richard Nixon had proposed an eight-point peace plan for Vietnam. Secretary of State Henry Kissinger had been secretly negotiating with the North Vietnamese.

But that wouldn't stop today's lottery.

Hanoi would reject Nixon's plan. The war went on.

The process of selecting the draft numbers in those days was what we now call "low-tech." Three-hundred-sixty-five blue balls — each imprinted with one date out of the year — were placed in a bin that was spun before selecting one of the balls and associating it with a birth date.

The first lottery was conducted in 1969. Prior to that, college students could obtain deferments. They wouldn't have to go into the military until they graduated from college. But Nixon ended the deferments in 1971, partly because of complaints that they discriminated against men who were black or poor, as they were less likely to attend college.

In 1969, 162,746 young men who drew numbers of 195 or lower were inducted into the military the following year. The inductions dropped to 94,092 in 1971 and to 49,514 in 1972. The rumor we heard was that in 1973 Selective Service would induct all of us with numbers up to about 90.

Needless to say, we were nervous.

To the best of my knowledge, none of the young men in that dorm room that day supported U.S. involvement in the Vietnam War.[1] We believed the war was being fought for the wrong reasons — to serve the interests of the "military-industrial complex," a popular pejorative in those days for corporations that made the bombs and the military generals who dropped them.

Even worse, we felt it was immoral that young men who opposed the war were being sent there against their will. A democracy, to be a democracy, should not force men to fight a war unless it could convince them that it was a just war. Of course, it couldn't do that. So it had to conscript. If you refused to fight, you were jailed.

The only other options for single men: become a conscientious objector, join the National Guard before you were drafted (like George W. Bush),[2] stay in college to get a deferment and then hire a doctor who will fabricate an illness (like Donald Trump),[3] join the R.O.T.C. and later refuse to serve (like Bill Clinton),[4] flee the country, or go underground in America.

The only sure way to avoid the military was to flee the country. By 1972, 70,000 young men had done just that. Most went to Canada.

What if I draw a low number? Would I run to Canada? How would I survive? What would my family think? Or should I just go? If I don't go, then someone else may die in my place. Is that immoral?

The men in the dorm room were quiet as the results of the lottery got underway. When a man in the room received a high number, the silence was broken with cheers and slaps on the back. When the number was low, the men cussed and moaned.

Jerry drew No. 292. He sighed. We cheered and shook his hand.

Johnny, the jackpot-raiser, was lucky, too, drawing 317.

Bob wasn't so lucky.

He drew No. 1.

"Shit," he screamed, as a half-dozen friends joined him in feigned agony and tried to console him. Bob tried to "take it like a man" and laughed as he took possession of the $44.37 jackpot, but I could see the terror in his eyes.

Then came my number — 128. *Was that good? Would Selective Service change its mind and go above 90?*

As the lottery came to an end, the young potential draftees returned to being young college students — joking, wrestling, shouting. Someone down the hallway put Crosby, Stills, Nash & Young's "Ohio" on the stereo and turned up the volume. The song was written about the four student protestors at Kent State University who were shot and killed by National Guardsmen on May 4, 1970, during an anti-war demonstration — an event that stunned America and solidified public opposition to the war.

Tin soldiers and Nixon's comin'
We're finally on our own
This summer I hear the drummin'
Four dead in O-hi-o ...

A second later the door to the room closed, muffling the music. The edge of a dark blue towel emerged from under the door. The room's occupants were lighting a joint. The towel helped block the smell of the weed from making its way into the hallway.

Were they celebrating or crying in that room?

I didn't know, but for months afterward I kept thinking about Bob and whether he would have to go to 'Nam.

Should young men be forced to die for a cause they didn't believe in? How can a country that enshrined the phrase "life, liberty and the pursuit of happiness" deprive its own citizens of these cherished values? How much does America embrace liberty?

Chapter 10 Endnotes

1. All of us, however, were strong supporters of the men who were fighting in Vietnam. We all had brothers, relatives or friends who were serving in or had served in Vietnam.

2. Bush finished college in 1968 and was commissioned into the Texas Air National Guard.

3. Mariana Alfaro, "Donald Trump Avoided the Military Draft 5 Times, But It Wasn't Uncommon for Young Men from Influential Families to do so During the Vietnam War," *Business Insider* (December 26, 2018), retrieved September 10, 2020, from <http://www.businessinsider.com/donald-trump-avoided-the-military-draft-which-was-common-at-the-time-vietnam-war-2018-12>.

4. Ralph Frammolino, "Clinton Joined ROTC After He Got Draft Notice," *Los Angeles Times* (April 5, 1992), retrieved September 11, 2020, from <https://www.latimes.com/archives/la-xpm-1992-04-05-mn-932-story.html>.

Chapter 11

Children of the Enlightenment

Friday, April 21, 1972
Central Michigan University

"Okay, people, we've reached downtown — now you have to decide," a long-haired male college student with patches on his blue jeans yelled out to 500 students or so who had just marched from campus to the center of downtown Mount Pleasant, Michigan. "Are you going with me and others to Mission Street to stop traffic — to really send a strong message to the establishment — or are you going to march back to campus?"

The "agitator," as the "establishment" would have called him in those days, and the students he was trying to persuade had just walked from CMU's campus to the downtown in an organized protest of the war in Vietnam.

It was Friday, April 21, 1972, about 7 p.m. Spring jacket weather. The march was a coordinated effort. Hundreds of other campuses across America also were protesting that day.[1]

A police cruiser had been leading the procession through the streets as protestors sang and chanted slogans and carried placards containing the peace sign. Many homeowners along the route emerged onto their front porches. They clapped, flashed the peace sign on one hand (a "V" consisting of the index and middle fingers) and cheered.

As one of those protestors, I couldn't help but think how times had changed.

Four years earlier, in 1968, anti-war protestors involved in violent confrontations with police and National Guard soldiers outside of the Democratic National Convention in Chicago were framed in news reports as "snotty-nosed brats who needed a little discipline," as one of my mass media professors would later say.[2] They were maligned by the mass media even though the Walker Commission concluded that police, not protestors, had initiated the riot and used excessive force on protestors as well as on more than 60 news media personnel.[3]

In February 1967, fewer than half of U.S. adults believed the United States had made a mistake sending troops to fight in Vietnam.[4] After Richard Nixon was elected president in 1968, public opinion polls showed that more than half of U.S. adults

(53%) approved of his handling of the war, compared with only a third (30%) who disapproved.[5]

But four years later, in 1972, about seven of ten adults believed the United States had made a mistake in getting involved in Vietnam. The older generation — the so-called "squares" — now were praising student protesters.

At the time, many of us college students felt we deserved some credit for this shift in sentiment. After all, until recently, the main player in the anti-war movement had been Students for a Democratic Society.

SDS's manifesto — based on the Port Huron (Michigan) Statement, which was written by student activist Tom Hayden[6] — criticized the United States government and mainstream political parties for failing to achieve international peace, for promoting the nuclear arms race, and for failing to end racial discrimination and poverty.

The manifesto also criticized corporate power and America's emphasis on career advancement and material possessions. SDS wanted participatory democracy, the kind where everyone gets a chance to participate in decisions that affect them.

By 1968, about 100,000 young people had joined one of SDS's campus chapters. But the organization began to fragment the following year.

At its 1969 convention,[7] some leaders wanted SDS to be more active in the labor and civil rights movements, while others wanted to go a more radical route by advocating overthrow of the U.S. government and installing a "dictatorship of the proletariat." The latter group called itself the Weather Underground Organization — Weathermen for short — and by 1972 had already bombed some government buildings in Washington, D.C., and other places. Some Weathermen leaders lost their lives in police raids and through accidents when making bombs.

In 1969, FBI Director J. Edgar Hoover told *U.S. News & World Report* that SDS perpetuates "a mood of disillusionment, pessimism and alienation. At the center of the movement is an almost passionate desire to destroy, to annihilate, to tear down. If anything definite can be said about the Students for a Democratic Society, it is that it can be called anarchistic."

Later it turned out that Hoover was the biggest lawbreaker of all.

"Hoover built his FBI files into an intimidating weapon, not just for fighting crime but also for bullying government officials and critics and destroying careers," writes Kenneth D. Ackerman, one of Hoover's biographers. "The files covered a dizzying kaleidoscope — Supreme Court justices such as Louis Brandeis and Felix Frankfurter, movie stars Mary Pickford and Marilyn Monroe, first lady Eleanor Roosevelt, physicist Albert Einstein, Zionist leader Chaim Weizmann and philanthropist John D. Rockefeller III, among others — often replete with unconfirmed gossip about private sex lives and radical ties."[8]

Hoover — like many politicians and the news media — misunderstood the anti-war student movement. Although it contained some radical elements, the vast majority of students, like me, were not interested in overthrowing the establishment. We just believed the war was unjust.

The Pentagon Papers, parts of which were released in June 1971, proved this point.[9] Four administrations, from Harry S. Truman to Lyndon B. Johnson, had lied to the American people and Congress about the U.S. role in southeast Asia.

"The existence of these documents," U.S. Senator Birch Bayh told the media in 1971, "and the fact that they said one thing and the people were led to believe something else, is a reason we have a credibility gap today, the reason people don't believe the government."[10]

Credibility was an issue for us students. But so was the idea of being forced to fight and die for an unjust cause. We believed that all people should have the right to choose their own destinies. For many of us, the purpose of life wasn't to make a lot of money. It was to create a better world — one in which racial minorities, women and the poor were treated on equal terms with rich and powerful white men.

We wanted government to be more transparent and accountable to its citizens. We cherished freedom of speech and the press and despised censors. We wanted — and the SDS manifesto called for — "participatory democracy." This was a political system in which everyone, not just a small elite made up of rich politicians and bureaucrats, plays a role in the political process.

"But we already have democracy," one of my conservative college acquaintances said when he heard I was going to participate in the anti-war march at CMU.

"We have representative democracy," I responded, "which means ordinary people like you and me play very little role in the vast majority of decisions that government makes. Our role, as citizens, is basically limited to electing politicians every couple of years who often serve the interests of campaign donors and powerful people rather than ordinary citizens."

"You sound like a communist," he said, snickering.

"I am not anti-capitalist or pro-communist. I am just pro-democracy."

"Sounds like communism to me."

Of course, the vast majority of protestors were not communists. They were activists — mainstream activists.

In fact, the "agitator" in downtown Mount Pleasant was having trouble convincing students to march to Mission Street, which was the busiest thoroughfare in Mount Pleasant, because most students there were opposed to the idea of using violence or unlawful conduct to protest the war.

"Hey, man, this is supposed to be a peaceful protest," responded one woman with long red hair and beads around her neck. "If we break the law, we hurt our cause. We should continue with the original plan and march back peaceably to campus, as we promised."

Several other students spoke for and against the plan to march to Mission Street. Most of the students, including me, agreed with the woman.

"A promise is a promise," I said, drawing on my sober, small-town Lutheran values.

About 10 minutes later, the gathering broke into two, with several dozen students trekking to Mission and the rest, including me, heading back to campus.

The students who went to Mission fulfilled their promise and disrupted traffic for a short time. They returned to campus and threw rocks and paint at the Reserve Officers' Training Corps building, breaking some windows. Police arrested two students who sat on the hood of a police car. But police later told the campus newspaper that the march overall was very "orderly."[11]

The event was the last major anti-war march at CMU as well as at many other colleges across the country. The Vietnam War was winding down. Soon many activist students would turn inward. Making money and getting rich would be fashionable again.

But it would be wrong to say the anti-Vietnam War movement had no impact on America. More American lives would have been lost in Vietnam had students across America not engaged in public protest. For a brief time, we students wielded a disproportionate amount of power. We embraced the ideals of the Enlightenment more than any cohort before or after us.

We were "children of the Enlightenment."

Chapter 11 Endnotes

1. Martin Arnold, "Campus Protests on War Continue," *The New York Times* (April 22, 1972), retrieved February 22, 2021, from <https://www.nytimes.com/1972/04/22/archives/campus-protests-on-war-continue-some-violence-occurs-but-most.html>.

2. The source of the quote is sociologist and mass communication professor Phillip J. Tichenor, who chaired my Ph.D. committee in the early 1990s. Public opinion polls showed that most Americans supported the police and military. See David Farber, *Chicago '68* (Chicago: The University of Chicago Press, 1988), p. 206.

3. Daniel Walker, later governor of Illinois, was appointed to investigate the Chicago convention riots. The Walker Commission concluded that the Chicago police, encouraged by Mayor Richard Daley, had provoked the crowd. The commission referred to it as a "police riot." Source: Daniel Walker, *Title Rights in Conflict; the Violent Confrontation of Demonstrators and Police in the Parks and Streets of Chicago during the Week of the Democratic National Convention of 1968*, a report submitted by Daniel Walker, director of the Chicago Study Team, to the National Commission on the Causes and Prevention of Violence, with a special introduction by Max Frankel (New York: Bantam Books, 1968).

4. Harold W. Stanley and Richard G. Niemi, *Vital Statistics on American Politics,* 4th edition (Washington, D.C.: Congressional Quarterly Press, 1994), p. 356. The Gallup Poll question was worded as follows: "In view of the developments since we entered the fighting in Vietnam, do you think the United States made a mistake sending troops to fight in Vietnam?" The poll-by-poll results are also available at <http://www.digitalhistory.uh.edu/learning_history/vietnam/vietnam_pubopinion.cfm>.

5. Gallup Poll, July 1969. The findings were published in the July 31, 1969, edition of *The New York Times.*

6. Hayden married actress Jane Fonda in the 1970s and later served for 18 years in the California state assembly and state senate. In recent years he has taught courses at colleges in the Los Angeles area.

7. SDS reorganized in the early 1970s but was never able to duplicate the political influence it had during the mid-1960s.

8. Quote is from Kenneth D. Ackerman, "Five Myths About J. Edgar Hoover," retrieved November 17, 2012, from a blog at the *Washington Post* <http://www.washingtonpost.com/opinions/five-myths-about-j-edgar-hoover/2011/11/07/gIQASLlo5M_story.html>. For more detail, see Kenneth D. Ackerman, *Young J. Edgar: Hoover and the Red Scare, 1919-1920* (Falls Church, VA: Viral History Press LLC, 2011).

9. Daniel Ellsberg, *Secrets: A Memoir of Vietnam and the Pentagon Papers* (New York: Viking, 2002).

10. Quoted from "1971 Year in Review: The Pentagon Papers" (New York: UPI, 1971), retrieved June 12, 2010 from <http://www.upi.com/Audio/Year_in_Review/Events-of-1971/The-Pentagon-Papers/12295509436546-7>.

11. The story appeared in *Central Michigan Life* on Monday, April 24, 1972.

Chapter 12

A Right Turn

June 1972
Saginaw, Michigan

"What are you doing, Dave?" one of my coworkers at a metal stamping plant in Saginaw asked one day in June 1972.

"I'm trying to see if I can do this job blindfolded."

Sure enough, I could.

My job at the plant was to check the width tolerances on some strange-looking metal parts twice the size of my hand. It was a boring job. I picked up the part and inserted an edge into a sleeve to see if it would fit. If it fit, it passed and I tossed it into a bin. It if didn't, I threw it into a separate bin. Presumably the rejects would be melted down and recast.

"Yes," I said, "I can do the job with my eyes closed."

"What the hell is going on?" a plant supervisor yelled, interrupting me.

I opened my eyes. "Sorry. I was just trying to see if I could do this job blindfolded," I said. "I'm — "

"Get back to work. We don't have to time to screw around here. If I catch you doing that again, you're out of here."

I should have responded: "What we've got here is a failure to communicate." But I didn't. I simply said, "Okay."

I managed to avoid a pink slip that summer. But it was the worst job I ever had.

Free-market advocate Adam Smith, author of *The Wealth of Nations*, and communist Karl Marx, author of *Capital*, were on opposite sides of the political spectrum, but both agreed that unskilled factory work could be very unsatisfying and alienating.

Adding to my pain was the fact that my hourly wage was only $3.10, which was less than half of what a permanent employee earned.[1] That made me a little resentful. Marx's supporters called my sentiment "class consciousness."[2]

But I didn't have the option of quitting. I had to work to pay for tuition, as my parents did not have a lot of disposable income. I was feeling the "dull compulsion of economic relationships."[3]

The summer of 1972 was less pleasant than other summers I spent during my college years. But events that summer would have a tremendous impact on my life. They helped me figure out what I wanted to be when I grew up.

ON JUNE 17, 1972, security guard Frank Wills was making his nightly rounds when he discovered a piece of masking tape over the lock of a door on the first floor of the building he was patrolling. He removed the tape and discovered several other doors had been taped. When he returned to the first door, he found the tape he'd removed had been replaced.

Wills called police at 1:47 a.m.

Together, they followed the trail of tape to the Democratic National Committee headquarters, whose offices were located in Wills's building — the Watergate office-apartment-hotel complex in Washington, D.C. Police arrested five men who had broken into the offices.

Later, it turned out four of the burglars were Cuban exiles and one was a former CIA surveillance expert. They were carrying cameras, pens filled with tear gas, eavesdropping equipment and $2,300 in cash.

For two years news reporters followed the story, which eventually tied the burglary to President Richard Nixon's reelection campaign. The burglars had been searching for information to embarrass Democratic presidential candidate George McGovern. They also intended to bug the phones and offices.

But the dirty tricks didn't end there. The reporters also discovered that Nixon's administration had been spying illegally on U.S. citizens, harassing political opponents, forging campaign literature, and attempting to obstruct justice through a cover-up.

Nixon won the 1972 election but resigned two years later, on August 8, 1974, under pressure of impeachment. Many of his assistants were convicted and spent time in prison.

But Nixon escaped a prison sentence. Vice President Gerald Ford, who became president after Nixon resigned, pardoned him. The pardon angered many Americans. Ford lost the 1976 presidential election to Democrat Jimmy Carter.

No story in the history of journalism has generated more praise for U.S. news media than Watergate, which has become the quintessential example of journalism's role as a guardian of Enlightenment ideals.[4] Bob Woodward and Carl Bernstein of the *Washington Post* took the lion's share of credit, helping their newspaper win a Pulitzer Prize. They also wrote a best-selling book, called *All the President's Men*, which was made into a successful movie starring Robert Redford and Dustin Hoffman.[5]

For a brief time, security guard Frank Wills, who earned $80 a week, was a hero. But he quit his job after his employer refused to give him a raise for helping catch the burglars. He traveled the talk show circuit and even appeared as himself in the Redford/Hoffman movie and several others. But after that he was unable to hold down a job. He died penniless in 2000 at age 52.

Had I not worked in the stamping plant, I am not sure I would have understood why Wills quit his job.

WHEN I RETURNED to Central Michigan University in fall 1972, I enrolled in courses in philosophy and history. They introduced me to the ideas of Plato, John Dewey and Walter Lippman.

Plato lived two thousand years before the Enlightenment. But his ideas are relevant to the debate in terms of solving social problems and protecting the rights of people.

In *The Republic*, Plato argued that people are easily corrupted by power. People should not rule for personal enjoyment but for the good of the state. He believed educated people — or a "philosopher king" — were best suited to rule.[6] He advocated a universal educational system for men and women.

But restrictions must be placed upon rulers and the military to prevent them from being corrupted. These restrictions include abolishment of wealth and the institution of family. Children would be reared in a group setting so none of them would have an advantage over the others, and the smartest and wisest would be groomed as guardians or rulers.[7]

Plato criticized democracy, because of its susceptibility to being ruled by unfit sectarian demagogues. The Nixon administration seemed to prove Plato's point, and many decades later the same charge would be leveled against President Donald Trump and his administration.

In contrast, Dewey had faith in democracy as a political system. He believed that education could enlighten ordinary people, not just the rulers. He was a strong advocate of Enlightenment ideals. He supported science and believed it should be used to solve social problems and to create a better world.

Lippman, an intellectual contemporary of Dewey and a syndicated newspaper columnist, disagreed. He argued that participatory democracy could not work, because it was impractical for the average citizen to be well-informed about many issues in a modern, complex society.[8] A successful democracy would have to rely heavily on trained experts in government and political science. The role of the press, Lippman argued, was to inform the public about the conclusions reached by these experts.

Dewey responded that Lippman's vision of democracy was elitist and that the basis of democracy is not information but conversation and debate. In other words, the process was just as important as the decision itself.

Yet, despite these disagreements, both Dewey and Lippman agreed that scientific knowledge was crucial for a well-run state.

Dewey argued that knowledge was best obtained through reflective thought, a process that involved identifying problems, proposing hypotheses (informally or formally), and testing the ideas. This way of thinking — that knowledge was best gained not from armchair theorizing or speculation but from interacting with the real world — was often called pragmatism.[9] Dewey believed that science could give humans control over nature for the purpose of improving human life.[10]

This was an intriguing debate. But my budding interest in the subject was cut short.

About six weeks into the semester I contracted a heinous cough that made it difficult for me to sleep, attend class and study. I had suffered from this ailment all my life. The cough would often persist for months.

A pulmonologist would develop a cure for me in 1986, and the medical industry would eventually label it reactive airway disease. But doctors in the 1970s didn't prescribe steroids or narcotics or steroids for my cough. I was forced to drop out of school for a while.

I RECOVERED from the cough about six weeks later and took a job at Chess King in Saginaw's Fashion Square Mall selling conservative suits and ties for men, mostly white men. I left that position several weeks later to work for the much hipper Merry-Go-Round store, which was located next door.

Merry-Go-Round was the first unisex chain clothing store in the United States. Bell-bottom and elephant-bottom men's jeans, psychedelic shirts, blouses, halter tops, and platform shoes were the staple products. Our customers covered the entire spectrum of racial and ethnic groups.

Working at Merry-Go-Round was fun. The managers and employees often partied after work, which created close bonds among everyone. The sales strategy was very aggressive: sell $30 or more an hour or get fired. About half of the people hired were fired within a month. Some would cry. Charles Dickens would have written novels about it had he been born a century later.

I survived using a low-key, nonthreatening sales approach. Customers seemed to trust me. Maybe it was because I would tell the truth.

"That blouse does not look good on you," I would say.

"What about this one?"

"Now you're talking. Groovy."

We played a lot of soul music in the store. African Americans made up at least one-third of our customers, but everyone loved the sound of Motown, especially Marvin Gaye, the Four Tops and the Temptations. Gaye and Four Tops member Renaldo Benson co-wrote "What's Going On," a 1971 song about an American soldier who returns from Vietnam to find life has changed in America.[11]

Mother, mother
There's too many of you crying
Brother, brother, brother
There's far too many of you dying ...
Picket lines and picket signs
Don't punish me with brutality
Talk to me, so you can see
Oh, what's going on
What's going on

To balance the seriousness of this song, we also often played the Four Tops' "Ain't No Woman (Like the One I've Got)" and the Temptations' "My Girl."

I decided to hold off before going back to college. I was having too much fun.

Within three months I was an assistant manager, and three months after that I was managing my own store in Indianapolis. At age 19, I had become the youngest manager in the chain of 42 stores.

I enjoyed flying to Baltimore for a company meeting, which was attended by about five dozen other long-haired men like me wearing freaky-looking platform shoes and psychedelic shirts. Only a couple of women worked in management for the company.

In those days, there were no formal procedures at Merry-Go-Round or other corporations for dealing with discrimination. Six more years would pass before Catharine MacKinnon would publish *Sexual Harassment of Working Women*, a book which argued that sexual harassment is a form of sex discrimination under Title VII of the Civil Rights Act of 1964.[12] That book changed the world, although it didn't end the problem. At the time, I never would have guessed that the problem would still be with us in 2020.

I enjoyed my manager job.

But there were two problems.

One was the long hours. I usually worked six or seven days a week and about 10–14 hours a day. The other problem was the pay — it was so low that I had trouble making ends meet. As a manager, I was earning only $160 a week before taxes.

I felt exploited.

It was time to go back to school.

I quit my corporate job in fall 1973.

In hindsight, a critic might convincingly point out that I had violated my vow to fight the military-industrial establishment. Although my bosses and I had long hair and liked to party, we were participants in corporate capitalism.

Of course, at the time I didn't see any contradiction in my behavior. I was simply trying to survive and pay the bills. And I also knew from my courses that all revolutions, to be successful, need resources, and those at the bottom of the social hierarchy almost always lack sufficient resources.

Merry-Go-Round eventually purchased Chess King and would continue to expand until it had more than 536 stores operating under the Merry-Go-Round, Dejaiz, Cignal, and Chess King brand names.

In 1994, the company filed for bankruptcy.

It had fallen out of fashion with the times.

Chapter 12 Endnotes

1. I found the job through a temporary work agency, which kept the other $3.10 an hour for its services.

2. Class consciousness is defined here as an awareness that people have of their own social and economic status in society. Marxists believe that workers' awareness of their subordinate status in capitalism was necessary to spark revolutionary action against capitalists, who owned the companies that produce goods and services.

3. See Chapter 7 for elaboration on this concept.

4. Some scholars argue that Watergate had little impact on changing the structure of the American political system. There is some validity to this argument, as the office of president became even more powerful with subsequent administrations. However, the event did serve warning that even a president can be subjected to the rule of law.

5. Carl Bernstein and Bob Woodward, *All the President's Men* (New York: Simon and Schuster, 1974).

6. Plato, *The Republic*, translated with introduction and notes by Francis MacDonald Cornford (New York: Oxford University Press, 1945).

7. A contemporary version of Plato's philosophy is "equality of opportunity" or "equality of fair opportunity" (EFO). This is the idea that all children should have access to the same resources, regardless of the wealth or status of their parents. Daycare centers for preschoolers may help promote equal opportunity when they bring together children from different social backgrounds. See, e.g., John Rawls, *A Theory of Justice*, revised edition (Cambridge: Harvard University Press, 1999).

8. See Walter Lippman, *Public Opinion* (New York: Harcourt, Brace and Company, 1922).

9. John Dewey, *Experience and Education* (New York: Touchstone, 2007, first published

in 1938), p. 54.

10. Dewey wrote: "That science is the chief means of perfecting control of means of action is witnessed by the great crop of inventions which followed intellectual command of the secrets of nature. ... Railways, steamboats, electric motors, telephone and telegraph, automobiles, aeroplanes and dirigibles are conspicuous evidences of the application of science in life. ... [Science] has brought with it an established conviction of the possibility of control of nature in the interests of mankind and thus has led men to look to the future, instead of the past. ... To subjugate devastating disease is no longer a dream; the hope of abolishing poverty is not utopian. Science has familiarized men with the idea of development, taking effect practically in persistent gradual amelioration of the estate of our common humanity." See John Dewey, *Democracy and Education: An Introduction to the Philosophy of Education* (New York, The Macmillan Company, 1916). Quote is taken from Chapter 17.

11. Hubpages.com ranked "What's Going On" as the No. 1 protest movement song of the 1970s. The song is from the album of the same name, Marvin Gaye, *What's Going On* (Motown Records, Detroit, 1971). At Hubpages.com, Chris J. Baker writes that "while many protest songs are angry indictments, 'What's Going On' is a mournful questioning. It is an earnest yearning for positive change. Sadly like most of the best protest songs of the protest movement, the song is more relevant than ever."

12. Catharine MacKinnon, *Sexual Harassment of Working Women* (New Haven, CT: Yale University Press, 1979).

Chapter 13

A Journalistic Calling

January 1974
Central Michigan University

A lot had changed when I returned to Central Michigan University in January 1974.

John McCain, who had spent six years as a prisoner of war in North Vietnam, was finally back home. He would later become a U.S. senator, campaign for president of the United States, and save health care for millions of Americans.

Nixon abolished the draft, which meant that Bob, the college student who drew the No. 1 position in the draft two years ago, didn't have to go to 'Nam. None of us did.

The war was still on, but the withdrawal was well under way. In two years, all U.S. personnel would be pulled out, and Saigon would fall to the communists.

The winding down of the Vietnam War brought an end to much of the student activism that had made the college campuses so vibrant. Many students abandoned their altruistic job goals. Writers Tom Wolfe and Christopher Lasch began calling them "Generation Me" and the "Prophets of Narcissism."[1]

Making money was fashionable again. Discos, polyester shirts and the Bee Gees were in. The "establishment" was no longer a dirty word.

But not everyone was selling out.

Some of us still had a desire to make the world a better place.

I took a course on social organization from a left-wing sociology professor who spoke highly of Mao Zedong's Cultural Revolution, which in the late 1960s attempted to purge China of anti-Maoist and anti-revolutionary (or pro-capitalist) sentiment. Many urban intellectuals, teachers and business people were sent to the rural areas to work in the fields. They also were forced to attend classes whose purpose was to re-indoctrinate them with Maoist ideas.

The Cultural Revolution led to widespread economic and political upheaval throughout China. Some historians and scholars estimate that up to three million people died or were killed. Millions more were displaced.[2]

I suspect that, today, the instructor, if he is still alive, has a different view from the one he had in 1974, when accurate information about the Cultural Revolution was still hard to come by.

I MOVED into a high-rise dorm room on campus. My three new roommates, who were two years younger than I and, thus, were never eligible for the draft, had little interest in politics or activism. They were jocks.

My roommates jokingly called me "commie pinko," because I had enrolled in that social organization class. I took the moniker as a badge of honor, but the truth was that I didn't really think much of Marxism or Maoism. After all, neither form of communism or other forms of collectivism had worked well anywhere in the modern world, and even communists often punished people who criticized them.[3]

Although there was no war to protest, I satisfied my drive for activism by helping to publish a dorm newspaper called *Quadrascope* in fall 1974, even though I had yet to enroll in a journalism class. I was managing editor.

I spent most of my remaining free time, about four to six hours a day, studying. I enjoyed it. I got good grades. I attended school in the spring and in summer, and then I began to worry about what I was going to do when I graduated.

I was a sociology major. Social work or criminal justice were possible options, but neither was very appealing. Too passive.

I enjoyed writing stories for the dorm newspaper.

Maybe journalism would be a better calling.

WHEN I ENROLLED in my first journalism classes in fall 1974, enrollments were soaring. From 1960 to 1971, the number of journalism majors grew from 11,000 to 33,000, partly as a result of the Vietnam War and increased student activism. But Watergate had an even greater impact. From 1971 to 1976, enrollments nearly doubled, surpassing the 60,000 mark.[4]

Everyone, it seemed, wanted to be Bob Woodward and Carl Bernstein, the two *Washington Post* reporters who helped the newspaper win a Pulitzer Prize for its reporting on Watergate.

I took two courses in journalism.

The first was an "introduction to mass media" course, which examined the role and function of media in society and was taught by Donald Bird, a dynamic professor who made the content very interesting. Among other things, Bird's class covered the role of media as an agent of change, promoting democratic ideals, free speech and openness in government.

These ideals were reinforced in my reporting class, which was taught by Suzanne Nichols, a former journalist whose effervescent personality drew many admiring students. I also liked the fact that she let us smoke in class.

Nichols often affectionately called me "deadline Demers," because I wasn't a very fast writer. I struggled for hours sometimes. But I persevered and it got easier.

Nichols had a knack of being able to extract the best from her students. She quickly sized up their strengths and weaknesses and then poured her energy into helping the students build on the former and overcome the latter.

On one occasion, I investigated a rumor that the university had used tax dollars to pay airfare expenses of alumni who attended away games. It turned out to be false.

"There's no story," I said.

"But that is a story," she pointed out.

Nichols, Bird and other journalism professors at CMU instilled in me a deep appreciation for the role and function of journalism in society.

First and foremost was the idea that journalists represented the interests of "the public," or ordinary people, especially people and groups with little or no voice in society. Although most news sources were political and economic elites in government and business, the journalist's role was to ensure the powerful followed local, state and federal laws and society's values when making decisions that affected the public. The journalist was, in other words, an emissary of Enlightenment ideals, especially democracy, openness in government and free speech.

Perhaps the single best example in the field of journalism, aside from Woodward and Bernstein, was I. F. (Isidor Feinstein) "Izzy" Stone, an investigative reporter who uncovered corruption and discrimination in government and who promoted civil rights and free speech.

In the early 1940s, Stone, who was editor of *The Nation*, revealed that J. Edgar Hoover's FBI was systematically denying civil service jobs to applicants who associated with Jews and minorities and who held liberal or anti-fascist attitudes. Stone was a harsh critic of fascism, but he also was a First Amendment absolutist and defended fascists' right to free speech.

On May 18, 1949, he wrote a commentary about a recent U.S. Supreme Court decision[5] that overturned the "breach-of-the-peace" conviction of a man who was espousing fascist ideas: "[Y]ou cannot have freedom without the risk of its abuse. The men who wrote the Bill of Rights were willing to take their chances on freedom. ... Everything we know from the past teaches us that suppression in the long run provides an illusory security, and this is why, though a socialist, I am also a libertarian."[6]

In 1950, Stone was blacklisted by mainstream journalism organizations because of his views on civil liberties, which included strong criticism of McCarthyism.

So he started up a weekly newsletter.

I. F. Stone's Weekly would go on to earn the distinction as one of the most influential publications in American history, even though its circulation never topped 70,000.

During the 1950s and 1960s, Stone championed the civil rights movement, writing in 1955 that "the American Negro needs a Gandhi to lead them." Eight years later Martin Luther King would emerge to fill that role.

When Stone and a black judge were refused luncheon service at the National Press Club, he quit the organization and joined the black newspapermen's club. Stone was given a standing ovation when he returned to speak to the National Press Club in 1980.

In 1964, after closely scrutinizing government and published accounts, Stone became the only American journalist to question the veracity of President Lyndon B. Johnson's account of the Gulf of Tonkin incidents, which claimed that North Vietnam had attacked a U.S. ship without provocation.

Stone scoured documents and government press conferences to identify inconsistencies which suggested, correctly, that Johnson and military leaders staged the incident to justify more U.S. involvement in Vietnam.

Stone also was an astute observer of organizational routines in journalism, writing that "reporters tend to be absorbed by the bureaucracies they cover; they take on the habits, attitudes, and even accents of the military or the diplomatic corps. Should a reporter resist the pressure; there are many ways to get rid of him. ... But a reporter covering the whole capital on his own — particularly if he is his own employer — is immune from these pressures."[7]

It was easy to love journalism with role models like Stone, Woodward and Bernstein. Plus, journalism allowed me to practice my activist ideals, albeit in a somewhat circumscribed manner. Journalism was no radical agent of change, to be sure.[8] But Watergate showed that journalism could change the world.

During the 1974–75 school year, I became friends with a student who ran for and was elected to the office of student body president. Robert Bixon asked me whether I would manage a media center to monitor and promote student involvement in government when he took office in fall 1975.

I accepted with enthusiasm.

If there was any doubt about journalism as a career, it was quickly erased the following year, when I uncovered a mini-Watergate-like scandal at CMU.

"WHERE IS the promissory note?" I asked Robert, president of the student government at Central Michigan University.

"It's back in my room," he said. "I'll bring it tomorrow."

Robert was my friend, or so I thought. After being elected president in spring 1975, he appointed me to head a new office called Media Information Services. Student government funded the office.

Part of my job involved publishing an eight-page newsletter called *3rd Faction*. I had a staff of about a dozen student volunteers.

The lead story in the second issue of *3rd Faction*, published November 13, 1975, attacked conservative-backed U.S. Senate bill S.1, formally called the Federal Criminal Justice Act of 1975 but more popularly known as the U.S. Official Secrets Act.

The bill sought to (1) prevent the prosecution of government officials who commit illegal acts under the order of a superior; (2) allow prosecution of union strikers and peaceful demonstrators where ten or more are gathered and property may be threatened; (3) permit wiretapping without a court order; (4) make it illegal to possess classified government documents, such as those associated with the Watergate scandal; and (5) criminalize possession of small amounts of marijuana.

In an editorial, I wrote:

> In an attempt to codify the Federal Criminal Code, supporters of Senate Bill No. 1 (S.1) have done no less than to place our Constitutionally guaranteed freedoms on the butcher's chopping block.
>
> If S.1 is allowed to become law, freedoms of the press, speech and assembly will be hacked to pieces. S.1 goes beyond revising the Federal Criminal Code to destroying our civil liberties and the Bill of Rights. ...

The bill, which was dubbed "Nixon's Revenge" (Nixon supported the bill but was forced to resign August 9, 1974, after the Watergate scandal), was never enacted.

That issue of *3rd Faction* also contained an advertisement for a concert performance by David Crosby and Graham Nash. Tickets cost $4.50 to $6.

As editor of *3rd Faction*, my job was to report student government news fairly and objectively, Robert told me.

"But if you ever find corruption," he said, "you must report it."

Robert would regret making that statement.

Three months later I heard a rumor that his running mate, *Barry Chevy*, the student government vice president, had been making personal long-distance phone calls using university phones.

I confronted Barry with the allegations. He confessed to the "crime," but said he would give me a better story if I didn't report that one.

I consulted with Sue Nichols, my journalism professor, and then I agreed to Barry's terms, with the proviso that the story would have to be more newsworthy.

Through the years, some colleagues have questioned whether my actions were ethical.[9] I still have mixed feelings about it. But I did get a better story.

Barry told me that Robert and the student government treasurer both had withdrawn money from a little-known student government bank account to pay their tuition. The bank account had been set up several years earlier after an insurance company donated several thousand dollars to student government for rights to promote its products and services to students.

I confronted Robert with the allegations.

"Yes, I took the money, and so did the student body treasurer," he confessed. "But we only borrowed it. We signed a promissory note a year ago when we took the money. We will pay it back."

The next day Barry gave me the note. (Robert, by the way, didn't know that Barry had "ratted" on him to save himself.)

I was immediately suspicious. First, why would he have Barry deliver the note? Second, the note was crisp and clean — too crispy clean to have been a year old.

Could it have been just typed?

I left Barry's office and went into an outer office area equipped with three IBM Selectric typewriters, all of which used one-strike ribbons. *Could they have been careless enough to type the letter on one of those machines?*

The first typewriters had new ribbons, and I didn't want to remove them for fear of ruining them. The ribbon was nearly used up on the third typewriter. I pulled it and transcribed the impressions, which were upside down and backwards. Sure enough, the promissory note had been typed up the night before — not a year earlier, as Robert had told me.

Coincidentally, at the time I was reading Woodward and Bernstein's *All the President's Men*, which told the story of Watergate from the perspective of two *Washington Post* reporters.

My story was Central Michigan Gate.

No, CMU Gate. That was better.[10]

A day later Robert obtained a vote of confidence from the Student Senate. Senators didn't seem to care that one of their own had secretly borrowed money from a student government fund and lied about when the promissory note had been created.

But Robert and the treasurer resigned from their student government jobs after *Central Michigan Life*, the student newspaper, covered the story. The university forced both of them to repay the loans.[11] Barry also resigned from his position.

Journalism could change the world.
And I had found my professional calling — at least for a few years.

Chapter 13 Endnotes

1. Tom Wolfe, "The 'Me' Decade and the Third Great Awakening," *New York Magazine* (August 23, 1976) and Christopher Lasch, *The Culture of Narcissism: American Life in an Age of Diminishing Expectations* (New York: W.W. Norton, 1979).

2. Jon Halliday and Jung Chang, *Mao: The Unknown Story* (New York: Random House, 2005).

3. Later I came to appreciate many of the ideas and theories that Karl Marx developed. In particular, his predictions about centralization and concentration of ownership have come true in many business sectors.

4. See Paul V. Peterson, "Journalism Growth Continues at Hefty 10.8 Per Cent Rate [and] Enrollment Data by Campuses," *Journalism Educator*, 26(4): 4-5, 56-60 (January 1972) and Ben H. Bagdikian, "Woodstein U: Notes on the Mass Production and Questionable Education of Journalists," *The Atlantic* (March 1977), retrieved Oct. 24, 2008, from <www.theatlantic.com/ doc/197703/journalism-school>.

5. *Terminiello v. City of Chicago*, 337 U.S. 1 (1949).

6. I. F. Stone, "Free Speech Is Worth the Risk," pp. 12-13 in I. F. Stone (edited by Karl Weber), *The Best of I. F. Stone* (New York: Public Affairs, 2006). The article was originally published on May 18, 1949.

7. I. F. Stone, *The Best of I. F. Stone*, p. 5. Stone's comments were originally published in 1963.

8. Many social scientific studies of journalism since then support this proposition. For a summary, see David Demers, *The Menace of the Corporate Newspaper: Fact or Fiction?* (Ames: Iowa State University Press, 1996).

9. I never wrote up the story about the "illegal" telephone calls. Media ethics experts could argue that I acted unethically by reporting one story of wrongdoing and not the another. As one former journalist put it: "Did you feel you were betraying your own ethics by agreeing (to Barry's terms)?"

10. I wrote a story about the events, but it was never published because the local campus newspaper usurped me on the breaking news.

11. Jim Harger and Jim Reindl, "[Student Leaders] Resign Positions," *Central Michigan Life* (February 9, 1976), p. 1.

Chapter 14

Journalism Daze

Monday, November 14, 1977
Rochester, Michigan

Anthropologist Margaret Mead pushed her eyeglasses up and uttered a phrase that would evoke cheers and wild applause from the audience of several hundred students, faculty and citizens.

"Men have more physical strength than women, but women have more stamina, because they bear the children and perpetuate the species."

It was November 14, 1977, and she was speaking at Oakland University in Rochester, Michigan.

At the time, Mead was the world's most famous living social scientist — so famous that many ordinary Americans, not just students or scholars, knew of her.

Her popularity shot up when she advocated that women in America should have the freedom to choose casual sex. She became a central figure in the women's movement of the 1960s, but she detested the label "women's libber."

The topic of her lecture today was supposed to be "The World Food Crisis," but I can't remember a thing she said about that. I was there to write a story for the *Rochester Clarion*, a small-town newspaper in a suburb north of Detroit. But I had a personal interest in her lecture, too, because I had taken an anthropology course at Central Michigan University two years before.

The audience included more women than men. I suspected they were there to pay homage to a woman who had done more to promote women's rights than perhaps any female scholar in history.

The foundation of her reputation was her 1928 book, *Coming of Age in Samoa*.[1] The book summarized a research project in which she looked at whether adolescents in a traditional culture have a difficult time making the adjustment from childhood to adulthood, as was the case for many American youths.[2]

Through an interpreter she interviewed 68 girls and women between the ages of 9 and 20 who lived in a village of 600 people on the island of Ta'u. She concluded that the transition from childhood to adulthood in Ta'u was smooth and not marked by emotional or psychological distress, as it is in America and most Western countries.

The book created a firestorm of controversy, however, when she reported that Samoan women engaged in casual sex before marriage. My, how things have changed.

Mead died a year and a day after her appearance at Oakland University. Five years later, in 1983, another anthropologist, Derek Freeman, challenged Mead's findings. Freeman spent four years in Samoa and interviewed some of Mead's surviving informants.

Freeman asserted that the women lied to Mead. They told him that they did not have casual sex as young women.[3] Freeman concluded that virginity was highly valued in Samoan culture, even though it was only required of women of high social rank.

Freeman's book touched off a debate that continues to this day.

I would later learn that disputes like this are very common in the social sciences. Some critics even argue that mainstream social science is incapable of generating knowledge and truth and, thus, incapable of fulfilling one of the key ideals of the Enlightenment. Years later I would write a book that challenged this assumption, but concluded that social scientists have had relatively little impact on public policy.[4]

Yes, despite the controversy over Mead's research, scholars widely agree that one of her greatest contributions was her argument that culture is a more important element influencing people than biology.

She changed the world.

I HAD BEEN WORKING at the *Clarion* for more than a year when I covered Mead's speech. I was one semester short of graduation but left Central Michigan University early because I was worried about getting a job.

The market was flooded with journalism graduates and the national unemployment rate was nearly 8 percent.[5] I reasoned it was better to get a job now and finish school later.

Rochester was home to many automobile executives. For a brief time I dated the daughter of one of them. She was the granddaughter of a retired high-ranking executive at Cadillac, who owned a beautiful cottage on the St. Clair River near Detroit — one of the playgrounds of the local well-to-do.

The upper-middle-class lifestyle was a new experience for me. But her family was kind and nonjudgmental, and my experiences with them were always positive, especially her mother, who was always a perfect host. We spent many hours at the kitchen table playing games and talking about books and news events.

A man named Charles S. Seed founded the *Clarion* in 1898. He passed ownership on to his kin. In 1976, the business was being run by two brothers, one of whom was publisher and the other the advertising manager.

My boss was Ridge Anderson, who was about seven years older than I and much more worldly. He understood politics in a small town. Although he wasn't a great writer, he was enthusiastic about journalism and enjoyed his work. I liked that about him.

Both of us spent many hours talking about local politics over a beer and a cigarette. Ridge's wife, Lynn, worked in public relations, and was a former student of and good friends with my journalism mentor, Sue Nichols.

Our weekly newspaper covered all of the news that the big newspapers didn't want to cover — school events, community functions and activities, library events, church functions, and city and township government meetings.

Few things I wrote about ever made news outside of Rochester. But there were two exceptions: the Mead story and the hockey coach molester.

WHEN I SAW the Oakland County Sheriff's incident report that deputies had arrested a hockey coach for molestation, I was horrified but not too shocked. Even my little hometown of Frankenmuth had its share of problems. A postal employee there was accused of molesting young girls, but he was never formally charged. Small towns have a penchant for hiding their warts.

The hockey coach had been charged, and although I didn't question the veracity of the incident report, my journalism teachers had taught me that there are two sides to a story.[6] The report said the coach was out on bail, and the incident report included his address. So I drove to his apartment complex and knocked on the door.

I was nervous.

I expected a monster to open the door.

But it was a man.

I identified myself and told him I was there to get his side of the story. He immediately confessed to the crime and said he needed psychological counseling.

"I'm a sick man," he said. "I need help."

Not what I was expecting to hear. I thought he would refuse to talk or declare his innocence.

In that brief moment, I pitied the monster.

I drove back to the newsroom and wrote up the story, which included the direct quotes listed above. The story wouldn't be published for another day because the *Clarion* was published once a week, on Wednesdays. The next day Ridge called me into his cubicle.

"Dave, the sheriff's office and the hockey coach's attorney are very upset," he said. "The sheriff said that if we publish comments from the conversation you had with the hockey coach, it could jeopardize the state's case against the accused. The defendant's attorney also said the comments could adversely affect the defendant's Sixth Amendment right to a fair trial."

"So what," I responded. "Journalists are paid to report the news fairly and objectively. I had every right to interview the coach. He did not have to talk to me. But he did, and the right thing to do is to publish his comments."

"Well, we can't. The sheriff said if we publish the defendant's comments, he would refuse our newspaper access to all incident reports in the future."

"That would be an abuse of his power," I responded.

Ridge shrugged.

He was sympathetic to my position, but he also knew our publisher would be very upset if we lost access to the sheriff's reports, because a competing newspaper in town would have exclusive access to the incident reports.

I didn't lose too much sleep over it. Small-town newspapers tend to shy away from controversy and conflict. I understood that because of my courses in sociology.

I filed it away in my mind as a good example of how even newspapers, whose Enlightenment mission is to tell the truth, can allow the bottom line and powerful sources to trump principle.

Despite this incident, I enjoyed my time at the *Clarion*. People treated me well wherever I went. Life as a big fish in a small pond wasn't disagreeable.

The only downside to my job was that it paid $105 a week. After one year, I was making $125, but that still was never enough to cover all the bills.

Was I being exploited?

I sure felt like it sometimes.

But I convinced myself that I was getting "paid in bylines," and this job would be a stepping-stone to a better position.

I was right.

In January 1978, I took a job at the *Huron Daily Tribune* in Bad Axe, Michigan — a city of 3,100 located smack-dab in the middle of the thumbnail of the state (Michigan looks like a left-handed mitten, in case you didn't know).

THE MICHIGAN DEPARTMENT of Social Services (DSS) was convinced that one or more administrators in an adult foster care home in town had used a cattle prod to punish residents who would not cooperate.

What's a cattle prod?

I didn't know because I didn't grow up on a cattle farm. But it's used to move cattle at stockyards. The end of the cattle prod has two blunt prongs on it. When the user pushes a button, it sends an electric shock to anything touching the prongs.

To do this story right, I had to see for myself how much shock is delivered by those prods. So I went to the local farm-and-feed hardware to test one out.

"May I test this cattle prod?" I asked the clerk, a twentysomething man with two or three days of stubble on his chin.

"Sure," he said, smiling.

"Does it hurt much?"

"No, when we was kids, we use to poke each other for fun all the time," he said. "Cattle don't even hardly feel it."

I believed him.

I put it on my left index finger, held my breath and pushed the button. A jolt of electricity shot through my arm up to the back of my head.

"Shit!" I screamed.

He laughed.

At the beginning of the cattle prod investigation, I was convinced a crime had been committed. After all, bureaucratic officials tend to be credible. Social science research provides strong evidence to back this up.[7]

However, the alleged perpetrators claimed that the incident was exaggerated. They said one of the mentally disabled residents became upset one day and they were just trying to calm him down. There was some talk that a roller from a window blind might have been used. But the caretakers denied that was the case.

When answering questions about the incident, the caregivers were always cooperative, and the alleged tool of abuse — the cattle prod — was never found.

State investigators speculated the prod had been thrown away and was at the bottom of a landfill somewhere. Most of their case was built on the allegations of the resident, however, which were never corroborated.

The investigators were not law enforcement officers, so the accused caregivers were never charged with a crime. But they also did not have due process rights. DSS eventually took control of the home. The caregivers eventually closed their facility.[8]

I wrote several in-depth stories about the incident.

In the end, I believe the DSS officials knew they had conducted a flawed investigation. But embarrassment and fear of retribution from higher-ups and the public kept them from admitting their screw-ups.

My series of articles on the alleged abuse won a first place investigative reporting award from the Michigan Press Association.

More important, though, was the lesson I took from this incident: Public bureaucracies have a great deal of power and are able to insulate themselves easily from public accountability.

I LOVED my job at the *Daily Tribune*. Bad Axe was a small city surrounded by farmland and dozens of small towns. Lake Huron and its hundreds of miles of sandy shoreline and endless cottages and cabins were a 20-minute drive due north. At one point, I thought I could live here for the rest of my life.

At the time, the newspaper had the distinction of having the highest level of "household newspaper penetration" in the United States. The newspaper sold about 1.2 copies for every household in its service area, nearly twice the national average.

My editor was Richard (Dick) W. Carson, who was about a decade older than me and a consummate story-teller. Carson was a reporter's editor. He could have a good argument with a reporter and still go out later and have a beer and a friendly conversation. Now that was professionalism — the ability to separate one's personal feelings from one's professional judgment. Some lawyers are blessed with that trait.

At the time I thought many editors were like that. On my next job, I would be proved wrong.

Carson gave me and other reporters a great deal of latitude to cover stories, including some critical of powerful people in Huron County, population 36,000.

One memorable story I wrote involved the president of the most powerful bank in the county. I spent six months researching the bank and its president, who had been sued over a business deal gone bad. The bank, which was the second-biggest advertiser at our newspaper, threatened to pull its advertising if we published the stories.

Carson refused to back down.

The *Tribune* published a two-part series and the bank never pulled its advertising. It needed us more than we needed them.

Carson had guts. He proved to me that even small-town editors can do their jobs without compromising their principles. He and I remained friends for the rest of our lives.[9]

In May 1979, I finally graduated from CMU after taking a semester of courses at Oakland University and one correspondence course. The latter was an early version of online education courses, except that everything was done through postal mail.

After the graduation ceremony, my journalism professor Sue Nichols wished me "an interesting life, not just a happy one." I didn't know exactly what she meant. But eventually I figured it out.

She was a smart woman.

I LOVED WORKING for Dick and the *Daily Tribune*. But I wanted to work someday as an investigative reporter for a large daily. To do that, I needed to work my way up the journalism food chain.

Dick was supportive.

In January 1979, I accepted a reporting position with the *Midland Daily News* in Midland, Michigan, home to Dow Chemical, the world's largest chemical manufacturing facility. The *Daily Tribune* and *Daily News* had just been acquired by the Hearst Corporation, one of the most controversial newspaper chains in American history (now known as Hearst Communications).

Throughout the Vietnam War and for many years after, anti-war protesters and environmentalists had been critical of Dow because it was one of the companies that made Agent Orange, the powerful and deadly herbicide that was used to defoliate jungles in Vietnam in a matter of days after a spraying. The purpose was to deprive the enemy of hiding places. It worked.

However, many Vietnam vets who were exposed to Agent Orange claimed years later that it gave them illnesses and even cancer. Vietnamese authorities also estimate the defoliant killed 400,000 civilians and troops and led to 500,000 birth defects.[10]

Needless to say, Dow didn't like being in the news.

I HAD ONLY BEEN on the job for a couple of months or so when one day in September 1979 a disgruntled citizen called the *Daily News* and said workers at the Midland landfill were illegally selling topsoil.

"Would you look into this?" my editor asked.

I covered city hall.

If the allegation were true, asking the landfill operators if they were illegally selling soil wasn't likely to elicit the truth. So I called the landfill office and asked whether I could have a tour of the facility. Even if there was no wrongdoing, I could still write a story about how the landfill worked.

The representative there was delighted to help me out.

The tour took about 45 minutes.

The landfill was basically a big pit. Earth diggers dumped dirt into large dump trucks that left the site. I asked where the trucks were going, and the tour guide said he didn't know.

Red flag.

After the tour, I waited along the roadside in my 1979 Plymouth Arrow, which cost $4,200 brand new. I followed one of the dump trucks. I had no idea how far the truck would go. Fortunately, the drive was only about 15 minutes on rural dirt roads outside of Midland.

The truck pulled onto an open field containing a lot of heavy earth-moving equipment. The site displayed No Trespassing signs and was surrounded by barbed-wire fencing. That seemed odd because there was no livestock in the area.

I continued driving past the site and stopped to interview a local resident walking down the dirt road. The resident said she didn't know what was going on at the site.

I went back to the office and called officials in Williams Township and Bay County, who said the property was owned by Dow but they, too, didn't know what was going on there.

I eventually spoke with a state Department of Natural Resources official, who said Dow had used the site as a landfill in the 1950s. He said the carcinogen ethylbenzene tar and other chemicals were leaking into underground aquifers. The problem came to the attention of the authorities after a dog drank standing water on the site and lost its fur.

I also learned that Dow had begun construction on the pit without obtaining the proper county and state permits. But the headline downplayed that problem.

Clay Lining Planned at Ethylbenzene Site

> An abandoned landfill near Midland — identified as the source of a leaking cancer-producing chemical — is the target of a massive cleanup effort by its owner, the Dow Chemical Co.[11]
>
> Construction of a clay-lined dike to isolate and hold the contaminants began Monday.
>
> But local officials said they were unaware of the $500,000 project and its purpose.
>
> When told of the work, a Bay County planning official said he would investigate to determine if the construction began before a permit required under state law had been issued.
>
> A Dow official confirmed the project began without obtaining any permits. Another said the permit would be sought if needed. ...[12]

The next day Dow said it started construction without the permits because it wanted to build the dyke before it rained. I wondered, however, if the company was attempting to solve the problem without drawing attention to it.

One Dow executive chastised me in a letter to the editor for using the word "abandoned." He was right. I should have used the word "inactive."

Dow allegedly sealed the leaking landfill and was never fined for failing to obtain the necessary permits. The lesson I learned is that powerful corporations operate under a different set of rules than the rest of us.

As a journalist, I covered other stories that I believed had an impact on making the community a better place. One involved a tenant protest over housing conditions and an infestation of cockroaches at a trailer park in Midland. The landlord refused to address the problem until the story was published. A judge eventually forced the landlord to make repairs to the trailer.

But I also learned that my newspaper was not insulated from community politics.

IT WAS SPRING 1980, to the best of my recollection. Mary, the police reporter at the *Midland Daily News*, informed me that she was working on a story about a Michigan State Police investigation of the Midland Police Department.

"Officers are accused of gambling and prostitution," she said. "But the state police won't release the results of the investigation. You cover city hall. Have you heard anything?"

"No, but I'll get back to you."

I called the city manager, William Castle, who didn't beat around the bush. "Yes, the state police are investigating, but you already know that. Your editor and publisher have already seen the state police report."

"What?"

"Mark has already seen the report," Castle said.

I placed a call to the city attorney's office, but he was not in.

I informed Mary.

She was puzzled, because she had just spoken with Mark, who gave her no indication that he had seen the report. "I'll ask Mark about it," she said.

Mary emerged from Mark's office and he called me in.

"Where did you hear that we have seen the state police report?" he asked.

"William Castle, the city manager. Have you seen the report?"

"No," he said. "I want you to stop investigating this story, Dave. This is not your story. It's Mary's. She's the police reporter."

I was dumbfounded.

Someone was lying.

Whom was I to believe?

A short time later the city attorney returned my call and confirmed what Castle had said.

Why would Mark lie?

The next day Mark called me into his office, where he confessed that he had seen the confidential police report. He said he lied because he had promised the police confidentiality. Apparently someone forgot to tell the elite bureaucrats at city hall.

I felt betrayed.

There was, I had always believed, a sacred trust between reporter and editor. That's the way it was with Dick Carson at the *Huron Daily Tribune*. *If you can't trust your editor, whom can you trust?*

I didn't lecture Mark. Although he deserved a good verbal lashing, I wasn't very good at confrontation in those days. I still had a lot of Lutheran boy in me. But I wondered later why, instead of lying to me, he didn't just say, "I can't talk about it."

Turns out the state police never charged any officers with a crime, which made the subterfuge even more perplexing. Why lie about a report that never found evidence of a crime? And why would police allow the publisher and editor to see the report but not the police reporter?

It was no secret in the journalism business that sources often bring journalists into their confidence to co-opt them. They do this to avoid bad press. But it still didn't explain why they excluded Mary from the private screening.

This wasn't the only occasion that Mark failed to live up to my journalistic expectations.

On another occasion, he backed me up when an attorney for a local bank threatened to sue the newspaper if I quoted him in a story. The attorney told me, on the record, that Chemical Bank, the only bank in Midland and one of his clients, was not happy that a competing bank from a nearby city was going to open a branch in Midland.

"What are you going to do?" Mark said.

"I'm going to write up the story."

"Good."

But Mark withdrew that support when the Chemical Bank attorney followed through on his threat. Mark, the publisher, the attorney and another bank representative met in closed session. I was not invited.

Our newspaper published a retraction the next day, saying that Chemical Bank welcomed the competing bank into the community.

Boy, was I angry.

The retraction suggested that I had written a false news account.

I contacted a local attorney to see what I could do to restore my good name. He said the issue wasn't big enough to fight. Instead, he suggested I write a letter to the bank attorney and give him a piece of my mind. The attorney advised, "Put the words 'personal and confidential' on the envelope and letter. That will protect you from a defamation lawsuit should others read the letter."

I followed his advice.

Of course, the bank attorney contacted my publisher and editor to complain about the letter.

Mark admonished me.

And I suppressed the good Lutheran boy in me.

"You have no grounds to criticize me. You approved the original story and then caved in when things got tough."

Mark walked away.

He knew he was wrong.

I surprised myself, because I was never good at telling people to go to hell even when they deserved it.

A third event that shook my confidence in Mark as an editor came after I started investigating cancer rates in Midland, where a large proportion of people work for Dow.

I had been dating an attorney who was a social activist, and she wondered why no one had ever investigated the cancer rates in Midland.

I went to the local hospital to get statistics on cancer rates. The public relations person there relayed my request to hospital administrators, who then informed the board of directors of the hospital, who in turn informed the publisher and editor of the *Daily News*.

Mark called me into his office.

"You are going to have to drop this investigation," Mark said.

"Why?"

"Because you don't have the expertise to investigate the health issue. It's very complex."

Mark's argument was weak. Journalists often cover complex issues. It wasn't my goal to determine whether the Dow facility was causing cancer, but to see if cancer rates differed in Midland compared with other communities. The cause was another issue, one for the experts.

But the incident demonstrated how naive I was about local politics. I should have realized that the local hospital board would be populated with Dow employees, since they were the biggest employer in town.

The censorship of the cancer rate story and the stories about the state police investigation and Chemical Bank raised questions in my mind about the ability of some journalism organizations to promote the Enlightenment project.

They also shook my confidence in Mark as an editor.

Two decades later pollsters would discover that my experiences with Mark were not unique in the news business. About four in 10 local and national journalists reported that they had purposely avoided covering newsworthy stories or softened the tone of stories to benefit the interests of their editors or news organizations.[13]

But I didn't dwell on these matters for long, for my short, yet intense, four-year-long career as a reporter was coming to an end.

Although I enjoyed news reporting and felt my stories often had a meaningful impact on public policy, the daily grind of cranking out two or more stories a day was losing its appeal. I wanted something more challenging.

I really wanted a full-time investigative reporting position.

So I applied for the Kiplinger Program in Public Affairs Reporting at The Ohio State University, hoping that program would open doors for me.

I left the *Midland Daily News* in August 1980.

Ten years later I encountered Mark at an academic conference in Minneapolis. He apologized for the way he treated me when I worked for him and told me I was the best reporter he ever had.

I thanked him.

Few people I know have that kind of courage.

He would have made a good Lutheran.[14]

Chapter 14 Endnotes

1. Margaret Mead, *Coming of Age in Samoa: A Psychological Study of Primitive Youth for Western Civilisation* (New York: W. Murrow and Company, 1928).

2. Ibid., p. 11.

3. Derek Freeman, *Margaret Mead and Samoa: The Making and Unmaking of an Anthropological Myth* (Cambridge, MA: Harvard University Press, 1983).

4. David Demers, *The Ivory Tower of Babel: Why the Social Sciences Are Failing to Live Up to Their Promises* (New York: Algora Publishing, 2011).

5. Ben Bagdikian, "Woodstein U," *The Atlantic* (March 1977), retrieved August 15, 2008, and October 29, 2020, from <www.theatlantic.com/doc/197703/journalism-school>.

6. The ethic of objectivity holds that reporters should get all sides to a story, provide an equal amount of coverage to all sides, and keep their personal opinions out of the story. Oddly, though, this rule does not usually apply to people charged with crimes. Generally speaking, only celebrities and powerful people are interviewed after they are charged. Ordinary offenders are rarely interviewed. Journalists defend this practice by pointing out that they don't have time to interview everyone who is charged with the crime. Another reason, though, is that most journalists accept at face value the credibility of police and the courts. They readily defer to the power structure, even though the history of those organizations is replete with many cases of abuse of power. See, e.g., Roger G. Dunham and Geoffrey P. Alport (editors), *Critical Issues in Policing: Contemporary Readings*, 6th edition (Long Grove, IL: Waveland Press, 2010), Section IV.

7. See, e.g., Mark Fishman, *Manufacturing the News* (Austin: University of Texas Press, 1980).

8. The series won a first-place investigative reporting award from the Michigan Press Association.

9. Dick Carson eventually became editorial editor of the *Columbus Dispatch* in Ohio. He also spent more than a decade writing a book about a murder in the Thumb area. See Richard Carson, *Murder in the Thumb* (Spokane: Marquette Books, 2009).

10. Geoffrey York and Hayley Mick, "Last Ghost of the Vietnam War," *The* (Toronto)

Globe and Mail (July 12, 2008), retrieved September 22, 2010, from <http://www.theglobeandmail.com/incoming/last-ghost-of-the-vietnam-war/article1057457/?page=all>.

11. David Demers, "Clay Lining Planned at Ethylbenzene Site," *Midland Daily News* (September 25, 1979), p. 1.

12. The series earned a first place aware for investigative reporting from the Michigan Associated Press.

13. Pew Research Center, "Self Censorship: How Often and Why Journalists Avoiding the News," A Survey of Journalists in Association with Columbia Journalism Review (April 30, 2000), retrieved November 17, 2020, from <https://www.pewresearch.org/politics/2000/04/30/self-censorship-how-often-and-why>.

14. Mark eventually completed his Ph.D. in history, left daily journalism, became a highly respected professor, wrote a number of poetry books, and retired to central Illinois.

Chapter 15

The Descent of Journalism

August 1980
The Ohio State University

When I arrived on the campus of The Ohio State University in August 1980, Willard Monroe Kiplinger, who created the Kiplinger Program in Public Affairs Reporting, had been dead 13 years.

But his legacy was very much alive.

He attended OSU from 1908 to 1912 and was one of the first two journalism graduates from the university. When he began working as a cub reporter for the *Ohio State Journal* in 1912, his fellow journalists didn't have much respect for him.

"The idea of a college-trained journalist was preposterous and presumptuous," he acknowledged later.[1] In those days, most journalists earned their stripes on the job and viewed college graduates as eggheads without street smarts.

But it only took him and the other graduate "six months to establish the confidence of our fellow reporters." That respect came after he covered the Columbus flood of 1913, commandeering a horse and buggy through thigh-deep water to obtain the names of 100 flood victims.

He spent the next five years covering the nation's capital for the Associated Press. He walked in the rain with Woodrow Wilson on the night he was nominated for the presidency. He obtained exclusive interviews with suffragettes who were locked up for parading without a permit.

He left AP in 1919 to become a correspondent for a national bank, and then he left that job to establish a "query service" to answer questions that clients had about what was happening in Washington, D.C. In 1923, he published his first weekly *Kiplinger Letter*, which continues to this day.

His newsletter was heavy on opinion and forecasting and light on sources. But that's how he got bureaucrats and politicians to talk. "Men in public life would often give you the straight story in private, then reverse their field in their pro forma public statements," he explained.

Kiplinger built an empire around his newsletters, which also covered tax issues and agriculture. He died in 1967 at the age of 76.

By the time I arrived in Columbus, there was little debate in my mind about the value of a college degree when it came to reporting the news. But unbeknownst to me, clouds were forming over the journalism program at OSU and the newspaper business in general.

MY FIRST DAY at the OSU campus was exciting.

The Oval, a football-sized grassy area peppered with sidewalks that looked like a spider's web, was bustling with pedestrians. I had never seen so much diversity in one place. People were wearing dhotis and colorful silk saris, shorts and T-shirts, bell-bottom blue jeans and polyester shirts, hot pants and halter tops, suits and ties, robes and hijabs.

Something very important was happening here. I was thrilled to be a part of it. Yet I was a bit scared, too, because in high school, I never dreamed of attending graduate school. I didn't think I would be smart enough. I was worried about doing well in my classes.

My fears subsided a lot after I met one of the Kiplinger fellows, Norma Steele, a gregarious, unpretentious and sometimes irreverent woman from Pittsburgh who loved to laugh and banter. She had worked as a newspaper reporter and, I would soon learn, didn't "take shit from nobody." We forged a platonic bond that turned into lifelong friendship.

There were nine fellows in the yearlong Kippy Program, five women and four men. All were experienced journalists looking for an educational adventure and maybe a boost in their careers.

The master's degree program was founded in 1972. Its purpose was to provide early-to-mid-career journalists with in-depth knowledge about public affairs issues — such as crime, poverty, the economy, education, and discrimination — so that they could become better reporters. The program was supervised by a seasoned journalist who usually worked there for five years or so.

Our Kippy professor was a gleeful, intelligent man named Henry Schulte, who had worked as a reporter and editor for several major southern newspapers. This was his second year as director.

The program was designed to provide a liberal arts graduate education. We took mostly graduate-level courses in different disciplines and met several times a week as a group to talk about issues facing society and journalists. Schulte moderated the discussions, which were often lively and sometimes irreverent.

On one occasion I was giving a presentation and everyone was looking at me. Norma was sitting across from me. When I raised my eyes from my notes and looked at her, she was grinning and giving me the finger. We both exploded with laughter. Everyone stared, wondering what happened.

Schulte admonished us, but he didn't hold a grudge. Newspaper people are like that.

That year in the Kippy program was glorious. I took courses in money and banking, administrative law, mass media theory, quantitative research methods, civil liberties and the courts, and criminology. We took a field trip to Washington, D.C., and sat in on a U.S. Supreme Court hearing and visited the Chinese and Russian embassies.

The year flew by.

ALTHOUGH WE KIPPIES believed the program offered a valuable education, some faculty in the journalism and mass communication program were skeptical.

No master's thesis was required — just an oral exam and an in-depth story project. Most of us completed the program in one year, compared with one-and-a-half to two years for a typical master's program.

As the years passed, criticism of the program mounted, mostly from Ph.D.-educated faculty who felt the program should have been more intellectually rigorous. Compared with other master's programs at the university, there was some validity to this charge.

But the strength of the Kippy program was that it linked a university education to the real world. Better journalists produce better news and information, which in turn helps public policymakers and citizens solve social problems.

Journalism enhances the Enlightenment project.

It helps protect democracy and liberty.

But some administrators and Ph.D. faculty at OSU failed to see these benefits. Ten years after we graduated from the program, the dean of the College of Social and Behavioral Sciences announced that journalism was not central to the mission of the college. The journalism and professional mass communication programs (public relations, advertising, broadcasting) would be downsized and merged with communication studies[2] and a unit called Academic Technology Services and University Systems.

The merger decision drew criticism from some former professors.[3]

Dr. John J. Clarke, a highly respected OSU journalism professor emeritus, sent a note to OSU president E. Gordon Gee:

> My Ohio State students wanted above all to learn how to be journalists. Their tax-paying parents sent them to Ohio State expecting them to become excellent

reporters and broadcasters, not to be tolerated pawns of professors who are mostly occupied with Tiddlywink academic games.[4]

Clarke's concerns were ignored.

The merger was completed in 1996.

The Kippy Program survived, but its master's degree was ended in 2003. Two years later the program was moved from the School of Communication to the John Glenn School of Public Affairs at OSU. Graduates now would receive a certificate rather than a degree.

The program was shortened to six months and emphasized the impact of digital media on public policy, according to Debra Jasper, who was director of the Kiplinger Program in 2008 and had earned a Ph.D. in educational policy and leadership. At that time, she said the Kips worked on in-depth public affairs projects to take back to their newsrooms.[5]

By 2008, the OSU journalism program had basically shed most of its professional full-time staff.

Twenty-nine of the 31 faculty now held the Ph.D. degree.

The program relied mostly on adjuncts (part-time faculty) to teach skills courses and it was no longer accredited by the Accrediting Council on Education in Journalism and Mass Communications.[6]

By 2013, the Kiplinger Program had been moved to University Communications and was supported by the office of the vice president for communications. The program now involved only one week of digital media training a year.

In 2019, the Kiplinger Program left OSU and found a new home at Ohio University in Athens. The program continues to offer weeklong training for journalists and other professionals.

The decline of the Kiplinger Program, one professor told me years later, reflected the fact that Ph.D. faculty had little interest in addressing real-world problems.

"They were more interested in building an ivory tower."[7]

The Enlightenment project also lost an important ally.

THE CHANGES taking place in the journalism program at Ohio State were not isolated events.

In 1977, former *Washington Post* editor-turned-journalism-professor Ben H. Bagdikian wrote a series of articles for the *Atlantic Monthly* that questioned the transition of power from what he called the "green eyeshades" professors to the "chi-squares."

Green eyeshades refers to the green-rimmed celluloid visor that many newspaper editors wore in the early twentieth century to cut down on glare from incandescent lights in the newsroom. Chi-square is a statistic that quantitative social scientists often use in their research.

"Today young Ph.D.s ... teach reporting and other practical journalism courses even though they have had little or no professional experience," Curt MacDougall, a then-73-year-old former journalism professor from the green-eyeshade camp, told Bagdikian. "The internal fight by those of us who warned against and resisted the influx of chi-square fiends is over. We did our best and we lost."

Bagdikian acknowledged that the chi-squares, who by then comprised roughly half of the journalism faculty at universities across the country, were winning the power struggle.

He lamented the change, arguing that journalists need a strong humanistically oriented education — one that drew heavily on history, literature, philosophy and the arts. He wrote that news companies "are in danger of sterility unless they are constantly fed generations of new journalists lively in spirit and mind, formed by something other than the corporate ethic. This kind of men and women will ... come from institutions that still nurture the humanities."

In 1981, I was not fully aware of the scope of this debate.

I did not realize that the slow death of journalism programs at many large-scale universities would reduce journalism's role in the Enlightenment project.

Nor did I realize that most research universities were devaluing the arts and humanities, partly because these disciplines were not generating a great deal of grant money from governmental and private sources.

With the decline in state funding of public universities, which started in the early 1980s,[8] universities increasingly were turning to science and technology, because these were the disciplines that were generating revenues through grants and patents.

Ironically, in 1981, I was about to join the chi-square camp.

I had taken a course in criminology that examined quantitative research about criminal behavior.

I loved it.

The instructor was Richard Lundman, who would be on my master's committee.

He would pace back and forth in the front of the room, feverishly writing the main points of his lecture on the blackboard and thrusting both of his arms through the air to emphasize point after point.

At the end of the 50-minute session, he was often perspiring, and my note-taking hand was sore from trying to keep up. If teaching was a sport, Lundman surely would have earned an Olympic gold medal.

I would stay on at Ohio State and complete a master's degree in criminology, but I would soon learn that the problems facing the field of criminology were not much different from those in mass communication. Criminology, too, was experiencing a purge of professional faculty, for essentially the same reasons as the field of mass communication.

In addition, criminology also was having difficulty solving the crime problem. I didn't know it at the time, but all of the social sciences in general were struggling to live up to the ideals of the Enlightenment. Some scholars were even calling for an end to the project.

Chapter 15 Endnotes

1. Biography of Willard Monroe Kiplinger (1891-1967), Harvard Square Library, retrieved November 3, 2020, from <https://www.harvardsquarelibrary.org/biographies/w-m-kiplinger>.

2. Professors in communication studies focus mainly on interpersonal, organizational and intercultural communication and rhetoric.

3. Interestingly, the journalism/mass communication faculty supported the merger but many communication studies faculty opposed it. A sociologist might use status theory to explain the opposition; that is, the Ph.D.-heavy communication studies may have viewed the merger with a professional program as lowering the status of their academic unit.

4. Quoted in John Wicklein, "No Experience Necessary: In the Battle for the Soul of Journalism Education, the Ph.D.'s Are Beating the Pros," *Columbia Journalism Review* (September/October 1994), retrieved October 7, 2008, from <http://backissues.cjrarchives.org/year/94/5/experience.asp>.

5. In a telephone interview on October 8, 2008, Jasper told me, "People are doing research here that really makes an impact. They focus on practical problems and team up with social scientists to help solve those problems. ... We're trying very hard to navigate between academic research and journalism. ... You want to do research that makes a difference. ... That's why people go into journalism."

6. ACEJMC accredits journalism and mass communication programs that meet a minimum set of requirements considered to produce a high-quality education program. For more details, visit <http://www2.ku.edu/~acejmc>.

7. The term "ivory tower" was first used in Song of Solomon 7:4, but its meaning today derives from an 1837 poem by French writer Charles Augustin Sainte-Beuve, who used it to describe the poetical attitude of Alfred de Vigny versus that of the more socially engaged Victor Hugo, author of the novels *Les Misérables* and *The Hunchback of Notre Dame*. Webster's defines ivory tower as "a place of mental withdrawal from reality and action"; Wiktionary.com defines it as "a sheltered, overly-academic existence or perspective, implying a disconnection or lack of awareness of reality or practical considerations."

8. Thomas G. Mortenson, "State Funding: A Race to the Bottom," *The Presidency* (American Council on Education, Fall 2012), retrieved January 8, 2014, from <http://www.acenet.edu/the-presidency/columns-and-features/Pages/state-funding-a-race-to-the-bottom.aspx>.

Chapter 16

More Truth Next Time?

Fall Quarter 1981
The Ohio State University

The white-haired professor stared at his class of four dozen criminology students, pausing briefly to transition to a new topic.

"On August 11, 1979, New York criminologist Robert Martinson hurled himself through a 15th-story window in his Manhattan apartment while his adult son was sleeping," Simon Dinitz solemnly told his undergraduate students.[1] "His suicide made national news, because five years earlier Martinson had become a celebrity in the field of criminology.[2] He appeared on CBS's *60 Minutes* and declared that, when it comes to rehabilitating people convicted of crimes, 'nothing works.'"

Dinitz paused and then added: "Was he right?"

I was a graduate student in criminology at OSU and the teaching assistant for Dinitz's class. I attended lectures, took notes, and created and scored tests. He was, in my opinion, the best lecturer I had ever known. He rarely looked at his notes, spoke in full sentences, altered the tone of his delivery to match the mood of a scene, smiled a lot, treated his students with genuine respect, and clearly knew what he was talking about.

In fact, today he was going to draw upon his own research to address the question he raised: Does rehabilitation work?

"Why do some boys engage in delinquent behavior while others don't? My colleague Walter Reckless concluded that a good self-concept was the answer. In high-delinquency neighborhoods, this is what distinguishes the nondelinquent boys from the delinquents. A good self-concept appears to insulate them from the social pressure to engage in lawless behavior."[3]

Dinitz added that he and Reckless devised a series of field experiments designed to instill a higher level of self-esteem in seventh-grade boys.[4] Boys with delinquent backgrounds were exposed to instruction that contained positive role models and positive self-image concepts. The control group of "good" boys had standard instruction.[5]

"But after two years of intensive treatment and four years of follow-up, the program had no appreciable effect on delinquency," Dinitz said, waving his left hand through the air to emphasize the point. "Boys who went through the program had the same arrest rates as those who did not. Our study supported much of the literature up to that point in time, which basically concluded that social intervention did not seem to have much impact. And that's where Martinson comes in. He and his colleagues reviewed more than 200 intervention and rehabilitation programs like ours over a two-decade period and concluded they had little or no effect."

A summary of Martinson's analysis was published in *The Public Interest* magazine in 1974. "With few and isolated exceptions, the rehabilitative efforts that have been reported so far have had no appreciable effect on recidivism. ... [O]ur present strategies ... cannot overcome, or even appreciably reduce, the powerful tendencies of offenders to continue in criminal behavior."[6]

Dinitz added that many other scholars previously had reached the same conclusion.[7] But those reports had little direct impact on public policy, because they had been published in scientific journals, which were read only by scholars, not politicians or the public.

In contrast, nearly 10,000 policymakers, journalists and citizens read the conservative-leaning *Public Interest*. This included producers at CBS's *60 Minutes*, who followed up with an investigative story and interviewed Martinson. The segment was titled "It Doesn't Work," and *60 Minutes* host Mike Wallace announced to the nation that the research "findings are sending shock waves through the correctional establishment."[8] Martinson told Wallace that treatment approaches have "no fundamental effect on recidivism" and that psychological counseling may be a "good way to pass the time" but "has no effect."[9]

No single event in the history of criminology has had more political impact, Dinitz said, quoting other scholars.[10]

"In fact, within one year many scholars and policymakers completely abandoned the rehabilitation model," Dinitz said, pacing back and forth in front of the blackboard. "Conservatives, in particular, seized upon the 'nothing works' conclusion to justify closing down rehabilitation programs and passing laws that increased the severity of punishment. Capital punishment was reinstated in the United States in 1976, even though other research had shown that it and increasing the severity of punishment for many other crimes had little impact on reducing recidivism rates."[11]

"So, Professor Dinitz, are you saying that policymakers failed to take the research evidence into account?" another student asked.

"Since when have public policymakers based their decisions mostly upon scientific evidence?" he responded and grinned. "Policymakers usually have their own agendas, which don't always coincide with scientific research."

"So why did Martinson kill himself?" another student asked.

"Good question. After the *60 Minutes* report, Martinson was severely criticized for overstating the lack of effects of rehabilitation programs. He also was having serious mental health issues, and the IRS was hounding him for failing to pay taxes on some of the income he earned through lectures. He was a civil rights advocate, but his fellow activists denounced him for ushering in a conservative public policy platform that treated offenders as non-redeemable. And the last book he wrote was a commercial flop."

The bell rang.

"More truth next time."

DINITZ ALMOST ALWAYS ended his formal lectures with that "more truth next time" remark, which could have sounded pompous coming from anyone else. But he never failed to impress students and, to the best of my knowledge, faculty and administrators as well.

In fall 1981, Dinitz was 55 and at the apex of his career. He had written or cowritten more than two dozen scholarly books and 120 peer-reviewed scientific articles. He had advised more than three dozen Ph.D. recipients and scores of master's students.

He had lectured at universities around the world and had won many awards for his research and service.[12] He was honored as the first faculty member in history at OSU to deliver a commencement address at the university. He also became the only professor in the history of OSU to earn all three of the highest awards that could be bestowed on faculty — Distinguished Teaching, Distinguished Research and Distinguished Service.

But Dinitz was a modest man. Compassionate, a great listener, quick to praise but slow to criticize, engaging, precise, witty, respectful and supportive.

His eyes were his most outstanding physical feature. They sparkled. I never met a man with eyes like that. Very dark, almost black — but that sparkle, it surely stemmed from the greatness of the man, not from genetics.[13]

As a former newspaper reporter who had covered more than a dozen different police beats, I was no novice when it came to the issue of crime.

However, I was puzzled when Dinitz made the comment in 1981 that policymakers often ignore research in criminology. After all, he had just told his class that policymakers abandoned the rehabilitation model after *60 Minutes* broadcast the program showing that rehabilitation programs aren't very effective.

I assumed, like most other graduate students and young faculty, that social science research was important and impacted public policy. After all, wasn't that how it was supposed to work under the Enlightenment project?

TWO DECADES WOULD PASS before I would have a good answer to that question (details to come). For now, let me just say that conservative politicians did respond to Martinson's report because the message — rehabilitation programs don't work well — reinforced their political agenda, which emphasized increasing the severity of punishment, not rehabilitation. When scientific evidence runs contrary to an agenda, politicians almost always ignore the research.

But in 1981, my big concern wasn't the efficacy of social scientific research; it was completing my master's degree. My master's committee was composed of Dinitz, Lundman, and Joseph E. Scott, a professor who had turned the criminology program at OSU into the largest major in sociology. Scott was chair of the committee.

Charismatic and gregarious, Scott was an expert on constitutional law and an ardent supporter of First Amendment rights. He occasionally was called upon to give expert testimony in court as to the socially redeeming value of pornographic materials.[14] Few college professors had that kind of courage, even among those who taught law in mass communication programs. I know, because I taught a course on obscenity and the law once, and a professor questioned the value of the class — and not just any professor, but a First Amendment professor.

As a former journalist, I admired Scott for his strong support of free speech rights. I also was grateful when he gave me the opportunity to teach an introductory criminology course that focused on constitutional law.[15]

For my master's thesis, I decided to examine the impact of exposure to mass media content on fear of crime.

At the time, the prevailing assumption was that mass media presented a distorted picture of crime in society, one that focused disproportionately on violent crime, especially murder, in both news and fictional programming.

The conventional wisdom was that people who watched a lot of TV and read a lot of news would be more fearful of becoming a victim of a crime. Thus, I hypothesized that the more time people spend consuming mass media content, the greater their fear of crime. I also hypothesized that the effects would be stronger for social groups or categories that are more fearful of victimization (e.g., the elderly, women, racial minorities, or the less educated).

To test the hypotheses, I analyzed data from three telephone surveys of voters in the Columbus, Ohio, area[16] and conducted an original survey of OSU students.

The results failed to support both hypotheses.[17]

Citing the work of social psychologist Fritz Heider,[18] I concluded that when it comes to fear of crime, mass media have limited effects because people often look for ways to explain away their own fear or victimization. They do this because, as Heider pointed out, people possess strong desires to establish stability in their social and physical environments.

They prefer and want the explicable and predictable; they want security; and they work hard to establish "balanced states of cognition" to structure that security into their world.

Consequently, they look for explanations (or "attributions," as Heider called them) to explain away the information that threatens their secure sense of being.

Thus, when news media report that a drug dealer has been shot and killed by other drug dealers, most people do not see that as a threat to their own security because "I'm not a drug dealer." Some may even reason that the dealer "deserved what he got."

Because street crime rates are higher in inner-city and poor areas, I concluded that people who live in the suburbs do not feel threatened (or as threatened) by most reports of crimes. Instead, they simply avoid driving through or walking in high-crime districts, which in turn reinforces self-perceptions of personal security.

Most news stories contain enough information (location of the crime, motivation and/or background of the offender and victim) to explain away the unpredictable, rudimentary nature of crime.

However, I pointed out that the so-called random crimes — where the perpetrator selects victims at random — are an exception to the rule. They prevent people from being able to make attributions that explain away the threat.

A good example at the time was the Atlanta child murders, in which at least 28 African American children, adolescents and adults were murdered in Atlanta, Georgia, from the summer of 1979 until the spring of 1981.[19]

The murders terrorized certain neighborhoods because the perpetrator appeared to randomly select his victims.

I never followed up and tested Heider's theories.[20]

But I never forgot his assumptions about the nature of human behavior — that people seek stability and predictability in their lives.

Years later, University of Minnesota sociologist George A. Donohue, who was a member of my Ph.D. committee, would reinforce this idea in one of his seminars.

"Do people prefer freedom or security?" he asked.

We students, sensing a setup, were quick to choose "security," much to his delight.

After watching people in action in social institutions for more than four decades, I believe Heider and Donohue are right.

I also believe that people who have a strong need for security have less commitment for Enlightenment ideals such as liberty and free speech.

IN JUNE 1983, I graduated from the master's program in sociology, with an emphasis in criminology.

Dinitz retired in 1991.

Lundman continued teaching at OSU.

Scott took early retirement in 1994, partly because he, as a professor, felt he had limited impact on the policymaking process. He obtained a J.D. and started up a successful criminal defense law practice in Columbus.

"Criminology has made so little progress in the last 30 and 40 years," Scott said many years later. "Policymakers pay no attention to it. The impact of criminological research has been minimal. That's the one nice thing about being out of it [the university environment]. It's nice to have impact [as an attorney]."[21]

Asked if he thought all of the research in the field was insignificant in terms of influencing public policy, Scott softened his criticism. He said Dinitz was an exception to the rule.

In 1993, the Ohio governor selected Dinitz to head a committee to conduct a comprehensive evaluation of all reports and information pertaining to the 1993 prison riot at Southern Ohio Correctional Facility in Lucasville, Ohio, where one guard and nine inmates were killed.[22]

Dinitz told me he was proud to be associated with such a project. However, he later expressed some ambiguity about the impact it had on public policy.

In an oral history interview at The Ohio State University in 2005,[23] Dinitz said that even though the legislature adopted many of the suggestions offered by the committees that studied the riots, most "were the easy ones" to adopt. The state did not implement suggestions that required substantial changes to the structure of the criminal justice system.[24] He added:

> I've had some influence in the political realm, but only because — I never kid myself — they [policymakers] wanted the changes to be made, or they wanted a "cover" [someone to blame or hold accountable if something went wrong]. You use task forces as a cover, right? [If] you want to go get more money, you bring a task force in to tell you that we're not doing well enough. That's what they do.[25]

In summer 1999, I visited OSU and Dinitz took me and a mass communication colleague of mine to lunch at the Faculty Club. At the time I had just begun research on a book about the impact of social science on public policy. I asked him whether much had changed in research in criminology since I had left the program in 1983 — whether any new solutions to the crime problem had been developed. Reinforcing Martinson's report and Scott's observation, he said there had been no major breakthroughs.

"How does that make you feel?" I asked.

"You do the best you can," he said.

That was the last time I spoke with Dinitz. Eight years later, on March 3, 2007, he died of complications from cardiovascular disease. Lundman died in 2015. As of this writing, Scott continues to practice law.

There's no question in my mind that Dinitz did his best.

But, I wondered in 1999, what if doing your best doesn't help solve social problems? Does this mean the social sciences are incapable of fulfilling one of the ideals of the Enlightenment?

I would spend the next decade trying to answer these questions.[26]

Chapter 16 Endnotes

1. Jerome G. Miller, "The Debate on Rehabilitating Criminals: Is It True that Nothing Works?" *The Washington Post* (March 1989), retrieved November 3, 2020, from <https://www.prisonpolicy.org/scans/rehab.html>.

2. Adam Humphreys, "Robert Martinson and the Tragedy of the American Prison, RibbonFarm.com (December 15, 2016), retrieved November 3, 2020, from <https://www.ribbonfarm.com/2016/12/15/robert-martinson-and-the-tragedy-of-the-american-prison>.

3. Walter Reckless conducted observational studies of crime in Chicago with sociologists Robert Park and Ernest Burgess. His 1925 dissertation was published as *Vice in Chicago* in 1933 and was a landmark sociological study of crime. In 1932, he and Mapheus Smith published the first book on juvenile delinquency. He took a position at Ohio State in 1940. Reckless retired in 1969 and died in 1988 at age 89.

4. Walter C. Reckless and Simon Dinitz, *The Prevention of Juvenile Delinquency: An Experiment* (Columbus: Ohio State University Press, 1972).

5. During the 1960s, Reckless developed "containment theory," which contended that people have inner and outer forces that restrain them from committing crimes. The inner forces stem from moral and religious beliefs whereas the outer forces come from family members, teachers and others. He believed that the effectiveness of containment forces can be influenced by effective supervision and by internal factors such as a good self-concept.

6. Robert Martinson, "What Works? Questions and Answers about Prison Reform," *The Public Interest, 35*: 22-54 (Spring 1974), p. 25 (first sentence) and p. 49 (second sentence). The full report was published as a book a year later. Douglas Lipton, Robert Martinson and Judith Wilks, *The Effectiveness of Correctional Treatment: A Survey of Treatment Evaluation Studies* (New York: Praeger, 1975).

7. See, e.g., Walter C. Bailey, "Correctional Outcome: An Evaluation of 100 Reports," *Journal of Criminal Law, Criminology and Police Science, 57*: 153-160 (1966); William C. Berleman and Thomas W. Steinburn, "The Value and Validity of Delinquency Prevention Experiments," *Crime & Delinquency, 15*: 471-478 (1969); and James Robison and Gerald Smith, "The Effectiveness of Correctional Programs," *Crime & Delinquency, 17*: 67-80 (1971).

8. CBS Television Network, *60 Minutes: It Doesn't Work* (Transcript), 7: 2-9 (August 24, 1975), p. 3.

9. Ibid., p. 4.

10. Two years after the article was published, criminologist Stuart Adams wrote that the work had "shaken the community of criminal justice to its root." See Stuart Adams, "Evaluation: A Way Out of Rhetoric," pp. 75-91 in Robert Martinson, Ted Palmer and Stuart Adams (editors), *Rehabilitation, Recidivism, and Research* (Hackensack, NJ: National Council on Crime and Delinquency (1976).

11. But increasing the certainty and severity of punishment for nonviolent crimes often works. The key is rational calculation of costs and benefits. Many violent crimes are committed in the "heat of passion." Drugs and alcohol are also often involved.

12. Dinitz was a recipient of the Society's Edwin H. Sutherland Award in 1974. In 1981, criminology scholars across the country wrote a book in honor of him. I. Barak-Glantz and C. Ronald Huff (editors), *The Mad, the Bad, and the Different: Essays in Honor of Simon Dinitz* (Lexington, MA: D.C. Heath, 1981).

13. In fall 1982, when Dinitz heard I was spending Thanksgiving alone (my family lived in Michigan), he invited me to dine in his home with his family and a few friends, one of whom was a professor and expert on Israel. Dinitz and his wife, Mildred, made all of the guests feel at home. At one point, shortly after the dinner, Dinitz's then 20-year-old daughter, Risa, a student at the University of Michigan, began ribbing her father. I can't recall what she said, but I can remember very clearly the intent of the jabs: to tease her father and perhaps me. She knew I had great admiration for her father, as did all of his students, and so she was playfully trying to bring his allegedly big ego down to earth. Dinitz just smiled through it all, and Risa kept looking at me to see my reaction. What I didn't know then was that Risa and other family members often ribbed their accomplished father, and he, in turn, would egg them on. This was another one-act play, and I was an unknowing member of the audience. Of course, I knew that Risa had the greatest admiration of all for her father.

14. Pornographic means "sexually arousing" material. Most pornographic material enjoys protection of the First Amendment. Obscene materials are those materials that do not enjoy First Amendment protection, according to the U.S. Supreme Court.

15. This included the First, Second, Fourth, Sixth and 14th Amendments. The Second Amendment deals with the "right" to bear arms; the Fourth with search and seizure rights; the Sixth with fair trial rights; the Eighth with cruel and unusual punishment; and the 14th with due process and the states.

16. Lee B. Becker, a professor in the School of Journalism and Mass Communication, generously added a question on fear of crime to three voter or adult population surveys he conducted on various media issues in 1982.

17. David K. Demers, "Fear of Crime and the Mass Media: Another Test of the Mass Media Effects Hypothesis," unpublished master's thesis, The Ohio State University (June 1983), p. 115.

18. Fritz Heider, *The Psychology of Interpersonal Relations* (New York: Wiley, 1958).

19. Wayne Bertram Williams was charged and convicted of two of the murders, although investigators disagreed whether he was responsible for all of the crimes. A more recent example of a random violence was the 24 Ohio highway sniper attacks around Columbus, Ohio, in 2003. One person was killed and many others were injured. The shootings caused widespread fear until a man suffering from schizophrenia was arrested, convicted, and sent to prison for 27 years.

20. When I entered the Ph.D. program at the University of Minnesota in 1987, I moved away from the social psychological perspective to a structural sociological perspective.

21. Telephone interview in fall 2008.

22. A summary of events surrounding the riots is contained in Reginald A. Wilkinson and Thomas J. Stickrath, "After the Storm: Anatomy of a Riot's Aftermath," *Corrections Management Review* (Winter 1997).

23. Oral history transcript of Simon Dinitz conducted by Adrienne Chafetz (November 8, 2005), retrieved September 18, 2008, from <https://kb.osu.edu/dspace/handle/1811/29289>.

24. Dinitz did not elaborate on those major changes.

25. Supra note 23.

26. David Demers, *The Ivory Tower of Babel: Why the Social Sciences Are Failing to Live Up to Their Promises* (New York, NY: Algora, 2011).

Chapter 17

Collective Manipulation

Fall 1985
Phoenix, Arizona

"What I can't understand is why owners of Ford automobiles are more likely than nonowners to remember our advertising," said Frank Fluxor, the director of marketing research for Ford Motor Company.[1]

Fluxor made the comment during a meeting in 1985 with me and two executives of Winona Market Research Bureau, Inc., a national market research company whose telephone calling facility was located in Phoenix, Arizona. I was senior research analyst for Winona and had been working there since summer 1983, shortly after graduating from the sociology/criminology master's program at Ohio State. I toyed with the idea of earning a Ph.D. in criminology, but my heart was in journalism. I really wanted to work as an investigative newspaper reporter, but there were few job openings.

So I packed up my car and drove to Scottsdale, Arizona, where my father was living at the time.

To pay the bills, I took a job as a security guard for minimum wage ($4.25 an hour). No benefits. I learned quickly that a quasi-military form of organization was not a good fit for me. I was reprimanded for helping tenants get into their apartment after one of the apartment managers went AWOL during his shift. The moral of the story is that organizational rules sometimes conflict with being a Good Samaritan.

Fortunately, six weeks later I landed the job at Winona, which paid a lot more ($27,000 a year) and offered health insurance benefits.

Winona specialized in conducting telephone interviews for major corporations that sold goods and services to consumers nationwide. Its clients included Ford, Burger King, Honeywell, 3M, the United States Postal Service, Group Health Foundation, Ore-Ida (the potato maker) and many other national companies.

The telephone calling facility in Phoenix was state of the art at the time. The interviewers were able to record everything via touchscreen computers.

My job was to analyze the data collected in those telephone surveys.

The surveys measured consumer attitudes, beliefs and purchase intentions toward automobiles, fast food, hobbies, health care, and many other products and services. The results of the Ford study being presented on that day in 1985 had been derived from a nationwide telephone survey that measured the impact of television, newspaper and magazine advertising on buying intentions.

Fluxor's question took me by surprise.

A well-documented finding in marketing research is that owners of various products almost always have higher awareness of advertising for those products than nonowners. Advertising reinforces and legitimates an owner's previous behavior or decision and helps reduce cognitive dissonance, a mental state in which people question the wisdom of their decision. People seek harmony between their beliefs and behaviors.

Shades of Fritz Heider, I thought, as Fluxor nodded his head, acknowledging my response.

MARKETING RESEARCH is big business in America. In the late 1980s, corporations were spending more than $10 billion a year to understand consumers and markets.[2] This figure is actually about three times greater than the U.S. government spends in total on research in health, space, energy, transportation, environment, agriculture commerce, and justice.[3] At the time, I wondered whether this disparity explained in part why America has so many social problems.

Although I had great respect for academic research, what I liked about marketing research is that it had immediate, practical applications. The results helped our clients improve their products and services.

But many scholars in American universities at the time were skeptical. Some, like the postmodernists,[4] even questioned the value of quantitative research. Postmodernists believe all knowledge about the social is not absolute but dependent upon time, place and culture.

"All knowledge is relative," they declared.

Of course, proponents of the Enlightenment enjoyed pointing out the paradox of that statement.

Other critics, especially leftist scholars, believed quantitative research exploited people and consumers. From their perspective, market researchers like me and mainstream social scientists were agents of the capitalists who created knowledge that would be used to manipulate consumers and citizens.

Were my research reports manipulating people?

I suppose, at least to some degree.

But I was also being manipulated.

I was simply following the "social ethic" that former *Fortune* editor-turned-professor William H. Whyte Jr. perceptively identified in his famous 1956 book, *The*

Organization Man.[5] To succeed in corporate America, Whyte argued, individuals must embrace the collective and give up much of their individuality and creativity.

As I entered my fourth year at Winona, that's how I began to feel.

WHYTE DEFINED the social ethic as that "contemporary body of thought which makes morally legitimate the pressures of society against the individual."[6] In plain English, the social ethic justifies the repressive power of the collective (organizations) over individuals.[7]

He said the social ethic encompassed three beliefs: (1) The group, not the individual, is the primary source of creativity; (2) Belongingness is the ultimate need of the individual; and (3) Scientific methods should be used to achieve belongingness.

Whyte's concept of belongingness is similar to Fritz Heider's concept of security — people want to be loved; they treasure security more than freedom.

The obverse of the social ethic is the Protestant ethic, which Whyte defined as the "pursuit of individual salvation through hard work, thrift, and competitive struggle."[8]

Modern complex bureaucratic organizations cannot function effectively if their workers or participants embrace the Protestant ethic. That's because cooperation and teamwork, not competition and individualism, are necessary to get things done, Whyte argued.

The social ethic assumes that group decision-making is superior to individual decision-making.

Whyte disputed that idea.

He studied top executives at major corporations and found that they were risk-averse, because they wanted to keep their high-paying jobs.

In modern organizations, workers give their loyalty to the organization. In return, they get "belongingness," or acceptance and respect from others, and the organization rewards them with long-term employment, raises, promotions, and homes in the suburbs.[9]

The social ethic also contends that there is no inherent conflict between the individual and society. Conflicts are just misunderstandings. And when they occur, the social sciences (e.g., organizational and management theories and research) can be used to solve them and restore harmony to the organization.

"Essentially, it is a utopian faith," Whyte wrote. ""[I]t is the long-range promise that animates its followers, for it relates techniques to the vision of a finite, achievable harmony."[10]

But Whyte argued that modern bureaucratic corporations were robbing the "organization man" of his individuality — of control over his life and thoughts.

Ironically, though, the organization man didn't even realize it was happening. In fact, he actually believed he was still pursuing the Protestant ethic, despite working in a collectivist environment.

> We do need to know how to co-operate with The Organization but, more than ever, so do we need to know how to resist it.[11] ... The fault is not in organization ... it is in our worship of it. ... In our vain quest for a utopian equilibrium ... it is in the soft-minded denial that there is a conflict between the individual and society. There must always be, and it is the price of being an individual that he must face these conflicts. He cannot evade them, and in seeking an ethic that offers a spurious peace of mind, thus does he tyrannize himself.[12]

Wow.

Whyte hit it on the head. And he didn't stop there. He argued that most people in organizations never escape the tyranny.

> [T]here are only a few times in organization life when he [an organizational man] can wrench his destiny into his own hands — and if he does not fight then, he will make a surrender that will later mock him. But when is that time? ... By what standards is he to judge? ... If he goes against the group, is he being courageous — or just stubborn? Helpful — or selfish? Is he, as he so often wonders, right after all? It is in the resolution of a multitude of such dilemmas, I submit, that the real issue of individualism lies today.[13]

Yes, Whyte had it right when it came to understanding bureaucracies. And so did several other social commentators who were publishing fiction and nonfiction books from the 1940s to the early 1960s.

One was Ayn Rand, who, despite her extremist individual-over-the-collective philosophy, understood in her novel *The Fountainhead* how organizations can apply intense pressure on individuals to conform to popular standards.[14]

Another was Sloan Wilson, whose novel *The Man in the Grey Flannel Suit* presents the story of a married World War II veteran who is trying to find meaning in life after killing 17 enemy soldiers and having an affair with an Italian woman who becomes pregnant.[15] He eventually rejects the social ethic, devotes more time to his family and takes responsibility for the child born out of wedlock.

A third commentator was an academic, a man who had escaped Germany when Adolf Hitler came to power. In his book *One-Dimensional Man*, Herbert Marcuse argued that industrial management, mass media, and advertising created false needs for material goods and integrated the working and middle classes, labor and management, and Democratic and Republican politics into a "one-dimensional" system of thought incapable of recognizing the exploitative features of "advanced industrialist society."[16]

And a fourth commentator was David Riesman, whose book *The Lonely Crowd* would become the best-selling sociology book of all time (1.5 million copies).[17]

LIKE WHYTE, Riesman argued that modern capitalism and the growth of the corporate form of organization were changing the character of American workers, turning them into passive, dependent sycophants.

Riesman maintained that, historically, the American character consisted of three major types: tradition-directed, inner-directed and other-directed. The tradition-directed personality emerged prior to the Enlightenment. Such people tend to obey rules and tradition and have a difficult time succeeding in a modern, industrialized nation, because of constant change.

Inner-directed people emerged during the Reformation and Enlightenment. They act not necessarily in accord with established norms but according to a set of principles, including the Protestant ethic, that they usually pick up during childhood from their parents or church. They have an "inner gyroscope" and tend to be confident, self-reliant, assiduous, but sometimes inflexible.

Other-directed people emerged after the Industrial Revolution, during the twentieth century, and act not on the basis of an abstract set of principles but in terms of cues from others in their world, especially peer groups, coworkers, and mass media. Riesman associates the rise of the other-directed character with the rise of the corporation and the middle-class consumer.

For other-directed people, tradition and values associated with organized religion, the family, or other institutions have less impact. They are focused on material needs and consuming goods and services, and define themselves in terms of the way others see them.

Other-directed people have a strong need to accommodate others to gain approval; as such, they fit well into bureaucratic organizations, which need pliable people.

"The other-directed person wants to be loved rather than esteemed," Riesman writes.[18] They dislike conflict and seek consensus.

"While all people want and need to be liked by some of the people some of the time, it is only the modern other-directed types who make this their chief source of direction and chief area of sensitivity."[19]

In today's world, other-directed people might include Facebook users who validate themselves through the number of "likes" they get for their postings.

Other-directed people are guided by "radar," or a concern about how others and the mass media see things.[20] Riesman argued that societies dominated by other-directed people have onerous shortcomings in terms of leadership, individual autonomy and knowledge.

Riesman's book was popular because it raised concerns that America's ethos of self-reliant freedom (under the Protestant ethic) was disappearing. The nation was becoming a land of anxious, oversocialized people who were incapable of thinking for themselves.

In *The Fountainhead*, Rand called them "second-handers," or people who derive their self-respect from others (second-hand) rather than from their own accomplishments or integrity. Second-handers, she argued, are people of mediocrity.

The title of Riesman's book was created by the publisher (the term "lonely crowd" is not used in the book) and was meant to convey the idea that in modern society other-directed people feel painfully alone because they define themselves through references to others and, thus, are unable to develop independent meaning for their lives.

Riesman attributed some of the blame for the rise of other-directedness to the mass media. However, there is ambiguity in his writing. Later in his book, he argues that media may also contribute to increased levels of autonomy.

"I believe that the movies, in many unexpected ways, are liberating agents, and that they need defense against indiscriminate highbrow criticism as well as against the ever-ready veto groups who want the movies to tutor their audiences in all the pious virtues the home and school have failed to inculcate."[21]

No doubt the movie *Cool Hand Luke* would have fit Riesman's definition of a "liberating agent." It was for me.

But the anti-Vietnam War movement in the 1960s seemed to call into question, at least for a while, Whyte's and Riesman's theories. Young people at the time were rejecting the social ethic. They were politically active and highly critical of the so-called establishment, which included major corporations, government and some dominant social values (e.g., no sex before marriage).

However, when the war ended in 1973, the social ethic and other-directedness seemed to make a comeback. By 1983, most college students were looking forward to working for major corporations and raising a family in comfortable suburban homes.[22] Social activists accused them of selling out.

I LEARNED a great deal about research and statistics during the four years I worked at Winona.

I also loved Phoenix.

For nine months out of the year, the weather is perfect. It gets a little hot in the summer, but "you don't have to shovel heat, eh?" as the Phoenix residents from Michigan and Canada love to tell each other.

For a time I confess I was taking on the characteristics of the other-directed personality. I was working 60–70 hours a week at Winona, partly under the belief that I would be justly rewarded for getting my reports out to corporate clients.

But just rewards never came for me and many of the other people who worked long hours at Winona. I made the equivalent of $10 per hour. Most of the profits of the business went to the owners and top executives, who built expensive homes, purchased fancy cars, and took lavish vacations.

By 1986, my third year at Winona, I was lonesome for the journalism business. But instead of doing journalism, I wanted to teach and do research. The latter would satisfy my need for challenging work.

Mona Pearce, a coworker at Winona, and I became engaged and in January 1987, we left Phoenix and moved to Minneapolis, where I entered the doctoral program in mass communication in the School of Journalism and Mass Communication at the University of Minnesota. She obtained a job as a market researcher at IDS Financial Services, which is now part of American Express.

The transition, in terms of weather, wasn't easy. On the third week in January, an Alberta Clipper[23] moved in and the temperature dipped to minus 32 degrees. The wind chill knocked that down to about minus 50 degrees.

I only had to walk two blocks to get to Murphy Hall, which housed the journalism and mass communication program. I was completely wrapped in protective clothing except for my eyes, nose and cheeks, but that still wasn't enough protection. The cold air seared my cheeks red.

Michigan has its fair share of snow and cold, but I had never experienced anything like this. *How in the world did Native Americans survive in this kind of weather during the 1800s?*

"Thick blood," one seasoned Minnesotan professor told me. "You get used to it."

Journalism may have given me a thick skin, but my blood never thickened much during the eight years I would spend in Minnesota. Fortunately, the winters only lasted six months. The other six months, as Minnesota's Garrison Keillor would say on the popular Public Broadcasting System radio show *Prairie Home Companion*, consisted of road construction.

LIKE OTHER NEW GRADUATE STUDENTS, I was required to take a number of theory and methodology courses. I particularly enjoyed a media and society course taught by Donald Gillmor, a mass media legal scholar who was popular with graduate students because he was so friendly, helpful and supportive.

As part of the course requirements, Gillmor asked us to read some scholarly literature, including sociologist Todd Gitlin's "Media Sociology: The Dominant Paradigm," which was highly critical of mainstream social science research.[24]

Gitlin had been a president of Students for a Democratic Society during the Vietnam War. He later achieved national fame with publication of his book, *The Whole World Is Watching*, which chronicles the student activist movement and media coverage of that movement during the Vietnam War.[25]

In that book, Gitlin wrote that mass media are "a significant social force in the forming and delimiting of public assumptions, attitudes, and moods ... . Such ideological force is central to the continuation of the established order."[26]

Gitlin was, in other words, a left-wing critic.[27]

His attacks on mainstream research were blistering and self-righteous, in my opinion. But they forced me to question what I was doing as a researcher.

I enrolled in several more courses at Minnesota that took a critical look at mass media and mainstream social science research.

In one of them, we students read some of the works of Jürgen Habermas, a German sociologist who had gained worldwide fame for his analysis of society and human communication. Unlike some of his critical colleagues, such as the postmodernists, Habermas supported the Enlightenment project.[28] He wanted more democratic participation.

In his book *The Theory of Communicative Action*,[29] Habermas criticized capitalism, including corporate capitalism, consumerism and the mass media, which, he wrote, generate cultural content that fails to stimulate an open and free discussion of many social issues and problems. He contended that political parties and interest groups are subverting democracy because they operate without much input from ordinary citizens.

Mainstream social science research cannot alleviate those problems because it narrowly defines knowledge through empirical observation and "falsely" assumes that science can be objective. Democracy can thrive only when institutions give all citizens the right to debate matters of public importance.

Habermas' "ideal speech situation" is one based on an open, free and uninterrupted dialogue involving everyone, not just a small band of experts working in the government or the private sector.[30]

He contended that modern society can still transform the world into a more humane and egalitarian place through what he called "discourse ethics." This essentially means that truths about the world and about what is right or wrong can emerge when everyone is given a chance to speak their minds, to engage in public discourse.[31] Participatory democracy is the goal, as the Students for a Democratic Society had also argued.

By the late 1980s, when I was attending the University of Minnesota, the ideas of Habermas and other social critics were exerting a major influence in the social sciences, especially in the disciplines of communication, sociology, political science, philosophy and English literature.

In America, the most prominent scholar in this group was Noam Chomsky, from whom I took a course in 1988.

Chapter 17 Endnotes

1. Not his real name.

2. Data obtained from the 2007 CASRO (Council of American Survey Research Organizations) Data Trends Survey, retrieved January 19, 2009, from <www.casro.org/pdfs2007%20CASRO%20Data%20Trends%20Survey.pdf>. Today the figure is twice as much, about $20 billion. See <https://www.researchworld.com/esomars-latest-global-market-research-report-values-global-research-and-data-industry-market-at-us-80-billion.>

3. "Domestic Research Priorities," National Science Foundation (April 1988), cited in Joan Petersilia, "Policy Relevance and the Future of Criminology — The American Society of Criminology 1990 Presidential Address," *Criminology, 29*(1): 1-15 (1991), pp. 3-4. The rank order of expenditures per capita is as follows: health, $32.04; space, $19.32; energy, $11.19; transportation, $4.34; environment, $4.34; agriculture, $3.47; education, $1.21; commerce, 53 cents; and justice, 13 cents. For long-term comparisons in funding across various content and disciplinary areas, see <http://www.clarkson.edu/dor/documents/summary%20FY09%20funding%20priorities.pdf>.

4. A postmodernist, for purposes here, is defined as person who rejects many or all ideals of the Enlightenment project, especially the role of free-market economics and the idea that social science can product meaningful knowledge about human behavior.

5. William H. Whyte Jr., *The Organization Man* (Garden City, NY: Doubleday Anchor Books, 1957; originally published in 1956 by Simon & Schuster).

6. Ibid., p. 7.

7. The "social ethic" that Whyte wrote about is similar to the American Dream ethos popularized earlier by James Truslow Adams in 1931: "A land in which life should be better and richer and fuller for everyone, with opportunity for each according to ability or achievement." See James Truslow Adams, *The Epic of America* (Boston: Little, Brown & Co, 1931), p. 214. But Whyte takes it a step further, examining the social control consequences of the American Dream for individual freedom and creativity.

8. Whyte, *The Organization Man*, p. 5.

9. Whyte's other intellectual interest was urban planning. In fact, Nathan Glazer argues that "possibly Whyte's greatest achievement was to revise our thinking about urban density. ... Whyte argued that density worked — it made the city attractive." Nathan Glazer, "The Man Who Loved Cities," *The Wilson Quarterly* (Spring 1999), p. 32.

10. Whyte, *The Organization Man*, p. 8.

11. Ibid., p. 13.

12. Ibid., pp. 14-15.

13. Ibid., p. 15.

14. Ayn Rand, *The Fountainhead* (New York: Signet, 1996; originally published in 1949). This endorsement of Rand's book does not include her extreme views on self-interest to the detriment of the other. But Rand did understand how organizations can suppress individual creativity.

15. Sloan Wilson, *The Man in the Gray Flannel Suit* (New York: Simon & Schuster, 1955).

16. In his introduction, Marcuse paid homage to William H. Whyte and other popular writers in the 1950s who raised concerns about the power of the collective (society) over the individual. Here is a good summary of Marcuse's critique: "Technical progress ... creates forms of life (and of power) which appear to reconcile the forces opposing the system and to defeat or refute all protest in the name of ... freedom from toil and domination. ... This containment of social change is perhaps the most singular achievement of advanced industrial society ... . At its origins in the first half of the nineteenth century, ... the critique of industrial society ... occurred ... in the political action of the two great classes which faced each other in the society: the bourgeoisie and the proletariat. ... However, the capitalist development has altered the structure and function of these two classes in such a way that ... [a]n overriding interest in the preservation and improvement of the institutional status quo unites the former antagonists." Quote from Herbert Marcuse, *One-Dimensional Man: Studies in the Ideology of Advanced Industrial Society*, 2nd edition (Boston: Beacon Press, 1991; originally published 1964), pp. xliv-xlv.

17. David Riesman, *The Lonely Crowd: A Study of the Changing American Character*, in collaboration with Reuel Denney and Nathan Glazer (New Haven, CT: Yale University Press, 1961, originally published in 1950).

18. Ibid., p. xx.

19. Ibid., p. 22.

20. Some writers have associated the multicultural movements on campus with the other-directed personality. The concern is that students are being taught to be so sensitive to the concerns of others that they lack the capacity to express unique thoughts are ideas on their own.

21. Riesman, *The Lonely Crowd* (2001), p. 291.

22. Riesman's theory became the basis for Stanford University's Values and Lifestyle (VALS) typology of consumer personalities, as well as many pop-psychology approaches.

23. An Alberta Clipper is a fast-moving cold low pressure system that originates in the Canadian province of Alberta and drops down into Minnesota and Wisconsin during the winter months and travels east southeast across other states.

24. Todd Gitlin, "Media Sociology: The Dominant Paradigm," pp. 73-121 in G. Cleveland Wilhoit and Harold de Bock (editors), *Mass Communication Review Yearbook*, Vol. 2 (Beverly Hills, CA: Sage, 1981) [originally published in *Theory and Society* 6(2): 205-253 (1978)].

25. Todd Gitlin, *The Whole World Is Watching: Mass Media in the Making and Unmaking of the Left* (Berkeley: University of California Press, 1980).

26. Ibid., p. 9.

27. As the years passed, Gitlin has become much more mainstream, often criticizing the radical left.

28. Jürgen Habermas, *Legitimation Crisis*, translated by T. McCarthy (Boston: Beacon Press, 1975).

29. Jürgen Habermas, *The Theory of Communicative Action*, Volumes 1 and 2, translated by T. McCarthy (Boston: Beacon Press, 1984 and 1987, respectively).

30. Jürgen Habermas, "On Systematically Distorted Communication," *Inquiry*, 13: 205-218 (1970) and Jürgen Habermas, "Towards a Theory of Communicative Competence," *Inquiry*, 13: 360-375 (1970).

31. For an application of discourse ethics to the mass media, see Theodore L. Glasser and Peggy J. Bowers, "Justifying Change and Control: An Application of Discourse Ethics to the Role of Mass Media," pp. 399-424 in David Demers and K. Viswanath (editors), *Mass Media, Social Control, and Social Change: A Macrosocial Perspective* (Ames: Iowa State University Press, 1999).

Chapter 18

Noam Chomsky and Me

Fall 1988
University of Minnesota

"Professor Chomsky," I said, clearing my throat, "in your book *Manufacturing Consent*, you state at one point that ownership of mass media is becoming more concentrated and that this impairs the diversity of ideas. Yet at another place you suggest that the diversity of ideas may be expanding because of the growth of new broadcast media. French sociologist Émile Durkheim and German sociologist Max Weber also suggested that increasing social complexity may generate greater diversity of ideas. Would you agree?"

That was the first and last scholarly question I ever asked Noam Chomsky, the world-famous professor of linguistics and America's most prominent anti-war and anti-mainstream mass media critic.

The date was April 5, 1988.

I was one of about 60 graduate students in an interdisciplinary course taught by Chomsky and other professors at the University of Minnesota. Students from four disciplines — mass communication, law, English and philosophy — met as a group about once a week. The groups also met separately with professors from their respective disciplines.

Chomsky, who then was a professor of linguistics at the Massachusetts Institute of Technology, flew in to lecture to the group four times during the quarter. This was his first visit.

To be honest, I didn't know much about Chomsky in those days. I recall reading something about him in the early 1970s, during the Vietnam War, when I was an undergraduate student and an anti-war protestor.

At that time, Chomsky was often referred to as America's most prominent anti-war protestor. He earned that distinction after his essay "The Responsibility of Intellectuals" was published in 1967 as a special supplement in *The New York Review of Books*. Chomsky criticized social scientists and technocrats for providing pseudo-scientific justification for U.S. involvement in Vietnam.[1]

His first political book, *American Power and the New Mandarins*, was published in 1969 and further cemented his dissident reputation. The book criticized intellectual liberals who supported the Vietnam conflict or who opposed it not because it was morally wrong but because of the high level of U.S. casualties.[2]

But Chomsky had built his worldwide reputation more on scholarship than on anti-war activities or writings. In fact, he was widely acknowledged as the father of modern linguistics.

During the 1950s, he argued that the linguistics scholars should focus more on describing a "universal grammar" than on formulating specific grammars for different languages. People, he argued, are "born knowing" and that allows children to acquire the language to which they are exposed. In other words, the basic structure of language comes from nature, not nurture.

Experts say his theory of generative grammar is a milestone.[3]

But Chomsky's passion since the Vietnam War had been analyzing the role and function of mass media. He and University of Pennsylvania economist Edward S. Herman had just completed the final draft of their book, *Manufacturing Consent: The Political Economy of the Mass Media.*[4]

In it, they argued that mass media were tools of propaganda for powerful politicians and corporate America. He and Gitlin shared common ground.[5]

Although *Manufacturing Consent*, which was published in 1988, contains no citations of the works of Karl Marx and only a few citations of works associated with neo-Marxist (variations of Marxism) literature,[6] it shares a great deal of common ground with them.[7] In fact, one could reasonably conclude that the Herman and Chomsky book plows no new theoretical ground. But empirical research, both neo-Marxist and mainstream, generally supports Herman and Chomsky's main thesis.[8]

One of the major shortcomings of the propaganda model, however, is that it fails to account for social change. Herman and Chomsky concede that the propaganda machine in the United States "is not all-powerful." A good example was public opposition to the Vietnam War after 1968.

But Herman and Chomsky do not provide an extended discussion about how oppositional ideas or groups or individuals form, nor do they provide an explanation for the many social changes that occurred during the twentieth century — changes that, in some cases, forced elites to give up some of their rights and privileges. These changes include expansion of rights to union workers, the poor, minorities, women, homosexuals, environmentalists, and immigrants.

Some scholars give much of the credit to social movements.

Others point out that elites themselves can sometimes alter the political process, as might have been the case when President Barack Obama publicly announced his support of same-sex marriage in 2013.[9]

Such changes often can be interpreted as being in line with the general ideals of the Enlightenment. However, conservative political movements in the United States have often dented or held back reforms, particularly with respect to global warming, universal health care, and income inequality.

On the first day of class for our mass communication group, our instructor, an affable, bearded assistant professor named Robert L. Craig, asked us to "come up with two questions that you'd like to ask Chomsky" when he comes to town.[10]

WHEN I ARRIVED at the Law Center on the West Bank of the UM campus to hear Chomsky lecture, I could feel the excitement. Everyone applauded when he entered the room. Few faculty get that kind of reception.

Chomsky's style of presentation wasn't what I expected. Because he was an activist, I expected a little fire and brimstone. Instead, he was staid and mostly humorless.

He talked about a half hour or so, then began answering questions. He never got around to reading and answering the questions we students had submitted to our instructors.

But the ad hoc approach was better.

More spontaneous.

Eventually, the journalist in me got the better of me. I mustered the courage to ask the question presented earlier: Is diversity in the marketplace of ideas expanding?

"I'm not going to answer that question," Chomsky responded, waving his hand through the air in a dismissive motion. The room filled with laughter — the kind where everyone is in on the joke except you.

Years later I wondered if I had recalled the incident correctly, and a colleague who was present confirmed, indeed, that Chomsky had made the dismissive gesture with his hand.

To this day, I'm not certain why Chomsky refused to answer my question. To the best of my knowledge, he was not hostile to the Enlightenment. In fact, his writings have a lot of affinities with social liberalism, which embraces civil liberties and contends that government is needed to ensure the populace has access to education, health care and welfare.

Since that incident, everything I have read about him suggests that his response that day was out of character. The only exception was a comment from the late libertarian media ethics professor John C. Merrill, who, after hearing about my experience, told me that "Chomsky did the same thing to me in Cairo many years ago. He refused to answer my question."[11]

As a scholar and as a man, Chomsky is widely respected and adored.

Years later I would invite him to speak at an international conference I had organized on global media. He declined but was very polite about it.[12]

Seventeen years later, in spring 2005, he gave a lecture at Washington State University, where I was teaching. The philosophy department professors organizing the event wouldn't let me join them at a pre-speech gathering because there "was not enough room."

But I sent him a copy of a story I wrote about his speech, which included a brief discussion of the incident in the classroom at Minnesota in 1988.[13]

He never responded.

Some reports say he has a policy of not responding to comments that criticize him, even those that are libelous or false. Perhaps he just had a bad day on April 5, 1988.

Whatever the cause of his taciturnity, I didn't take it personally.

I had worked too long as a journalist to be that thin-skinned.

ALTHOUGH SCHOLARSHIP critical of capitalism and consumerism was extremely popular in the 1980s and 1990s,[14] it had relatively little impact on the lives of ordinary Americans.

One of the proponents' original goals was to convince people that capitalism was an economic system that exploited them.

But that goal has never been achieved.

Critical scholars might argue that mass media and political and economic elites have subverted their attempts to make people aware of the problems of capitalism. Certainly mainstream media are not very receptive to Marxist ideas or criticism of capitalism.

But there are other possible explanations.

One is that capitalism has simply succeeded in making people happy. Capitalism eventually accommodated labor unions, created a middle class whose material needs were well met, and supported other social institutions (churches, schools, volunteer organizations, neighborhood groups) that met people's spiritual and emotional needs. In other words, the flexible nature of modern capitalism — not ideology — may better explain why Chomksy and critical scholars have failed to convince people that they are being manipulated or exploited.

But I wondered if there was another, more pragmatic reason for the inability of these critics to mobilize the ordinary people behind their cause: The critics never really tried.

The vast majority of critical scholarship, including Chomsky's work, appeals to scholars, not ordinary people.

Like mainstream social scientists, critical scholars publish mostly in academic journals or write books that are marketed to academics, not the public. They publish esoteric works for the same reasons as mainstream social scientists: to get tenure, promotion, raises and the adoration of colleagues.

As former history professor Carl Brauer put it at the time I was a Ph.D. student at Minnesota, "[T]he vast majority of academics in traditional arts and science disciplines rarely venture forth to confront, enlighten, or change the world."[15]

In short, critical scholars might have been more successful if they had tried harder to take their message directly to ordinary people instead of preaching to the choir of academics.

A day would come when, paradoxically, I would level a similar criticism at mainstream research, including my own research. In the meantime, as a graduate student in the late 1980s and early 1990s, I was still very much concerned with changing the world and tried to practice what I preached.

Chapter 18 Endnotes

1. Noam Chomsky, "The Responsibility of Intellectuals," *The New York Review of Books,* 8(3), (February 23, 1967).

2. Noam Chomsky, *American Power and the New Mandarins* (Harmondsworth, England: Penguin, 1969).

3. Noam Chomsky, *Syntactic Structures* (The Hague/Paris: Mouton, 1957).

4. Edward S. Herman and Noam Chomsky, *Manufacturing Consent: The Political Economy of the Mass Media* (New York: Pantheon, 1989).

5. Ibid., p. 306: "The mass media of the United States are effective and powerful ideological institutions that carry out a system-supportive propaganda function by reliance on market forces, internalized assumptions, and self-censorship, and without significant overt coercion."

6. Neo-Marxism is a term that has different meanings, but most often it refers to revisions that scholars have made to fix flaws in Marx's economic theories or extend Marx's economic theories of inequality to other non-economic categories, such as gender, race, ethnicity, sexual orientation and age.

7. The absence of such citations is perplexing, because Herman and Chomsky's research shares much common ground with the neo-Marxist scholarship. One possible explanation is that Herman and Chomsky feared being marginalized under the label "Marxist." Chomsky has stated many times that he is not a Marxist.

8. See, e.g., Karen E. Altman, "Consuming Ideology: The Better Homes in America Campaign," *Critical Studies in Mass Communication, 7*: 286-307 (1990); J. Herbert Altschull, *Agents of Power* (New York: Longman, 1984); W. Lance Bennett, *News: The Politics of Illusion,* 2nd edition (New York: Longman, 1988); Stanley Cohen and Jock Young (editors), *The Manufacture of News* (London: Constable, 1981); Edward Jay Epstein, *News From Nowhere* (New York: Random House, 1973); Stuart Ewin, *Captains of Consciousness: Advertising and the Social Roots of the Consumer Culture* (New York: McGraw Hill, 1976); Mark Fishman, *Manufacturing the News* (Austin: University of Texas Press, 1980); Doris A. Graber, *Mass Media and American Politics,* 3rd edition (Washington, D.C.: Congressional Quarterly Press, 1989); Herbert J. Gans, *Deciding What's News* (New York: Vintage, 1979); Gitlin, *The Whole World*

Is Watching, op. cit.; David L. Paletz and Robert M. Entman, *Media Power Politics* (New York: The Free Press, 1981); David L. Paletz, Peggy Reichert and Barbara McIntyre, "How the Media Support Local Government Authority," *Public Opinion Quarterly*, 35: 80-92 (1971); Fred Powledge, *The Engineering of Restraint* (Washington, D.C.: Public Affairs Press, 1971); Leon Sigal, *Reporters and Officials* (Lexington, MA: Heath, 1973); and Phillip J. Tichenor, George A. Donohue and Clarice N. Olien, *Community Conflict and the Press* (Beverly Hills, CA: Sage, 1980).

9. See, e.g., Marco Giugni, Doug McAdam and Charles Tilly (editors), *How Social Movements Matter* (Minneapolis: University of Minnesota Press, 1999) and T. K. Oommen, *Protest and Change: Studies in Social Movements* (New Delhi: Sage, 1990).

10. I kept the syllabus and other materials I produced for the course.

11. E-mail from John C. Merrill on February 26, 2009.

12. The conference was cosponsored by the Center for Global Media Studies, a 501(c)3 nonprofit corporation that I managed, and the Korean Communication Association. The Association offered $4,000 and all expenses paid to lure Chomsky.

13. David Demers, "Questioning Chomsky 17 Years Later," *Global Media News*, 7(1): 6-8 (Winter/Spring 2005).

14. By the way, in my opinion, critical theories have contributed a great deal of knowledge about society and human behavior. My own structural theory of the mass media is built partly on the Marxian notion that competition in capitalism paradoxically leads to less competition in many sectors of business over time. The bigger company can usually produce goods and services for a lower cost, and this gives it a competitive advantage. This leads to the growth of powerful bureaucracies that stifle creativity and dissent.

15. Carl Brauer, "More Scholars Should Venture Forth to Confront, Enlighten or Change the World," *The Chronicle of Higher Education* (March 14, 1990).

Chapter 19

Are Minneapolis Police Racist?

Spring Quarter, 1989
University of Minnesota

"Dave, the Minneapolis Police Department refused to give us access to the complaints filed against police officers," one of my students said at the beginning of class one day during spring quarter 1989.

"Yeah," said another. "And they weren't very nice about it."

The students were enrolled in a public affairs reporting course I was teaching at the University of Minnesota. I had just started my third year in the Ph.D. program.

My adviser was Phillip J. Tichenor, a tall, soft-spoken, modest man who grew up on a farm in Wisconsin. Some of his brothers went into farming. Phil worked as a correspondent before earning a Ph.D. from the Stanford University. His adviser was Wilbur Schramm, who founded some of the first Ph.D. programs in communication. At Minnesota, Phil was part of a research team that also included George A. Donohue and Clarice N. Olien in sociology.

I had a lot of teachers before Phil, but none who could compete in terms of saying things that would stick in my head — like the time during my first semester when I said a society that allows freedom of expression doesn't control information like a totalitarian society.

"Oh," he said, gently correcting me, "when you give people the freedom to speak, that is a form of social control. It makes them feel powerful and cools down the revolutionary potential of a society."

BINGO.

As part of the requirements for my journalism class, I asked the students to come up with a group investigative project. At the time, several community leaders had accused the Minneapolis Police Department of using excessive force on minorities. The story attracted coverage in local news media, including the main newspaper in town, the *Minneapolis Star Tribune.*

Community leaders also alleged that police discriminated against minorities who filed complaints of misconduct or unlawful behavior against individual police officers. The leaders said police were more likely to uphold complaints filed by whites.

Our class didn't have the resources to assess whether police had used excessive force, although research in criminology showed that excessive force was not an uncommon event in large police departments.[1] However, we could answer two questions: Were police less likely to sustain complaints filed by minorities? And when an investigation finds that police officers have committed criminal acts, are they punished and, if so, how?

Minnesota state law required police agencies to release information on incident complaints filed against citizens after they are resolved or become inactive. In other words, incident complaints become public data when police finish their investigation.

The students and I assumed the same standards applied to complaints filed against police officers who are accused of violating the law.[2] Why would they differ? No one in America is above the law, right?

However, the police refused to give the students the records.

On March 21, 1989, I wrote a letter to Minneapolis police chief John Laux, formally requesting access to the records over a 10-year period. Five weeks later the chief responded and said information about the complainants, the police officers, and the complaints was not public data. However, the department would give us access to everything else at a cost of $2,322.50. It wasn't clear what he meant by "everything else."

Police argued that most of the information in the records was confidential because they were "personnel records." They also asserted that police are often wrongly accused of using excessive force or violating the law and, consequently, they deserve special protection from public scrutiny.

We argued just the opposite: The records on allegations of criminal wrongdoing should be public because the same information for citizens is public. In fact, police should be more accountable because they are the only nonmilitary institution in our democratic society authorized to use deadly force on citizens. Enlightenment advocates would expect nothing less.

Minnesota state law specifically stated that citizens did not have to pay for records if they just wanted to inspect them and did not want photocopies. But attorneys for the city maintained that citizens should be required to pay the city for the time it took to generate the records — and to redact information in them — because local government could not afford to absorb such costs.

We were at an impasse.

A lawsuit was the only option available to my students and me.

I asked several campus organizations and a national journalism association for assistance in filing a lawsuit. No one responded.

I mentioned the problem to UM media law professor Don Gillmor. He suggested I contact Mark Anfinson, the attorney for the Minnesota Newspaper

Association, a nonprofit organization that represented the interests of newspapers in the state.

Anfinson was an energetic thirtysomething attorney who said he would put the paperwork together at no charge. I would just have to pay the filing and paperwork costs, which amounted to about $150. He suggested I argue the case *pro se*, meaning I would represent myself without an attorney.

If I lost the case, or if I won and the city appealed, Anfinson said he would then take over and argue the case in the appeals courts.

I agreed.

THE LAWSUIT was filed in October 1989, long after the public affairs reporting course had disbanded. The students ended up working on individual in-depth projects.

As expected, the attorney for the city of Minneapolis argued in court that the records were not public because they were personnel records. I responded that a democracy is predicated upon openness and accountability in government. This requirement is even more crucial when it comes to police records, I said, because police have the power to use deadly force.

The judge listened patiently to my idealistic arguments about democratic processes. What I didn't realize was that the judge would make his decision based not on abstract theories about democracy but on how the law was worded.

"Save that stuff for the classroom," the judge could have told me. But he didn't. He was very polite and professional. And, fortunate for me and advocates of government accountability, he could find nothing in Minnesota law that restricted release of the records.

I won the case.

The city appealed.

Anfinson argued the case before the Minnesota Appeals Court, which also ruled in our favor. The city then appealed to the Minnesota Supreme Court, the highest court in the state.

Meanwhile, in late June 1990, the *Toledo Blade* published a series of stories detailing 17 years of police misconduct that had been hidden in internal affairs police records.[3] The investigation came after Ohio courts ruled that everything in the records was public data under the state open-records law.

Blade reporters found scores of cases of police abuse of authority. Internal affairs investigators had documented many cases of administrative rule violations and unlawful conduct, including domestic abuse, drunken driving, theft, and assault.

However, few officers were punished or prosecuted. Critics alleged that police refused to prosecute the officers in court because of fears the cases would tarnish the reputation of the police, hinder efforts to obtain more resources from taxpayers, and lead to expensive lawsuit settlements.

"There was a long list of incredible misdeeds by cops that would have resulted in big problems if you or I had committed them," said John Robinson Block, co-publisher and editor in chief of *The Blade*. "We needed to show internal affairs was a long-standing whitewashing operation."[4]

Several months later, Anfinson appeared before the Minnesota Supreme Court. Mona and I and a handful of other citizens were in the audience. But only the attorneys were allowed to speak to the justices.

At one point, a judge asked Anfinson what kind of information we were seeking from the court. Anfinson responded that the lawsuit was only concerned about obtaining access to information on the complainants, not on the police officers or other information in the records.

That was incorrect.

The students and I wanted access to all of the information in the records that accused officers of violating the law — the same information that was already public data under Minnesota law when citizens were accused of violating the law.[5]

I felt betrayed, for a time.

But I didn't hold a grudge against Anfinson.

He had spent a lot of time helping me obtain access to the records, and I appreciated his help. Besides, the court probably would have ruled the same way regardless of how Anfinson answered the question.

On April 19, 1991, nearly two years after the students first asked for the records, the Minnesota Supreme Court ruled that information about the complainants was public data and that the city could not charge fees for inspecting the records.[6]

Most of the information in the complaints — including the names of the officers, the charges, and facts about the case — would not be disclosed. So we could not duplicate what investigative reporters did in Toledo.

But at least we could answer the first question our class set out to answer: Are police more likely to sustain complaints filed by whites than nonwhites?

In July 1991, while I waited to get the records from the police, I wrote a commentary for an alternative weekly newspaper in the Twin Cities, suggesting that Minneapolis police, like the Toledo police, had a history of brutality that had been effectively hidden from the public view.[7] In September 1991, I also wrote a commentary for *Minnesota's Journal of Law & Politics* raising the same issue.[8]

When the police turned over the data, Mark Engebretson, two journalism students and I began analyzing the internal affairs complaint information that we were allowed to see.

In March 1992, we published our findings in the *Twin Cities Reader,* an alternative weekly newspaper. The story was titled "The Color of Justice: White People Are Almost Twice as Likely to Prevail in a Complaint Against a Minneapolis Police Officer — and Critics Claim Racism Is the Reason." As community leaders had suspected, we found that police were less likely to sustain complaints filed by nonwhites (11%) than whites (19%).[9]

Needless to say, police chief Laux wasn't pleased with the findings.

He and I debated the issue on WCCO's *Jim Rogers Show.* WCCO was the most prominent talk and news radio station in town and was one of the most respected talk radio stations in the nation.

Laux asserted that his officers were not racist.

I said the data did not say they were. Community leaders had made that assertion. The data simply showed that internal affairs officers are more likely to sustain complaints by whites. The cause of that disparity was unknown.

Our radio debate was cordial and polite. But I did drive slower than the speed limit for the next couple of months.

Meanwhile, several weeks after the Minnesota Supreme Court decision, I filed another *pro se* lawsuit that specifically requested access to criminal complaint records involving police as the accused offender. I excluded administrative complaint records. I focused only on criminal complaints, the kind that are already public when a citizen is the alleged offender.

I lost at the trial court level.

I appealed to the Minnesota Court of Appeals.

On June 26, 1992, the Minnesota Court of Appeals ruled against my request to obtain access to criminal complaints against the police.[10] The court said that the records are "personnel data" and, thus, are confidential, even for allegations of criminal conduct.

That evening I consoled myself with John Mellencamp's "Authority Song," which he wrote for his 1983 *Uh-Huh* album.

I fight authority, authority always wins
I fight authority, authority always wins
I been doing it, since I was a young kid
I've come out grinnin'
I fight authority, authority always wins

Sometimes you win, sometimes you lose.

In September 1992, Mark Engebretson, one of the students who worked on the project, and I presented the findings on the differences between white and nonwhite complainants to the Minnesota Human Rights Commission.[11]

Commissioners showed a lot of interest in the data and asked a lot of questions. But no formal action was ever taken by the commission, the police or the city council.

To this day, criminal complaints against police in Minnesota are nonpublic. They are public only when authorities decide to prosecute the officer or the case becomes inactive.

Another step backward for the Enlightenment project.

Chapter 19 Endnotes

1. Two separate studies in the 1960s and 1970s showed that police use excessive force in about 1 percent of all contacts with citizens, or about one-third of all contacts in which force is used. See Robert J. Friedrich, "Police Use of Force: Individuals, Situations, and Organizations," *The Annals of the American Academy of Political and Social Science*, 452: 82–97 (1980) and Robert E. Worden, "The 'Causes' of Police Brutality: Theory and Evidence on Police Use of Force," in *Police Violence: Understanding and Controlling Police Abuse of Force*, William A. Geller and HansToch, editors. (New Haven, CT: Yale University Press, 1996).

2. Complaints about administrative misconduct, however, would not be public data because they would be considered personnel data.

3. Reporters Sam Roe and Dave Murray reviewed 1,000 formerly confidential internal affairs files from 1973 to 1990. See "The Secret Files of Internal Affairs," *Toledo Blade* (June 24 to July 1, 1990). The series won a Pulitzer Prize for Investigative Reporting.

4. Eight police officers and two wives filed libel lawsuits against the newspaper, but all of the cases were dismissed by the courts, including the Ohio Supreme Court and U.S. Supreme Court. The newspaper sought to recover more than $1 million in legal fees from the plaintiffs and their attorneys, but one of the attorneys filed for bankruptcy.

5. Of course, some information in those records, such as the names of juveniles, is nonpublic. But names of victims and suspects and the nature of the crime are generally public information in Minnesota as well as other states.

6. *Demers v. City of Minneapolis*, 468 N.W.2d 71 (1991 Minn.).

7. David Pearce Demers, "Commentary: What Are the Police Hiding?" *Twin Cities Reader* (July 17-23, 1991), pp. 7-8.

8. David Pearce Demers, "Violence in Blue: Does the Minneapolis Police Department Have a History of Brutality that Has Been Effectively Hidden from the Public?" *Minnesota's Journal of Law and Politics* (September 1991), pp. 20-22.

9. David Pearce Demers, Mark Engebretson, Jeanne Fitzsimmons, and Darcy Dennison, "The Color of Justice: White People Are Almost Twice as Likely to Prevail in a Complaint Against a Minneapolis Police Officer — and Critics Claim Racism Is the Reason," *Twin Cities Reader* (March 25-31,1992), pp. 8-11.

10. *David Pearce Demers*, Appellant, v. *City of Minneapolis*, et al., Respondents, and

Minneapolis Police Officers Federation, intervenor, Respondent, Court of Appeals of Minnesota, 486 N.W.2d 828; 1992 Minn. App. LEXIS 712; 20 Media L. Rep. 1545, June 26, 1992. Decided July 7, 1992.

11. David Pearce Demers and Mark Engebretson, "Report to the Minneapolis Civil Rights Commission on Differences Between IAD Record Studies Conducted by the *Twin Cities Reader* and the Center for Urban and Regional Affairs," Minneapolis, MN (September 1993).

Chapter 20

Unfair Assessments

Summer 1990
Shoreview, Minnesota

Mona and I decided to purchase a house in the Twin Cities area in summer 1990. We narrowed our search to a St. Paul suburb called Shoreview.

I spent an inordinate amount of time researching the purchase. As I was looking at home prices, I noticed that property taxes on high-priced homes frequently were no higher than those on less expensive homes. I entered some data into a computer program and found that my intuition was correct. In fact, the data indicated that most owners of high-priced homes were paying substantially less in taxes than they should be.

Although my main job at the time was being a Ph.D. student, I could not suppress my journalistic impulses. I had to look into this some more.

I contacted one of my former students, Mark Engebretson, who was now a reporter for Lillie Suburban Newspapers, a Twin Cities publisher of community newspapers. We obtained data on 5,508 real estate sales recorded in the Minnesota Department of Revenue's 1989 State Board of Equalization Study. The data were statistically representative of all sales in the state during that year (about 23,000 total sales) and excluded so-called distress sales—foreclosures and other factors that might confound values.

I ran the statistical analysis.

Mark did the interviewing.

On March 20, 1991, our results were published in the *Twin Cities Reader*, the largest weekly arts and entertainment publication in town.[1] The results were startling.

ASSESSING DAMAGE:
UNFAIR PROPERTY TAX ASSESSMENTS CAUSE WORKING-CLASS HOMEOWNERS AND RENTERS TO PAY TOO MUCH, WHILE OWNERS OF BUSINESSES, FARMS AND EXPENSIVE HOMES DON'T PAY ENOUGH

A computer analysis of 5,508 property sales in Minnesota in 1989 shows that, as a group, people who own high-priced properties are paying less than their fair share in taxes, while many of those with low-priced properties are paying too much. ... How much? ... People who own residential property valued at $68,000 or less are typically paying about 25 percent more than they should. ... about $170 a year. The owner of a home valued at $100,000 is paying about 16 percent too much, or $205. In contrast, ... people who own a $310,000 home ... are paying about $1,000 less than they should be if the system were equitable.

The analysis also found that businesses and farms were paying far less than they should be (about 18% and 38%, respectively), and homeowners and apartment complex owners were paying much more (about 21% and 75% more, respectively).

Most of the assessors Mark interviewed conceded that the assessing system favors owners of more expensive properties. Mark also found that these assessors believe high-priced properties receive lower assessments because they are more difficult to assess. However, the data in our study showed that is not the case. The amount of variation or range between the selling price and the assessed valuation between medium-priced and high-priced properties did not differ.

We offered three reasons for the assessing disparities:

(1) Assessors are under pressure to keep taxes on high-priced properties lower because Minnesota has a progressive tax system, in which higher priced homes are taxed at a higher rate (3% instead of 1% for lower-priced properties);
(2) Owners of higher-priced properties are more likely to appeal and, because they are more highly educated and have more income, they wield more political power;
(3) In wealthy neighborhoods, assessors are reluctant to raise prices of all homes after one home sells for much more than its assessed valuation, saying that "one sale does not make a market."[2] But because there are fewer sales among high-priced homes, it appears that this practice may keep assessed values artificially low for that category of homes."

The story drew the attention of state officials and assessors.

In October 1991, the Minnesota House of Representatives assigned a six-member task force to investigate unfair property assessments.

Mike Wandmacher, director of local government services for the Revenue Department, told the *Twin Cities Reader* in the October 23, 1991, issue that he doesn't think there is anything wrong with the current assessment system. "We [Revenue Department officials] felt there was a problem with the report (TCR's investigation)."

But his comments contradicted earlier ones made by two officials within Wandmacher's department. Both said our "study was accurate."[3]

In December, Rep. Paul Ogren, chair of the Minnesota House Tax Committee, declared that Minnesota homes are valued in an "arbitrary and capricious" manner. He speculated that assessors sympathize with owners of expensive property.

Rep. Andy Dawkins, chair of the task force, added: "The higher the value of a property, the more likely it's underassessed."

However, Dawkins said the committee would investigate only residential property assessments, not business or farm assessments, even though they benefit most from the inequitable assessment system. In fact, the problem could not be solved without addressing all types of properties.

Hearings were conducted, but no action was taken.

The disparities in assessing continue to exist to this day in Minnesota as well as in most states across the nation.

Another setback for the Enlightenment.

THE LACK OF POLITICAL ACTION in this case as well as the Minnesota Appeals Court decision that denied the public access to criminal complaints filed against police caught me off guard.

The assessing problem could be explained as a power struggle. Assessors and state officials knew that if they were to take corrective action, the shit would hit the fan. Most of those adversely affected would be powerful elites who own a lot of property or expensive properties. Those elites also donate a lot of money to the election campaigns of state political leaders.

But what explains why the appeals court would allow criminal complaints against citizens to be open to the public but not criminal complaints against police officers?

The ruling seemed to contradict the theories of German sociologist Max Weber, who argued that bureaucracies discharge their business through an impersonal, objective process. "Bureaucratization offers above all the optimum possibility for carrying through the principle of specializing administrative functions according to purely objective considerations ... without regard for person."[4]

Yet in the Minneapolis Police case, the courts seemed to reject the doctrine of "objective discharge of business." In fact, the courts appeared to be showing their loyalty to, or perhaps affinity with, the police.

How could that be?

There are at least two answers to this question.

The first came from my Ph.D. adviser, Phil Tichenor, who was a sociologist and had a joint appointment in mass communication and rural sociology at Minnesota. "Your success in the lawsuit may very well depend upon whether you are able to convince other elites in the system that there is a problem of police misconduct."

Tichenor's reasoning was dead-on.

The "system" was not convinced that there was a problem.

None of the local media were paying attention to the misconduct issue or to the second lawsuit I had filed to get access to criminal complaints. Although I wrote two articles drawing attention to the misconduct issue, those articles appeared in publications with limited readership.

If police misconduct wasn't perceived to be a significant problem, then why change the status quo?

I was a coyote howling in the wilderness.

The second reason the appeals court failed to open the records might be traced to the fact that bureaucratic organizations, including the courts, tend to monopolize information, because information is power. This argument comes from Max Weber.

WEBER WAS a German sociologist who penned what have become the classic works on bureaucracy, or what he sometimes called the corporate form of organization. He defined a corporate organization as "an associative social relationship characterized by an administrative staff devoted to such continuous purposive activity."[5]

Corporate organizations may or may not pursue economic profits (the Minnesota court system and Minneapolis police being an example of the latter),[6] but they all establish and maintain boundaries for admission and continued membership and expect members to abide by their rules. The rules are enforced either by the chief or head (*Leiter*) or by an administrative staff.[7]

According to Weber, a bureaucracy is a specific type of corporate organization — one in which behavior is goal-directed and decision-making is rational. By rational, he means that bureaucratic organizations try to reduce the production and distribution of goods or services into routines so as to find the most efficient and effective way to reach a goal.[8] "Precision, speed, ambiguity, knowledge of the files, continuity, discretion, unity, strict subordination, reduction of friction and of material and personal costs — these are raised to the optimum point in the strictly bureaucratic administration."[9]

In addition to rationality, Weber says bureaucracies are characterized by a hierarchy of authority, employment and promotion based on technical qualifications, a set of rules and procedures that define job responsibilities and show how tasks are accomplished, formalistic impersonality, and a division of labor and role specialization.[10]

Although Weber believed bureaucratic organizations are very efficient, he did not see them as utopian. One shortcoming is that they tend to monopolize information.

"Every bureaucracy seeks to increase the superiority of the professionally informed by keeping their knowledge and intentions secret."[11] This characteristic certainly applied to the Minneapolis Police, which denied my students access to internal complaint reports.

Bureaucracies also resist change. "Once it is fully established, bureaucracy is among those social institutions which are hardest to destroy."[12]

A third problem, according to Weber, is that bureaucracies are powerful social entities whose actions are often in conflict with democratic principles. He was, in fact, very pessimistic about the long-term consequences that bureaucracies would have for individual freedom and autonomy and democratic decision-making.[13] He even suggested that a bureaucracy can be an "iron cage."[14]

I was not surprised to learn that the iron cage argument was picked up in the 1950s by both William H. Whyte and David Riesman, who wrote about the organizational man and the other-directed personality, respectively.[15]

Weber's student Robert Michels took the iron cage argument a step further. He developed what he called the "iron law of oligarchy," which contends that bureaucracies are incompatible with democratic processes. Although the leaders of new organizations often start with a commitment to democracy, they are compelled, as the organization grows, to hire a bureaucracy of professional staff and to centralize power.

To retain their power, these leaders often oppose efforts to democratize their organizations through free elections or other means.[16] This produces an oligarchy — a handful of elites who control most of the power. Here is Michels's classic statement on this topic:

> It is organization which gives birth to the domination of the elected over the electors, of the mandataries over the mandators, of the delegates over the delegators. *Who says organization says oligarchy.*[17] [emphasis added]

To test his theory, Michels examined socialist parties in Germany and elsewhere, which were committed to the principles of direct democracy, free speech and equality. Of course, he found ample evidence that the organizations themselves didn't practice what they preached. But the most damning evidence came from political events in 1914 and 1917.

The first was a decision of the German Social Democratic Party, which had opposed German militarism for years, to support the kaiser's declaration of war. The second was the Russian Revolution, the first successful socialist revolution in the world, but one which eventually led to brutal suppression of democratic principles and individual rights.

A number of empirical studies also have questioned the extent to which bureaucracies or corporations are rational or efficient. Sociologist Robert K. Merton has argued, for example, that employees of bureaucracies often place more importance on following the rules than on achieving the goals of the organization.[18]

One example of this in higher education involves the tenure process. The ultimate goal, or terminal value, of social science is to solve social problems. However, candidates for tenure are not evaluated on how well they solve social problems but on how many scholarly publications they can accumulate. This rule, or instrumental value, has, over time, increasingly insulated scholars from the public policymaking process.[19]

Another sociologist, Michel Crozier, even contends that bureaucracies are self-destructive and are unable to acknowledge their faults.[20] "A bureaucratic organization is an organization that can not correct its behaviour by learning from its errors."[21] He adds that a bureaucracy is "not only a system that does not correct its behaviour in view of its errors; it is also too rigid to adjust, without crises, to the transformations that the accelerated evolution of the industrial society makes more and more imperative."[22]

One of the most striking contemporary examples of the anti-democratic tendencies of bureaucracies involves the American Civil Liberties Union. This organization is dedicated to preserving the liberties of Americans, often through free speech lawsuits, yet its members do not have the right to vote on issues facing the organization.[23]

Many other criticisms of bureaucracies have been leveled.[24]

But I would end up taking a more sanguine view of bureaucracies in my Ph.D. dissertation in 1992 and my research that followed.[25]

I hypothesized that the more structurally complex a community, the more the local newspaper would exhibit the characteristics of the corporate form of organization and the more emphasis it would place on product quality and the less emphasis on profits. My national probability surveys and content analyses repeatedly support these hypotheses.[26]

Consistent with Noam Chomsky's propaganda model and Phil's theories and research, my data showed that U.S. daily newspapers produce content that generally helps political and economic elites achieve their goals, often to the disadvantage of less powerful, alternative groups.

But in contrast to Chomsky's research, my data showed that newspapers become more, not less, critical of political and economic elites as they grow and become more "corporatized." They publish a larger number and proportion of editorials and letters to the editor that are critical of mainstream values, institutions and elites.

One of my surveys also showed that mayors and police chiefs in communities served by large corporate newspapers also viewed those newspapers as being more critical of them and their policies. In contrast, mayors and police chiefs in communities served by entrepreneurial, or less bureaucratic, newspapers perceived their newspapers as being more supportive.

I never collected any empirical data linking corporate structure and media content to social change, which is a far more difficult empirical question to answer than the one I addressed. But the historical record provides a great deal of prima facie evidence to support the idea that corporate mass media have played a role in facilitating or legitimizing many of the social changes that took place during the twentieth century.

During the muckraking era at the turn of the century, it was the largest newspapers and magazines — the ones that began to exhibit the characteristics of the corporate form of organization — that investigated abuse of power by big business and government.

During the 1950s, big corporate newspapers like the *New York Times,* the *Atlanta Constitution* and the *Nashville Tennessean* were the ones that investigated racial discrimination and violence against blacks in the South.

And today, the largest, most "corporatized" media are the ones that give more editorial support to the civil rights, women's rights, environmental and gay rights movements.[27] Small-town papers often ignore or belittle such movements.

Of course, my research contradicted the theories of William H. Whyte, David Riesman and the other writers critical of corporations and bureaucracies. My research showed that corporations can do good things and the people working in them (journalists) can have a lot of autonomy and freedom.

Two decades would pass before I would solve this conundrum. The solution was in the organization's culture; that is, if an organization places a high value on principles like democracy, free speech, truth, honesty, fairness and due process, then it can do good things. Newspapers and universities have the capacity to embrace and promote Enlightenment ideals. But this goal can be lost when the culture in the organization does not value such ideals and fails to reward its employees for embracing them.

I did not fully understand this when I graduated from the Ph.D. program in mass communication at the University of Minnesota in December 1992. I had a good "book understanding" of how bureaucracies function. However, my practical knowledge was sorely lacking, as I would soon learn the hard way in my first full-time faculty position at the University of Wisconsin–River Falls.

Chapter 20 Endnotes

1. Mark Engebretson and David Demers, "Assessing Damage: Unfair Property Tax Assessments Cause Working-class Homeowners and Renters to Pay Too Much, While Owners of Businesses, Farms, and Expensive Homes Don't Pay Enough," *Twin Cities Reader* (March 20-26, 1991), pp. 10-13.

2. Assessors call this practice "spearing," saying it is unfair to raise the value of one home in a neighborhood without raising the others.

3. Mark Engebretson, "Task Force May Yield Fairer Property Taxes," *Twin Cities Reader* (October 23-29, 1991), p. 4.

4. H. H. Gerth and C. Wright Mills (editors), *From Max Weber: Essays in Sociology* (New York: Oxford University Press, 1946), p. 215.

5. See, e.g., Gerth and Mills, *From Max Weber*, pp. 196-244; and Max Weber, *The Theory of Social and Economic Organization*, translated by A. M. Henderson and Talcott Parsons (New York: The Free Press, 1964, originally published in 1947).

6. Bureaucracy is a term that historically usually referred to the state or governmental entities, but now it is widely used to refer to any large organizational structure, including businesses.

7. Weber, *The Theory of Social and Economic Organization*, pp. 145-51.

8. Ibid. It is important to point out that rationality as defined by Weber involves a means-end calculus — that is, behavior that begins with the objective of finding the most efficient way to reach a goal, not whether the behavior itself is considered "rational" by some sort of moral standard.

9. Gerth and Mills, *From Max Weber*, p. 214.

10. Authority in a bureaucracy is vested in the position rather than in the individual. This minimizes the disruption that occurs when an individual leaves the organization. Selection for employment or promotion is based on technical competence or expertise rather than patronage or social position, and loyalties are given to the organization and its set of rules and procedures, not individuals. In exchange, employees are given monetary compensation, promotions or other rewards. Interpersonal relations in bureaucracies are more impersonal than those in non-bureaucratic organizations, but this was perceived as being necessary to efficiently accomplish the goals of the organization. Tasks in a bureaucracy are highly specialized and delegated to individuals who are ultimately accountable for their performance. Rules and regulations control and standardize behavior, enabling managers to control the actions of a large number of workers. And the division of labor and role specialization generate economies of scale and increase the productive capacity of the organization far beyond that of small, less diversified organizations. The list of characteristics is distilled from Gerth and Mills, *From Max Weber*, pp. 196-8, and Weber, *Social and Economic Organization*, pp. 329-36.

11. Ibid., p. 233.

12. Ibid., p. 228. Weber also writes on p. 229: "The ruled, for their part, cannot dispense with or replace the bureaucratic apparatus of authority once it exists. For this bureaucracy rests upon expert training, a functional specialization of work, and an attitude set for habitual and virtuoso-like mastery of single yet methodicly integrated functions. ... More and more the material fate of the masses depends upon steady and correct functioning of the increasingly

bureaucratic organizations of private capitalism. The idea of eliminating these organizations becomes more and more utopian."

13. Gerth and Mills, *From Max Weber*, p. 224-228. Also see Robert Michels, "Oligarchy," pp. 48-67 in Frank Fischer and Carmen Sirianni, *Critical Studies in Organization and Bureaucracy* (Philadelphia: Temple University Press, 1984).

14. Weber called it *stahlhartes Gehäuse*, which was translated by American sociologist Talcott Parsons to mean "iron cage." Other sociologists dispute this translation, saying "shell as hard as steel" or "steel-hard housing" would be more appropriate. Iron cage is a better metaphor.

15. See Chapter 17 of this book for more details.

16. Robert Michels, *Political Parties: A Sociological Study of the Oligarchical Tendencies of Modern Democracy*, translated by Eden Paul and Cedar Paul (New York: Free Press, 1962, originally published in 1911).

17. Ibid., p. 365.

18. "Adherence to the rules," according to Merton, "originally conceived as a means, becomes transformed into an end-in-itself; then there occurs the familiar process of displacement of goals whereby 'an instrumental value becomes a terminal value.'" Robert K. Merton, "Bureaucratic Structure and Personality," pp. 195-206 in Robert K. Merton (ed.), *Social Theory and Social Structure* (London: The Free Press, 1957 [1949]), p. 199.

19. David Demers, *The Ivory Tower of Babel: Why the Social Sciences Are Failing to Live Up to Their Promises* (New York, NY: Algora, 2011). To enhance the connection between social science research and solving social problems, universities could require tenure candidates to have direct involvement in the policymaking process; however, to the best knowledge of this author, none do. Some require professors to obtain state and federal research grant money, but this does not ensure that their research will solve social problems.

20. Michel Crozier, *The Bureaucratic Phenomenon* (Chicago: The University of Chicago Press, 1964).

21. Ibid., p. 187.

22. Ibid., p. 198.

23. I joined the ACLU for a short time in the 1990s and dropped my membership because it refuses to give members voting privileges.

24. For a summary, see Dean J. Champion, *The Sociology of Organizations* (New York: McGraw-Hill, 1975), pp. 36-40.

25. David Kevin Pearce Demers, *Structural Pluralism, Competition and the Growth of the Corporate Newspaper in the United States,* Minneapolis: University of Minnesota (Doctoral Dissertation, December 1992).

26. The results of these studies are summarized in David Pearce Demers, *The Menace of the Corporate Newspaper: Fact or Fiction?* (Ames: Iowa State University Press, 1996) and David Demers, *History and Future of Mass Media: An Integrated Perspective* (Cresskill, NJ: Hampton Press, 2007).

27. Masahiro Yamamoto, "Corporate Newspaper Structure and Same-Sex Marriage: An Empirical Test of the Editorial Page Vigor Hypothesis," unpublished master's thesis (Washington State University, August 2006) and Taehyun Kim, "Corporate Newspaper Structure, Global Warming and the Editorial Vigor Hypothesis," unpublished Ph.D. dissertation (Washington State University, July 2007).

Chapter 21

The $64,000 Apology

Summer 1995
Shoreview, Minnesota

The summer of 1995 offered respite from the controversy at the University of Wisconsin–River Falls. I was less stressed because I didn't have to teach at UW–RF in the fall. I accepted a visiting professorship at the University of Minnesota.

I was also less worried about the legal matters related to my lawsuit, because I hired a new attorney who had a strong background in First Amendment law. Mona and I threw a couple of fun dinner parties. And we added a new member to our family: a Bichon Frise, a fluffy white dog that charmed the French nobility in centuries past.

Although I was one-fourth French (Demers means "of or by the sea"), I had no affinity for fluffy white dogs.

But Mona wanted that breed.

I begged her to consider a more masculine dog, like a Labrador or a German Shepherd. After all, my reputation was on the line. Anti-free speech administrators would never see me as a fearless, menacing activist if I were holding a fluffy white dog.

Mona keenly pointed out that even with a German Shepherd, no one would see me as a fearless, menacing free speech activist. Too much Lutheran boy still in me.

She had a point. So I gave in, and Pouché (pronounced poo-shay) joined our family.

Of course, I fell in love with her, and she with me. In fact, Pouché followed me everywhere I went, like a hellhound minus the hell part. I mean everywhere. To my office. To the living room. To the bedroom. And to the bathroom.

"Turn your head, would you please?" I begged.

It's true what they say about dogs.

They bring out the best in people, especially when they are at their worst. Even Mona noticed.

"You've been acting almost normal this summer, Dave."

"That's odd," I responded, stone-faced. "I thought I was going to the dogs."

Mona rolled her eyes.

Okay, so my newfound personality wasn't so funny.

But it was useful in terms of entertaining friends. I loved to cook, so we invited a number of people over for dinner, including First Amendment scholar Donald Gillmor, journalism historian Hazel Dicken-Garcia, and graduate student Giovanna Dell'Orto, who was from Italy.

We talked about Italy and other parts of Europe, movies, theater, politics, and food. And one of those evenings had a major impact on my life.

I recall we were talking about Europe, and I mentioned, "Isn't it funny when you're in a restaurant and you order ice for your water and the server only drops two ice cubes in your glass?"

"Sometimes you only get one cube," Don said.

"Americans are strange when it comes to ice," Giovanna pointed out in her charming Italian accent. "They put more ice in the glass than water."

Everyone laughed and agreed.

Then someone said, "If you drink water that is freezing cold, it can kill you."

"Is that true?" I asked.

"Yes."

I was aware that if you drink too much water, it can kill you. It's called hyponatremia. So the idea that ice-cold water could do the same thing seemed logical.

Later I did some fact-checking and apparently cold water can't kill you. But it does slow down the rehydration process, so if you are very dehydrated, there is a chance you can die from dehydration.

Since that time, I almost always drink water at room temperature.

And whenever I see someone filling up their glass with ice and I want to start a conversation, I say, "Did you know that can kill you?"

HAZEL WAS A HISTORIAN in the School of Journalism and Mass Communication at Minnesota (the program is now called the Hubbard School), a brilliant woman who had high standards for her students but a tender heart.

Giovanna was one of her students and one of the rising stars in the UM graduate program. Her parents lived in the area, too, and they were as delightful as their daughter.

A decade later Hazel and Giovanna would coauthor a book which found that during the Civil War, newspaper editors were very intolerant when it came to free speech. "[E]ditors consistently supported the larger political system over any professional journalism ideology, the 'common good' over individual rights, and the military 'discretion' over constitutional principles."[1] Their finding joined a growing body of research showing that the press has never been a staunch defender of First Amendment rights during crises.[2]

These studies also supported the general "social system theory" that I learned from my Ph.D. adviser, Phillip J. Tichenor, and sociology classes. Mass media are institutions of social control, Tichenor and his colleagues pointed out in many of their writings, but not the way most people think. They don't deliberately produce overt propaganda or false content. They rely heavily on powerful elites and government leaders for the news, which means reality is framed from their perspective. News media play a system-maintenance role, producing content that generally supports powerful institutions and dominant values in our society.

Yet this support is not all-encompassing (or hegemonic, as scholars like to say). The news media also generate content that is critical of those in power, and that, in turn, can lead to social change that benefits disadvantaged groups and the less powerful.

In fact, my research over the past seven years had found that the more newspapers exhibit the characteristics of the corporate form of organization, the more they produce content that is critical of dominant institutions and elites. Corporate newspapers, my theory maintained, produced information and knowledge that enabled other institutions to adapt and change.

Yet that summer I was becoming increasingly aware of a discrepancy between my theory and the real world.

My personal experiences with bureaucracies at the *Midland Daily News*, the Minnesota court system, the Minneapolis Police Department, the Minnesota Department of Revenue, and now at the University of Wisconsin–River Falls suggested that they put political interests and personal loyalties before truth and justice.

Maybe I was wrong, and sociologists Max Weber, Robert Michels and Michel Crozier were right. Bureaucracies monopolize knowledge, resist change, destroy democracy (iron cage), and never admit their mistakes. Even my new attorney, Marshall Tanick of Minneapolis, seemed to back them up when he outlined our legal strategy in the summer of 1995.

"If we file a lawsuit in Wisconsin, we'll lose. The state courts will identify strongly with the UW administrative system. Instead, we'll file in federal court. We'll have a chance there. We'll file a federal First Amendment lawsuit."

TANICK AND I MET for the first time in April 1995. He was an employment attorney but also an expert in First Amendment law. He had represented several professors at UM in employment disputes. He also represented the student newspaper at the

University of Minnesota (*Minnesota Daily*) in several high-profile legal cases that expanded free speech, and he had written many articles about the First Amendment.

I hired him on the spot and immediately informed Jay Willardson, my attorney in Madison. Jay wasn't upset, because he acknowledged he didn't have an extensive legal background in First Amendment law.

Tanick was a pit bull in a three-piece suit.

Decisive, commanding, smart — very smart.

He earned his law degree from Stanford, graduated summa cum laude and was a member of the Order of the Coif, an honor society for U.S. law school graduates who rank in the top 10 percent of their class. I heard he graduated third in his class, but I never had the nerve to ask him whether that was true.

Tanick's mind always seemed to work twice as fast as everyone else's in the room. As such, sometimes he was a bit impatient with people who couldn't express an idea in ten seconds or less — people like me.

But this flaw, if you want to call it that, was nothing more than a blemish. Tanick could see opportunity where others could not. He loved a challenge. And my case certainly offered that, given that the law and the courts readily defer to universities when it comes to tenure decisions.[3]

Tanick told me that filing in federal court meant that financial remedies would be limited.

"We can fight to keep your job. Is that what you want?"

"Yes," I said. "This isn't about the money. It's about protecting First Amendment rights. All I want is an apology, and I can continue to work at River Falls, if I have to."

If Tanick thought I was naive and idealistic, he never told me.

The first thing he did was to file an amended Notice of Claim, which gives the government a chance to settle the dispute before a formal lawsuit is filed. Jay had filed the original notice in April. The revised notice added several more complaints, including a defamation claim against John Smith as well as the First Amendment claim.

The UW system denied the claim.

MEANWHILE, I WAS preparing to teach at UM, my alma mater.

Dan Wackman, the director of the journalism and mass communication program there, had asked me in spring if I wanted to teach in the program during the 1995–1996 school year.

"We need someone," he said. "Besides, it will give you a break from the controversy at River Falls. It's a visiting professorship and we can match or beat your pay at River Falls."

I accepted his generous offer.

As a graduate student, I took several courses from Dan and we had conducted research and published a paper together. He was a kind, family-oriented man. He and his wife had six kids and invited faculty and students to parties at their home on several occasions.

That year at Minnesota turned out to be one of my best years of teaching. I attribute that mostly to the students. They were bright.

Minnesota admits only about 50 percent of applicants, compared with about 85 to 90 percent at UW–RF and most other public institutions. The UM students were far more serious about learning and studying. Most read the material assigned for the day and were prepared to discuss it. That made my job much easier.

My favorite class that year was an introduction to mass communication course I taught in fall 1995. One-hundred and twenty students enrolled in that class, but it was like teaching a seminar of ten. I served more as a moderator or facilitator than a teacher. Once an issue was introduced, students took over. The discussions were lively and intelligent.

On the final day of the course, I was surprised when many stood and clapped. They were the ones who deserved the applause.

TANICK FILED the free speech lawsuit on September 4, 1995, in Federal District Court in Madison,[4] and named John Smith, journalism chair, and the University of Wisconsin Board of Regents as defendants.[5]

The complaint claimed the university refused to renew my contract because I helped students publish a series of articles about student evaluations of faculty and faculty salaries.

"Because of his involvement in those articles," the complaint stated, "he encountered hostility from other members of the faculty, including his colleagues and superiors within the Department of Journalism and other administrators at the university."

I wrote a news release about the lawsuit. Local newspapers, the Student Press Law Center, and *Quill* magazine, which is published by the Society of Professional Journalists, covered the story.

The media coverage upset many university officials, because privacy laws limited their ability to comment to the press. I talked freely and openly about the case. It was one of the few advantages I had over the powerful UW System bureaucracy.

A week after the lawsuit was filed, John resigned from his position as chair of the journalism department, saying his workload was too heavy. However, he rescinded that decision two days later, after an administrator in the dean's office asked him to reconsider.

IN LATE JANUARY or early February 1996, I received a telephone call from William Glaberson, a reporter at the *New York Times*.

"Dr. Demers, I am working on a story about the loss of family-owned newspapers and I see you have just published a book about corporate newspaper ownership. May I ask you some questions?"

"Hell yeah!" I wanted to shout, but instead responded, "I'd be delighted to help you, Mr. Glaberson."

Wow, the *New York Times*. Calling me. Most scholars who develop theories about the social world live their lives in relative obscurity. They publish in journals that are read by a small number of scholars in their fields. As such, many good theories and research findings have little or no impact on changing the world, because public policymakers don't know about them. Some scholars are content to live a low-key professional life. But, to me, making the world a better place is what scholarship is all about.

Glaberson said he had not yet read my book, but he had ordered a copy. The book summarized my research over the past seven years and was titled *The Menace of the Corporate Newspaper: Fact or Fiction?*[6] The publisher was Iowa State University Press.

I spent the next hour or so answering Glaberson's questions and explaining my theory and the results of my research. Not surprisingly, he was a critic of chain or corporate ownership. In fact, I later learned that he was an expert on the newspaper industry, having covered it for more than five years.[7]

By the end of our conversation, I could tell I had not persuaded him as to the validity of my theory. But he said he would withhold judgment until he read my book.

A week passed and we chatted by phone again. Glaberson said he had read parts of my book. I spent another 15 minutes making my case, but to no avail.

"I don't know if I can buy into your theory," he said.

"You don't have to," I said. "As a journalist, your role is report all sides of the story."

His story was published February 19, 1996, on page one of the business section.[8]

The story quoted critics of chain and corporate newspaper ownership. And it quoted some newspaper executives, who said consolidation "is a symptom of an industry reshaping itself to compete with new competitors like electronic information distributors." Bigger means economies of scale.

But most of the story focused on the adverse impact of chain and corporate ownership.

And what about the empirical evidence from my book?

Not there.

I wasn't even quoted.

Some might argue that Glaberson refused to quote my research because he was biased.

Perhaps.

But as the years passed, I told my graduate students that I believe my research was less a victim of bias than of failed credibility. When activists, scholars or citizens have a point of view that contradicts well-established beliefs, whether right or wrong, it's extremely difficult for their voices to be heard. Knowledge is not self-evident. It also involves discourse about the credibility of sources and information.

Glaberson was an expert on the newspaper industry.

As an expert, he was more difficult to persuade than a layperson. In short, it would take more than one book to get 15 minutes of fame in the *New York Times*, and I returned to being one of the professors whose research would live on in relative obscurity.

BY FEBRUARY 1996, Mona and I had spent more than $12,000 on legal fees, and it was estimated we would spend another $10,000 before the deposition stage. Going to trial would cost about $50,000, and if the case were appealed, Tanick said the figure could easily top $100,000. That was a lot, but the alternative seemed even worse: the end of my career as a professor.

If we won, the best-case scenario was that all attorney fees would be paid by the university with perhaps some compensation for lost time. But all I really wanted, outside of attorney fees, was an apology.

I was well aware that few court cases go to trial. Most are settled.

But what I didn't realize then was that bureaucracies rarely apologize. They'd rather spend taxpayers' money.

While attorneys on both sides of *Demers v. UW–RF* were preparing the case, I was applying for jobs at other universities. Washington State University in Pullman, Washington, had a position open. I told my wife about it.

"Why don't you apply?"

"But Pullman? Where the hell is that? Are you sure you want to go there?"

"It's south of Spokane."

I applied and got an interview.

Needless to say, WSU faculty had heard about the lawsuit in River Falls. Some were uneasy about interviewing a faculty member who might be a troublemaker. One of those faculty was a public relations expert and would later become the director of the Murrow School at WSU.

I suspect that I survived the interviewing process because one of my Ph.D. adviser Phillip Tichenor was a highly respected scholar in the field.

At any rate, the interview went well and a month later I was offered a position.

IN LATE MARCH 1996, I received a call from Tanick.

"Dave, the attorney for the UW system and I have reached a possible settlement in your case."

I was surprised, because I didn't even know a settlement was in the works.

"Is the university going to apologize?" I asked.

"No. Bureaucracies don't apologize. The legal system doesn't operate like that. The courts are a place where money is exchanged for a wrong that is committed. The UW system is offering you a $62,000 cash settlement. In exchange, you'll have to drop the lawsuit and leave your job."

I was disappointed.

What I really wanted was an apology.

"Dave, take the money and declare victory," Tanick said. "The payment will be interpreted by others as a sign that the university wronged you. You can use that to your advantage."

He pointed out that the alternative was a long and drawn-out lawsuit with an ending that couldn't be guaranteed. The settlement, on the other hand, would cover my costs and I could give some to a scholarship fund.

Tanick suggested that I ask the university to increase the settlement to $64,000, to draw attention to the crooked game show from the 1950s, *The $64,000 Question.*

I laughed and consented.

The university accepted the change.

After the settlement, Tanick and I issued a press release to various media. The story was widely covered in local newspapers and professional media in journalism, including SPJ's *Quill* magazine:

JOURNALISM PROFESSOR VINDICATED

What is a journalism professor entitled to when he is terminated from his position for exercising his freedom of expression?

In the case of David Demers, the answer is $64,000. That's the amount the University of Wisconsin in River Falls is paying Demers to get him to drop a First Amendment lawsuit against the university and journalism chair ...

"I am extremely pleased with the settlement," says Demers, an assistant professor who was fired for helping journalism students cover some controversial stories. "I hope this settlement serves as a warning to administrators at other institutions that violations of the First Amendment cannot be tolerated."

Demers filed the lawsuit in federal district court in Madison last September. ... Internal administrative memos obtained after the lawsuit was filed also showed that administrators were trying to fire Demers because he had hired an attorney to help him fight for his job and protect his reputation.

"This was an important case because it demonstrates that colleges must respect First Amendment rights," says Demers' attorney, Marshall H. Tanick of Minneapolis. "It is ironic that a journalism department, which supposedly teaches students about the First Amendment, should have to learn such a costly lesson this way."[9]

John Smith was furious.

On May 8, he wrote a letter to the *Quill* editor, accusing her of publishing a one-sided story.[10] Smith was especially angry about Tanick's comment.

"We found it to be offensive to the faculty and students in this department and completely erroneous in its implications of the quality of journalism education students expect and deserve at UW-River Falls."

Smith was right.

The story was one-sided.

Quill published Smith's response.

But Tanick was also right.

The settlement was nearly as good as an apology.

ALL TOLD, I PILED UP about $31,000 in attorney fees and court costs. I gave Mona an extra $5,000 for her "pain and suffering."

I gave $9,000 in scholarships to River Falls journalism students. I gave $2,000 in bonuses to Tanick and his assistant attorney. The rest, which amounted to $17,000, I used to pay off my three-year-old Mazda 626.

Tanick's law firm gave several $500 scholarships to UW–RF students.[11]

From a financial standpoint, the lawsuit was a "no-gainer." No amount of money can compensate one for the stress and mental anguish of fighting a bureaucracy. Ask anyone who has been through it.

However, if I had to do it all over again, I wouldn't change a thing. I have a deep commitment to defending the First Amendment and other civil liberties.

Did UW–RF officials learn a lesson from my lawsuit?

Hard to say.

But back then I told myself that things would be different at Washington State University. After all, it was four times bigger than UW–RF, and social theory predicts that larger institutions are more likely to tolerate conflict, disagreements and activist professors.

Chapter 21 Endnotes

1. Hazel Dicken-Garcia and Giovanna Dell'Orto, *Hated Ideas and the American Civil War Press* (Spokane, WA: Marquette Books, 2007), p. 247.

2. John Lofton, *The Press as Guardian of the First Amendment* (New York: Columbia University Press, 1980).

3. State and federal courts, by the way, have repeatedly allowed universities to use collegiality as a criteria for dismissing faculty. But because the UW system had eliminated that clause from system rules, it could not use collegiality to defend its decision.

4. *David Pearce Demers v. Board of Regents of the University of Wisconsin System, and John Smith** (U.S. District Court, Western Division, Court File No: 95C 0648). *John Smith is a pseudonym.

5. Brett Longdin, "Professor Files Lawsuit in Fight for Job Security," *Student Voice* (September 7, 1995), p. 1.

6. David Pearce Demers, *The Menace of the Corporate Newspaper: Fact or Fiction?* (Ames: Iowa State University Press, 1996).

7. William Glaberson, "Media: Press; Corporate Veils of Secrecy Limit Access to Important Stories," *The New York Times* (November 27, 1995, p. D7) and William Glaberson, "'60 Minutes' Case Part of a Trend of Corporate Pressure, Some Analysts Say," *The New York Times* (November 17, 1995, p. B1).

8. William Glaberson, "Newspaper Owners Do the Shuffle; Communities Worry as Dailies Pass from Chain to Chain," *The New York Times* (February 19, 1996, p. D1).

9. "Journalism Professor Vindicated," *Quill* magazine (May 1996).

10. Letter to Maggie Balough, editor, *Quill*, dated May 8, 1996, on University of Wisconsin–River Falls stationary.

11. In 2008, about 13 years after the lawsuit, I attended a conference and met one of the new faculty who was teaching at UW–RF. "Oh, you're the guy who secretly tape-recorded people," she said. Not unexpectedly, I had been framed in the program as an unethical professor, not as one defending free speech rights of faculty.

Part IV

Censored in the Palouse

Chapter 22

Murder in the Palouse

Monday, July 22, 1996
Pullman, Washington

I was unpacking a box of books when someone knocked on my apartment door. My mother answered.

"Dave, it's a police officer."

"I'm with the Pullman Police Department," the officer said as I arrived. "A woman died in a condominium across the courtyard last night. We're going door-to-door to see if anyone heard any strange noises last night or saw anything that looked suspicious."

My mother, Joanie, and I shook our heads.

"I just moved in here. What happened? Was she murdered?"

My mother and I had arrived in Pullman, Washington, two days earlier after a three-day, 1,400-mile drive from Minneapolis. She had graciously volunteered to accompany me on the trip to my new job at Washington State University. I would start teaching in three weeks. In two days, she would fly back to Saginaw, Michigan, where she lived on a farm with my stepfather.

I was 43 and soon to be single.

Mona, who had encouraged me to apply for the faculty position at WSU, decided not to move to Pullman. We mutually agreed to part. It was bittersweet, but we remained friends.

I enjoyed my mother's companionship on the trip. For the last two decades I had spent less time visiting with her or other members of my immediate and extended family. Since leaving home for college, I had lived in six different cities. I had some regrets about that. Family has always been important to me and to Lutherans in general.

The decline in familial ties is one of the costs of the Age of Enlightenment. Progress needs educated people who are mobile, and the siren call of a meaningful career now replaces the close bonds of family connections. People define themselves by their careers, and they move from city to city, climbing the economic ladder and acquiring more occupational prestige. For some, though, the experience isn't always positive. The disconnect with family has led to an increase in divorce rates, single parenthood and depression.

The police officer standing outside of my apartment door had no knowledge of what I was thinking. He simply handed me a business card and answered my question. "Her death is suspicious, but we don't know exactly what happened. If you have any information that might help our investigation, please call us at the number on this card."

"Yes, we will."

Welcome to Pullman. To what kind of town had I just moved?

The journalist in me couldn't wait several hours to read the answer in the evening *Moscow-Pullman Daily News*. I darted out the door and tracked down the manager of the apartment/condominium complex, Walt Begstone, who was pruning a hedge.

"Hey, Walt, the police just stopped by my apartment. What's going on?"

"The woman living in the condominium next to mine was apparently murdered last night," Begstone said. "She was suffocated, possibly with a pillow."

The victim was Dorothy Martin, an 89-year-old widow in extremely good health who lived alone. She was found lying in her bed in her nightgown.

"Wow," I said. "Are murders common in Pullman?"

"No, she's the first in 15 years. Someone broke into my apartment yesterday and stole the master key to her condominium and several others. My wife and I were at our cabin yesterday and last night."

Walt had discovered Martin's body early that morning.

He later told me that police had several suspects.

But police would not solve the case for five years.

A handyman who worked for Martin, Bradley Marion Steckman, confessed in 2001 to suffocating her with a pillow. The breakthrough came after Steckman's ex-wife gave crucial information to police.[1]

He then confessed to police that Skye M. Hanson, 44, of Post Falls, Idaho, paid him $1,000 to steal a diamond ring owned by Martin. Steckman pleaded guilty and was sentenced to 18 years in prison.[2]

Steckman also confessed to the 1998 hot-tub electrocution of Barbara Loesch of Post Falls, the mother of Hanson's lover, Tina R. Loesch, 37. Tina took out a $500,000 life insurance policy on her mother and paid Steckman $10,000 to kill her.

According to police, Tina watched as Steckman dropped a "live" television into the hot tub in which her mother was soaking, electrocuting her.

Police initially ruled the death an accident.

Tina collected the insurance money.

Then she, her 5-year-old son, and Hanson left the area before Steckman confessed to the crimes. He was sentenced to life in prison for the hot-tub murder. Police said Tina Loesch also may have been involved in the shooting death of her father in the 1990s.

For the next seven years police searched for Hanson, Loesch and Loesch's son, Kristopher.

Then, on November 15, 2008, the television show *America's Most Wanted* featured pictures of fugitives Hanson and Tina Loesch in an episode, linking them to the murder of Barbara Loesch. The next day, the lovers committed suicide.

Police are still searching for Kristopher, who was last seen by Tucson neighbors several months before the deaths. He would be 30 in 2021.[3]

DESPITE MY MACABRE introduction to Pullman,[4] I was grateful to have landed the job at Washington State University, which is located about 75 miles south of Spokane and 250 miles southeast of Seattle and eight miles from Moscow, Idaho (pronounced moss-koe, long "o," rather than moss-cow, as many Americans pronounce the Russian capital), which is home to the University of Idaho.

About 25,000 people lived in Pullman, which was founded in 1886 under the name Three Forks. Within three years, the town was renamed after George Pullman — the inventor of the Pullman sleeping (railroad) car — who now is remembered more for tyrannical treatment of his employees than his business successes.

When business revenues declined in 1894, George Pullman cut wages by 30 percent, increased the length of the working day, laid off workers, and refused to cut rent and utility bills for workers who lived in the Illinois town he built to support his factory.

In response, the workers went on strike. National Guard troops eventually quashed it, killing 34 strikers. Adding insult to injury, the strikers were blacklisted.

A short time later, a national commission concluded that Pullman's paternalistic town was "un-American." In 1898, the Illinois Supreme Court forced the company to divest ownership of the town. The city of Chicago then annexed the village.

A small victory for the Enlightenment.

THE CITY OF PULLMAN was built on four hills (the university is on College Hill) and is surrounded on all sides by prairie-like rolling hills known as the Palouse (rhymes with "caboose"). The name may have come from a Native American tribe called the Palus,[5] who lived in the area before the white people came.

Geologists believe the hills were created when glaciers ground up rock and wind blew it into the area. The area gets only about 20 inches of rain a year,[6] so deciduous trees survive only near creek or river beds or from yard watering. Conifers, which need less water, survive best on shady slopes or in low-lying areas.

Winters are mild, with moderate amounts of snowfall that usually melt in a day or two. Summers are dry and pleasant, with temperatures mostly in the 78-to-92-degree range.

Before farmers began growing wheat, barley, peas and lentils on the Palouse, various Native American tribes, including the Palus, Cayuse and Walla Walla, lived in or roamed the area. Traveling down to Pullman from Spokane, drivers pass the town of Rosalia, where the Battle of Pine Creek, also known as the Battle of Tohotonimme, was fought.

On May 17, 1858, about 900 Native Americans from various tribes attacked 164 United States Army forces under the command of Lt. Col. Edward J. Steptoe. Seven soldiers were killed; about a dozen were injured. Nine to 50 Native Americans, according to varying accounts, were killed. The remaining soldiers escaped during the night.

Nearly four months later, the U.S. Army sent Col. George Wright and his 600 troops to suppress "native resistance."[7] Armed with the new Springfield Model 1855 rifle, which could kill at a distance of more than a hundred yards, the troops inflicted heavy casualties on 5,000 warriors in two separate battles.

To further punish the Native Americans, Wright's troops on September 8, 1858, rounded up 800 of their horses and shot them dead. The troops also destroyed the Indians' food stores. The Native Americans quit fighting and eventually were forced to live on reservations in the area.

But a century later some of the tribes opened casinos on their lands, extracting a small measure of financial retribution from the mostly white European American gamblers.

WASHINGTON STATE UNIVERSITY was founded in 1890 as Washington Agricultural College and School of Science. The university received 190,000 acres from the federal government under the Morrill Acts of 1862 and 1890, which helped establish land-grant universities across the nation. The university changed its name to Washington State College in 1905.

The only major disadvantage of Pullman is its geographical isolation. The state capital, Olympia, and Seattle are a six-hour drive to the west. The nearest major city is Spokane (population 210,000), which is more than an hour to the north.

Many professors privately concede that geographical isolation has hindered the university's impact on state and national politics.

News story citations back up their claims.

The University of Washington, which is located in Seattle and a one-hour drive from Olympia, was cited in 82,392 stories published from 1990 to 2012 in *The Seattle Times*, the state's largest and most influential newspaper. WSU was mentioned only 8,388 times.[8]

In the early years, Washington State College was known for its programs in agriculture, veterinary medicine, engineering and mining. Like other land-grant institutions, students often referred to WSC as a "cow college" — a pejorative appellation often coming from urban students.[9]

As Washington State and the nation became more industrialized, urbanized and "informationized," the curriculum at WSC became more diversified. Today, about three-fifths of students major in business, education, history, communication, social science or one of the humanities.[10]

Reflecting this transition, WSC changed its name to Washington State University in 1959.

The typical student admitted to WSU in 2009 had a combined SAT score of 1600 (critical reading + math + writing). This is slightly higher than the national mean of about 1500 for all universities but significantly lower than the 1745 average score for national research universities. WSU ranked in the bottom fourth (172 out of 226).[11] University of Idaho edged out WSU by five points (1605).

By 2012, the average SAT score at WSU had dropped twenty-five points, to 1575. The likely cause was a decision by administrators to increase enrollments to extract more money from the state treasury. State universities in Washington are funded in part based on enrollments.

WSU HAS MANY GRADUATES who have distinguished themselves.

They include Phil Abelson, father of the atomic submarine; Jacob Bigeleisen, founder of modern isotope chemistry; John Fabian, astronaut on the second Challenger space shuttle mission in 1983; Gary Larson, creator of *Far Side* cartoons; Jerry Sage, the World War II prisoner of war played by Steve McQueen in the movie *The Great Escape*; and William Julius Wilson, a Harvard University professor selected by *Time* in 1996 as one of America's 25 Most Influential People.

Timothy Leary — the 1960s counterculture proponent of the drug LSD who coined the phrase "Turn on, tune in, drop out" — obtained a master's degree in psychology at WSU in 1946. Leary lectured at Harvard University until 1963, when he was fired partly for advocating the use of psychedelic drugs.

Not surprisingly, the university does not mention Leary's name when promoting itself to donors or students. Instead, the university relies heavily on broadcast news pioneer Edward R. Murrow, who WSU administrators say is WSU's most famous graduate.

Murrow is best known for helping to end in 1954 the pernicious investigatory practices of anti-communist Republican Senator Joseph R. McCarthy, who had falsely accused many Americans of being traitors or communists.

Murrow attended Washington State College from 1926 to 1930. He graduated with a bachelor's degree in speech. Journalism wasn't an option back then.

I confess that I didn't know much about Murrow before I began teaching at WSU. My heroes were print journalists like Watergate sleuths Bob Woodward and Carl Bernstein, muckraker Ida Tarbell (whose stories helped break up John D. Rockefeller's oil trust), socialist Upton Sinclair (author of *The Jungle* and a Pulitzer Prize winner), and investigative journalist I. F. (Izzy) Stone (publisher of *I. F. Stone's Weekly* newsletter).

Like many print journalists and print journalism professors at the time, I had a snobby attitude toward broadcast journalism. Broadcast news was superficial, self-aggrandizing, and full of "snappers" — a term Henry Schulte, my Kiplinger Professor at The Ohio State University, coined to refer to the value-laden comments that come at the end of many stories (like "this tragedy has affected everyone in this community, but it has also made them stronger and more determined to rebuild"). Readers don't need to be told that a tornado that kills people is a tragedy, and opinionated statements about strength and determination are best attributed to sources, not reporters.

Nevertheless, if I were going to teach in the Edward R. Murrow School of Communication, I should have some knowledge of its namesake. So I purchased copies of biographies written by A. M. Sperber (1986) and Joseph E. Persico (1988)[12] and read them during the three weeks before my first day of work.

Ironically, Murrow would have a far bigger impact on my thinking than all of the other print heroes combined.

Chapter 22 Endnotes

1. Editorial, "Pullman Police Demonstrate Patience Pays," *Moscow-Pullman Daily News* (July 30, 2001), p. 71.

2. Staff report, "Women Sought in Connection with Pullman Slaying Found Dead," *Moscow-Pullman Daily News* (November 18, 2008), p. 3A.

3. More information about Kristopher Loesch can be found on the MissingKids.com website: <http://www.missingkids.com/servlet/PubCaseSearchServlet?act=

viewChildDetail&caseNum=986992&orgPrefix=NCMC&seqNum=1&caseLang= en_US&searchLang=en_US>.

4. In December 2005, three people were found shot to death in the same apartment/condominium complex in an apparent murder-suicide. As with the Dororthy Martin murder, someone broke into the manager's office and stole a key to the condominium. Walt Begstone also discovered these bodies.

5. Various spellings have been associated with this tribe, including Palloatpallah, Pelusha and now, today, Palouse.

6. Precipitation data obtained from Western Regional Climate Center, 2215 Raggio Parkway, Reno, Nevada 89512-1095, retrieved September 20, 2011, from <http://www.wrcc.dri.edu/summary/puw.wa.html>.

7. William Stimson, *A View of the Falls: An Illustrated History of Spokane* (Northridge, CA: Windson Publications, 1985), pp. 14-19.

8. These statistics were derived from a search of *The Seattle Times* archives, conducted on October 27, 2012. A search of the Spokane *Spokesman-Review* archives revealed that, as might be expected, WSU is cited more often than UW (17,562 vs. 7,198 from 1994 to the present). However, the ratio is only about 2 to 1, versus 1 to 7 in the *Seattle Times*.

9. The term "cow college" emerged around the year 1910, at the height of the industrial revolution. Source: Dictionary.com, retrieved Oct. 29, 2012, <http://dictionary.reference.com/browse/cow+college>.

10. College Profile Data, Institutional Research, Washington State University (January 26, 2012). Data retrieved September 29, 2012, online from <http://ir.wsu.edu/Student%20Data>.

11. The university ranks 84th of 150 public and private and research universities in terms of in terms of annual expenditures of funding from federal sources. Source: John V. Lombardi, Elizabeth D. Phillips, Craig W. Abbey and Diane D. Craig, *The Top American Research Universities* (Tempe, AZ: Center for Measuring Performance at Arizona State University, 2011), p. 12. Available online at <http://mup.asu.edu/ research2011.pdf>.

12. A. M. Sperber, *Murrow: His Life and Times* (New York: Freundlich Books, 1986) and Joseph E. Persico, *Edward R. Murrow: An American Original* (New York: Laurelm, 1988).

Chapter 23

The Enlightened Journalist

August 6, 1996
Pullman, Washington

It was sunny and 92 degrees near the swimming pool at my apartment complex in Pullman, Washington, where I was reading Joseph E. Persico's 1988 biography of Murrow, titled *Edward R. Murrow: An American Original*.[1] In two weeks, I would teach my first class at Washington State University.

Sweat was dripping from my chin.

Four decades earlier, on March 9, 1954, Murrow also was sweating, but for a different reason.

He was in New York City, just minutes away from telling his national television audience of 12 million *See It Now* viewers that U.S. Senator Joseph R. McCarthy was a bully and rumormonger.

McCarthy first garnered national attention on February 9, 1950, when he told a Republican women's club in Wheeling, West Virginia, that "the State Department is infested with communists" and that he had a list of 205 of them.[2]

Although McCarthy never produced the names — a pattern of behavior he would repeat often over the next four years when making allegations — the news media gave his speech a lot of attention. He was, after all, a powerful U.S. senator, and powerful people make news.[3]

But Murrow was not impressed.

For four years he had watched McCarthy level false or misleading allegations against hundreds of U.S. citizens, including some of his colleagues at CBS. On several occasions, Murrow helped save the careers of these colleagues.[4]

Some journalists and politicians had drawn attention to McCarthy's baneful tactics. But the criticism seemed to have no impact on his popularity. In fact, polls showed that McCarthy's ratings had steadily risen since 1951. In January 1954, just two months before Murrow's broadcast, a poll found that one-half of American adults had a favorable opinion of McCarthy.[5]

Murrow was apprehensive the evening of his broadcast, partly because he knew McCarthy would retaliate. Murrow was an easy target. Even though he had rejected radical politics all his life, he had associated with many known communists. Some were friends.

Murrow had a lot to lose. He owned two homes and was earning more than $1 million a year (in today's dollars) at CBS.

A make-up assistant wiped sweat from Murrow's chin and face.

Then the on-air cue.

"Good evening," he said. "Tonight, *See It Now* devotes its entire half hour to a report on Senator Joseph R. McCarthy, told mainly in his own words and pictures."

After a commercial break, Murrow said *See It Now* would offer McCarthy equal time if "he believes we have done violence to his words or pictures."

Republican presidential candidate Dwight Eisenhower is then shown after a meeting with McCarthy. Eisenhower comments on how he would deal with subversives: "This is America's principle: trial by jury of the innocent, until proved guilty."

McCarthy's response to Eisenhower's comments is odd, even "chilling," according to the biographer. McCarthy repeatedly giggles and ends up simply saying that he thinks Eisenhower will make a "great president."

Murrow then comes on camera and says McCarthy often "operates as a one-man committee. He has traveled far, interviewed many, terrorized some, accused civilian and military leaders of the past administration of a great conspiracy to turn the country over to communism, investigated and substantially demoralized the present State Department, made varying charges of espionage at Fort Monmouth. The Army says it has been unable to find anything relating to espionage there."

The time remaining in the half-hour slot is filled mainly with film clips of McCarthy making outrageous accusations against mainstream politicians and organizations, none of whom has ties to communism. They included Democratic presidential candidate Adlai Stevenson II, a U.S. Army general, the mainstream press, the Voice of America, the American Civil Liberties Union, and the Institute of Pacific Relations.

McCarthy is incriminating himself. That's what Murrow and his *See It Now* co-producer Fred Friendly had intended when putting the show together.

As the show came to a close, Murrow added perspective.

> [T]he line between investigating and persecuting is a very fine one and the junior senator from Wisconsin has stepped over it repeatedly. ...
> We must not confuse dissent with disloyalty. ...
> We will not walk in fear, one of another.
> We will not be driven by fear into an age of unreason if we dig deep in our history and doctrine and remember that we are not descended from fearful

men, not from men who feared to write, to speak, to associate and to defend causes which were for the moment unpopular. ...

The actions of the junior senator from Wisconsin have caused alarm and dismay amongst our allies abroad and given considerable comfort to our enemies, and whose fault is that? Not really his. He didn't create this situation of fear; he merely exploited it, and rather successfully.

Cassius was right: "The fault, dear Brutus, is not in our stars but in ourselves. ... Good night, and good luck."[6]

THE *SEE IT NOW* SEGMENT about McCarthy, then as today, is often heralded as one of the greatest examples of broadcast journalism.[7]

Shortly after the broadcast, *New York Times* TV writer Jack Gould called the show "crusading journalism of high responsibility and genuine courage."

John Crosby of the *New York Herald Tribune* wrote that Murrow "put his finger squarely on the root of the true evil of McCarthyism, which is its corrosive effect on the souls of hitherto honest men."

Variety said Murrow was "practically ... a national hero."

Alistair Cooke, writing for the British *Guardian Weekly*, said "Mr. Murrow may yet make bravery fashionable."

And *I. F. Stone's Weekly*: "Hats off to Ed Murrow."[8]

CBS and its affiliates received more than 75,000 calls, telegrams and letters after the show — the highest number of responses for a TV show to date. By a 10-to-1 margin, they supported Murrow.

Well-wishers mobbed Murrow the following day when he left the CBS building, and 1,500 journalists attending the Overseas Press Club at the Waldorf gave him a standing ovation a week later.

"Murrow did not kill off McCarthy or McCarthyism," Joseph Wershba, who worked under Murrow and helped produce the McCarthy segment, said years after the broadcast. "But he helped halt America's incredible slide toward a native brand of fascism."[9]

The McCarthy broadcast remains one of the greatest examples of broadcast journalism in history.

But the episode, as some observers have pointed out, also is one of the greatest examples of a journalist breaking the rules of conventional journalism.[10]

"Is it right in principle for television to take a clear stand on one side of a great issue?" *Newsweek* magazine asked its readers in a cover story soon after the McCarthy show.[11]

"The McCarthy broadcast was not objective reporting," Persico pointed out three decades later. "It was subjective polemicizing. To those who would insist on purist rules governing even a fight with a barroom brawler, Murrow was wrong. But to millions, it had been satisfying to see the bully thrashed at last."[12]

The ethic of objectivity admonishes journalists to keep personal biases and opinions out of stories, to cover all sides of a story, and to give roughly equal amounts of coverage and space to all sides.[13] The assumption is that readers and viewers can sift through the information presented and find the truth.

The New York Times at the time reinforced this ethic, declaring that even if McCarthy's charges "are usually proved false," he was still news, because separating innuendo from truth and accusation from guilt "lies with the readers," not the newspaper.[14]

But, Murrow and other critics asked, how can the public discern the truth if sources are lying and journalists are unable to get all of the facts?

A massive amount of research in mass communication over the next five decades eventually revealed that the ethic of objectivity is not objective in any absolute sense. It produces its own bias, which is neither radical nor aligned with a particular political ideology, per se. The bias is mainstream. The ethic of objectivity tends to reinforce the status quo, which usually means support for powerful people and organizations and mainstream values. Objective reporting tends to marginalize radical or unorthodox ideas. That's partly because it relies very heavily on powerful elites who have an interest in maintaining the status quo.[15]

Interestingly, some "objective" news reporters in Murrow's time could see the shortcomings of their reportorial method.

"It [Murrow's show] speaks for scores of us who must stifle our opinion even when it hurts," John Scali of the Associated Press cabled Murrow.[16]

"When you sailed into McCarthy," the news personnel at an affiliate wrote, "we in this business who are arbitrarily confined to straight reporting ... raised our voices to shout, 'at last.'"[17]

Murrow "did not possess the cardinal virtues of the journalist, objectivity and balance," Persico writes. "His power lay rather in his subjectivity, in the passionate moral biases, however coolly concealed, that he brought to his work."[18]

Murrow believed the news needed to be interpreted, not just presented. Stenography was not good journalism.

But Murrow's brand of subjective journalism was not unbounded. It eschewed speculation and hyperbole, unlike many editorials and commentaries. Murrow's journalism was grounded in facts and logic, like academic scholarship. And although Murrow held a liberal perspective on many issues, he did not define his journalism through his personal ideology.

In fact, when a reporter from *Look* magazine asked him to explain his motives for going after McCarthy, Murrow replied: "I wouldn't say it was liberalism. ... I think it stems from my feeling about the sacredness of due process of law. I saw in Germany and Czechoslovakia that the law is destroyed first and then, after the law is gone, the freedom of the people is destroyed. The thing about McCarthy that bothers me is his disrespect for the due process of law."[19]

When I read this comment in Persico's book, I realized then that Murrow's most significant contribution to broadcast journalism wasn't the McCarthy broadcast, even though it helped turn the tide against McCarthy; nor was it his courage or integrity, as he had a number of personal and professional lapses during his lifetime; nor was it his sensate coverage of World War II, which made him a household name.

Murrow's most significant contribution to broadcast journalism was his activist brand of journalism.

MURROW WAS a tireless advocate of democracy, free speech, due process, egalitarianism, transparent government, education, rule of law and civil liberties.

These values are reflected in many other stories he covered through the years, such as the "Harvest of Shame" investigative report, a powerful indictment of America's agricultural system, which mistreated migrant workers.

The civil liberties theme is echoed by Gary R. Edgerton, professor and dean of the College of Communication at Butler University:

> In words evocative of America's original Founding Fathers, Murrow frequently used the airwaves to revivify and popularize many democratic ideals such as free speech, citizen participation, the pursuit of truth, and the sanctification of individual liberties and rights. ... Resurrecting these values and virtues for a mass audience of true believers during the London Blitz was high drama — the opposing threat of totalitarianism, made real by Nazi bombs, was ever present. ... Ed Murrow's persona was thus established, embodying the political traditions of the Western democracies, and offering the public a heroic model on which to focus their energies.[20]

In other words, Murrow was an activist for the Age of Enlightenment and one of its most important prodigies, the Bill of Rights.

But Murrow's activist journalism eventually got him into trouble.

His bosses at CBS weren't happy when the targets of Murrow's stories — most of whom could be identified as enemies of the Enlightenment project — demanded equal time for a rebuttal of his reports. CBS executives cringed and pushed his programming into low-audience time slots. They eventually cut his shows, and Murrow struck back with a speech at a convention that provided the final nails in his professional coffin.

On October 15, 1958, Murrow criticized CBS corporate bean counters in a speech he gave at the Radio-Television News Directors Association convention in Chicago.

> [I] can find nothing in the Bill of Rights of the Communications Act which says that they [news corporations] must increase their net profits each year, lest the Republic collapse. ... I would just like to see it reflect occasionally the hard, unyielding realities of the world in which we live. ... This instrument can teach, it can illuminate; yes, and it can even inspire. But it can do so only to the extent that humans are determined to use it to those ends. Otherwise, it is merely wires and lights in a box.[21]

CBS executives were furious.

Murrow was biting the hand that fed him.

Asked later by a Chicago journalist why he gave that speech, Murrow replied: "I've always been on the side of the heretics against those who burned them, because the heretics so often proved right in the long run. Dead — but right!"

Murrow fell into a depression.

He took a sabbatical and traveled with his family for nearly a year. After he returned, he left CBS for good, accepting an offer from President John F. Kennedy in 1961 to head up the United States Information Agency, the international propaganda arm of the U.S. government.

Early on, Murrow tried to prevent the BBC from broadcasting the "Harvest of Shame" report, fearing the Soviets would use it as an example of the how capitalism mistreats its citizens. Murrow was harshly criticized for this ethical lapse.

He held the position at USIA for three years.

Illness forced him to retire in 1964.

Murrow, who had smoked three packs of cigarettes a day for most of his adult life, died of complications from lung cancer in 1965, two days before his 57th birthday.[22]

Most analysts argue that corporate greed played the key role in why Murrow was pushed out of CBS. But a more nuanced interpretation is that the executives failed to see the importance of "Enlightenment journalism." In other words, to them, protecting civil liberties was far less important than making money.

I was really hot now.

Time to dip in the swimming pool.

"What a splash!" exclaimed one 10-year-old boy who watched me turn into a human cannonball.

AFTER READING ABOUT MURROW, I wondered whether Murrow's Enlightenment journalism was embodied in the Edward R. Murrow School of Journalism curriculum and the university as a whole.

Were journalism students being taught to become advocates of the cause of the Enlightenment — a role that challenged, at least to some degree, the conventional objective model of journalism? Did university administrators and faculty embrace this model as well as civil liberties and freedom of speech in general? Was decision-making at the university more democratic or autocratic?

The director of the Murrow School was Alexis ("Alex") Tan, who grew up in the Philippines and exhibited the best characteristics of its people. Filipinos are widely recognized as some of the most hospitable people in the world. In times of food shortage, they are even known to feed guests before themselves.

Tan made me and three other new hires feel very welcome.

His management style was a mix of East and West. He avoided public criticism of staff or faculty and was never paternalistic or condescending. An autocrat he was not.

"Do your job" was his only mandate.

He gave faculty and staff a great deal of freedom and autonomy. This endeared him to most of the faculty, some of whom had worked for corporations or government bureaucracies, where autonomy is often limited. Tan always tried to accommodate individual faculty needs; however, because of resource shortages, not everyone was happy all the time.

Tan earned his Ph.D. from the University of Wisconsin, where he worked with Steven Chaffee and Jack McLeod, two internationally renowned mass communication social psychologists.

The year I started, Tan had been elected incoming president of the Association for Education in Journalism and Mass Communication, the most prominent professional organization in journalism and mass communication. At that point in his career, Tan had published one research methods textbook and had written or co-written 27 scholarly papers and book chapters. He also played a key role in changing the name of WSU's communication program.

In 1990, he and other administrators at WSU persuaded Murrow's wife, Janet, and his son, Casey, to allow the school to change its name to the Edward R. Murrow School of Communication.

Prior to that, the five general degree programs that made up the school — advertising, broadcast journalism, print journalism, public relations and speech communication (interpersonal and organizational communication and rhetoric) — were simply called the School of Communication.

After Murrow's death in 1965, Janet spent much her time promoting Murrow's legacy in the United States and around the world. She donated pictures and other materials to the WSU library.

She was still alive when I started teaching at WSU in 1996.

But I never met her.

She died two years later at age 88.

Casey, who was 45 in 1990, had worked briefly as a journalist decades earlier, but he found education was a better vocational fit. He became executive director of Synergy Learning International, Inc., a nonprofit organization that promotes science, math, and technology in grades K–8.[23]

Although Murrow earned a good salary working at CBS, he did not accumulate a massive fortune. Nevertheless, in the world of academia, big names like Murrow have "brand value" and often make it easier for development fund managers to raise money and resources for academic programs.

To facilitate this process, WSU administrators created the Murrow Symposium, an annual event held to honor journalists, scholarship donors and WSU students.

Administrators had high hopes that the Murrow name would draw more resources to the university.

As it turns out, the Murrow program certainly needed it.

IN 1996, THE MURROW School was composed of two dozen faculty, three full-time staff and about 900 majors and 500 pre-majors. Nearly 1 of 12 students at WSU was affiliated with the Murrow School. The only program bigger than communication was business, which had more than 1,000 majors.

Although I didn't know it at the time, the Murrow program was substantially underfunded compared with other programs of its kind across the country as well as with similar programs at WSU. Its annual budget was 25 to 50 percent less than other comparable journalism and mass communication programs.

Arizona State University's Cronkite School of Journalism and Mass Communication, for example, employed 75 full- and part-time faculty who taught about 1,000 majors. The WSU College of Education had slightly fewer majors than the Murrow School but about 50 percent more funding and a dozen more faculty.

The Murrow School was poorly funded because it was being used as a "cash cow"[24] for other programs, several WSU administrators conceded over the years.[25]

The Murrow School was housed in the College of Liberal Arts and had to compete with 17 other programs for funding. The university overall at the time was spending an average of $6,500 to educate a student. Some programs, like music, spent more (as much as $12,000 per full-time student). That stemmed partly from the fact that music majors often had one-on-one lessons with instructors. Programs in the natural sciences, like chemistry, physics and biology, also spent more per student, partly because of the costs of operating and equipping laboratories.

The Murrow School, according to an accreditation report issued by the Pacific Northwest Newspaper Association during the 1990s, was receiving about $2,700 per student, compared with $3,600 for the average department in the College of Liberal Arts, which included English, art, philosophy, history, music, foreign languages, political science, sociology, geology and seven other fields of study.

To compensate for the lack of funding and faculty, class sizes for some courses in the Murrow School were big. The introduction to mass communication course, for example, packed 350 to 600 students into an auditorium per semester. Several other introductory courses also enrolled more than 300 students. Media law and media history classes often had 50 to 70 students — twice as big as at comparable schools across the country.

TAN ASSIGNED ME to teach two courses during my first semester: introductory news reporting and a senior seminar in journalism.

Academically, my WSU students were more competent than their counterparts at the University of Wisconsin–River Falls. But WSU students were no match for University of Minnesota students, especially when it came to inquisitiveness. Minnesota students were self-starters, always asking questions. WSU students often needed a little prodding.

But they were very likable.

They also seemed to be taller, especially the women.

"Is it possible," I asked one faculty member, "that the students here are taller because they are descended from Seattle-area lumberjacks?"

"I think they are normal height," my colleague said. "It's probably because you are getting shorter as you age."

Indeed, at my most recent doctor visit, I was told I was one-quarter inch shorter than I had been telling people all my life (five-foot-seven and three-fourths instead of five-foot-eight).

Was I shrinking or did the nurse make a mistake?

I was never able to confirm the lumberjack-height theory, but I did enjoy teaching at WSU. The load was 50 percent less than I had had at River Falls, which gave me more time to conduct research on newspapers. I surveyed editors across the country and asked them how much emphasis their newspapers placed on product quality, profits, and keeping employees happy, and I examined the relationship between complexity of the organization and editorial-page vigor.

The results reinforced the findings in my previous research: as newspapers acquire the characteristics of the corporate form of organization, they place more emphasis on product quality as an organizational goal and less emphasis on profits, and they treat their employees better[26] and are much more vigorous editorially, meaning top news sources in their communities (mayors, police chiefs) tend to see the local newspaper as being more critical of them and their policies.[27]

I eventually wrote a summary article for *Newspaper Research Journal*, a peer-reviewed journal oriented in part to explaining the results of social scientific research to working professionals.[28] I argued that corporatization of the newspaper industry — and the decline of family ownership — appears to enhance rather than diminish diversity in the marketplace of ideas.

As I expected, reaction from the academic community was muted.

At conferences, scholars and students listened, but most could not accept the idea that the rise of corporate newspapers could be a good thing for democracy in America. I attributed some of the skepticism to the fact that, politically, most social scientists are liberal. Some were neo-Marxists who believed that mainstream mass media almost always produce content that inhibits rather than facilitates social change that can help disadvantaged groups.[29]

I certainly didn't argue that mass media content produces radical change. Media are better characterized as "reformist." And reform is one of the reasons why the United States is one of the most politically stable countries in the world. Instability tends to be associated with societies that repress civil liberties and freedom of speech.

Of course, I knew that it was unreasonable to expect scholars who have spent their lifetimes developing and building their own theories critical of the mass media to accommodate the controversial ideas of an upstart parvenu like me. I realized that if I were to have any impact on the field, it would have to be on students who had not yet committed themselves to theories highly critical of the mass media.

There was just one theoretical snag.

As I noted earlier in this book, my corporate newspaper theory didn't jive with some of my personal experiences with corporate organizations. How could corporate newspapers enhance the Enlightenment project when my personal experiences and the theories of David Riesman and William H. Whyte suggested just the opposite?

The answer, I would discover sometime later, was culture: most newspapers, unlike many other types of bureaucracies, have a very strong organizational commitment to finding the truth, to defending democratic principles and civil liberties. This culture insulates the newspaper from the adverse effects of bureaucratic organization and enhances its prosocial effects, even though the ethic of objectivity has its flaws. I would develop this theory in more depth later.

Meanwhile, I was happy at WSU, despite the funding shortfalls at the Murrow School.

Like other faculty, I worked a lot — about 65 to 80 hours a week. And I was productive as a scholar, publishing three scholarly books and six refereed journal articles during my first three years at WSU.

As I told one senior faculty member on one occasion, "I love my job so much I don't know if I will ever retire."

He chuckled. "You might change your mind someday."

In 1996, the only flies in the ointment at WSU, aside from funding, that I could see were an isolated case of censorship and weaker than desired ties between the school and the newspaper industry.

Chapter 23 Endnotes

1. Joseph E. Persico, *Edward R. Murrow: An American Original* (New York: Laurelm, 1988).

2. There is a dispute about the actual number of names on the list. The event was not recorded. But most reports cite 205. Historians point out that McCarthy frequently changed the number of alleged communists on his lists.

3. The relationship between power and news is one of the most documented findings in mass communication research. See, e.g., J. Herbert Altschull, *Agents of Power* (New York: Longman, 1984) and David L. Paletz and Robert M. Entman, *Media Power Politics* (New York: The Free Press, 1981);

4. Persico, *Edward R. Murrow*, see Chapters 22 and 25.

5. Nelson W. Polsby, "Towards an Explanation of McCarthyism," *Political Studies*, 8 (October 1962), p. 252.

6. Edward R. Murrow, "A Report on Senator Joseph R. McCarthy," *See It Now* (aired March 9, 1954, Columbia Broadcasting System).

7. The responses in this section are taken from A. M. Sperber, *Murrow: His Life and Times* (New York: Freundlich Books, 1986), pp. 440-443.

8. The pro-McCarthy press criticized Murrow's McCarthy show, and some of the praise in the mainstream press was qualified. But since then, the show has been elevated to mythical status.

9. Joseph Werschba, "Edward R. Murrow and the Time of His Time," *Eve's Magazine* (2000), retrieved October 22, 2020 from <http://www.evesmag.com/murrow.htm>.

10. CBS had a policy requiring its reporters to be objective. But management issued a statement after the McCarthy show saying it was making an exception. Persico, *Murrow*, pp. 382-383.

11. Quoted in Persico, *Murrow*, p. 382.

12. Ibid., p. 383.

13. For a discussion of the ethic of objectivity, see Chapter 16 in David Demers, *History and Future of Mass Media: An Integrated Perspective* (Cresskill, NJ: Hampton Press, 2001).

14. Quoted in Persico, *Edward R. Murrow*, p. 8. Original Source: Richard H. Rovere, *Senator Joe McCarthy* (New York: Harcourt, Brace and Company, 1959), pp. 137 and 166.

15. For a discussion of the mainstream bias, see Chapter 16 in Demers, *History and Future of Mass Media*.

16. Sperber, *Murrow*, p. 442.

17. Ibid.

18. Persico, *Edward R. Murrow*, p. 496.

19. Ibid., p. 8.

20. Gary Edgerton, "Edward R. Murrow: U.S. Broadcast Journalist," The Museum of Broadcast Communications, retrieved November 3, 2012, from <http://www.museum.tv/eotvsection.php?entrycode=murrowedwar>.

21. Persico, *Edward R. Murrow*, p. 434.

22. Janet Murrow kept a diary that has been a valuable source of information to historians about Ed. She died in 1999. Ed attended Washington State College, which is now Washington State University and houses the Edward R. Murrow College of Communication.

23. Synergy Learning's website is at <http://www.synergylearning.org>.

24. In the 1960s, management expert Peter F. Drucker coined this metaphor (cash cow) to refer to a product or business that can continue to produce profits without further investment and with little maintenance. A dairy cow, for example, can be milked on an ongoing basis with little expense after being acquired. See Peter F. Drucker, *The Frontiers of Management* (New York: Truman Talley, 1986).

25. In 2006, WSU Dean Erich Lear confirmed to me in an e-mail in 2006 that the Murrow College was being used as a cash cow.

26. David Demers, "Revisiting Corporate Newspaper Structure and Profit-Making," *Journal of Media Economics, 11*(2): 19-35 (1998).

27. David Demers, "Structural Pluralism, Corporate Newspaper Structure and News Source Perceptions: Another Test of the Editorial Vigor Hypothesis," *Journalism & Mass Communication Quarterly, 75*: 572-592 (1998).

28. David Demers, "Corporate Newspaper Bashing: Is It Justified?" *Newspaper Research Journal, 20*(1): 83-97 (1999).

29. Ironically, a decade later many of these same scholars, even some neo-Marxists, would bemoan the decline of the large-scale metropolitan newspaper, a victim of increasing competition from new media and cheaper, alternative sources for advertising.

Chapter 24

Censorship, Weak Ties and a Crisis

November 1, 1996
Washington State University

"Have you seen today's *Daily Evergreen*, Professor Demers?" one of my students asked me on November 1, 1996.

"Not yet. Why?"

"The newspaper is blank. The editors say the WSU administration is trying to censor them."

Sure enough, that day's issue of the WSU student newspaper was blank — no text or headlines or pictures, except for advertising and a short front-page commentary about the controversy.

"This is an issue of protest," the commentary stated.[1]

The student editors were angry because the new university general manager of student publications "went back on two of the most important promises made before he was hired: That he would not censor this newspaper, and that he would not attempt to take the student out of Student Publications," the editorial stated.[2]

The new manager, John Contrilman, had asked the newspaper's adviser, Jeff Hand, a university staff employee, to prevent publication of an article about a search for a new university provost. Contrilman's boss, interim provost Geoffrey Gamble, was one of the candidates for the provost position at WSU and had complained to Contrilman about the story.

"That marriage to the administration makes him [Contrilman] a tainted gatekeeper," said *Evergreen* editor-in-chief Isamu Jordan. "As soon as the staff and faculty gets involved, it gets tainted with a lot of politics that shouldn't be in the newspaper."[3]

The student journalists refused to obey Contrilman and published the article about the provost search. Contrilman then suspended Hand for three days.

"He was being punished for our actions," one of the student editors told the Student Press Law Center in Washington, D.C.[4]

Students also were upset because several months earlier Contrilman killed a column that was critical of the residence halls. The column appeared in a special issue distributed to incoming freshman, who were attending summer orientation. Among other things, the column criticized the quality of the food served in the residence halls.

I had been teaching in the WSU program for only two months when the controversy erupted. I didn't know Contrilman very well. He was a former newspaper editor and a professor in WSU's Murrow School.

I was surprised, though, that Contrilman did not seem to recognize the generally accepted "hands-off" norm of advising for student newspapers. But, as I learned at the University of Wisconsin–River Falls, loyalty often trumps principles.

In response to the incident, the Board of Student Publications, which oversaw the newspaper and other student publications, created an ad hoc committee to draft new rules for protecting the First Amendment rights of the students. The members included Contrilman, a law professor in the Murrow School, another staff administrator at the newspaper, two students and myself.

Our committee met a half-dozen times over a three-month period.

Because U.S. courts have ruled that administrators at universities and high schools may, under certain conditions, control the content of student publications that obtain funding from the university, our committee drafted strong language to protect against that.[5]

> Students of Washington State University have the undeniable right as guaranteed by the First Amendment of the U.S. Constitution to speak, write and publish their sentiments freely on all subjects and shall be free from censorship, advance review or approval. Student editors and managers shall be free to develop their own editorial policies regarding news coverage, or content without interference by the university or its administrators, faculty, staff or agencies. ... Washington State University shall make no rule, regulation or policy that abridges students' freedom of speech and of the press.

In terms of the censorship controversy, Ed Murrow no doubt would have sided with the students. But in terms of assessing whether the school or university honors the legacy of Murrow and shows respect for the ideals of the Enlightenment, this incident surely was not enough to indict WSU officials or the Murrow program.

THE NEXT 10 YEARS at WSU were wonderful.

Well, mostly.

Three months after I arrived, I attended a conference of newspaper publishers in Seattle. My goal was to try to reconnect the Murrow journalism program to the professional community.

But the newspaper publishers were giving me the cold shoulder.

I asked Frank Blethen, publisher of the *Seattle Times*, if he knew why the publishers were less than eager to interact with me. Blethen's response to my question hit me like a blind-sided punch.

"Don't you know?" he said. "You've got a Ph.D."

"You're kidding. The publishers here dislike me because I have a Ph.D.? What about the fact that I worked as a newspaper reporter? Doesn't that count?"

"Not really," Blethen responded. "WSU's decision to hire you as well as another Ph.D. in the journalism school this year instead of a professional sent a bad message to the publishers. Let me give you some background."

During the 10 minutes that were left in the break, Blethen tried to summarize three decades of the relationship between the University of Washington, WSU's big sibling institution in Seattle, and the Pacific Northwest newspaper industry.

Publishers were angry because over the years UW had been replacing professional faculty — faculty with significant experience in journalism — with Ph.D. research professors, many of whom had little or no professional experience. There was, of course, too much history to cram into that short period of time.

But the message was clear: Publishers were angry because UW administrators were de-professionalizing the mass communication programs at UW. In fact, the administrators were planning to eliminate the professional programs in advertising, public relations and broadcasting. Print journalism would be saved partly because of strong support from Blethen and other newspaper publishers attending this conference.

The situation at the University of Washington was nearly identical to what happened at The Ohio State University in the 1980s.

As the 1996–97 school year came to a close, it did not appear to me that Director Tan or WSU administrators were trying to eliminate the mass communication programs. In fact, they were encouraging more students to enroll, because that translated into a bigger cash cow.

But my attempts to improve relations with the professional community fell flat. A year later I spoke to the publishers and argued that journalistic skills and mass media theory were compatible, but my message was not warmly received. It was too late to repair the damage. And soon the publishers would turn their attention toward preserving their organizations, as competition from the internet and cable news systems cut deeply into their bottom lines.

Meanwhile, mass communication scholars would soon face their own crisis — a crisis of relevance.

THE REVEREND JESSE JACKSON entered the hotel banquet room, embraced the lectern, and preached about the struggles and successes of the civil rights movement.

At one point, he told his audience of more than a thousand journalism and mass communication professors that people often asked him how he could remain optimistic when so many of the movement's goals remained unfulfilled.

"Because," he said, "the civil rights movement has achieved many of its goals and has had a significant impact on public policy."

The audience of mostly liberal professors attending the annual meeting of the Association for Education in Journalism and Mass Communication at the Chicago Marriott gave him a standing ovation. I was among them.

It was August 8, 1997.

After Jackson left the room, former Illinois Senator Paul Simon, who was a professor of political science at Southern Illinois University in Carbondale, and five leading scholars in the field of mass communication — including Steven Chaffee of Stanford University — took the stage.[6]

The purpose of the panel was to comment on the impact of mass communication research on public policy.[7] But in striking contrast to the upbeat presentation of Jackson, the panelists were unable to identify examples of mass communication research having a significant impact on public policy. In fact, the discussion focused more on the lack of impact.

"Chaffee tried really hard," said my boss Alex Tan, who was president of AEJMC at the time and organizer of the panel, years later.[8]

Unfortunately — or perhaps fortunately for the panelists — the session ended early, because Jackson had used more than his allotted time.

At the time, I was nose-deep into my research, because I was scheduled to go up for promotion and tenure in less than two years.

But I couldn't stop thinking about that session.

It reminded me of my days in the early 1980s, when I was a master's student in criminology and sociology at The Ohio State University. If the panel had been composed of criminologists, they, too, would have been at a loss to produce evidence that their research was having much of an impact on solving the crime problem.[9]

In time, I might have forgotten about the plenary session conducted after Jackson's speech. After all, there is no great incentive for social scientists like me to question the value of what we do. We all assume that the research we conduct is important to society, and scholars who question that assumption undoubtedly invite criticism from their colleagues, no matter how much evidence they amass.[10]

But curiosity — a trait that journalism helped drive into me in the 1970s — kept this possible sanction at bay. *Is it possible that mass media researchers, and social scientists in general, are incapable of having a significant impact on public policy or on solving social problems? Are they failing to fulfill the goals of the Enlightenment?*

Those questions would eventually become part of my research program. But in the fall of 1997, I faced another problem central to the Enlightenment: a police department that refused to give public information to my students.

Chapter 24 Endnotes

1. Richard Roesler, "WSU Students Print Blank Newspaper: Evergreen's Student Editors Protest Alleged Censorship by Administrator," *Spokesman-Review* (November 2, 1996), retrieved December 3, 2012, from <http://www.spokesman.com/stories/1996/nov/02/wsu-students-print-blank-newspaper-evergreens>.

2. Staff Report, "Paper Publishes Blank Copy: Editors Protest Adviser's Censorship Policies," *Student Press Law Center Report Magazine*, 18 (1) (Winter 1996-97), p. 22.

3. Isamu Jordan committed suicide on Sept. 5, 2013, according to Jess Walter, a colleague who worked with Jordan at the *Spokesman-Review* in Spokane, Washington. Jordan was 37, married and father of two children. SR editor Anne Walter said Isamu suffered from severe depression. She and husband Jess, an award-wining writer of nonfiction and fiction works, were godparents to his children. Jordan worked at the *Spokesman-Review* until he was laid off with other reporters in a downsizing in 2008. Source: "Spokane Musician, Writer Isamu Jordan Dies at 37," *Spokesman-Review* (Sept. 6, 2013), retrieved Sept. 28, 2013, from <https://www.spokesman.com/stories/2013/sep/06/isamu-jordan-spokane-dj-and-entertainment-writer>.

4. Ibid.

5. Ted McDonough, "New Policy Leaves Students in Charge at Evergreen," *Moscow-Pullman Daily News* (April 2, 1998), p. 8A.

6. The other panelists were Sharon Dunwoody of the University of Wisconsin–Madison, Oscar Gandy and George Gerbner of the University of Pennsylvania, and Ellen Wartella of the University of Texas at Austin

7. Everette Dennis, who was at the time executive director of the Freedom Forum, moderated the panel. I contacted him and several members of the panel but they were not able to recall much detail from the session. Chaffee and Simon have died since the panel was conducted, but I did contact Chaffee shortly after the session and he provided more comments about the issue. See Chapter 26.

8. Personal conversation in fall 2008.

9. See Chapter 16 for more details.

10. Some of my colleagues have refused to respond to my questions about the relevance of social scientific research in terms of its impact on public policy.

Chapter 25
Democracy Foiled Again

September 1997
Washington State University

"Professor Demers, the Pullman Police are refusing to give us access to incident reports," one my reporting students told me one day in September 1997.

Not again, I whined, remembering my experience with the Minneapolis Police.[1]

As is customary in an introductory reporting class, I assigned the students to cover the police beat and write up basic stories about car accidents, thefts, drunken driving arrests, and disorderly conduct arrests.

Several days later students reported that the police refused to give them the names of the people who filed the complaints, the victim's names and addresses, and factual information about the complaints and offenders. In one case, the police were refusing to release the name of a woman who had been found dead in her home several days earlier. Police would only provide a complaint number and a brief statement about this and other incidents.

At the time, several journalists and one faculty member told me that the state of Washington had the most liberal open-access public records law in the country. How, then, could Pullman police justify refusing to give my students access to basic information that journalists routinely use to write up police stories?

I wrote to the police chief and pleaded my case before city council.

But the city continued to withhold basic information about the reports. To me, this was even more insidious than my experience with the Minneapolis Police Department, because these were routine police reports, not internal affairs criminal complaint records.

So, in October 1997, I filed a freedom of information lawsuit in Superior Court. The Associated Press covered the story.

WSU PROF SUES POLICE OVER ACCESS TO REPORTS

> A college professor has sued the Pullman Police Department for records that he claims are being unfairly withheld from students seeking them for a class assignment.

"Like I told my students, now you know what it's like dealing with bureaucracies," a frustrated David Demers said Tuesday. "All we want to do is cover the police beat. Why are they making it so hard?"[2]

The city attorney told the reporter that the police had complied with the students' request for information. But the records failed to include things like when the crime occurred, victims' names, or what was taken in thefts. State law required that this information be made available for public inspection.

About a month after I filed the lawsuit, however, the Washington Supreme Court ruled, in a separate case, that police have the authority to withhold any information from police records they consider to be part of "active" or "open" investigations.[3] The case involved the investigatory records connected to the 1969 assassination of Edwin Pratt, a civil rights leader in Seattle.[4] A freelance writer was investigating the unsolved murder and wanted access to the records. But the high court ruled police could even withhold newspaper articles and other public documents in the files.

So much for the country's most liberal open-access law.

I immediately dropped my lawsuit and instructed the students to cover the campus police instead. WSU Police were very cooperative and provided access to all of the information students needed to cover their stories.

I explained to the students that bureaucracies often try to monopolize information, because that is a major source of their power.[5] Journalists and citizens often have difficulty getting information from state and public bureaucracies, but a democratic society depends upon it. And that's one of the most important roles of the press: to ensure government is accountable to the people.

This was a step back for the Enlightenment.

As was the process of hiring of a new dean.

IN THE FALL 1997, a search was on to replace the dean of the College of Liberal Arts, who resigned to accept an administrative position at another university.

As is the case with most searches, university administrators and faculty began the process with declarations that the search would be conducted in a fair, impartial, objective and democratic fashion.

Academics pride themselves on process.

Process also is the lifeblood of the Enlightenment project, which places a high value on democratic decision-making. The means to an end is just as important as the ends themselves.

In fact, Stephen Joel Trachtenberg, the retired president of George Washington University, even contends that faculty are more committed to process and tradition than to outcomes. "Faculty generally do not see themselves as responsible for proposing new institutional departures," he writes in his memoir. "Rather, they see themselves as guardians of tradition. ... They are more committed to process and less committed to outcomes."[6]

Many faculty would challenge Trachtenberg's proposition.

But with respect to this job search, one WSU administrator clearly fit the reverse proposition: She was less concerned with process and more concerned with outcomes.

The WSU dean search committee, which was composed of both female and male faculty and administrators, rank-ordered the candidates. The top five would be brought in for interviews.

All turned out to be men.

The highest-ranking woman was ninth.

The provost, who was a woman and to whom the new dean would report, demanded that at least one of the candidates brought in for an interview be a woman.

The committee agreed.

Four male candidates and one female candidate were interviewed.

But the committee didn't like any of them, including the woman, and recommended that a new search be conducted the following year.

That wasn't acceptable to the provost.

She hired the woman.[7]

Needless to say, this angered some faculty, but, to the best of my knowledge, no one filed a formal protest or complaint. Despite their image as independent, outspoken people, most faculty are reluctant to challenge administrators, fearing retribution even though the faculty manual allegedly protects such speech.

History would repeat itself in 2007, when WSU circumvented "process" again in the hiring of a new president, Elson Floyd (see Chapter 32).

In the world of university politics, process and democratic decision-making are often sacrificed for other ideals or objectives, so much so that one can easily be convinced that decision-making in universities is better characterized as autocratic than democratic.

THE HIRING of the new dean in winter 1998 opened the door for the Murrow faculty to seek independence from the College of Liberal Arts. The logic was that maybe the new dean, unlike the old dean, would be amenable to new ideas.

By this time, most Murrow faculty were aware that other universities of our stature were getting far more funding per student. In fact, a comparison I conducted with other programs across the country showed that the Murrow School employed about 50 percent fewer faculty and had 50 percent less funding than other comparable programs nationwide.[8]

"Ed Murrow no doubt would turn over in his grave if he knew," one faculty member said when I presented the statistics.[9]

At a faculty retreat, Murrow faculty decided to do something about it: They voted unanimously to become a College of Communication or an independent school, which would report directly to the provost's office and presumably get more funding.

Of course, as expected, the new dean of liberal arts rejected the recommendation. She also denied allegations that the Murrow School was being used as a cash cow.

"Then why not let us become our own college?" was our collective response.

"Because you're not big enough — you don't have enough faculty," was the standard response from administrators for the next decade.

Catch-22.

We don't have enough faculty because the college is underfunding us, and we can't get enough faculty because we're being used as a cash cow for the college.

Later, another new dean would confirm in writing that the Murrow School was a cash cow for the college.[10] But, in the meantime, the plan for college status was lifeless. The Murrow faculty did not push the administration. A formal protest and fight would have required the expenditure of political capital, and most faculty do not have the stomach for that. I, too, was among the sheep, because I was working hard to ensure I would be tenured in 1999.

Although faculty have a fair degree of control over the curriculum (a process that is somewhat democratic), they have relatively little input or power over the budgetary process and other administrative decisions. In fact, during the 16 years I worked as a professor at WSU, administrators never once presented a detailed Murrow budget to faculty. The process of setting budgets is top-down and done behind closed doors, with the exception of a few public hearings, which makes the process appear to be more democratic than it really is.

THE LACK OF FUNDING for the Murrow School was a problem that wouldn't go away during the 1998–1999 school year. Administrators had nixed the idea of increasing funding for the Murrow programs. But I knew of another way to extract resources.

National accreditation.

I learned this at the University of Wisconsin–River Falls.

The criteria for obtaining accreditation is usually set by nonprofit organizations that represent the interests of a real-world profession as well as in the academy. These criteria include minimum standards for teaching, classroom size, research, service, diversity (ethnic and racial), scholarships, and internships. Schools that meet these criteria are "accredited." Those that don't lose accreditation or are put on probation.

Accreditation in journalism and mass communication is not mandatory. But to obtain it, an academic unit has to prove that it has the resources to provide a high-quality education. Accreditation site teams always find problems in a program, and the solution almost always calls for more funding.

Administrators, not wanting to be accused of opposing "quality education," rarely oppose the allocation of funds to a program that seeks accreditation.

I suppose I could be accused of being Machiavellian here.[11]

But I viewed my role as a professor as one of attempting to create the best possible educational program for students, and that means drawing upon all possible strategies to fight for a fair share of the financial pie.

The accrediting authority in mass communication is the Accrediting Council on Education in Journalism and Mass Communication,[12] the same group that visited UW–RF when I was there. Most of the top-rated journalism and mass communication programs are accredited.[13]

None of the mass communication programs at WSU (print journalism, broadcasting, public relations or advertising) had ever been accredited. And there were some serious problems in the print journalism curriculum.

One of the most notable was that many of our graduates were not good writers. One factor contributing to this problem is that our program did not offer enough writing courses. Most students took an intro general writing course and two reporting courses. That was it.

Another factor was that most students weren't allowed to take their first reporting course until their junior year. Two years was not enough time to turn them into good writers.

The curriculum required students to take a series of five general mass communication courses and to certify for the major. Only one of those courses involved intensive writing.

In the meantime, freshmen and sophomores who were really interested in a print journalism career were working at the student newspaper, the *Daily Evergreen*, where they were picking up bad habits. This included the dreaded "no-content lead," in which a hard-news story begins with a statement that contains no real news value.

But getting bylines in the *Evergreen* seemed to confirm for many students that they didn't need to take the writing courses during their junior and senior years. They were, in their own minds, already journalists. "Why do I have to take these classes?"

The negative attitude toward classes was a major problem at WSU, as well as a lot of other journalism programs where students are not allowed to take writing courses in their early college years. The problem was minimal at the University of Wisconsin–River Falls, because students there took their first writing course freshman year.

In spring 1998, I proposed to journalism faculty that we change the curriculum to allow students to take a reporting course during their first semester sophomore year and that we seek formal accreditation.

I thought the idea would be warmly embraced. After all, it would mean more money and a better reputation for the Murrow School.

But Murrow faculty rejected the idea.

"But you can use accreditation to get more money from the college," I pleaded. They refused to change their minds.

"The real reason most faculty reject accreditation is that they are afraid that there won't be enough money for the graduate program," one faculty member told me later. "They are more concerned about their own research programs and working with graduate students than in improving the quality of the undergraduate program."

Maybe it was impossible to have both accreditation and a high-quality graduate program, but I didn't think so. Without accreditation, though, one thing was certain: The Murrow School would have a difficult time arguing that it provided the highest-quality education to its students.

As the years passed, I tried several more times to get the Murrow faculty to see the importance of accreditation, but to no avail. In 2007, I submitted a formal plan for seeking accreditation and other changes to improve the quality of the journalism program. That, of course, led to *Demers v. Austin*, a story to be picked up in depth in later chapters.

Meanwhile, I was granted tenure in spring 1999, which was my third full year at WSU. Normally, tenure candidates go up in their sixth year. The university gave me three years credit for the five years I previously taught full-time at the University of Wisconsin and University of Minnesota.

By this time, I had published three scholarly books, 18 first or sole-authored peer-reviewed journal articles and one coedited book, and earned five conference paper awards.

Most of my scholarship was theoretical.

But soon I would alter my research program in a way to make it more policy friendly.

Chapter 25 Endnotes

1. See Chapter 19.
2. "WSU Prof Sues Police Over Access to Reports," Associated Press (November 20, 1997).
3. *David Newman v. King County*, 133 Wn.2d 565; 947 P.2d 712; 1997 Wash. Lexis 805.
4. The case was never solved.
5. Pullman Police never fully explained why they refused to release the records. One theory was that the department was angry because students didn't follow a strict protocol that they had created for releasing information to student journalists. This is probably the best explanation, because one broadcast faculty member in the Murrow School who was friends with many of the people at City Hall said his students never had difficulty obtaining access to the records.
6. Stephen Joel Trachtenberg, *Big Man on Campus: A University President Speaks Out on Higher Education* (New York: Touchstone, 2008), p. 111.
7. The woman went on to become president of another university.
8. See David Demers, "The More You Give WSU's Communication School, The More It Loses: Writer Urges Donors to Put Funds into Escrow Until School Achieves College-Level Status" (unpublished commentary, Spokane, WA, June 2003).
9. But, of course, the university did not publicly reveal this information. It continued to promote the school as being "one of the best communication programs" in the United States, and the affiliation with Murrow helped sustain that perception.
10. Dean Erich Lear confirmed that the Murrow School was a cash cow for the college on two separate occasions: one in an e-mail to me and another in an e-mail to a university official who asked whether "Demers was right" about the school being a "cash cow." Of course, Lear offered little in the way of support to help the Murrow School become independent, telling faculty at a meeting that the school did not have enough faculty or resources to become independent. But several years later he and the provost both did an about-face and supported independence after the new president of the university, Elson Floyd, decided to turn the Murrow School into a college. At a faculty meeting, the interim Murrow School director then issued a statement thanking the dean for his help on turning the school into a college. "I wanted to put my finger down my throat," one faculty member told me later.
11. Machiavelli (born Niccolò di Bernardo dei Machiavelli) was an Italian Renaissance philosopher and politician (1469-1527) whom scholars consider to be one of the founders of modern political science. His enduring work, *The Prince*, provides a list of methods that an "aspiring prince" can use to acquire and maintain power. Machiavelli argues that the greatest moral good is a stable state, and actions to protect that stability are justified even if they are cruel and brutal. See Niccolò Machiavelli, *The Prince*, translated by N. H. Thomson. (New York: P. F. Collier & Son, 2001). *The Prince* was first published in 1532, five years after Machiavelli's death.
12. The organization's website is <http://www2.ku.edu/~acejmc>.
13. They include Arizona State University, University of Missouri, Northwestern University, University of California at Berkeley (graduate program in journalism), University of Florida, University of Illinois, Indiana University, University of Iowa, Louisiana State University, University of Minnesota, Columbia University (graduate program), and Syracuse University.

Chapter 26

An 'Enlightened' Research Program

May 1999
San Francisco

The professor from a Southern university glanced at me and smiled moments before he began speaking. "In contrast to the research just presented by Dr. Demers," he said, "I am going to argue for and test a theoretical model which holds that corporate media are hegemonic institutions of control."

A few grins emerged on the dozen or so scholars in the audience.

The presenter and I were two participants in a paper session at the International Communication Association conference in San Francisco in May 1999.

I had just finished presenting a paper titled, "Corporate Newspaper Structure and Control of Editorial Content: An Empirical Test of the Managerial Revolution Hypothesis."[1] Not exactly the kind of topic that would generate interesting conversation at a cocktail party.

But the paper had implications for public policy.

It suggested that, contrary to conventional wisdom,[2] power and control of newspapers and other news organizations actually becomes more decentralized as they grow and become more structurally complex. Creating policies or rules that inhibited such growth could actually lead to more, not less, centralization of power and decision-making.[3]

Needless to say, this conclusion was controversial, because the vast majority of scholars and professionals in mass communication — including the presenter in that room that day — believe corporate media imperil democratic principles and good journalism.

But here's the odd thing: His research actually showed that news media under corporate ownership produce content that is MORE, not less, diverse.

The inconsistency between what his research found and what he was saying did not go unnoticed. During the question-and-answer period at the end of the session, the presenter continued to defend his approach until someone from the audience spoke up: "But your data support Professor Demers' model."

A few people chuckled.

I suppose I should have been one of them. But I was dumbfounded. Here was a scholar whose data supported my theory but who continued to argue the opposite. *Aren't social scientists supposed to be open-minded?*

THAT INCIDENT at ICA was the beginning of the end of my decade-long program of empirical research on corporate media and the beginning of new research program, one that aligned more closely with the Enlightenment project.

That ICA conference session opened my eyes to a new truth: No matter how much empirical data I could produce to support my model, I probably would never convince professors who already held an opposing view of corporate media.

Facts do not speak for themselves.

Science is discourse and politics, as philosopher Thomas Kuhn,[4] sociologist Jeffrey Alexander,[5] and many others have pointed out.

The history of science and politics is filled with many examples of ideology trumping facts.[6] My story was no exception.

Instead of trying to change the minds of my scholarly colleagues, I decided a better approach was to write more books and other materials targeted not just to academics but to students, citizens and policymakers — people who presumably would be easier to influence because they had not already taken a position on an issue.

I initiated the process by signing a contract with Pearson Education, a major academic publisher, to write an introductory mass communication book.

I also decided to write a book that would examine the impact of social science research on public policy and try to find ways to increase it. This line of research was prompted in part by the plenary session in Chicago — when mass communication scholars had a difficult time producing evidence that their research influenced the public policymaking process.

At conferences, in e-mails and in telephone conversations, I began asking my colleagues about the role and function of social science. I would tease them with the following scenario:

> Imagine a world without physics, chemistry, mathematics, and biology. Technology, as we know it, would cease to progress or even exist. No electricity, running water, sewage treatment, gasoline, roads, modern farming techniques.
>
> Similarly, imagine a world without research on diseases and new medicines. If the medical sciences were eliminated from the academy, we would

have no new doctors, nurses, drugs, treatments. Lives would be directly and immediately affected.

Now imagine a world in which literature, art, theater, dance, music, linguistics ... and philosophy are no longer taught or critiqued in an institution of higher learning. Although the humanities may have a difficult time showing how they have a direct impact on social problems or public policy, they have always been able to justify themselves in inspirational terms — or as a "secular religion." After all, who hasn't felt inspired or moved by a quality piece of literature or art? That could be enough to justify an entire discipline.

But now imagine the world without the social sciences — a world without sociology, political science, communication research, economics, social history, or cultural anthropology as formal disciplines in the university. How much would that impact people and society? Could the world survive without the social sciences?

None of the two dozen or so colleagues to whom I posed these questions were able to respond with a good argument to defend the social sciences. To be fair, I didn't give them much time to think about it. Most had never envisioned the world without the social sciences. They always assumed that what they do is important to society. How could it be otherwise?

But few would have disagreed with the comments of Peter Demerath, associate professor of educational policy and administration at the University of Minnesota, to whom I posed the same question some years later:

> What would happen if we eliminated the social sciences? A haunting question for social scientists, no doubt. I don't think I would disagree there are very large and haunting questions for knowledge transmission and ... utilization, and probably all of this was slowed in the big picture by the postmodern critique of knowledge and the extent to which knowledge is possible. ... So ... yeah, you have hit upon something that is quite important.[7]

To be clear, I did not begin the research process with the assumption that the social sciences are incapable of generating knowledge meaningful to the policy-making process. I believed they do.

The bigger problem, as Demerath pointed out, was the "transmission" and "utilization" of knowledge.

Did policymakers really use the knowledge that was being generated, and did that knowledge help solve problems?

This was the question that drove part of my research program for the next decade. I began reading about the impact of social science research on public policy, and I began collecting newspaper clippings of stories about social science. I e-mailed and talked with scores of scholars in the fields of communication, sociology, education, economics and political science.[8]

Results of this initial stage of research were not encouraging. It showed that social science generally has little impact on public policy or on solving social problems — a point that social scientists who actually study the policymaking process had already been making for more than two decades.[9] As University of Illinois law and political science professor Robert F. Rich put it in the late 1970s:[10]

> Scientists, philosophers, and sociologists have argued that social change is directly related to changes in modes of knowing. ... But with the exception of studies carried out during World War II, the influence of the social sciences as a field and social scientists as experts was limited. The field developed as an autonomous social system and it continued as such with minimum regard for its social utility.[11]

Public administration professor Cheol H. Oh expressed similar sentiments in 1996:[12]

> Despite the tremendous increase in attention to the importance of information in the decision-making process, recent research indicates that governmental policymakers make little use of information;[13] at best, social science research findings alter policymakers' understandings and/or definitions of policy problems over a long period of time (the "conceptual use").[14]

In short, the consensus among those who had studied the impact of social science research is that research plays a relatively minor role in public policy decision-making processes.

One reason for this is that policymakers are turned off by the jargon of social science. Another, more important reason, is that policymakers are driven more by ideology than science. Facts are far less important than what "my party, my constituents or the special interests say."[15]

Many policymakers, especially conservatives, even harbor an outright dislike of university researchers, believing their research has little relevance to solving real world problems. The literature also directed some of the blame to social scientists themselves, who, it is said, are often reluctant to become involved in policymaking processes and believe their role ends with the generation of knowledge.

This head-in-the-sand position raises some difficult ethical questions. If policymakers ignore social scientific research and make decisions that harm people, do social scientists have a moral obligation to intervene? Should scientists help make the world a better place? Or is the search for knowledge simply an end in itself?

NOW, A REASONABLY intelligent person might think social scientists would have been concerned and upset that their research had so little impact on public policy.
 But they weren't in the late 1990s (nor are they today).
 Most of the professors I spoke with said their role was not to set public policy, but to produce the research. If policymakers didn't use that knowledge, then that was their problem. They also pointed out that their universities do not reward them for influencing public policy, but for publishing refereed journal articles and books.
 They had a damn good point.
 Why would anyone be motivated to do something that isn't likely to be rewarded?
 But what about professors who are rewarded for producing applied research? Do they feel they are making a difference?
 I put that question to Darío Menanteau-Horta, a professor in the School of Social Work at the University of Minnesota.
 "No," he said. "I think that they would say they are not having enough impact. They would like to have more impact, but the problem is that some of them don't have the conceptual or theoretical tools to have a greater impact."[16]
 Menanteau-Horta said he became a social scientist because he wanted to help make a difference in his own country, Chile. He worked in a rural sociology unit at Minnesota for many years.
 However, he said "the social sciences have failed keep up with the times and some of the theoretical tools are not well equipped to deal with social complexity." As a consequence, even applied research units such as that at Minnesota have had a relatively weak impact on public policy, he said.
 Yet, during the 1990s, there was no significant national debate about the role of social science research in public policymaking, nor is there one now. Part of the problem is that the social sciences themselves do not define solving social problems as the ultimate goal of social science. Research universities emphasize publications, not results.[17] In fact, some faculty are not even rewarded in annual reviews for producing research or scholarship that tries to educate or influence the public or policymakers.
 A comment I frequently heard from faculty is that "we get no rewards for writing books or articles that try to inform the public and policymakers about what we are doing. Publish in academic journals or perish." This state of affairs helps fuel the criticism that most of the activities and practices of social scientists are better characterized as ritualistic than strategic, meaning they have no more impact on

solving social problems than the act of throwing rice over the bride and groom has on conception.[18]

But perhaps I was being overly critical.

Maybe these conclusions don't apply to all of the social sciences.

To test this idea, I suggested to my colleagues at the Association for Education in Journalism and Mass Communication (AEJMC) that they use the impact theme as the topic of their plenary session at their annual convention in Phoenix in 2000. They liked the idea and asked me, a member of the AEJMC Research Committee, to organize it.

So I did.

"DOES JOURNALISM and Mass Communication Research Matter?"[19]

That was the title I gave to the plenary session I was moderating in August 2000 at the AEJMC annual meeting in Phoenix.

I had asked Robert F. Rich, a leading expert in the field of science and public policy, to join three mass communication scholars on the panel.[20] They were Theodore Glasser, a professor of communication at Stanford University; Kasisomayajula Viswanath, an associate professor of mass communication at The Ohio State University who had just accepted a new job as a researcher at the National Cancer Institute (and who later became a research professor at Harvard University); and Joanne Cantor, a professor of communication arts at the University of Wisconsin–Madison (now retired).

About three hundred professors attended — far fewer than the thousand who came to see Jesse Jackson three years earlier. But I was still impressed, given that none of us was a national celebrity.

As moderator, I began the session with a brief discussion about what happened in Chicago in 1997 and then added:

> Public policy studies show that social science research plays a relatively limited role in public policy decision-making. ... If research has relatively little impact on public policy, then what can be its expected impact on solving social problems like poverty, malnutrition, poor health care, child abuse, crime, drug abuse, and discrimination?

In contrast to the 1997 conference, the panelists provided at least two examples of the impact of social science research. Viswanath said research played a key role from the 1950s onward in raising awareness about the hazards of smoking cigarettes and the causes of cardiovascular disease. He pointed out that increased public awareness saved lives.

After the session, one member of the audience said that doctors and medical scientists played a much bigger role in influencing the public agenda than social scientists. He pointed out that mass media give far more coverage to medical scholars and physicians than to social scientists.

But Viswanath had noted that the process through which social science influences public policy is often complex, involving an interplay among medical researchers, social scientists, public policymakers and social activists.

Cantor, an expert on television and its impact on children, said her research in the 1990s contributed to the development of a content-based rating system for television programs and the V-chip, a computer hardware device in television sets that allowed parents to restrict what their children watch. But she conceded most parents don't use it.

She pointed out that during the 1990s she spent more time writing materials that reached out to other audiences, including doctors and the general public. For example, she published a book called *Mommy, I'm Scared*[21] and wrote articles for *Family Circle* and *Our Children* magazines.

However, Cantor conceded that "academia does not usually weigh these forms of public service very heavily in merit and tenure decisions." She pointed out that even though her university rewarded her for publishing a book that reached a broad audience, "there are subtle ways in which our field looks down on the popularization of one's work."

After the plenary session, one attendee pointed out that even though communication scholars may have influenced legislation on the television ratings system, they have been relatively powerless to do anything about the amount of sex and violence on television.

Indeed, more than 70 percent of children's shows and nearly 60 percent of other shows contain at least one act of violence.[22] Moreover, some evidence shows that the amount of violence is increasing,[23] even though one of the most strongly documented findings in the history of research on media is that children who watch violent programming on television have a substantially higher risk of engaging in aggressive behavior.[24]

Unlike Viswanath and Cantor, Glasser didn't provide examples of research affecting public policy. His comments involved a critique of motives or reasons that social scientists employ to study the world. Many researchers, he said, do not understand or appreciate the political interests behind their research. The implication was that a lot of research is used to help powerful corporations or governments make more money or control people.

Years later Glasser also told me via e-mail that "I like to think that my work in and beyond the classroom makes a difference in the practice of journalism. But who knows? It's a difficult thing to monitor. Does inspiring one journalist count as evidence of influence? Does changing one editor's mind matter?"[25]

Robert F. Rich, the non-media professor of the plenary group, pointed out that government and science, including social science, historically worked under the assumption that science would produce knowledge and policymakers would use that knowledge to address particular problems or issues.

But government began to question the utility of this social contract[26] in the 1960s, according to Rich. "What is the return on our investment? What is the utility of the research that is being financed out of public funds? There seemed to be a growing feeling that funded research should ... have utility and that researchers applying for government funding should address the question: How is this information going to be used?"

Although the U.S. government has spent billions of dollars on social scientific research, Rich pointed out that the governmental and scientific "cultures" have a "deep distrust for each other."

One consequence is that policymakers often ignore that research.

There are many reasons for this, including poor communication and a policy-making bias that elevates ideology over facts. Research also shows, Rich pointed out, that the source of the information (e.g., a trusted aide versus an unknown social scientist) is far more important than the quality of information itself.

However, Rich's research has shown that social scientists are most likely to have an impact on public policy when policymakers themselves specifically request their advice or when the research fits into the ideological needs of the policymakers. This proposition was the main conclusion of his 1981 book, *Social Science Information and Public Policy Making*, which was reprinted shortly after the Phoenix plenary session.[27] Rich found that if the research information promoted the ideological interests of the policymakers or could advance the career of a staffer within the policy-making organization, then its probability of influencing the policymaking process was enhanced.

These findings and others have helped debunk the "rational" model of knowledge effects, or the idea that policymakers will make decisions based upon knowledge that social scientists create.[28]

NEEDLESS TO SAY, the plenary did little to quell my concerns about the relevance of social science in solving social problems or impacting public policy.

Although it was clear that social science can and does have an impact on public policy, its impact is far less than what it could or should be, as Cantor pointed out.

Other scholars I spoke with agreed.

Social scientists can play a key role in identifying or legitimating social problems. Some mentioned the progress that has been made in reducing racial discrimination, although that assumption was called into question during the presidency of Donald Trump.

But most of the credit for ameliorating social problems goes not to the social scientists who study them but to social activists like Jesse Jackson and to social movements like the National Association for the Advancement of Colored People. Playing an active role in the political arena is crucial.

Although such movements can and do draw upon social science research, I could not find a scholar who could identify a clear example of social science research playing the lead role in the political process or in resolving a social problem. In fact, years later I attended a journalism historians conference in Seattle, where a panel of four media historians was examining media coverage of racism from the 1930s to the 1950s, and I asked each of them whether they had, in their research, found any evidence showing that professors at local universities played any role in the civil rights struggles at that time.

None had.[29]

The best defense of the academy I could find came from the late mass communication scholar Steven Chaffee, who was a member of the first plenary in 1997 and was now, in 2000, distinguished professor of communication at the University of California, Santa Barbara. After briefly tracing the history of violence in mass media, he wrote in an e-mail to me:

> [A]t least the research findings on effects of media violence are not being dismissed as the work of a small claque of goody-goodies. They are given wide credence in our society. I notice that a lot of high school kids believe that TV violence is bad for them and for their peers and siblings. If norms must underlie policy shifts, as a lot of social scientists argue, this is an area of success to me. ... We tend to underestimate the influence of our research because we look for dramatic and controversial policy pronouncements from on high. If we look at how people conduct their life and work, we can often see the results of the research in action.[30]

Chaffee's point is valid.

The field of policy studies has created two concepts to refer to the idea that the impact of social science research is either long-term or indirect.

The first is called the serendipity rationale, which is the idea that at the time the research is done, the researchers have no idea how it might be used, but someday somebody finds something that can be applied somewhere. The second is the enlightenment argument, or the idea that social science research does not lead directly to policy decisions but broadens the understanding of policymakers and therefore makes some positive contribution.

Although the enlightenment argument is comforting to defenders of social science, Cornell University professor William Foote Whyte points out that "some works of fiction also offer enlightenment."[31] (Actually, a lot of fiction does.)

But is the enlightenment argument strong enough to appease taxpayers, whose tax dollars often support research? I don't know about other people, but I would not be satisfied if scholars tried to justify their roles by arguing that their research has "serendipitous," "enlightening," or "subtle" impacts.

I spent the next decade studying the impact of social science research on public policy and writing materials and creating service projects that were geared toward educating students and the general public about research in the social sciences. The pinnacle of that process was my 2011 book, *The Ivory Tower of Babel: Why the Social Sciences Are Failing to Live Up to Their Promises.*[32]

In the early 2000s, meanwhile, I began the process of creating a nonprofit center to promote research on the origins and effects of global mass media. The Center for Global Media Studies sponsored two international conferences, published an edited book of papers from the conferences,[33] and published a 12-to-28-page newsletter every three months for five years.

I would spend $25,000 of my own money to help fund the center. This included creating a book publishing company called Marquette Books that paid the costs of printing up the conference book.

The plan was to make the center self-supporting. It was never able to achieve that goal, even though it did raise about $60,000 on its own, through conference registration fees, membership fees, donations and sales of books. I was unable to obtain a big grant from a foundation.

The grant-making process, I learned, doesn't work from the bottom up; it works from the top down. Most of the agencies giving grants, especially the private foundations, already have their own "world" and if your "world" doesn't fit precisely with their "world," then you're "worlds apart" or, to be more blunt, "shit out of luck."

But the center did accomplish its goal of producing and distributing knowledge about global mass communication. That was enough for me.

Chapter 26 Endnotes

1. David Demers and Debra Merskin, "Corporate Newspaper Structure and Control of Editorial Content: An Empirical Test of the Managerial Revolution Hypothesis," paper presented at the May 1999 International Communication Association conference in San Francisco (May 1999). A revised version of the paper was published in *World Futures*. See David Demers, "Who Controls the Editorial Content at Corporate News Organizations? An Empirical Test of the Managerial Revolution Hypothesis," *World Futures: The Journal of General Evolution, 57*: 103-123 (2001).

2. The term *conventional wisdom*, which means generally accepted belief or opinion about a particular matter, has been around since 1850, but came into popular usage in the 1950s after publication of economist John Kenneth Galbraith's book, *The Affluent Society* (New York: Houghton Mifflin Co, 1958).

3. My paper hypothesized that publishers and owners would have less control over editorial content as a newspaper becomes more "corporatized, because of increasing role specialization. As an organization becomes more complex, publishers and owners increasingly focus on other goals, leaving the editorial decisions to professional journalists." The data — which were based on a national probability survey of newspaper publishers, owners, editors and reporters — showed that publishers and owners play less of a role in deciding what kind of stories to cover and story placement the more their organization exhibit the characteristics of the corporate form of organization. For a summary of this and other research which shows that corporate media structure may enhance democratic processes, see David Demers, *History and Future of Mass Media: An Integrated Perspective* (Cresskill, NJ: Hampton Press, 2007).

4. Thomas S. Kuhn, *The Structure of Scientific Revolutions* (Chicago: University of Chicago Press, 1962).

5. Jeffrey Alexander, "The New Theoretical Movement," pp. 77-101 in Neil J. Smelser (editor), *Handbook of Sociology* [Newbury Park, CA; Sage, 1988]).

6. Jonathan M. Gitlin, "Does Ideology Trump Facts? Studies Say It Often Does," *Ars Technica* (September 24, 2008), retrieved November 9, 2008, from <http://arstechnica.com/news.ars/post/20080924-does-ideology-trump-facts-studies-say-it-often-does.html>.

7. The interview with Peter Demerath, associate professor of educational policy and administration and professor of education, was conducted October 22, 2008.

8. My Ph.D. is in mass communication but most of my course work was in sociology.

9. Bent Flyvbjerg, *Making Social Science Matter: Why Social Inquiry Fails and How It Can Succeed Again* (Cambridge, United Kingdom: University Press, 2001), p. 166; Cheol H. Oh, *Linking Social Science Information to Policy-Making* (Greeenwich, CT: JAI Press, 1996), pp. 9-10; C. E. Nelson, J. Roberts, C. Maederer, B. Wertheimer, and B. Johnson, "The Utilization of Social Science Information by Policymakers," *American Behavioral Scientist, 30*: 569-577 (1987); W. E. Pollard, "Decision-making and the Use of Evaluation Research," *American Behavioral Scientist, 30*: 661-676 (1987); and A. L. Schneider, "The Evaluation of a Policy Orientation for Evaluation Research," *Public Administration Review, 46*: 356-363 (July/August 1986); Robert F. Rich and N. Caplan, "What Do We Know about Knowledge Utilization as a Field/Discipline — The State of the Art," paper presented at the Research Utilization Conference, University of Pittsburgh (September 1978); Carol Weiss, "Introduction," pp. 1-20 in *Utilizing Social Research in Public Policy Making*, edited by Carol Weiss (Lexington, MA: D.C. Heath, 1977); Carol Weiss, "Knowledge Creep and Decision Accretion," *Knowledge, 1*: 384-404 (1980); and Robert Formaini, *The Myth of Scientific Public Policy* (New York: Transaction Publishers, 1990), p. 1.

10. Robert F. Rich, *Social Science Information and Public Policy Making* (New Brunswick,

NJ: Transaction Publishers, 2002, originally published in 1981 by Jossey-Bass), p. 2.

11. For this sentence, Rich cites N. S. Caplan, "The State of the Art: What We Know About Utilization," in L. A. Braskamp and R. D. Brown (editors), *New Directions for Program Evaluation: Utilization of Evaluative Information,* No. 5 (San Francisco: Jossey-Bass, 1980).

12. Cheol H. Oh, 1996. *Linking Social Science Information to Policy-Making* (Greeenwich, CT: JAI Press, 1996), pp. 9-10.

13. Oh cites these scholars to back up his statement: C. E. Nelson, J. Roberts, C. Maederer, B. Wertheimer, and B. Johnson, "The Utilization of Social Science Information by Policymakers," *American Behavioral Scientist, 30*: 569-577 (1987); W. E. Pollard, 1987. "Decision-making and the Use of Evaluation Research. *American Behavioral Scientist, 30*: 661-676 (1987); and A. L. Schneider, "The Evaluation of a Policy Orientation for Evaluation Research," *Public Administration Review* (July/August 1986), pp. 356-363.

14. Robert F. Rich and N. Caplan, "What Do We Know about Knowledge Utilization as a Field/Discipline — The State of the Art," paper presented at the Research Utilization Conference, University of Pittsburgh (September 1978); Carol Weiss, "Introduction," pp. 1-20 in *Utilizing Social Research in Public Policy Making,* edited by Carol Weiss (Lexington, MA: D.C. Heath, 1977); and Carol Weiss, "Knowledge Creep and Decision Accretion," *Knowledge, 1*: 384-404 (1980).

15. President George W. Bush's administration was often accused of ignoring not only social science but natural science research when it comes to making policy decisions (e.g., global warming). But his administration is not the first nor the last to do this. See David Demers, *The Ivory Tower of Babel: Why the Social Sciences Are Failing to Live Up to Their Promises* (New York: Algora, 2011).

16. Telephone interview, February 27, 2009.

17. Paul Dicken, an academic who has been trying to write a book to reach a popular audience, cautions: "If serious academics do not attempt to reach a wider audience, someone else will, and there is no guarantee that they are going to uphold the intellectual standards that we desire. Without a change in the existing academic culture, we will continue to see public debate on important issues derailed by factual errors and invalid reasoning. If we really are committed to the old-fashioned ideals of education and the pursuit of knowledge — and in today's corporate environment, that is no longer a given — it seems that we should be rewarding the attempt to reach a broader audience." Paul Dicken, "You Want to Write for Popular Audience? Really? *The Chronicle of Higher Education* (June 9, 2015), retrieved June 11, 2015, from <http://chronicle.com/article/You-Want-to-Write-for-a/230781/?cid=at&utm_source=at&utm_medium=en>.

18. The term *ritual* is defined here as a pattern of behaviors expressed through symbols a public or shared meaning whose function is to bond social actors together, as opposed to achieving some utilitarian purpose, such as solving problems.

19. This section was adapted from my earlier book, Demers, *The Ivory Tower of Babel,* pp. 166-178.

20. The plenary was conducted August 10, 2000, at the Hyatt Regency in Phoenix.

21. Joanne Cantor, *"Mommy, I'm Scared": How TV and Movies Frighten Children and How We Can Protect Them* (San Diego, CA: Harvest Books, 1998).

22. B. J. Wilson, S. L. Smith, W. J. Potter, D. Kunkel, D. Linz, C. M. Colvin, and E. Donnerstein, "Violence in Children's Television Programming: Assessing the Risks," *Journal of Communication, 52*(1): 5-35 (2002), p. 63.

23. Bruce D. Bartholow, Karen E. Dill, Kathryn B. Anderson and James J. Lindsay, "The Proliferation of Media Violence and Its Economic Underpinnings," pp. 1-18 in Douglas A. Gentile (editor), *Media Violence and Children: A Complete Guide for Parents and Professionals*

(Westport, CT: Praeger, 2003). On page 18, the authors write: "As media play more prominent roles in our lives over the coming decades, history shows that we can expect the violent content of media to increase as well."

24. Ibid.

25. E-mail from Theodore Glasser (November 10, 2008).

26. The term "social contract" generally implies that people give up some rights to a government and other authority in order to preserve social order.

27. Robert F. Rich, *Social Science Information and Public Policy Making* (New Brunswick, NJ: Transaction Publishers, 2002).

28. Perhaps the best modern example of this was President George W. Bush's refusal to recognize the research on effects of pollution on global warming and to sign the Kyoto Protocol.

29. One sociologist who clearly did have some impact, however, was W. E. B. Du Bois. However, he became disillusioned with the pace of change in the United States and moved to Africa, where he died a short time later.

30. Personal e-mail from Steven Chaffee (October 13, 1999).

31. William Foote Whyte, "On the Uses of Social Science Research," *American Sociological Review 51*: 555-563 (Augustin 1986), p. 555. I often tell my students that some of the greatest works in sociology are fiction, such as John Steinbeck's *The Grapes of Wrath* and Charles Dickens' *David Copperfield*. Both books resulted in legislative changes to protect laborers.

32. Demers, *The Ivory Tower of Babel*.

33. David Demers (editor), *Terrorism, Globalization & Mass Communication: Papers Presented at the 2002 Center for Global Media Studies Conference* (Spokane: Marquette Books, 2002).

Chapter 27

Family Matters

December 5, 1999
Pullman, Washington

While attending a midwinter business meeting of the Association for Education in Journalism and Mass Communication in December 1999, I noticed that one of my colleagues was missing.

"Where's Carol?" I asked a colleague who also was a member of the research committee, like me.

"She's in China adopting a baby."

I was 46, single and childless.

I had always wanted kids, and I knew that China allowed single people, including men, to adopt. My clock was ticking. The older I got, the more difficult it would be to find a partner who would be willing to have a child. So when Carol returned from China, I called her.

"It's a wonderful experience," she said. "You should look into it."

She gave me the name of her adoption agency and suggested I search the internet for more information.

When I did, I found four other single men who had adopted baby girls from China and asked them about their experiences. All of them had wonderful experiences. Their children were healthy and thriving.

That was good enough for me.

In spring 2000, I filed the paperwork to adopt a baby girl from China.

After extensive background checks from the FBI, local police, state police and adoption agencies, my application was approved.

But I wouldn't pick up my baby girl until August 2001. I timed it so that I could go on a short sabbatical to work on my introduction to mass communication book project.

As fate would have it, Carol and her husband decided to adopt another Chinese baby, and the three of us and five other sets of would-be parents would also make the trip.

MEANWHILE, in February 2001, I decided to sell my townhouse in Pullman and move to Spokane, a metropolitan area of 400,000 located 72 miles to the north.

Pullman is a nice town. Good schools. People are friendly. But it's not a great place for people who are single, because there isn't much to do there.

Spokane was better. More restaurants and night life. At the time, three of the 29 Murrow faculty lived in Spokane.

I found a split-level house on the South Hill, an area about 14 square miles just south of downtown Spokane and about 500 feet higher than city's 1,800-foot elevation. The area behind the house was vacant except for a newly paved road.

Before buying, I contacted Spokane County, which sent me a site plan that showed the developer was going to build duplexes and two-story apartment complexes. A year later a massive three-story assisted-living facility would be constructed there instead. The developer changed the plan even though he had signed a private contractual agreement with a local neighborhood association saying he would not change the plan without the association's permission.

That incident eventually would trigger the resignation of a county official and lead to allegations of censorship against the Spokane *Spokesman-Review*, the major daily in town. But before these controversies erupted with full force, I went to China to pick up my adopted daughter.

"BABA, BABA," said the nanny ("Daddy, Daddy" in Chinese) as she delivered 17 pounds of toddler into my arms.

The tiny girl's face flushed. Her nose and eyes crinkled. Then her mouth opened wide — so wide I thought a 747 was taking off, except she was louder. Tears streamed down her cheeks.

I knew 17-month-old Xiang Jun He would cry when she met me for the first time. She had spent her entire life in an orphanage in Hefei, China, surrounded by female caretakers. Contrast that with her new dad: a middle-aged, single, bearded, balding Caucasian.

Yes, she was scared.

But that was nothing compared to what I was going through.

What if she cried all the time? What if she didn't like me? What if she hated me as she grew up, pierced every part of her body, and became a drug addict? Or worse yet, what if she became a fan of Rush Limbaugh or Bill O'Reilly? Is it too late to get a refund?

Okay, I was a bit irrational at the moment. But who wouldn't be? My entire life was about to change.

Everything was so uncertain, except for one thing: At some point I would have to change her diaper. The other families accepting their crying bundles of joy looked as if they understood diapers. But I had never changed one before.

Was I insane?

Why would a divorced man with a great job and good life in Spokane, Washington, take on a lifelong commitment to raise a Chinese baby girl on his own?

These questions weighed heavily on me as I left the hotel conference room in central China with my sobbing daughter on that hot, muggy afternoon.

It was August 26, 2001.

I tried to convince myself I had made the right decision. But that isn't easy to do when you have 17 pounds of screaming flesh in your arms.

THAT SUMMARY ABOVE introduced a story I wrote in 2004 for *The Local Planet*, a weekly newspaper in Spokane, Washington.[1] To make life a bit easier for her in the states, I renamed my daughter "Lee Ann," using the middle names of my mother and aunt, respectively.

Fortunately, the story has a very happy ending.

She graduated valedictorian of her high school class of 304 in 2018. She got a full ride scholarship to University of Arizona, where she graduated with a bachelor's degree in spring 2021, one year early. Can you tell I'm a proud daddy?

Almost everyone who adopts from China has the same experience. However, what took them to China often varies.

In my case, I had always wanted children but my marriage was childless. In 2000, I decided that if I wanted to become a father, I would have act quickly on my own.

I was forty-six and my options were limited. It's virtually impossible in the United States for a single man to adopt a baby. However, back then China allowed single men over age forty to adopt abandoned children.[2]

So I filed the paperwork.

As any parent will tell you, there is nothing like a child to give you perspective on what is important in life. It was time to stop working 70-plus-hour weeks.

My job at the university was still very important, of course, but it was time to build a family world, one that also included Theresa, a very kind, thoughtful woman whom I married two years after the adoption. She became a great mom for Lee Ann.

So, after I returned to work in winter of 2002, I reduced my hours to about 40–50 per week. That reduction would have felt like a vacation, except for the fact that I now had another full time job: taking care of a 17-month-old baby.

Fortunately, that turned out to be fun, too, with the exception of changing those stinky diapers.

MY ACADEMIC WORLD during 2002 and 2003 included managing the Center for Global Media Studies and Marquette Books, which, as noted earlier, was initially founded to publish papers from the CGMS 2002 conference in Spokane.

The conference book contained 19 chapters written by scholars from England, Scotland, Canada, Taiwan, and France. Lee B. Becker, the director of the James M. Cox Jr. Center for International Mass Communication Training and Research at the University of Georgia, wrote an afterward that offered comments and constructive criticism.[3]

The book sold about 300 copies over the next five years — not much of a success by book industry standards. Total costs for publishing and distributing the book were about $5,900. The book generated about $6,500 in revenues, so I was able to give $600 to the center.

Not much, but, to me, it was still a big success, because higher education libraries across the United States and Canada were the major buyers, and the book is now available for generations to come. The major goal of CGMS was to distribute information, not make money.

Around the same time, I also published another edited book of readings taken from the *Global Media News*, CGMS's newsletter. This book was less academic and more accessible to a general audience. It included an article from Steve Bell, the former ABC news anchor who was now professor of telecommunications at Ball State University. This book also didn't sell many copies, but it was readable and could be used in undergraduate classes.

Then, in spring 2003, Melvin DeFleur, a media sociologist at Boston University, called and asked if I could publish a book he and his wife, Margaret, had written, which was titled *Learning to Hate Americans*.[4]

The DeFleurs asked their foreign graduate students to conduct surveys of more than 1,300 teenagers in their 12 home countries. They found that teenagers around the world believed Americans were extremely violent and criminally inclined, and they believed American women were sexually immoral.

The DeFleurs placed most of the blame for these negative attitudes on U.S. mass media, especially Hollywood, which produces many negative images of Americans. They concluded that unless something is done to correct the problem, future generations of foreign teenagers will grow up "learning to hate Americans."

"Why would you want my small company to publish your book, Mel?" I asked him. "It has no prestige."

"We want to get the book out at soon as possible," he said. "The topic is very newsworthy right now. It takes too long for a big publishing house to do that."

I was able to publish their book in three months.

That book opened the floodgates.

Ralph Berenger, an American who was teaching at the American University in Cairo, was looking for someone to publish his edited book about global media and the 2003 Gulf War, titled *Global Media Go to War*.

John C. Merrill, one of the most prominent libertarian First Amendment scholars in the United States, also wanted me to publish his book *Media Musings: Interviews with Great Thinkers*.

I worked on these and other books mostly in the summer, when I was not on appointment. WSU, like most colleges, allows faculty to work jobs in the summer but limits the amount of time that faculty can work on consulting or on non-university business during the regular school year to the equivalent of one day a week.[5]

None of the books generated much in the way of profits. In fact, in the first five years of operation, Marquette Books lost $16,634.[6] By the year 2008, the losses would total $42,458.[7]

Although my goal was to make the business profitable someday, the losses didn't bother me greatly. It felt good to publish works that were contributing to the advancement of knowledge and to help other faculty achieve their publishing goals.

But what I failed to realize at the time was that many Murrow faculty were becoming resentful.

"They are envious," one professor friend later told me.

"I don't believe it," I responded. "Why would they be envious? They are all very accomplished people. Marquette Books is simply disseminating knowledge to the public and scholars. Isn't that one of the goals of our profession?"

"Yes, your company is a win-win for everyone. But you know human nature. Faculty can be just as petty and insecure as any other professional group. And they don't like to be upstaged. They are fiercely competitive."

I guess I didn't know people very well. Perhaps it was because of my working-class origins or my educational training. I was still drawing on the model of human nature presented to me by my elementary Lutheran schoolteachers: "Treat others as you would have them treat you."

If any of my colleagues needed their book published, I was there to help out.[8] In fact, I made the offer to all of the faculty, including one who was having a difficult time finding a publisher for his book.[9]

I also offered the resources of Marquette Books to the university. I told the dean and provost that if they needed any assistance, Marquette Books would be there to help out — at no charge. No one took advantage of the services, however.

IN SPRING 2002, the WSU professor who taught the Introduction to Mass Communication course told Tan that he was stepping down.

By pure coincidence, I was at the time writing a textbook for such a course. *An Interpretive Introduction to Mass Communication* was part of my revised program of research, which sought to influence students and the general public, not just scholars.

I had signed a contract with a major book publishing company in 2000 to write the introductory book.[10] Needless to say, I jumped at the chance to teach the intro course, and Tan assigned me as instructor of the course in fall 2002.

A first draft of my book was nearly finished. My publisher suggested that I use it in my classes, because I could get some feedback from the students. The publisher would publish hard copies of the book for use in my class and make the book available to other scholars across the country who also might want to use it.

I told Tan I would defer any royalties from the sale of the book to the nonprofit Center for Global Media Studies. But he said that wasn't necessary. WSU rules allowed faculty to earn royalties on the sale of their books. To do that, the book had to be published by a reputable publisher, it had to be available to other faculty across the country, and the department chair/director and the dean's office had to approve the request.

Tan said many faculty in the Murrow School had used their own books in their classes and all kept their royalties. This included one faculty member who was publishing his own books[11] and another faculty member who eventually would become director of the Murrow program.[12]

Alex encouraged me to accept the royalties.

I thought that to do otherwise would make the other faculty look greedy and generate more resentment of me. Besides, as he pointed out, Com 101 was one of the hardest courses in the curriculum to teach. More than 600 students enrolled in the course in the fall and 300 in the winter/spring semester, and the instructor of the course had to manage a half-dozen graduate student teaching assistants.

I didn't argue with him.

In hindsight, that was a mistake, even though I faithfully followed all of the rules at the university. And I donated the proceeds in profitable years to CGMS.[13]

Nevertheless, a year or so later a Murrow faculty member filed a complaint, alleging that I was violating university and/or state ethics codes. It also alleged that Tan was giving me "release time" for my work at CGMS, meaning that I didn't have to teach as many courses as a regular faculty member. But I received no release time. All of my work at CGMS was volunteer. I never earned a penny in compensation.

The complainant happened to be a faculty member who was coming up for tenure. During his third and fifth year reviews, I raised some questions about the quality and quantity of his research record.[14]

WSU's internal auditor was called in to investigate. On Oct. 8, 2004, he issued a report to Tan, exonerating me. But the university controller told me in a telephone conversation that even though I was not benefiting financially from the books used in my classes, he said there could be a nonfinancial benefit through CGMS, and that was still prohibited under state and university rules. The internal auditor confirmed this in a follow-up memo.

So I created PDFs of the books and gave them to students free of charge,[15] and royalties from the intro book were used to help fund CGMS, even though university rules allowed me to keep those royalties for my own use.

Chapter 27 Endnotes

1. David Demers, "China Girl: One Man's Adoption Story," *The Local Planet Weekly* (December 5, 2002), pp. 8-11. Four years later I also wrote a book about my experiences. See David Demers, *China Girl: One Man's Story* (Spokane, WA: Marquette Books, 2006).

2. Single people are no longer allowed to adopt children from China. In many areas in China, if a couple has no male child, they will have no one to care for them when they reach old age. Thus, female babies are often abandoned shortly after birth, and couples will often keep trying until they have a male child. It is against the law to abandon a child.

3. Lee B. Becker helped me with my master's thesis at The Ohio State University in the 1980s.

4. Melvin DeFleur and Margaret DeFleur, *Learning to Hate Americans: How U.S. Media Shape Negative Attitudes Among Teenagers in Twelve Countries* (Spokane, WA: Marquette Books, 2003).

5. One of my colleagues in the Murrow School who was a consultant to business argued that "one day" meant 24 hours per week. Indeed, the dictionary defines "day" as 24 hours. However, I interrupted it as meaning eight hours a day. I think that's how university officials would have interpreted the rule, although there is room for ambiguity here.

6. This is based on annual federal tax returns.

7. If you subtract the value of the assets, which include book binding and printing equipment, the total loss would be approximately $25,000 to $30,000. Here's a year by year accounting: 2002, lost $2,563; 2003, earned $3,511; 2004, earned $12,044; 2005, lost $16,200; 2006, broke even; 2007, lost $13,426; and 2008, lost $25,824. On the advice of an attorney, my wife became sole owner of the business in 2008 to avoid potential conflict of interest charges. I returned as owner in 2013, after I left Washington State University.

8. I discouraged some assistant professors across the country from publishing with Marquette Books, because the prestige of the publishing house can affect the tenure decision. But after tenure the name of the publishing house has less impact.

9. The faculty member took a sabbatical to write the book but never completed it.

10. I originally was writing the book with another colleague in the field, but she backed out and signed with another publisher.

11. At the time, this faculty member told me that the university allowed such royalties because it wanted to encourage faculty to write books for their courses. "Faculty salaries are lower than in the private sector," he said. "This is one way in which they try to reduce that gap."

12. Actually, his wife ran the company.

13. The DeFleur book was a perfect fit with the Com 101 course, because it raised questions about the role and function of American mass media around the world.

14. I eventually voted in favor of the candidate's tenure.

15. I gave the students free hard copies or gave them free PDF files of the books. Needless to say, they loved this.

Chapter 28

Censored in Spokane

Spring 2002
Spokane, Washington

I was still on sabbatical in spring of 2002 when my neighbors and I noticed that the construction behind our homes wasn't complying with the county-approved site plan.

Instead of one-story duplexes and two-story apartments, a massive three-story 100-unit assisted-living facility more than a football field in length was going up. The developer had reneged on a promise not to change the plan and secured approval from Spokane County building officials without going through normal protocol, which would have required another public hearing.

My neighbors and I were angry.

But the neighborhood association refused to sue, because a former president of the group was now the neighborhood liaison for the mayor of Spokane, and "if word got out that the mayor's neighborhood liaison opposed this developer, other developers in town would stop contributing money to the mayor's reelection campaign and she would lose her liaison job," one member of the association later told me.

Once again, loyalty trumps principle.

I wrote a letter to the county and appeared at several meetings, but county officials said they were not willing to file a lawsuit to stop the development.

I decided some media attention to the issue might help. So I took out a classified advertisement in the *Spokesman-Review*.

The ad would criticize county officials who approved the project as well as the developer who violated the private contractual agreement.

I figured I'd have no problem getting the newspaper to publish my little classified ad. After all, the owners of the *Spokesman-Review*, the Cowles family, had placed half-page advertisements in their own newspaper on several occasions criticizing City of Spokane officials for their role in what came to be known as the River Park Square Garage scandal.

That case is complicated, but basically what happened is that the Cowleses family, one of the wealthiest families in Spokane, built a shopping mall in downtown Spokane and asked the city to give it a free parking garage. The Cowles and their consultants said the parking garage would generate enough revenue to pay for itself.

But it didn't.

And the you-know-what hit the fan.

The case eventually produced hundreds of news stories, led to investigations by the Internal Revenue Service and the FBI, and made national news several times.[1] In a confidential report, the IRS accused Elizabeth A. (Betsy) Cowles, an attorney who headed up the Cowles TV and radio broadcasting operations, of orchestrating a deal designed to benefit her business rather than the community.

In the end, the taxpayers were stuck with the tab, which amounted to more than $35 million.

No one went to jail.

At any rate, I thought I'd have no problem placing my classified ad.

But the newspaper rejected it.

A spokesman there said the newspaper doesn't publish political advertisements. So I wrote a letter to the editor, criticizing the newspaper for being hypocritical — for publishing its own political advertisements defending itself in the River Park Square Parking Garage scandal but for refusing to publish those submitted by citizens.

To my surprise, the newspaper also refused to publish my letter to the editor.

What the hell?

When I worked as a reporter in Bad Axe, Michigan, my editor Dick Carson never once refused to publish a letter to the editor critical of us or our newspaper, even if the letter contained false allegations. Had the editors at the *Spokesman-Review* skipped Journalism 101 in college?

I called *S-R* publisher (William) Stacey Cowles.

Stacey was the son of the former publisher William H. Cowles III, who had died in 1992 at age 60 while jogging. Control of the newspaper went to Stacey. His sister, Betsy, got the broadcasting operations.

Stacey defended the decision of the newspaper not to publish my letter.

"We don't publish every letter we receive," he said.

"But is your decision not to publish my letter based on the fact that you don't have enough space or because you're afraid it will make your newspaper look hypocritical, because you publish your own political ads?"

Cowles refused to answer the question but he began talking about the boundaries of what a newspaper would publish.

"We would never publish a letter from a neo-Nazi in Idaho," Cowles said at one point.

"Why not?" I responded. "As the Supreme Court once noted, the best remedy for 'bad speech' isn't censorship, it's more speech.[2] If you published such a letter, you might be surprised at the positive result that could emerge from that."[3]

Cowles rejected my appeal.

But then something totally unexpected happened. As news of the decision spread through e-mail, friends and colleagues began telling me about other people who had similar experiences with the *Spokesman-Review*.

Within weeks I had sixteen examples of censorship. Doctors, professors and activists in the community told me that the *Spokesman-Review* had refused to publish their letters and columns. Within months I had posted 30 examples to a website I titled Censored in Spokane.

Two categories of censored works emerged.

About half of the letters and commentaries came from people who had written letters criticizing the newspaper or its staff, some for its role in the garage scandal. The other half had written letters that were pro-environment. The newspaper owned a printing plant near town that was one of the biggest polluters of the river, according to state officials.

The editorial page editor at the time, it turns out, was a political conservative who was very loyal to the Cowles family. The editorial page editor eventually was reassigned. The editor-in-chief said the decision was unrelated to my criticisms of the newspaper.[4]

Over the next two years, I wrote a series of articles for *The Local Planet Weekly*, a local alternative newspaper, that drew attention to the censored works as well as the conflict of interest posed in a community when its newspaper owners also have other economic investments in the community.[5] The Cowleses owned a substantial number of properties in downtown Spokane.

These commentaries, I confess, didn't have any noticeable impact on the newspaper or its journalists. However, they no doubt marginalized me even more among newspaper publishers in the Pacific Northwest.

Loyalties run deep.

Years later one publisher told me that he thought it was inappropriate to talk about the censorship incidents in my classes. He didn't say why, but his comments demonstrated that open, frank discussions aren't always appreciated, even among those who earn a living at trying to keep the government honest and open.

After the *Spokesman-Review* rejected my "political advertisement," I approached the *Seattle Times*. The newspaper agreed to run the advertisement as long as I removed the name of the developer.

I agreed, referring to him only as a "Spokane developer."

I took my case back to the *Spokesman-Review*, which then capitulated and agreed to run the same advertisement. To the best of my knowledge, the advertisements had no effect on either the developer or the county.

The developer never commented publicly on the dispute. He sold the assisted living facility several years later and reportedly made a handsome profit.

I eventually had a meeting with one of the county commissioners, who suggested that my neighbors and I file a claim with the county. The county paid $5,000 to each of us for the "wrong" that had been committed.

At one point, an anonymous e-mailer who had visited the "Censored in Spokane" website sent me a message saying, "You must really be a kook."

I responded that many other people probably would agree with him. I noted that it often takes a lot of bizarre actions to get media coverage for a good cause. I said the county eventually agreed to pay $5,000 for the wrong committed.

The e-mailer sent back an apologetic e-mail. "I didn't know about that," the critic contritely responded. The principle here, like the situation I experienced at the University of Wisconsin–River Falls, is that payment of money usually legitimates protests or causes.

I gave $900 of the money from the settlement to the association attorney, who had not been paid for his role in the assisted living controversy. He initially didn't charge for the visit, but I thought it was only fair that he receive something for his time. I spent $1,600 for other costs associated with fighting the case (advertisements, gas). I used the remaining $2,500 to purchase trees and shrubs, which grew quickly and blocked out most of the view of the building.

Chapter 28 Endnotes

1. City of Spokane taxpayers eventually were forced to pay more than $30 million to the bondholders. The City will turn the garage over, free of charge, to the Cowles family in 20 years.

2. The direct quote from Justice Louis D. Brandeis is as follows: "If there be time to expose through discussion the falsehood and fallacies, to avert the evil by the process of education, the remedy to be applied is more speech, not enforced silence." *Whitney v. California*, 274 U.S. 357 (1927).

3. When I was teaching at the University of Wisconsin–River Falls, the student newspaper published an advertisement from a man who said the holocaust never happened. The students who posted the ad admitted they didn't read it. The ad caused an uproar in the community. The chancellor at the university criticized the newspaper for being insensitive, and there were many other letters to the editor after the event. The students apologized, but the incident actually brought the community closer together. It reaffirmed the community's commitment to values that embrace different ethnic groups and races. See Chapter 5 in this book for more details.

4. One unanticipated consequence of this is that the unsigned editorials were less fun to

read, as they were more liberal and less inflammatory.

    5. I collected the articles and published them in a book. See David Demers, *The Media Essays: From Local to Global* (Spokane, WA: Marquette Books, 2003).

Chapter 29

Post-Tenure Affairs

2002–2006
Washington State University

The next four years at WSU were good, productive years.

I wrote one book, revised a second, and worked on a third during my sabbatical from fall 2001 to spring 2002.[1] When I returned to the university in fall 2002, construction of a $13 million building to house Murrow faculty and staff and provide more classroom space was underway.

The building was slated to be completed in 2004. Oddly, though, the building wasn't big enough to house all of the faculty and staff. The university didn't have enough money to build a bigger building. So some Murrow faculty, including me, stayed in the old Murrow Hall, which was a block to the east of the new building. Murrow was one of the first four buildings built on campus in the late 1880s. It originally was the science building.

On July 16–17, 2004, the Center for Global Media Studies sponsored its second conference, this time in Seattle and this time the Korea Press Foundation was a co-sponsor.[2] The Foundation donated $20,000 and so we were able to bring in some top-notch speakers and panelists. My Ph.D. student, Taehyun Kim, deserves the credit for bringing in the grant money.

The conference was titled "Communication and Globalization," and ten journalists and scholars from South Korea and the United States participated on two panels that examined media coverage of North Korea's nuclear arms program.

One of the participants was Charles L. Pritchard, a visiting fellow at the Brookings Institution in Washington, D.C., where he conducted research and wrote about political and security issues involving Japan and Korea. He was a top aide to President George H. W. Bush in the administration's negotiations with North Korea and was the U.S. representative to the Korean Peninsula Energy Development Organization.

Another panelist was Steven R. Weisman, chief diplomatic correspondent of the *New York Times*. In 2003, his book, *The Great Tax Wars: Lincoln to Wilson — The Fierce Battles Over Money and Power that Transformed the Nation*, won the Sidney

Hillman award for the book that most advances the cause of progressivism and social justice.

In 2004, I finished the first full draft of *An Interpretive Introduction to Mass Communication*. I also began work on a reference book titled *Dictionary of Mass Communication & Media Research*.

Universities generally do not give faculty much in the way of rewards for editing books or writing dictionaries or encyclopedias, especially those that are self-published.

But I didn't care.

As a graduate student, dictionaries and encyclopedias were a great starting point when I encountered a new topic or term. As such, they can play a big role in influencing a field of study, and my goal was to have as much impact as I could. Marquette Books published the book in 2005.

In late spring 2004, Murrow director Alex Tan informed me that the faculty member who had filed a complaint about Marquette Books two years before was filing another complaint against me and one of the full professors who used his own published books in his classes.

The full professor quietly retired that summer.

I had nothing to hide. I didn't profit from the books I used in my classes. I gave students free PDF files. The complaint was dismissed.

In fall 2004, I conducted a pilot study for the director of the Murrow School that compared research and publication productivity of tenured faculty in the Murrow School.[3] Follow-ups to that study would later play a crucial role in defending me against ad hominem attacks from WSU administrators and faculty.

By 2005, Marquette Books had published nearly 30 titles, about half of which were academic monographs, or theoretically driven books. Another dozen were in the works.[4]

I hired copy editors and book binders to do the production work.

The books were solid contributions to the field of mass communication, but most didn't sell well. Part of the problem is that libraries were buying fewer books.

During the 1980s, a publisher could expect to sell about 2,000 copies of a typical scholarly monograph. By the 2000s, it was down to 400. Some of ours were less than 200.

But that didn't concern me too much. Although Marquette Books wasn't making much money, it was able to pay the bills, mostly because of contract work from mostly older men who needed someone to publish their memoirs. And, more important, MB was contributing to the growth of knowledge in the field and was helping professors achieve their publishing goals.

A year later I announced that Marquette Books would begin publishing a half-dozen open access scholarly peer-reviewed journals in the field of communication.

Unlike most of the other scholarly journals in the field, these would be available free of charge to the public and scholars. In addition, the authors, not the publishing house, would own the copyright to the articles published.

It had always bothered me that publishing houses made huge profits from the sale of academic journals,[5] and the faculty who wrote the content for them received nothing at all. They at least deserved to own the copyright to their works.

In late 2005 and early 2006, the dean's office asked the Murrow School to rank order its top accomplishments in 2005.

The school selected my *Dictionary of Mass Communication & Media Research* as the second most important scholarly contribution in 2005.[6] That angered some faculty, although I didn't know it at the time. I would find out during the discovery phase of the lawsuit.

At the beginning of the 2006 calendar year, I was ranked among the top three most productive faculty members in the Murrow School. I had written and published 10 books, 20 sole or first-author refereed journal articles, and more than 100 professional papers and articles. I had won five national research awards for my research on corporate media and four journalism writing awards. And my teaching evaluations were higher than the departmental faculty average.

I present this information not to brag, but to prepare you for another principle: that the objective conditions of one's performance in a bureaucracy can have little bearing on how bureaucratic administrators see you.

Chapter 29 Endnotes

1. David Pearce Demers, *Global Media: Menace or Messiah?* (Cresskill, NJ: Hampton Press, 2002 revised); David Pearce Demers, *The Media Essays: From Local to Global* (Spokane, WA: Marquette Books, 2003); and David Pearce Demers, *An Interpretive Introduction to Mass Communication* (Boston: Allyn & Bacon and Pearson, 2004).

2. Much of the credit for getting the Korea Press Foundation involved goes to my Ph.D. students at that time, Taehyun Kim. He helped negotiate the deal.

3. The report up the research productivity of the Murrow faculty. The data were derived from the curriculum vitae of each of the 14 tenured or tenure-track faculty members.

4. They included works on media ethics, media research, global media, and Hollywood. For more details, visit <www.MarquetteBooks.com>.

5. Scholarly journals are the most profitable arm of the academic publishing industry. Many journals turn an 80 percent profit on sales.

6. David Demers, *Dictionary of Mass Communication & Media Research: A Guide for Students, Scholars and Professionals* (Spokane, WA: Marquette Books, 2005). The book also received favorable reviews from two academic journals and one trade publication.

Part V

WSU's Ivory Tower of Babel

Chapter 30

Purging the Palouse

September 1998 and January 2006
Washington State University

They came without warning. Tiny black particles, no bigger than the head of a pin, moving swiftly through the screen of a window in a second-floor bedroom of my townhouse in Pullman, Washington.

It was late September 1998.

I shut the window within seconds.

But it was too late.

The motes, thousands of them, blanketed a window sill, a desk and the surrounding carpet. A fast-moving thunderstorm with strong winds propelled them into the room.

But what created them?

Although I had lived in Pullman for two years, it took me several minutes to answer my own question.

Field burning.

The specks were ash from burning the stubble in wheat fields.

The controversial farming practice of crop burning was often in the news in the 1990s and early 2000s. On my occasional trips from Pullman to Spokane along U.S. 195, I could see huge plumes of smoke in shades of light to dark gray, rising hundreds of feet into the sky.

But until now I had never personally experienced the effects of field burning.

In Washington State, farmers most often torched the stubble in wheat fields after the fall harvest. In 2006, the Washington State Department of Ecology issued more than a thousand burn permits to Washington farmers, who set ablaze more than 180,000 acres. About one-fifth of those acres were right in Whitman County, where Pullman is located.

Farmers burned for three major reasons: to get rid of pesky insects, to reduce field stubble, and to create a natural fertilizer for the soil. Burning was a cheap alternative to pesticides and fertilizers. It also reduced chemical pollution to streams and underground aquifers. Most environmental groups didn't dispute the merits of burning for farmers, and they liked the idea of using fewer chemicals on crops.

But environmentalists were concerned about the effects on human lungs. For people with respiratory illnesses, those pesky motes were making it harder to breathe.

In fact, during the first month I arrived in Pullman an asthmatic woman in a nearby Idaho community died a day after her backyard was inundated with smoke from a grass farm stubble burn.[1] She awoke with breathing problems after camping overnight with her children.

In Oregon in 1988, smoke from field burning blanketed Interstate 5, causing a 23-car collision that killed seven people and injured 37.[2]

Oregon banned field burning in 2009.

But farmers in Washington State and Idaho still purge to this day.[3]

And, unbeknownst to me and most other faculty at Washington State University in January 2006, administrators at WSU had been doing some purging of their own.

They were firing tenured faculty.

WSU OFFICIALS HAVE NEVER RELEASED the exact number of tenured professors who were ousted from their jobs during the first decade of the new millennium. It's somewhere between "five and 10," according to Frances McSweeney, who was vice provost for faculty affairs at the time.

She revealed the existence of the termination practice when giving a deposition under oath in 2010.[4] Operating behind closed doors, university administrators were giving targeted faculty two options: resign or be fired.

Is that two choices?

Firing a tenured faculty member normally isn't easy.

At most universities across the country, tenure means job for life unless you commit a felony or kiss a graduate student.

But none of the fired WSU faculty was a mugger or a sex fiend. Their crime, according to McSweeney, was low evaluations from their unit heads in at least two annual reviews. WSU actually had a draconian rule on the books that allowed administrators to fire any faculty, including tenured ones, if they received below average ratings in annual reviews. This is not a common practice in American universities.

Nobody likes employees who don't do their jobs.

But using annual reviews to fire tenured faculty violates American Association of University Professors' rules on academic freedom, because it is very easy for administrators to terminate outspoken faculty with this rule.[5]

The Association emphasizes that no procedure for evaluation of faculty should be used to weaken or undermine the principles of academic freedom and tenure. The Association cautions particularly against allowing any general system of evaluation to be used as grounds for dismissal or other disciplinary sanctions.

The assumption behind the AAUP policy is that truth and knowledge can flourish only when professors are fully insulated from undue political, economic and administrative influences.[6]

Of course, the fired WSU faculty could have requested a formal appeal.

But none did, to the best of my knowledge. They probably feared a public airing of their alleged incompetence. When a powerful bureaucracy labels someone as incompetent, the stigma is hard to shake.

In exchange for resigning, the university gave the canned professors one year's salary, McSweeney said.

After word of the firings got out, the vice provost became known on campus as "the terminator." Indeed, there was no more feared person walking College Hill in Pullman, even though she was probably six inches shorter and 50 pounds lighter than me.

"I would rather tangle with an alligator in open water," one faculty member told me later.

"Make that two, for me," said another.

I wasn't a great swimmer, so I respectfully disagreed with my colleagues.

But that didn't mean I was ready to tangle with the terminator.

In January 2006, I didn't even realize there was a terminator was on campus. I was busy writing a book about the history and future of mass media.

But I would eventually lock jaws with the terminator.

I'll get to that story later.

In the meantime, the existence of a culture of termination at WSU makes it easier to explain why administrators would, over the next several years, force more than a half-dozen Murrow faculty to resign from their positions.

And the origins of that purge can be traced to a decision on whether to renew the administrative contract of the current Murrow director.

IN THE SPRING OF 2006, Murrow Director Alex Tan was never in jeopardy of losing his tenured position at WSU. He was a good researcher and teacher.

But he could be removed from his post as director of the program.

His four-year contract was up for renewal.

Tan had spent more than two decades at the helm of the school. That's no small feat when you consider the conflict and turmoil that characterize academic life.

Departmental heads are often ousted and replaced. Research universities like WSU also are more likely than teaching universities to deny tenure to faculty who fail to publish. Faculty often compete with each other for resources and recognition. And administrators and faculty are often at loggerheads over the direction of a program or how to spend resources.

Some outsiders see this social conflict as dysfunctional.

"I've never understood why there is so much political turmoil and in-fighting at universities," one employment attorney who had represented faculty in labor disputes once told me. "The stakes seem so small. The battles rarely revolve around things worth fighting about. Why can't faculty just get along?"

"Because their universities are structured to encourage conflict," I replied.

The tenure system and the concept of academic freedom explain in part why universities usually have more visible social conflict than other types of institutions.

I qualify that proposition with the word "visible" because interpersonal conflict and complaints are present in virtually all large-scale and most small-scale organizations.

But in private business and non-academic governmental agencies, dissatisfaction with higher-ups is more likely to be expressed behind closed doors or around the water cooler, because employees of these organizations can be easily fired from their jobs for the things they say and do. They have no First Amendment protection.

In contrast, social conflict and criticism are more visible in the public university, because academics and the courts have carved out some free speech protection for university professors. More on that later. The important point here is that this legal protection, along with the fact that most university rules contractually provide free speech protection to faculty and students, means social actors in universities often engage in robust debates, usually without fear of reprisal. And even without constitutional or contractual protection, most university administrators tolerate a lot of flak from faculty, partly because they know that freedom of expression is a way to control people and, sometimes, a robust debate can produce better ideas and decisions.

Viewed from this perspective, then, social conflict is good thing. It can solve social problems and help an organization adapt to change.

That's how some professors and I see the university.

If there were no conflict, there would be greater abuse of power. And the best place to find social conflict at a university is in its power structure. One can hypothesize, in fact, that the more power[7] an administrator or group has, the greater the potential for conflict.

At the top of the pyramid are university presidents or chancellors, who often report that they are under attack from all kinds of groups and people, including faculty, staff, students, donors, policymakers, journalists and the public.[8] Making one decision that positively affects one group may adversely affect another.

Lower-level administrators face similar problems when they make decisions, but, in relative terms, the levels of conflict tend to decline as one moves down the hierarchy.[9]

At the bottom of the power pyramid, professors and students also can find themselves in a conflict, often over grades. However, faculty have much less power over a student's life than administrators have over faculty. The interaction between faculty and students is short-lived as each semester comes and goes. In relative terms, faculty-student conflicts rarely escalate into something big, with the notable exception of sex scandals.[10]

In contrast, the potential for conflict is much greater between department chairs or directors and their faculty, because they interact with each other over longer periods of time and because chairs usually evaluate the performance of faculty.

A chair or director of a program can make many decisions that positively or adversely affect each faculty member. Because departments usually have limited resources, a gain or benefit for one faculty member often means a loss or detriment for another (a zero-sum outcome).

Larger departments also tend to have more social conflict because they have more social actors and, thus, more chances for conflict.[11] I have called this phenomenon the "Quadratic Theory of Social Conflict." Conflict increases at a faster pace as organizational size increases.[12]

The high levels of social conflict in universities makes them ideal laboratories for studying a phenomena known as coup d'état — or the sudden overthrow of a government (or department head) by a part of the state (or faculty and administrators). Of course, one significant difference between political coups and academic ones is that the latter are nonviolent (at least most of the time, thankfully).

So I call them petits coups d'état.

THE CAUSES OF petits coups in academia vary. But they almost always involve a higher-level administrator and sometimes a group of faculty who are unhappy with the decisions of an administrator.

Petits coups are most successful when the supervisor of the administrator under attack is aligned with the unhappy dissidents. That's because all supervisors or administrators dislike making decisions that look capricious or undemocratic. This is particularly true for high-profile decisions, such as removing a lower-level administrator from power. The more support bosses can get from the rank-and-file, the better they look.

World history shows that after political coup d'états, many non-elite supporters of an ousted regime can be quickly co-opted into the new regime.

Fear motivates, as Machiavelli pointed out.

But some elites in the previous regime cannot be trusted, and so they are sometimes executed. Before the twentieth century, the British preferred hanging and the firing squad. The French preferred the guillotine.

Fortunately, universities today are less barbaric, although you'd have a tough time trying to convince me they are more civil.

When an administrator is removed from office, he or she usually returns to his or her department and resumes teaching and research responsibilities. Appealing these removal decisions is difficult because many administrative positions are limited-term appointments.

To remove faculty who fall out of favor with administrators in power, the preferred form of punishment in modern academe is banishment — in other words, dismiss the nontenured faculty and pressure the tenured ones to leave.

As Sophocles wrote in his play *Oedipus the King*:

OEDIPUS: What is the rite of purification? How shall it be done?
CREON: By banishing a man, or expiation of blood by blood ...[13]

In the academy, to banish non-tenure-track faculty (often called contract employees), you fire them or refuse to renew their work contracts. They are "at-will" employees, which means they don't have a right to due process as do tenure-track professors.[14]

To banish newer faculty who are working to obtain tenure, you give them poor performance reviews and then deny them tenure, usually when they reach their third or sixth year. They can appeal the decision, but the faculty member usually loses. Upper-level administrators who consider the appeal usually don't break ranks.[15]

To banish tenured faculty, you take away all of the privileges you can and you give them poor performance reviews. The goal is to make their lives miserable. If possible, you enlist the help of your colleagues to turn the faculty member into a pariah — into a target of ridicule and rolling eyes. Mobbing can work.

Sometimes you give the targeted faculty a severance package if they will agree to resign. That can be far cheaper than a lawsuit.

If the tenured faculty member still refuses to resign, you fire them and force them to file an administrative appeal, which can take a year or more to adjudicate and will stress them out. Even if they win the appeal, top-level administrators usually have the power to overturn the decision, which then forces the faculty member into filing an expensive lawsuit. Without a job, however, few have the resources to do that.

Attorneys will not take free speech cases on a contingency-fee basis, as it is very difficult and sometimes impossible in such cases to obtain punitive damages (financial compensation meant to punish the losing party and deter others from committing the same civil offense).

But attorneys will often represent on a contingency-fee basis faculty who claim they were fired because of the color of their skin, their religious beliefs, or their sex or age. Under various laws, these are called "protected categories," and punitive damages are far more common and sometime result in very large settlements.

Because the courts are often reluctant to interfere with the internal operations of universities, administrators overall enjoy a big advantage over fired faculty in a court of law.

But once in a while a professor prevails.

Administrative purges, like burning fields to wipe out pests, can result in car wrecks.

MURROW DIRECTOR ALEX TAN had support from most of the faculty when his contract came up for renewal in spring of 2006.

However, faculty did not have final say on the matter.

The dean of the College of Liberal Arts, Erich Lear, oversaw the selection process and made a recommendation to the provost and president, who in turn made the final decision. In most cases, upper-level administrators rubber-stamp a dean's choice. But on occasion, the higher-ups will take control and call the shots.

Lear was a WSU insider who had just been appointed to his position. Since 1989, he had been a professor in the School of Music and Theatre Arts and had also been its director.

As director of that program, he developed music-degree options with several other departments, including business, theater, electrical engineering and computer science. He also secured a $625,000 grant from the Allen Foundation for Music to pay for studio equipment and maintenance.

Administrators love faculty who bring in money.

Lear was an amiable man.

He appeared to be receptive to complaints from faculty. Not all administrators are like that.

But one of his first acts as dean did not endear him to some of the department heads that reported to him.[16] When the college received funding for nine new faculty positions, Lear notified everyone that he intended to give three to music and six to the remaining programs. At most universities, music is one of the most expensive programs to maintain because some of the instruction is one teacher to one student.

The Murrow School was one of the lucky programs in the college. It received one faculty position.

Rules at WSU required deans to consult with faculty before making a decision about whether to renew a director's appointment. Oddly, though, the rules did not call for a simple vote on whether to retain Tan.

Instead, faculty were asked whether they wished to fill the director position through an inside search or outside search. If the faculty selected an inside search, then rules required another vote on eligible faculty, which might include other possible candidates.

Lear met with faculty on several occasions to discuss procedure.

The details of those meetings are confidential.

But I can tell you that several faculty were confused by the process.

At least one wanted to change his or her vote. Lear wouldn't allow it.

As the final stages of the appointment process were drawing to a close, Tan circulated to Murrow faculty a copy of an article published in *The Chronicle of Higher Education*, the most prestigious general circulation (weekly) newspaper serving universities.

It was titled, "Mob Rule."

Chapter 30 Endnotes

1. Kevin Keating, "Growers Say They're Blameless In Death Of Asthmatic Woman," *The Spokesman-Review* (August 26, 1996), retrieved March 10, 2014 from <www.spokesman.com/stories/1996/aug/22/growers-say- theyre-blameless-in-death-of>.

2. Holley Gilbert, Michael Rollins and Cheryl Martinis, "Smoky 21-vehicle pileup kills 7 on I-5," *The* (Portland) *Oregonian* (August 4, 1988), retrieved March 10, 2014 from <http://www.oregonlive.com/data/2015/02/smoky_21-vehicle_pileup_kills.html>.

3. In 2002, university researchers and state officials monitored 33 asthmatic adults for eight weeks during the burning season and were unable to identify significant health effects. But peak exposures were lower that year than in previous years. See Tina Hilding, "Field-burning Study Proves Inconclusive," *Washington State Magazine* (no date provided), retrieved March 9, 2015, from <http://researchnews.wsu.edu/environment/35.html>. Environmentalists, no doubt, were not pleased with the results of the health study. But, to its credit, the state Department of Ecology never argued that field burning smoke was not harmful. Its website in 2015 stated: "While it is legal to burn for approved agronomic reasons with a permit, it is not legal to allow smoke to impact others. The agricultural burning of field crop residue and orchard tear out

residue can directly impact the safety and health of citizens breathing the smoke-filled air."
(Retrieved March 7, 2015, from the Department of Ecology's webpage on agricultural burning <http://www.ecy.wa.gov/programs/air/aginfo/agricultural_ homepage.htm>).

4. Deposition of Francis McSweeney, September 30, 2010, 332 French Administration Building, Pullman, Washington, commencing at 9:58 a.m., before Jeffory A. Wilson, Court Reporter and Notary Public, Accurate Court Reporting, for *Demers v. Austin* et al., Case No. CV-09-334-RHW.

5. Source: The American Association of University Professor's existing policy on post-tenure review, approved by Committee A and adopted by the Council in November 1983. In 1999, AAUP argued that "'post-tenure review ought to be aimed not at accountability, but at faculty development.' Colleges and universities already have procedures for disciplining and dismissing tenured faculty, the AAUP argued, and post-tenure review policies could be consistent with academic freedom only if they had no power to impose consequences on underperforming faculty." Quoted from Anne D. Neal, "Reviewing Post-Tenure Review," *Academe*, 94:5 (September-October 2008), retrieved September 10, 2012, from <www.aaup.org/AAUP/pubsres/academe/2008/SO/Feat/neal.htm>.

6. Purging of tenured faculty is revisited again in Chapter 45, when McSweeney gives her deposition.

7. Power is defined here as the authority and ability to control others.

8. See, e.g., Stephen Joel Trachtenberg, *Big Man on Campus: A University President Speaks Out on Higher Education* (New York: Simon & Schuster, 2008).

9. In absolute terms, conflict can increase at lower levels in the organization, because interaction between social actors may be greater. An example: A professor who teaches a large lecture class increases the chances of conflict with students. However, in relative terms, that conflict is usually less intense than conflict between faculty and administrators because the social contact is much shorter, normally ending when the class ends.

10. Much of the conflict between faculty and students is over grading. Students are at a disadvantage, because the system gives faculty a great deal of latitude in assigning grades. Most students know this and instead of fighting the issue will avoid taking courses from that professor.

11. This proposition is central to my theory of mass media, which expects larger, corporate media to produce content that is more critical of the power structure than smaller (entrepreneurial or family owned) media.

12. The "quadratic theory of social conflict" basically holds that as the number of people or social actors (such as organizations) increases in a system, social conflict increases at a quadratic (faster) pace. If you have two people, you have one potential case or set of ideas at any one point in time. Now let's add one more person to the setting. The number of cases or sets increases to three, because you have three pairs of relationships. When you add a fourth, the potential cases or sets increase to six, and so on. Mathematically, as you add more people to the setting, the potential for conflict increases at a faster pace. The mathematical equation for this model is quite simple: $[n \times (n-1)]/2$, where n equals the number of social actors. For example, if one has 10 social actors in an organization, the potential for social conflict is $[10 \times (10-1)]/2$, or $90 \div 2$, which equals 45.

13. Sophocles, *Oedipus the King* (Chicago: University of Chicago Press, 2010; translated in 1942 with a 1991 Introduction by David Grene), pp. 14-15.

14. Contract employees at public universities do have the same academic freedom protections as tenured faculty, but such protection exists only to the end of the contract, at which time administrators may oust the faculty member for any reason or no reason at all.

15. There are notable exceptions to this rule. At one California public university several years ago, a faculty member was denied tenure by the department head and the dean. The

provost overturned their decisions and granted tenure to the faculty member.

16. This story was relayed to me by a department head in the college.

Chapter 31

Workplace Mobbing

April 2006
Washington State University

"In departmental disputes," *Chronicle of Higher Education* reporter John Gravois wrote in 2006, "professors can act just like animals."[1]

Gravois explained that some bird species, when threatened by predators, will actually fly toward the threat rather than away. The birds will swoop down and harass the predator. Birds "mob" to teach younger birds whom to fear and, more importantly, to drive the predator away.

> Sometimes, especially in winter, Kenneth Westhues can hear a flock of crows tormenting a great horned owl outside his study in Waterloo, Ontario. It is a fitting soundtrack for his work. Mr. Westhues has made a career out of the study of mobbing. Since the late 1990s, he has written or edited five volumes on the topic. However, the mobbers that most captivate him are not sparrows, fieldfares, or jackdaws. They are modern-day college professors.

> Westhues, a professor of sociology at the University of Waterloo, Canada, told Gravois that universities are ideal places for workplace mobbing, because mobbing is one of the few ways to force tenured faculty out of their jobs.[2]

Although no two mobbings are identical, Westhues identified five stages:

> (1) "increasing isolation," where targeted faculty members might be left off of certain guest lists and the mobbing faculty ignore them and often roll their eyes at meetings when the targeted faculty speak; (2) "petty harassment," where the faculty member's administrative requests are delayed or misplaced or where classes or meetings get scheduled at odd times; (3) "critical incident," in which the faculty member is accused of making racially or sexually insensitive remarks or is accused of plagiarism, spending university money improperly, or a "rumor of some impropriety with a student gets traction," and the mobbing faculty demands that some action be taken; (4) "adjudication," where the allegations are either legitimized or dismissed by a university official or committee; and

(5) resignation, where the targeted faculty member, even if he or she wins, often leaves office.

Studies by psychiatrists show that many people who are victims of workplace mobbing often suffer from post-traumatic stress disorder. About 10 to 15 percent of the mobbed workers commit suicide, according to studies in Sweden.[3]

In the summer of 2020, this included Michael Adams, a conservative criminology professor at the University of North Carolina Wilmington who shot himself in the head after sending out a controversial tweet.[4] Adams tweeted about the statewide COVID-19 crackdown on dining as he ate and drank with six men: "I almost felt like a free man who was not living in the slave state of North Carolina." He added, "Massa [Governor Roy] Cooper, let my people go!"

More than 60,000 people signed a petition asking the university to fire him for his tweet. Adams previously had published two books criticizing political correctness on campus. The university tried to fire him once, but he sued and the courts ruled that his speech was private rather than job-related.[5] He was granted tenure and back pay.

In rare cases, the victims of mobbers also have attacked their mobbers, sometimes killing them.

Professors with foreign accents and those who frequently file grievances and "make noise" are often victims of mobbing.

But, interestingly, the victims usually are not underachievers.

The "most common single trait of mobbing targets," Westhues told Gravois, "is that they excel."

> To calculate the odds of your being mobbed, count the ways you show your workmates up: fame, publications, teaching scores, connections, eloquence, wit, writing skills, athletic ability, computer skills, salary, family money, age, class, pedigree, looks, house, clothes, spouse, children, sex appeal. Any one of these will do.[6]

Westhues also told Gravois that mobbing is rarely successful unless administrators back the mobbers.

"But because mobbers tend to be so impassioned and sloppy in their reasoning," Gravois wrote, quoting Westhues, "administrators who side with them may suffer for it later. Mr. Westhues's research provides numerous examples of mobbing victims who have walked away with fat court settlements, and of administrators who have walked away without their jobs."

As I read the story, I realized that Westhues nailed it.

Director Alex Tan distributed copies of the *Chronicle* article to all of the faculty. I wondered whether he did for my sake or his own, but I never asked him.

THE DECISION ABOUT Tan's contract renewal came in late April 2006.

Dean Lear announced that the Murrow School would search for a new director. Tan was out, but he would keep his professor position.

The details of this petit coup are irrelevant and nonpublic.

My purpose is not to assign blame, but to draw some lessons.

The first is a reminder that, despite the concept of shared governance, decision-making at universities does not depend solely or principally on democratic processes.

University bureaucracies are far more autocratic than democratic.

Almost every decision at a lower level can be overturned by upper administration. Obtaining consent of faculty is sometimes desired but not necessary.

This doesn't mean shared governance, or the idea that faculty should play a role in management of the university, is illusory. Faculty usually play a big role in curriculum development. But shared governance does not mean faculty share power equally with administrators. Power still flows from the top down.

The second lesson, as Machiavelli pointed out, is that no amount of kindness can appease your enemies. When it comes to holding on to power, love is less important than fear.

Tan was a kind man — one of the kindest I've ever met. He was, in my opinion, just as kind to those who helped oust him from power as he was to people who supported him.

But that didn't matter when it came time to cast a ballot.

Machiavelli elaborates:

From this arises the question whether it is better to be loved more than feared, or feared more than loved. ... [O]ne ought to be both feared and loved, but as it is difficult for the two to go together, it is much safer to be feared than loved. ... [M]en in general ... are ungrateful, voluble, dissemblers, anxious to avoid danger, and covetous of gain; as long as you benefit them, they are entirely yours; they offer you their blood, their goods, their life, and their children ... when the necessity is remote; but when it approaches, they revolt. And the prince who has relied solely on their words ... is ruined. ... [M]en have less scruple in offending one who makes himself loved than one who makes himself feared; for love is held by a chain of obligation, which, men being selfish, is broken whenever it serves their purpose; but fear is maintained by a dread of punishment which never fails.[7]

To his credit, Tan took his ousting with dignity, even though Dean Erich Lear told the *Lewiston* (Idaho) *Morning Tribune* that Tan took "too long to make decisions" and made "wrong decisions."[8]

Tan could have filed a defamation lawsuit.

But he didn't.

The university offered him another administrative post, which he accepted. Offering an alternative position is another common practice that administrators use to reduce conflict after a petit coup.

Shortly after Tan was removed from his administrative position, I had a chance meeting with Erica Weintraub Austin, a Murrow faculty member, and I suggested she run for the position of interim director of the Murrow School.

She smiled.

Was she flattered or had she already been offered the position?

I didn't know.

THE FIRST TASK after a petit coup is to select an interim director.

Two people ran for the office: Austin and a male professor in the communication studies sequence who was a vocal critic of Tan.

The voting was done by secret ballot.

Austin was the only woman in the communication program with full professor status. Her father is Stanley Weintraub, a Penn State University historian who gave a series of lectures at WSU during the first week of March 2006. Weintraub has written biographies and histories of the American Revolution and both world wars and is an expert on George Bernard Shaw.

He also apparently expected a lot out of Austin.

She told me that he told her that a competent scholar reaches full professor status before turning 40.

She didn't disappoint.

Austin was an accomplished mainstream quantitative social scientist, conducting research in an area of specialization referred to as health communication. Part of her research focused on children and the effects of alcoholic beverage advertising. She taught in the public relations sequence, which eventually was renamed "strategic communication."

At the time, Austin was coauthor of more than three dozen refereed journal articles and one textbook on public relations. She was one of the most published scholars in the Murrow School, according to a 2005 analysis of faculty productivity I conducted for the school.[9]

A national mass communication association once gave Austin an award for being the most promising researcher under age 40. She was smart, confident and well-liked by most Murrow professors, including me.

Her only shortcoming, some faculty would argue, is that she had few sole authored articles and no theoretically based books.[10] Almost everything she published had coauthors.

Austin's opponent for the director's position, who was a speech communication professor, hadn't published anything in several years.

He was an intelligent man; a good teacher; well liked by students and most Ph.D. faculty. He was working on a book but didn't have a publisher.

He also told me that he was not a big supporter of democracy. Plato was like that. He believed that ordinary people did not have the intelligence to rule effectively. An educated elite should call the shots.

Dean Lear collected the votes[11] and announced Austin had won, but he refused to release the final tally.

Only a couple of faculty, myself included, openly criticized the dean for refusing to release the results.

Plato won this time.

Chapter 31 Endnotes

1. John Gravois, "Mob Rule," *The Chronicle of Higher Education* (April 14, 2006), p. A10.

2. Westhues writes that "workplace mobbing is the collective expression of the eliminative impulse in formal organizations. It is a conspiracy of employees, sometimes acknowledged but more often not, to humiliate, degrade and get rid of a fellow employee, when rules prevent achievement of these ends through violence. It is a shared outpouring of irrationality upon the mundane, bureaucratic landscape of modern work." See Kenneth Westhues, *The Envy of Excellence: Administrative Mobbing of High-Achieving Professors* (Lewiston, Canada: The Edwin Mellen Press, 2005), p. 42.

3. Heinz Leymann and Annelie Gustafsson, "Mobbing at Work and the Development of Post-Traumatic Stress Disorders," *European Journal of Work and Organizational Psychology*, 5: 251-275 (1996), and Heinz Leymann, "The Content and Development of Mobbing at Work," *European Journal of Work and Organizational Psychology*, 5:165-184 (1996).

4. Robert Shibley, "In Memoriam: Professor Mike Adams, 1964-2020," Foundation for Individual Rights in Education (August 1, 2020), retrieved December 7, 2020, from <https://www.thefire.org/in-memoriam-professor-mike-adams-1964-2020>, and Ian Miles Cheong, "Woke Media Celebrates Suicide of Professor Who Was Fired for Controversial Tweet," The Post Millennial (July 26, 2020), retrieved September 22, 2020, from <https://thepostmillennial.com/woke-media-celebrates-suicide-professor-fired-controversial-tweet>.

5. *Adams v. Trustees of the University of North Carolina–Wilmington*, 640 F.3d 550 (4th Cir. 2011)

6. Gravois, "Mob Rule," quote excerpted from Westhues, *The Envy of Excellence*.

7. Niccolò Machiavelli, *The Prince* (New York: Alfred A. Knopf, 1992) [originally written circa 1505].

8. Joe Mills, "WSU Officials Explain Removal of Tan," *Lewiston* (Idaho) *Tribune* (April 26, 2006), p. 3.

9. I analyzed the vitae of tenured and tenure-track faculty and presented the results to Murrow Director Alex Tan and later to the faculty. No action was ever taken on the results. I updated the study in 2011 as an exhibit for the *Demers v. Austin* lawsuit. For details, see <www.marquettebooks.com/productivity.html>.

10. Some departments give lower ratings to publications with coauthors. There are two reasons for this. One is that the workload is reduced with coauthors. So some departments only give a coauthor 50 percent credit if there is one other coauthor. The second reason is to deter faculty from adding coauthors in an effort to help them get tenure or a promotion.

11. This is his real name. I use real names for higher level administrators because they occupy positions with high public visibility and generally have access to mass media, where they may defend themselves.

Chapter 32

Another Undemocratic Search

Summer/Fall 2006
Washington State University

In the summer of 2006, WSU President Lane Rawlins announced he was retiring. The WSU Board of Regents and top administrators began a formal search for a replacement.

Presidential searches are quite involved and, normally, relatively democratic, at least in terms of appearances.[1]

A professional search firm is hired to identify and screen some candidates. Then they are brought to campus, where they spend several days interviewing with various administrators, faculty, students, alumni, and citizens.

Of course, this is a time when administrators love to talk about the importance of "process" in making decisions. Committees are a must. Everyone's opinion must be taken into account. The process must be as democratic as possible.

Well, that's the talk.

In practice, as I've noted before, administrators don't always walk the walk. But to better understand how this anti-democratic story at WSU played out, you need a little background.

The campus is located in an area of the nation that has often been associated with racist groups and organizations. Although the number of people in these groups is quite small, no one disputes the fact that the Inland Northwest, which includes eastern areas of Washington State and northern areas of Idaho, is politically conservative, especially outside of the city of Spokane.

In the 1920s, various individuals, including Christian pastors, tried to encourage local residents to create chapters of the Ku Klux Klan in Pullman and Colfax.[2] Until recently, nearby Coeur d'Alene, Idaho, was home to the largest neo-Fascist Aryan group in the nation.

In the 1960s, the first African American to be admitted into a fraternity at WSU charged that some white members of the fraternity harassed him.[3]

In May 1970, a group of WSU students went on strike to protest racism on campus.[4] The action came after police shot and killed two black students and wounded 12 others on the Jackson State College campus. Unlike the shooting at

Kent State 10 days earlier, the shooting at Jackson State drew little news coverage, according to WSU professor emeritus of English Paul Brians, who studied protest events on the WSU campus during the 1960s and early 1970s.[5]

"Black students here drew the conclusion that white radicals identified only with other whites, and decided the time had come to press some of their urgent concerns about the racial climate on campus," Brians said during a lecture at WSU in 2006. "They drew up a list of demands. ... While the rest of the country was convulsed with demonstrations and strikes against the war in Southeast Asia, WSU students and faculty launched a strike against racism. ... Although few of the initial demands were realized, there were solid gains during this period, including the strengthening of minority studies programs, recruiting, and the establishment of a series of racism workshops which were extremely well attended and very intense."[6]

WSU administrators, by the way, fired all of the history graduate students who canceled the classes they were teaching to allow students to participate in the strike against racism. The president of the university at that time, W. Glenn Terrell, canceled final exams across the entire university, but he was not fired.

In 1978, five WSU students and the Japanese American Citizens League filed a class-action discrimination suit against WSU, claiming it violated the 1964 Civil Rights Act. The settlement required the administration to maintain an Asian American studies program.[7]

In 2005, two varsity basketball players were accused of making racist gestures and animal calls toward three Asian American female students working at a campus counseling center. After several investigations, the university concluded the accusations were not serious enough to warrant a full investigation. The incident ignited a storm of protest across campus and accusations of a cover-up. At least one administrator lost his job.

On April 2, 2005, the Washington State Democratic Central Committee passed a resolution which alleged that 20 incidents of racial harassment on campus had been inadequately addressed in the last 10 years.

At its meeting in late June 2005, the Washington State Human Rights Commission was informed that an investigation of racism was underway. "There is an urgent need at WSU to address the allegations of racism on the campus," the minutes of that meeting reported.[8]

Other details notwithstanding, the upshot was that in 2005 racism was perceived to be a major problem on campus, even though it was never documented that WSU had a more racist environment than other universities in the country.

If sociological theory is consulted, one might even predict that the problems were less serious at WSU than at other campuses for one simple reason: There were fewer minorities at WSU and, thus, fewer opportunities for discriminatory acts.[9] African

Americans made up only 2.4 percent of the WSU student body[10] and 1.4 percent of the faculty.[11]

In the 16 years that I worked at WSU, I never personally witnessed any incidents of racism on campus. My experience had been that every employee at the university, from faculty to staff to administrators, had tried very hard to make the campus a friendly place for people of all colors and ethnic groups.

To me, the biggest problem at WSU wasn't racism, it was trying to convince professors and students of color to come to WSU. After all, why would racial minorities want to attend or work at a university where resources and cultural activities for people of color were limited?

On Wednesday, December 13, 2006, long before the search process was completed, the WSU Board of Regents voted to give the job to Elson S. Floyd, who was president of the University of Missouri.

Floyd didn't even interview on campus.

The decision came after two days of closed-door sessions with top-level administrators and board members and took almost everyone by surprise.

"It's not how we do any other hires in the university," Ken Struckmeyer, a former Faculty Senate chairman who later became an ombudsman at the university, told the *Spokesman-Review*.[12] One outspoken communication professor sent an e-mail to many faculty and administrators on campus, strongly criticizing the regents for scuttling the search process and usurping the interests of faculty and others. She also copied Murrow faculty on the e-mail.

Administrators ignored the complaint and told the news media that the regents had to move quickly.

"With other high-profile schools out trolling for candidates," the newspaper reported, "and many top-flight administrators eager to avoid appearing to be out job-hunting, regents said that moving quickly to hire Floyd was the best way to ensure WSU got its top candidate."

Even the current chairman of the Faculty Senate, Charles Pezeshki, who oversees a faculty group that sometimes is at odds with the administration, supported the decision. Pezeshki told the newspaper he "understands that some on campus complain that the process wasn't more democratic." He admitted: "I've gotten some flak from people."

But Pezeshki defended the decision, saying a private search is sometimes necessary because administrators are afraid they will lose their current jobs if word gets out that they are searching for another job. "I feel that Dr. Floyd is going to be one of the more open, egalitarian presidents we've ever had at WSU," he said, apparently unaware of the irony of his comment.

Two days later, Gary Crooks, a columnist for the *Spokesman-Review*, pointed out that the searches for the last three presidents hired at WSU and Eastern Washington University were all conducted in public. The candidates came to the campuses and visited with students and faculty.

"The rationale for this speedy, secretive hire [of Floyd] is that no leaders worth having would subject themselves to a public process," Crooks wrote. "Do you buy it?"[13] Crooks's column and the news story announcing the selection of Floyd never mentioned the alleged racial problems at WSU, nor did any administrator link the regents' decision with that issue.

But the issue of racism on campus faded very quickly after Floyd came to campus.

Why?

Because Floyd was African American.

The regents had made a brilliant move, even though democracy was sacrificed in the process.

EARLY IN FALL SEMESTER 2006, Austin, the new interim director of the Murrow School, invited faculty to meet with her one-on-one to discuss issues and concerns.

She and I met for about 20 minutes.

I told her the school would benefit if it would appoint one of the non-tenured professional faculty members to the position of associate director of undergraduate studies. I recommended someone. I said some of the professional faculty feel like second-class citizens, and the appointment would help ease this concern.

Austin then changed topics.

"You know, the faculty have concerns about Marquette Books."

"Those issues were settled years ago," I responded. "The university attorneys and controller investigated and found no wrongdoing. If I use a Marquette Book textbook in my class, I give them out free of charge to students. I give them hard copies or a free PDF of the book."

She didn't respond.

I assumed the issue was settled.

I was wrong.

Meanwhile, the Murrow School was bustling with activity in fall semester 2006. More than a half-dozen committees had been formed to correct perceived problems in the curriculum and structure of the program.

There also was talk that the Murrow School might be converted into a college. If so, how should that be structured? One of the Murrow committees would address that issue.

"Here we go again," one faculty member who had been around for a couple of decades told me. "We're going to restructure the program for the umpteenth time, and no doubt we'll do that again in several more years."

There was, unfortunately, a lot of truth to that statement.

In the decade that I had been there, I had seen the faculty restructure various aspects of the program and, in some cases, revert back to a previous structure. Each administrator and faculty member had his or her own idea of how to construct the ideal program, and most of us felt entitled to do that.

I was no exception.

In my opinion, there were two major problems.

First, the Murrow School mass communication programs were not nationally accredited. Accreditation is the best and most logical way to improve the quality of the programs and gain national standing.

Second, the school needed to remove communication studies courses (formerly known as speech communication) from the curriculum. Those courses were draining too many resources from the mass communication programs.

At the time the Murrow School employed seven full-time communication studies faculty, but only about 25–40 students were majoring in communication studies (a 1:4 ratio). In other words, about one-fourth of the school's resources were going to 5 percent of the Murrow students.

In contrast, the school employed about 21 full-time mass communication faculty who served more than 650 majors (a 1:31 ratio).[14] This discrepancy meant that mass communication undergraduate students had fewer course offerings in their major.

At most universities, mass communication programs and communication studies are housed in different departments, because they have different goals and serve different real-world constituencies.[15]

I raised the accreditation issue at a faculty meeting and, once again, was unable to convince my colleagues that this was an important issue.

"They are worried about their graduate program," one faculty member explained again. "They don't want the undergraduate program to take resources away from their precious graduate program."[16]

As I expected, my plan to separate the communication studies program from the mass communication programs also was not well-received by many of the faculty, especially the communication studies faculty. They knew that if their unit were converted into a stand-alone department, the number of faculty would have to be reduced.

Austin did not initially appoint me to the structure committee. I think she and others were worried I would be out of step with the other faculty members of the committee. Of course, that was true.

But I requested the appointment because, I argued, my specialty in sociology was organizational structure. Maybe I could influence some of the other committee members.

Reluctantly, she agreed.

But by the time I joined the committee, it had already met twice. The meeting time conflicted with my daughter's school schedule, so I joined the meetings via telephone hook-up for most of the semester.

For nearly two months, faculty on the committee talked about ways to structure the school. From my perspective, the big problem was that none of the faculty were thinking like administrators. In a time of budget cutbacks, no plan for restructuring a program can succeed if it doesn't focus on securing donations and grants.

At one meeting, one of the communication studies professors made a disparaging remark about the Murrow School's professional advisory board, which was composed of about 30 working mass communication professionals who provided advice about the curriculum.

"We aren't going to let them tell us what to do," the faculty member said.

I had heard enough.

It was time to formally propose a plan to re-professionalize and improve the quality of the undergraduate mass communication programs — a plan that would make fundraising and servicing the needs of the professional community key components. To get higher-level administrators to take notice, I would donate, in my role as a book publisher, $50,000 to the university if administrators would implement the plan. I would send the plan, which contained seven steps for improving the undergraduate mass communication programs, to them after the holidays, in January 2007.

MEANWHILE, Austin sent an e-mail in late December 2006 informing faculty that they should not cancel their classes. Her e-mail, which was based on a conversation that one of the Murrow administrators had with Vice Provost for Faculty Affairs Frances McSweeney, said university rules prohibited the canceling of classes.

Canceling classes is not an unusual event at a university. Some faculty do it for legitimate reasons, such as compensating students for other class-based activities (e.g., extra library research, attending certain lectures and events). Some do it for illegitimate reasons, such as to skip out of a semester early.[17]

Although the e-mail was sent to all faculty, Austin's order was clearly directed at me. It was no secret that I canceled the last two days of classes in my Com 101 courses. I had it written right into my syllabus. I did it for pedagogical reasons: to deter students in my large-lecture Com 101 class from missing exams. I had been doing it for several years. Former Murrow Director Alex Tan was aware of the practice, and no other WSU administrators had ever raised the issue.

One of the biggest problems in a large lecture course is trying to get students to take the exams on time. To deter illegitimate reasons, I only allowed students to make up exams at the end of the course, during final exam week.

Faculty at WSU are not required to give final exams, so I used the final exam session for make-up exams. Because students are anxious to leave the university at the end of the semester, this was an effective deterrent. The vast majority of students, more than 90 percent, took every exam at the scheduled time.[18]

The faculty manual did not prohibit faculty from canceling classes for pedagogical reasons, which I had been doing for nearly four years without objection from administrators. I e-mailed Austin and asked her if she could identify the rule or regulation. She didn't respond.

So I e-mailed McSweeney and asked her if faculty were prohibited from canceling classes for pedagogical reasons.

On December 20, 2006, she responded: "I don't know of a University regulation that sets a numerical limit on the cancellation of classes. For a variety of reasons, I don't think that we'd want to assign a specific number." But, she added, that if faculty were canceling a lot of classes, that would be of grave concern.

No argument there.

I sent an e-mail to Austin, passing along the information I learned from McSweeney. I suggested that she send an e-mail to Murrow faculty, correcting her previous comments. I said I would be willing to defend my policies before a university grievance committee.

Austin didn't respond, nor did she send a follow-up e-mail to faculty.

A day later I cooled down. I decided that even if faculty had the authority to cancel classes for pedagogical reasons, it was best to change my Com 101 syllabus and hold classes during dead week. The teaching assistants would review material for students and allow them to check their grades.

I needed to pick and choose my battles more carefully.

And my 7-Step Plan was one battle worth a good fight. I would reach retirement age in less than eight years. It was now or never.

Chapter 32 Endnotes

1. By democratic, I mean various groups and constituencies are consulted. A formal vote of all members of those groups is never conducted.

2. "Pullman Needs Klan, Says Local Pastor," *Pullman Herald* (Dec. 22, 1992), p. 7, and "Klansmen Do Not Tar and Feather," *Colfax Gazette* (Dec. 1, 1922), p. 1.

3. He was an athlete who left the university after his first year. This information was obtained from a member of the fraternity.

4. The strike against racism occurred during the nationwide protests over the bombing in Cambodia, which led some people to incorrectly associate the strike with anti-war protests.

5. Paul Brians, "Images of the Counterculture: WSU in the 60s," an oral presentation, Fine Arts Auditorium, Washington State University (November 2, 2006). Professor Brians provided me with a copy of the presentation.

6. Ibid., pp. 73, 74 and 76.

7. These facts were taken from Alex Kuo, "How Much Progress Against Racism Has WSU Really Made?" *Seattle Post-Intelligencer* (March 1, 2009; guest columnist). Kuo, a professor of English at WSU for three decades, argues in his commentary that racism toward Asians is a major problem at WSU. He says his own department often discriminated against him.

8. Washington State Human Rights Commission, minutes of meeting June 23, 2005, held at Kitsap County Fairgrounds, Eagles Nest, Silverdale, Washington, retrieved April 24, 2009, from <www.hum.wa.gov/documents/Minutes/2005/June23-24,%25202005%2520Minutes.pdf+washington+state+human+rights+commission+june+2005+report+wsu&cd=2&hl=en&ct=clnk&gl=us>.

9. See Peter M. Blau, *Inequality and Heterogeneity: A Primitive Theory of Social Structure* (New York: The Free Press, 1977).

10. This figure includes the 18,000 or so students enrolled in Pullman as well as the 5,000 additional students at satellite campuses around the state.

11. The only tenured black faculty member on campus at the time worked in the communication school.

12. Shawn Vestal, "New Top Coug," *The Spokesman-Review* (December 14, 2006), p. 1.

13. Gary Crooks, "Gary Crooks: Smart Bombs," *The Spokesman-Review* (December 16, 2006).

14. The school also had about 700 pre-majors, mostly freshman and sophomores. So there were 60 students for each faculty member.

15. At the time, only three of 30 Ph.D.-granting mass communication programs in the United States housed communication studies programs.

16. The Murrow School was granted its own Ph.D. program in the early 2000s. It focused on intercultural communication and later was expanded to include mass communication.

17. One of our female faculty did that one semester and told two other faculty about it at a meeting one day, but she was never called out for it. Even Austin let her students out of some classes early at the end of the school year, her students told me.

18. I thought about giving the make-up exams during the last week of regularly scheduled classes, but I wasn't sure this was enough deterrent and the university had a policy that faculty cannot give exams during the final week of classes in a semester. Other Murrow faculty who taught large lecture sections with labs and I would also cancel some lab sessions during Veteran's Week, because the holiday meant some of the labs could not be conducted and fairness dictated that all students be presented with the same material. None of the other faculty, however, were scrutinized by the administration.

Chapter 33
My 7-Step Plan

January 2007
Washington State University

I sent my 7-Step Plan for improving the undergraduate mass communication programs to WSU Provost Robert Bates on January 16, 2007.

I would have sent it to President Lane Rawlins, but he was a lame duck. Incoming President Floyd wouldn't assume the helm until May 2007.

The plan was four pages, full color, 5.5 by 8.5 inches in size. The cover (first page) contained a picture of the new communication building, a headline and attribution:

A 7-STEP PLAN FOR MAKING THE EDWARD R. MURROW SCHOOL
OF COMMUNICATION FINANCIALLY INDEPENDENT AND A $50,000
DONATION TO KICK OFF A FUNDRAISING CAMPAIGN
Prepared by Marquette Books LLC, Spokane, Washington

In the cover letter on the second page, I said Marquette Books would donate $50,000 to the university if it implemented the 7 steps. The purpose of my donation was to jump-start a formal fundraising campaign for the Murrow School, to re-professionalize the mass communication programs.

The third page included a brief history of mass communication programs and the conflict between the green eyeshades and chi-squares. The fourth page, which also included a small picture of the Murrow Center building, outlined the 7 steps, which are condensed below.

1. Separate the mass communication program from the communication studies program at WSU ... to send a very strong message to the professional/business community that WSU is committed to enhancing its undergraduate program in mass communication.
2. Hire a director of the Edward R. Murrow School of Communication who has a strong professional background ... to improve its relations with the professional community.

3. Create an Edward R. Murrow Center for Media Research that conducts joint research projects with the professional community ... [and] non-accredited educational programs ... that enhance the careers of media professionals.
4. Give real-world professionals an active (rather than the current passive) role in the development of the curriculum in the School.
5. Give professional faculty a more active role in the development of the undergraduate curriculum for mass communication students.
6. Seek national accreditation for the "new" mass communication programs. ... [to] enhance the quality and visibility of the School at WSU.
7. Hire more professional faculty with substantial work experience.

I composed a press release announcing the details of the plan and sent it to three dozen news media and university officials. I was hoping to get some support from the professional community.

Seattle Times Publisher Frank Blethen responded: "Very ambitious. And, yes, thankfully, you are not one to follow the most trodden path. ... I understand the issue but am not versed on the particulars. Under the current WSU president (Lane Rawlins), we have lost all our connection with the school. Hope to reconnect with the new 'pres.' I will keep this top of mind. Journalism does matter."[1]

Blethen and other professionals had complained for years that the mass communication programs at University of Washington and Washington State University were losing touch with the real world, but, interestingly, not one professional organization or journalist openly supported the 7-Step Plan or any elements of it.

A month passed with no response from the Provost's office.

In late February, Dean Erich Lear said he'd given the plan to Austin.

She was not pleased, nor were the communication studies faculty.

At a faculty meeting, Austin announced that "communication studies was central to the mission of the Murrow School." Some faculty wanted to vote down the plan right there. But Austin said the plan had not been submitted to them for review. It had been submitted to the provost's office.

Several more weeks passed and still no response from the provost.

Only two faculty expressed some support for the plan, but neither would go public with their opinions.

I didn't blame them.

The plan was very controversial because of the call for the removal of the communication studies sequence.

The irony was that, outside of WSU, the other elements of my plan were mainstream. But inside, my plan was perceived as being radical.

After nearly two months of no response from WSU, I decided to sweeten the pot. I increased the donation to $100,000.

I composed a new letter on March 29 and sent it to incoming president Elson Floyd. He responded immediately and said he would like to meet to discuss the plan, but that he would be very busy that summer. I said fall semester would be fine.

At the Murrow Symposium in April 2006, Provost Bates said he never received the plan, even though postal records showed the university had signed for the package. But he said he was aware of the plan.

He then asked, in a disapproving tone of voice, "Why did you circumvent the Murrow administration and submit the plan directly to me?"

"Because I had no other choice," I said calmly, anticipating the question. "The Murrow School administration has refused to acknowledge the value of national accreditation as well as the other ideas in my plan for improving the undergraduate program."

MEANWHILE, unbeknownst to me, resentment was stirring in the department over another issue.

After the election of Austin for director of the Murrow School, Dean Lear had appointed the losing candidate to the part-time position of "associate director" in the Murrow School and given him a $10,000 raise.

That prompted one of the other current "associate directors" in the Murrow School to ask for a $10,000 raise, but the dean refused. Until now, associate directors were paid with time off from classes, meaning they were given one less class to teach per semester.

Several faculty also were angry because they felt faculty should have been given the chance to apply for the position given to the losing candidate.

Lear said the appointment was designed to bring the factions together.

Obviously, not everyone agreed.

In late February 2007, someone wrote an anonymous memo criticizing Lear's decision to appoint the losing candidate without giving other faculty a chance to apply.

Austin responded by sending an e-mail to faculty and threatening punishment if faculty continued to write anonymous letters.

"I want to assure you that I will not tolerate harassment of our faculty and staff. ... I want you to know that I will not let incidents like this go unaddressed."

Of course, no overly idealistic advocate of the First Amendment like me could allow a comment like that go unanswered. I e-mailed:

"If you, acting on behalf of the university, punish the individual for expressing those opinions, regardless of whether they are true or not, you and the university will be violating the First Amendment and the author's academic freedom."

Dean Lear then e-mailed: "We have an obligation to protect those we supervise. We would, if the action of the message's author is inappropriate, operate within the university's disciplinary processes. These sometimes elicit legal action outside of the university, but we need to be brave enough to call things to question."

Frances McSweeney, vice provost for faculty affairs, then backed up Lear.

She said in an e-mail that she wasn't advocating punishment for the faculty member who wrote the memo, but "if the comments are serious enough, as Erich (Lear) says, we do have a disciplinary process."

I responded: "The university can discipline faculty for unethical action and behavior but not for expressing a point of view on a political issue, even if that view contains errors or falsehoods. The 1940 Statement on Academic Freedom from the American Association of University Professors and the U.S. Supreme Court have made that very clear."

Actually, there was a good chance I was wrong on the latter point, at least in terms of how the courts were interpreting free speech in 2006.

Unbeknownst to me, ten months before our lively e-mail exchange, the U.S. Supreme Court issued a ruling that appeared to support the administrators' arguments.

In *Garcetti v. Ceballos*, the conservative majority of the court ruled 5–4 that public employees generally do not deserve free speech protection when speaking in their official roles — even when they report wrongdoing among governmental officials.[2] The case involved an assistant district attorney in Los Angeles, Richard Ceballos, who was disciplined after he discovered police had submitted false information to obtain a search warrant.

The five conservative Supreme Court judges who penned the majority opinion essentially said it is better for the government to control employees than to root out misconduct or corrupt public employees. In other words, only citizens and politicians, not government employees, have the right to criticize the government.

But because of the long-standing principle of academic freedom, the majority opinion left the door open on the issue of whether professors have more protection than other government employees. The opinion said: "We need not ... decide whether the analysis we conduct today would apply in the same manner to a case involving speech related to scholarship or teaching."

Prior to *Garcetti*, the courts had relied on what came to be known as the Pickering balancing test.[3]

This involved balancing the interests of a public employer with employees' right to free speech using the following three questions:

1. Did the employee's speech address a matter or matters of public interest and concern?
2. Was the employee's speech a significant or motivating factor in the employer's decision to punish or terminate the employee?
3. Did the interests of the individual commenting on matters of public concern outweigh the public employer's interest in "promoting the efficiency of public service?"

To prevail, an employee had to convince the court that the answers to all three questions were "yes."

Garcetti basically mooted the first two questions and assumed that all speech from employees was contrary to the efficiency of public service.

The *Garcetti* decision eventually would figure prominently in my own case against WSU administrators; in fact, my case would nullify the decision for nine states in the West.

But the exchange of e-mails between WSU administrators and me clearly demonstrated to me that administrators were more concerned about social order than academic freedom.

The author of the mysterious letter that criticized Dean Lear never revealed his or her identity.

I'm sure some Murrow faculty thought I wrote it, but I didn't.

I asked two faculty whether they had written it, but both denied authorship.

I e-mailed Dean Lear at one point to explain that some faculty saw his appointment of the losing candidate as a political payoff.

Lear denied the charge.

I think he was being honest.

He saw it as a way of trying to calm a conflicted situation, but things don't always turn out the way you predict.

IN FEBRUARY 2007, I submitted my annual review for the 2006 calendar year to Austin. Other Murrow faculty did the same.

Annual reviews affect merit raise increases, promotion and tenure.

The review contains three major areas: one for research and scholarship, one for teaching and one for service (to the community, university and profession).

Because WSU is a Ph.D.-granting institution, scholarship is clearly the most important (40%). That's what usually decides whether a faculty member gets tenure. Teaching is also very important (40%). Service is a distant third (20%).

When Alex Tan was the director of the Murrow School, he reviewed the material and rated faculty in terms of their performance.

However, the new administration opted for a different procedure: It created a four-member faculty committee that would review the performance records and make recommendations to Austin. The committee would be composed of faculty from various ranks.

This was an ill-conceived plan, for four reasons.

First, faculty of lower ranks should not be allowed to rate faculty of higher ranks. This was inconsistent with university rules on tenure, which only allow faculty of higher rank to rate the performance of other faculty.

Second, because the faculty review committee was a unit that did not have formal authority under WSU's faculty manual, giving some faculty the authority to see the performance records of other faculty could violate privacy laws on the release of personnel records.

Third, giving some faculty the authority to evaluate other faculty could generate a lot of resentment and conflict among faculty. In fact, faculty who disliked other faculty would have an incentive to serve on the committee, because as members of the committee they could "grind their ax."

Fourth, the faculty review committee approach might also encourage the Murrow director to displace responsibility for the ratings. The director could even play the role of Pontius Pilate and blame the committee for any errors that might crop up later.

Not surprisingly, Austin ignored my objections.

The plan was implemented.

At least two of the four faculty on the committee did not like my 7-Step Plan or the idea of removing communication studies from the Murrow program.

During the previous decade, I had received an average annual rating of 4.8 on a 5-point scale, with 5 representing extraordinary performance. I received a perfect 5.0 rating in two of those years.

My analysis of faculty vitae showed that I was the most productive scholar in the Murrow School on two of three measures and I ranked second on the third.[4] On average, I had published the equivalent of more than five social scientific articles per year since obtaining my Ph.D.

In 2006, I had just completed the first draft of a 370-page theoretically grounded book titled *History and Future of Mass Media.* This was my 10th academic book. I had signed a contract with Hampton Press of Cresskill, N.J., to publish the book in late summer.

In spring 2006, the Murrow School also chose my *Dictionary of Mass Communication & Media Research* as the second-most important contribution from the Murrow School faculty during 2005.[5] My teaching evaluations averaged 4.4 on a five-point scale, which was above departmental averages for faculty.

The year 2006 had been one of my best years as a professor.

But it wouldn't matter.

Chapter 33 Endnotes

1. E-mail dated February 1, 2007.
2. *Garcetti v. Ceballos,* 547 U.S. 410 (2006).
3. *Pickering v. Board of Education of Township High School District, 205, Will County,* 391 U.S. 563 (1968).
4. Faculty Productivity data was updated as part of the evidence for the *Demers v. Austin* lawsuit and is available for viewing at <www.marquettebooks.com/productivity/html>. All faculty names except Demers have been redacted.
5. David Demers, *Dictionary of Mass Communication & Media Research: A Guide for Students, Professionals and Scholars* (Spokane, WA: Marquette Books, 2005). The book also received good reviews from two scholarly journals and one trade publication.

Chapter 34

My Crummy Annual Review

9:34 a.m., March 22, 2007
Washington State University

I could feel my face flush as I read my 2006 annual review on the morning of March 22, 2007.

A 2.7 on a 5.0 scale.

How could the new director give me such a low annual review rating?

That was the lowest or second-lowest faculty rating in the entire Edward R. Murrow School of Communication at Washington State University.[1] Anything lower than 3.0 means a faculty member is failing to meet minimum expectations and can be fired for incompetence — even if they, like me, are tenured.

Incompetence?

Okay, I concede I'll never win a Pulitzer or Nobel prize.

But I was a good teacher,[2] and on two of three measures of faculty research productivity I was even rated the top researcher in the entire Murrow School.[3]

I am tempted — really tempted — to start calling Erica Austin a bunch of nasty names, like asshole or *scheissekopf*. That's German for shithead. I learned that when I was a kid, because I grew up in a small working-class German town in Michigan.

But now I'm a professor, and we professors are expected to control ourselves and our language. Our motto, if we had one, would be "cool and calm complements scholarly and sagacious."

So I'm trying my best to turn indignation into compassion. Maybe someone gave Austin faulty information.

Yeah, I bet that's it.

Now I'm even feeling a tinge of Lutheran guilt for thinking about calling her names. She's actually a very pleasant person. I even supported her candidacy for director of the Murrow School last summer. The least I can do is read the rest of her review before I fly off the handle.

"The committee and I ," Austin writes, "are concerned that ... [Dr. Demers] has had a class policy of cancelling lab sections. ... When asked by [me] to make a change for future semesters, Dr. Demers declined to alter this schedule. Because failure to comply with expectations regarding class contact time may be constructed as 'serious and repeated neglect of duty' as set for in the faculty manual, Dr. Demers' unresponsiveness on this issue is of concern."

Serious and repeated neglect of duty?
Unresponsiveness?
Is she kidding?

Previous WSU administrators have sanctioned my class policies, and I changed my syllabus to conform to her request not to cancel classes during dead week for pedagogical reasons. *Why didn't she look at my syllabus or contact me before issuing this review?*

The average rating in the department was 3.95. Ninety-five percent of the faculty were rated higher. I received a 2.8 rating in terms of research, even though I had completed my *History and Future of Mass Media* book and had secured a reputable publisher.[4]

One tenured Murrow faculty member chuckled when I told him the results.

"Gee, I didn't publish anything and I received a 3.0 rating on research," said Joey Reagan, a full professor.

In the review, Austin indicated she was giving me a low rating because I didn't publish any refereed papers. In my formal written response, I told her that she would be violating Murrow School rules if she punished me or other faculty for writing refereed theoretical books, because the rules place as much value on refereed books as on refereed papers.

She did not respond.

Austin's review also criticized me for not performing enough service, even though I served on two departmental committees, reviewed four papers for journals or conferences, chaired three master's committees and was a member of a fourth, and put in the required eight hours minimum per week.

In my response, I accused Austin of penalizing me not because of poor performance, but because I had supported the previous director (Alex Tan), proposed the 7-Step Plan, and criticized her policies and other administrators' policies regarding the administration of the school.

I asked her to change my ratings.

She refused.

I contacted one member of the faculty review committee in an attempt to find out how Austin could have made the error about my canceling classes in Com 101. The committee member wasn't sure, but he said when the committee discussed the issue, one of the other committee members (a friend of Austin) confessed that she had canceled classes during dead week in one spring semester to leave early for a vacation.

The faculty review committee member also told me that the committee did not issue any written findings to Austin. The committee's evaluation of faculty was transmitted verbally, he said.

Very odd.

UNIVERSITY RULES allow faculty to "appeal" the director's decision to the Dean of Liberal Arts.

Although Dean Lear did not defend Austin's review, he refused to change it.

I asked him if I could appeal his decision. He said there was no formal appeals process for annual reviews.

What?

Indeed, the faculty manual contained no statements about how to correct errors in annual reviews if the Dean refuses to correct them.

At one point, Dean Lear and Austin asked to meet with me. I agreed if they would give me permission to tape-record the meeting.

They refused.

I declined to meet, because without accountability they could use the meeting to generate more evidence against me.

The only other possible option was the Faculty Status Committee (FSC), which can hear grievances but cannot force administrators to correct errors. FSC only has the power to make recommendations.

I filed a complaint in May 2007, because I knew that if I needed to file a lawsuit to protect my job, I would have to exhaust all administrative reviews.

The committee sat on my complaint for nine months.

I contacted the committee chair and he sent me a letter saying the committee had declined to review the case. No reason was given.

Later I learned that the FS committee refused to hear complaints about annual reviews because it did not have enough time to evaluate them. It was too busy hearing appeals from faculty who were denied tenure and perhaps some who were being fired for low annual review ratings.

University rules also did not allow a decision of the FS committee to be appealed.

So it ended there.

IN SPRING 2007, I learned that I was not the only faculty member who was being targeted by WSU administrators.

Within a year or so, several Murrow faculty were gone. Within three years, more than a half-dozen had left. All of those who left except one had been Tan supporters.

I might have left, too, except that my wife couldn't leave the area.

She had only seven more years before she was fully vested in her retirement plan at a state-run hospital for the mentally ill where she worked. Another disincentive to leaving was that Lee Ann was doing well in school.

I believe that Austin and other administrators initially had good intentions when they took control of the Murrow School. They believed some faculty were not very productive or were poor teachers. They wanted to improve the quality of the Murrow School.

But all purges have risks.

Two faculty eventually filed discrimination complaints, one based on race and the other on age. The race case was dismissed and the university paid a small sum to settle the age case. And there is always the chance that someone, a person who is very passionate and quixotic, will file a lawsuit that will drag on for many years.

Chapter 34 Endnotes

1. The review provided the mean rating for the entire faculty and a standard deviation, from which I was able to calculate my relative position.

2. For ten years straight I received annual review ratings no lower than 4.5. Most were between 4.8 and 5.0. Last year's was 4.8. During that time, I wrote six scholarly books, twenty refereed papers, and more than a hundred professional papers.

3. David Demers, "Productivity of Tenured Faculty in the Murrow College of Communication Since Obtaining Ph.D. and Between 2006 and 2008," Washington State University (February 2011), Exhibit 24 of documents submitted in *Demers v. Austin* (746 F.3d 402 (9th Cir., Jan. 29, 2014). A PDF of the report is available at <www.marquettebooks.com/productivity.html>.

4. The publisher was Hampton Press of Cresskill, New Jersey, which at that time had published several hundred books in the field of journalism and mass communication.

Chapter 35

Murrow School Becomes a College

Summer 2007
Washington State University

Elson Floyd assumed the presidency of WSU in the summer of 2007, and one of his first acts was to announce that the university would consider turning the Murrow School into a college.

Floyd previously was president of the University of Missouri, which has one of the best undergraduate mass communication programs in the United States.

College status for the Murrow program presumably would mean more funding. The Murrow faculty, myself included, were pleased about that.

But Floyd's announcement was another reminder of how power in a university flows from the top down, not from the bottom up.

For a decade WSU administrators had been telling the Murrow School that it was too small to become a college — and then, overnight, one individual at the top changed everything. Presumably Floyd knew that converting the school into a college was a way to bring greater visibility to the entire university, because Edward R. Murrow was its most famous graduate.

MEANWHILE, I WAS preparing to move Marquette Books out of my basement and into a commercial location. The goal was to hire more workers to reduce my time in the business. During the school year, faculty are allowed to work one full day at a consulting or other non-university business. During the summer, there was no limit on work hours, as long as a faculty member wasn't teaching.

On September 18, 2007, I distributed a news release stating that Marquette Books would be moving into a commercial location two blocks from my home.

Unbeknownst to me, Murrow interim Director Erica Austin had been meeting with Vice Provost Frances McSweeney, internal auditor Heather Lopez and university attorneys about Marquette Books and about the issue of online quizzes and exams. I don't know the content of those meetings, but I received an e-mail from Lopez on September 20, 2007, asking for more information about the company.

I was surprised, because she was asking the same questions that had been answered nearly four years earlier, when the university controller investigated and found I had been following university rules. I assumed her inquiry was simply routine follow-up. I told her what I had been telling Austin. If I use a Marquette book in my class, I give them free to students. MB is my summer employment.

I also e-mailed Lopez and pointed out that Austin was penalizing me in my annual reviews for proposing the 7-Step Plan.

In November, I submitted an application to take a sabbatical to write a book about the lack of impact of social science research on public policy.[1] I informed WSU officials that the book could contain content "critical of WSU." I wanted them to be fully informed before approving the sabbatical.

Austin had reservations about granting the leave.[2]

But the provost's office approved it.

ON OCTOBER 24, 2007, I met with Floyd to talk about the $100,000 donation and the 7-Step Plan. I did a little background research on him before our meeting.

Since 1978, he had held 15 different administrative positions at various universities, including the presidential positions at University of Missouri and Western Michigan University. He earned all of his degrees from the University of North Carolina at Chapel Hill: a bachelor's degree in political science and speech, a master's of education, and a Ph.D. in higher and adult education.

His curriculum vitae indicates that he never held a full-time teaching position and had no refereed journal publications or books. Some faculty see the lack of scholarship and teaching experience as a flaw. They believe "managerial administrators" are less likely to identify with the concerns and issues of faculty. They might not, for example, see academic freedom and shared governance as being as important as "academic administrators" would see them. But Floyd was too new to the university for anyone, including me, to draw such conclusions.

He cordially escorted me into his spacious university office, which had yet to be adorned with WSU "Go Cougars" paraphernalia. He apologized for that.

Physically, Floyd reminded me of Laurence Fishburne, the actor who is perhaps best known for his role as Morpheus in the 1999 science fiction film *The Matrix*.

Fishburne is charismatic on screen; Floyd is equally impressive in real life. News reports did not exaggerate. He was charming and gracious.

The only discomfort I felt during his visit was his shifting gaze. He seemed to focus on every gesture I made as if looking for clues to flaws in my character. Another university administrator later told me he felt the same way when he spoke with Floyd.

But it surely wasn't fair to judge a man after one encounter, and, after all, this was the man who several weeks earlier announced that the university might turn the Murrow School into a college. Actually that statement was only partially correct. He had already made the decision.

"I am going to turn the Murrow School into a college," he said.

I told him the Murrow faculty had been trying to do that for 10 years.

I spent most of the half-hour in his office talking about the 7-Step Plan. I'm not sure he was all that interested.

But he was interested in the $100,000 donation I offered if the university accepted the plan.

At one point, he interrupted me and radically altered the conversation.

"Why do you get into it with the faculty over there? I think you enjoy taunting them."

I smiled but ignored his allegation. I continued with my presentation.

What was interesting about his comment is that it implied that I had power over other faculty — that I had the power to taunt. But I had very little power. When it came to implementing the changes I suggested for improving the Murrow programs, I always lost.

Floyd clearly had no clue that mobbing is a top-down phenomena, not bottom up.

But we parted with a handshake and smiles.

AFTER THE MEETING with Floyd, Austin sent an e-mail to faculty saying four deans from mass communication programs at other universities in the United States would visit the campus to make a recommendation about turning the Murrow School into a college.

I e-mailed Austin and other faculty and told them that it was a done deal. "Floyd already told me that he was going to turn the school into a college."

Austin responded via e-mail to all of the faculty that the decision had not been made. Formally, she was correct. The Board of Regents would need to approve the action. But I wondered if Floyd had told her what he told me. If so, she never revealed it.

The college proposal did not change my 7-Step Plan, which was oriented toward restructuring and re-professionalizing the mass communication programs.

I personally knew two of the outside deans who would visit WSU.

One of them, Jean Folkerts, had been editor of a scholarly journal where I had published eight of my refereed journal papers.[3] I also interviewed for a job once at her university, where she was director of the program. "We need someone like you," she said. But I was never offered the position.

The other dean was Tim Gleason of the University of Oregon. He was a First Amendment scholar and a pleasant man.

I contacted the four deans and gave them copies of the 7-Step Plan.

I specifically mentioned the importance of separating communication studies from the mass communication program and the issue of accreditation. All four journalism programs in their colleges were accredited. None included a communication studies (or speech communication) program.

I didn't know how they would react to the plan, but I knew they would endorse the college-status proposal. That's how it works in the politics of higher education. Committees are used to endorse and legitimate a decision. Ohio State University criminology professor Simon Dinitz taught me that one.

But the visiting deans' committee recommended that communication studies be included in the new college. The committee also informally advised that the new Murrow College should not seek accreditation. Was that comment intended to marginalize my 7-Step Plan?

The Murrow School officially became a college on July 1, 2008.

When the news was announced at a faculty meeting, most faculty were jubilant. One of the communication studies faculty who had strongly supported the college proposal and the ouster of Alex Tan jokingly said: "I suppose we should be careful of what we ask for, because we might just get it."

Little did he realize how prophetic that statement would be.

That professor had not been productive in terms of research and later was pressured to publish more research. He left WSU and became an administrator at another university.

Chapter 35 Endnotes

1. At WSU, professors are eligible for sabbaticals every five years. When they take a one semester sabbatical, they receive full pay. They receive three-fourths pay for a full school year sabbatical. I took a full year.

2. Her concerns were expressed in e-mails that were obtained through a freedom of information request several years later and through documents supplied during discovery after the lawsuit (*Demers v. Austin*, et al.) was filed.

3. Jean Folkerts was editor of *Journalism & Mass Communication Quarterly* (formerly known as *Journalism Quarterly*) from 1992 to 2003.

Chapter 36
More Censorship and Questions

Fall 2007
Washington State University

When Elson Floyd took over as president of WSU in summer 2007, one of the first controversies he encountered was a planned protest from a student group on campus during Islamo-Fascism Awareness Week, Oct. 22–26, 2007.

On Oct. 12, Floyd issued a preemptive strike: He said the university would punish students if they engaged in speech that was hateful or demeaning to other groups on campus.

> Universities must be places where the free exchange of ideas is not just protected, but encouraged. At the same time, we do not want individuals on our campuses to feel threatened because of their ethnicity or their religious beliefs. Sometimes these two principles appear to be in conflict. At those times, we must rely on the good-faith efforts of all members of the university community to assure that the resulting *dialog is both constructive and civil*. ... I fully understand concerns raised, in this post-9/11 era; however, *civility and constructive discourse must always prevail*. ...[1] [emphasis added]

Floyd clearly did not know the First Amendment or American history.

Civility is never a term applied to the colonists when they were hammering out the Constitution and the Bill and Rights. There was a lot of incivility in politics at that time.

Floyd's attempt to squelch the speech of students was not the first time WSU administrators had misunderstood the First Amendment.

In 2005, Ed Swan, a 42-year-old Washington State University elementary education student, wrote "diversity is perversity" in the margins of a book. A devoted Christian, Swan also told his professors that he didn't believe in the concepts of "white privilege" or "male privilege" or that there was bias any longer in favor of the majority. Swan also opposed adoption by gays.

In an evaluation to determine if he was fit to teach in public schools, one of his professors called him a "white supremacist." Officials threatened to dismiss Swan if he didn't undergo diversity training and sign an agreement stating he would respect community norms and diversity values.

Swan refused to sign.

"I didn't know I was a white supremacist until I read my file," Swan, who is the father of four biracial (Hispanic) children, told the Spokane *Spokesman-Review*.[2]

WSU dropped its threat of dismissal after the Foundation for Individual Rights in Education accused it of failing to protect the speech rights of students who have controversial or unpopular opinions. FIRE said the university failed to distinguish between speech and action when trying to punish Swan.

"I think Washington State is not too different from all too many other schools around the country," said David French, president of FIRE. "They have a real inability to handle a certain kind of controversial or dissenting speech." French also told the newspaper that Swan was being judged not on his behavior but on his opinions.

"That is incredibly dangerous," French said. "They focused on various expressions, whether it was writing phrases in notebooks, the T-shirt he wore ... Even wearing a camouflage hunting cap led one person to conclude he was threatening."

The Swan incident was the second time in 2005 that WSU had been reprimanded for violating free speech rights of students. The other incident occurred in April, when WSU administrators paid for and trained students to disrupt student playwright Chris Lee's satire, *Passion of the Musical*, a play that the writer said was deliberately designed to be "offensive or inflammatory to all audiences."

About 40 hecklers stopped the play and threatened physical violence against the cast members. Former university president Lane Rawlins also publicly criticized the play.

WSU originally defended its actions, saying heckling was an exercise of students' free speech rights. But WSU reversed its position after FIRE filed a complaint against the university.

WSU adopted a new policy, which stated: "Please be aware that disruption to this performance, or any program will not be tolerated and will be dealt with accordingly, up to and including participants being escorted from the venue."[3]

"WSU has apparently been embarrassed into respecting free artistic expression," said Greg Lukianoff, director of legal and public advocacy at FIRE. "It is long past time that WSU recognized that shouting down a play, like wantonly tearing down controversial artwork, is the very opposite of free speech."

Although WSU corrected its actions in both the Swan and Lee cases, the university never formally apologized for its actions.

The general rule, by the way, is that speech is protected, action is not. In other words, you can say just about anything you want — your speech can be unruly, raucous, mean, contemptuous, scornful, insulting, abusive, and even hateful and unconstructive — but the moment you translate that speech into violent or aggressive action, you've crossed the line.[4]

Floyd did not understand this when he e-mailed the statement at the beginning of this chapter to all of the faculty, staff and students at the university. He implied that the students would be punished for what they said, not just for what they did.

I was not the only faculty member to recognize this problem.

One of my colleagues, communication professor Joey Reagan, posted the comment below to his website, which, by the way, was and still is maintained by WSU.

> Elson S. Floyd, WSU's new president, has issued "A Call for Civility" in which he ... gives lip-service to "Universities must be places where the free exchange of ideas is not just protected, but encouraged." Unfortunately, there is always a caveat. In his case it's, "We do not want individuals on our campuses to feel threatened" and "civility and constructive discourse must always prevail." Administrators make these attempts to stifle speech when they disagree with the content of the speech in question. Buzzwords like "disrespect," "degrade," "feel threatened" and "offend" are used when they want an excuse to censor. ... Nothing in the First Amendment or Supreme Court opinions says that ideas need to be expressed civilly, responsibly or respectfully. Nothing in the First Amendment says you have to consider other people's feelings or opinions. It's only when someone wants to censor what they don't like that we have to be civilized. Maybe Dr. Floyd should be more concerned about actions rather than speech.[5]

I also sent an e-mail to one of Floyd's assistants, informing them that Floyd's statement was inconsistent with First Amendment law. The assistant did not respond.

As it turned out, the students never conducted the protest, because reportedly they were afraid of being punished.

Another example of how WSU administrators violated the "civility rule" came in February 2008. The university was rewriting its 2008–2013 strategic plan and was asking for feedback from faculty and students. Item number six on the list, "Freedom of Expression," stated that students, faculty and administrators should be "civil" when they discuss issues and problems on campus.

I sent an e-mail to the administrators who were rewriting the strategic plan, suggesting they eliminate the words that imply students, faculty and staff must be civil. To my surprise, they changed it to, "We are committed to being a community that protects the free exchange of ideas while also *encouraging* dialog that is constructive and civil."

Much better. There's nothing wrong with "encouraging" civil speech — the university just should not require it.

Unfortunately, though, when WSU created its 2014–2019 Strategic Plan (I was no longer working at the university), it reverted to the original wording:

> Freedom of Expression: We are committed to the free exchange of ideas in a constructive and civil environment, including the canons of academic freedom in research, teaching and outreach.[6]

Legal scholars Erwin Chemerinsky and Howard Gillman have studied the problem of free speech on campus and succinctly observe:

> Campuses must accommodate the battle of ideas but not actual battles. That certain ideas are considered inherently hateful or threatening cannot be the basis for censoring or punishing their mere expression. But we should not confuse the requirement to protect the expression of all ideas with the need to stand helpless when mobs gather to initiate or provoke violence. ... There is no right to conspire with others to organize violent confrontations.[7]

ON DECEMBER 20, five days before Christmas, Internal Auditor Heather Lopez called me again and grilled me about Marquette Books.

I spent an hour and half on the phone with her.

I asked if she had read the reports issued several years earlier about Marquette Books. She said she had access to them.

I should have tape-recorded the conversation, but I didn't realize she was going to write a formal report.

Of course, I had nothing to fear from a legal or ethical standpoint.

But my experiences at the University of Wisconsin–River Falls showed that administrators can quickly jettison facts and truth when they get in the way of other goals. In this respect, administrators were no different from policymakers, whose decisions were often based on factors others than empirical evidence or the truth.

Lopez's phone call did confirm one thing for me: Now I knew without question that there was a concerted effort in the administration to discredit me or my company or fire me. Question after question was accusatory. I reiterated my positions over and over.

I sent a follow-up e-mail to Lopez two days later to leave no doubt about the issues. I also pointed out that Murrow professor Joey Reagan published nothing in 2006 and got a 3.0 ("meeting expectations") rating from Austin, whereas I finished writing a 360-page theoretically based textbook (*History and Future of Mass Media*) and got a rating of 2.8.

But that didn't matter.

Lopez had already made up her mind.

I also began to notice that many faculty in the Murrow School were reducing their interactions with me. No one wanted to be associated with a professor who challenged the power structure, even if he was doing it for good reasons (national accreditation for the mass communication program).

"They're all cowards," one of my non-WSU friends would often remark. "They are envious of your accomplishments, and you are shaming them. There's no good defense for not seeking national accreditation for the professional programs."

"I find it hard to believe that faculty are motivated by envy," I responded. "These are smart, competent people. They need not fear each other or me. Each is very accomplished."

But other friends and colleagues would continue to use the "envy theory" to explain what was becoming a campaign against me. Although I almost always discounted it, I didn't have a better explanation. And sociologist Kenneth Westhues's theory of workplace mobbing listed envy as an important cause.

To deal with the stress and the thought that I could lose my career (a second time), I spent as much time with my seven-year-old daughter, Lee Ann, as I could.

She made me laugh every day. She was full of life — a constant reminder of what is important in life. On one occasion, when she was about four, she looked up at a large, bright moon low on the horizon and, comparing it to a light bulb, said, "Who turns off the moon?"

My wife, Theresa, also was very supportive, which meant a lot to me.

"They're angry because they can't control you, Dave," she would say, over and over again for the next couple of years. "You're like the little boy who tells the crowd that the emperor has no clothes."[8]

That Christmas I also decided to purchase a model train to set up around the Christmas tree. When I was a kid, I loved my HO gauge train set. I had no idea what a slippery slope that purchase would become.

I fell into model railroading with a passion, and I would spend many hours over the next two years working on my 8-by-8-foot layout. I also began playing my guitar again and created a homemade CD of classic blues music.

The CD included Eric Clapton's "Before You Accuse Me (Take a Look at Yourself)," the Allman Brothers' "One Way Out," B. B. King's "The Thrill Is Gone," and Blues Traveler's "Run-Around."

My family, the train, and the music were far more effective at keeping depression at bay than antidepressant drugs or therapists.

I was no Howard Roark, the overly confident architect in *The Fountainhead*, but I was tougher now than I had been at River Falls.

IN JANUARY 2008, I completed my second annual review for Austin.

I again emphasized that I never canceled any classes in 2007, including Com 101. I pointed out that my book on the *History and Future of Mass Media* had been published by Hampton Press in September 2007.

I also noted that I had made substantial progress on this book and another theoretical book. My teaching evaluations again were better than the school average, and I performed more service, working more than 10 hours a week.

She gave me a 2.5 overall rating, compared with 2.7 in 2006.

I again received the lowest or second-lowest rating in the school.

She criticized me for allegedly failing to follow university rules on outside work activities. And she falsely accused me again of canceling classes.

> The average teaching evaluation scores for his classes were positive, but Dr. Demers repeatedly cancelled classes despite warnings that the level of cancellations was unacceptable.

In my response to her review, I informed her that her facts were wrong — I did not cancel any classes in 2007, not one. I told her again that I had attendance records and quizzes and exams from all of my classes. They were time-stamped, which meant I could prove my classes were never canceled.

Austin did not respond.

But on April 6, 2008, before the errors could be resolved, I received a telephone call from Internal Auditor Heather Lopez.

Chapter 36 Endnotes

1. The full text of President Elson Floyd's statement can be found at <http://president.wsu.edu/perspectives/101207.html>.

2. Shawn Vestal, "WSU Takes Hit on Free Speech," *Spokesman-Review* (October 22, 2005), p. A1, A12.

3. "Victory for Freedom of Expression at Washington State," Foundation for Individual Freedom (December 12, 2005), retrieved August 10, 2009, from <http://www.thefire.org/case/683.html> and <http://www.thefire.org/article/6582.html>.

4. For a review of the literature on free speech and the First Amendment, see Chapter 12 in David Demers, *An Interpretive Introduction to Mass Communication* (Boston, MA: Pearson, 2005).

5. Reagan's comments are available at <http://www.wsu.edu/~reagan/Rants.html#president>.

6. Retrieved February 22, 2015, from <https://strategicplan.wsu.edu/wp-content/uploads/sites/153/2014/07/WSU-Strategic-Plan-2014-2019.pdf>.

7. Erwin Chemerinsky and Howard Gillman, *Free Speech on Campus* (New Haven: Yale University Press, 2018 edition), p. xv.

8. The "no clothes" metaphor is taken from a fairy tale written by Danish poet and author Hans Christian Andersen. The plot involves an emperor of a prosperous city who cares more about clothes than other affairs of state and hires two swindlers who promise him the finest suit of clothes from beautiful cloth. They tell him that the cloth is invisible to anyone who was either stupid or unfit for his position. The Emperor himself is unable to see the non-existent cloth but pretends he can for fear of appearing stupid. The swindlers pretend to dress the Emperor who then goes on a procession through the capital showing off his new "clothes." At one point, a small child cries out, "But he has nothing on!" The crowd realizes the truth, but the Emperor holds his head high and continues the procession.

Chapter 37

The Internal Audit Report

Spring 2008
Louisiana State University

"Dr. Demers, this is Heather Lopez from the Washington State University's Internal Audit Office. I'm sorry it has taken so long to get the results of our investigation back to you. I've been very busy."

"No problem."

"I've just finished the report, which contains two conclusions. The first is that you should have submitted an annual report on your involvement in your book company, Marquette Books. The second is that you violated university rules when you refused to comply with a department directive and canceled classes in your introduction to mass communication course in spring 2007."

"You're kidding me," I responded. "I never canceled classes in my communication course in spring 2007; in fact, I never canceled any classes in 2007, and I've got the records to prove it. I'm being targeted because of my 7-Step Plan."

"My job isn't to investigate the politics, Dr. Demers, but to examine the facts."

"But what if your facts are wrong?"

"My investigation is finished."

"Can I appeal your charges?"

"No, there is no appeal process. But you can write a response and we'll include it in the official record. As far as punishment, that's up to the director of your program. The report will be given to her. Goodbye."

I WAS IN LOUISIANA when I received that phone call from WSU's internal auditor. I had been invited to interview for an endowed chair position in the journalism and mass communication program at Louisiana State University.

I was not at my best during my time at LSU. My dreaded cough had returned and ruined my presentation.

I was never offered the position.

But in my discussions with faculty at LSU, it became clear the program there was structured in a way that was very consistent with my 7-Step Plan. The program had generated more than $20 million in endowment funds, compared to less than $3 million at WSU.

I obtained a copy of Lopez's written report several days after returning from Louisiana. The most disturbing aspect of her investigation was that she never asked me if I had deliberately violated Murrow School director Erica Austin's order not to cancel classes in spring 2007.

Why would someone presumably trained in investigatory techniques make an accusation without first asking the accused if he was guilty of the offense?

This question haunted me for several days until I recalled a conversation I had had with an administrator several months earlier.

"Dave, you know that Lopez's sister reports to Austin, don't you?"

"I didn't."

Lopez's sister was a staff member in the Murrow School.

She worked for Austin.

I thought I had a good working relationship with Lopez's sister. We used to joke a lot and talk about our kids.

But what I didn't know at the time was that Lopez's sister was the one who got Lopez involved in the investigation of Marquette Books in the first place. I learned that several months later after I reviewed university documents obtained through a freedom of information act request.

In August 2006, Lopez's sister sent an e-mail to the Murrow School office manager and to Austin, informing them that her sister was the internal auditor at WSU. Later I also learned that Lopez's sister had been sent to see if I was holding class. She reported back on one occasion that my class wasn't in session.

That was true — because the class was being conducted online. My students were taking a test that day. Austin incorrectly assumed I had canceled classes and erroneously passed that information on to Lopez.

"Wow, the internal auditor clearly had a conflict of interest," one retired state auditor in Seattle told me.

A dozen other professors, colleagues and attorneys I spoke with later echoed that same sentiment. Ironically, the university official who was responsible for investigating alleged violations of state laws on conflict of interest had herself overlooked the fact that her sister's role in the investigation compromised her own investigation, at least in terms of appearances.[1]

This is not to suggest that a conspiracy was in the works. I suspect that Lopez didn't even see the potential conflict of interest.

However, the problem, as I would write in many reports to university officials months later, is that her sister's relationship with Austin may have enhanced the credibility of Austin's false allegations, thus compromising Lopez's ability to objectively investigate the charges.

That could explain why Lopez never asked me whether I had canceled classes in Com 101.[2] She was already thoroughly convinced that Austin was correct and credible; after all, her own sister reported to her.

Before I had a chance to respond Lopez's report, though, I was blind-sided again.

ON APRIL 16, 2008, Austin drafted a letter, titled "Notice Concerning Serious or Repeated Neglect of Duty."

The letter falsely claimed that I gave a final exam in the 14th week of the semester in one of my classes, rather than during finals week; that I conducted only two and not three class sessions per week in my classes in fall 2007, which also was false; and that I had failed to file a form about my involvement with Marquette Books.

The last item was correct and part of Lopez's internal audit, but I was waiting for the university to explain why it believed I had to submit the form. (I never did get an explanation.)

Where the hell is Austin coming up with these facts? Why doesn't she contact me before making such charges?

No investigative reporter I know would ever accuse an individual of wrongdoing without first giving him a chance to respond.[3]

"It's a madhouse," I said to my wife, quoting a famous line from the movie *Planet of the Apes*.

I followed up with a response refuting each charge and repeating again that a high-level university administrator, the vice provost for research, told me that Marquette Books did not have to file the report. I also included an e-mail in which he confirmed that my interpretation of his conversation to me was correct.

Once again, there was no response from Austin or the university.

On April 24, 2008, I wrote a formal response to Lopez's report, providing details and evidence to contradict all of the allegations.

I also informed Lopez that she had made several other factual errors in her report and I asked her to correct the errors.

I also said I would file the annual reports on Marquette Books if it was determined that the company was subject to the reports.[4] I asked her in an e-mail if I could dispute her interpretation of university rules.

I thought about raising the conflict of interest issue.

But, after talking with two attorneys, I decided not to, at least not at that time.

INTERNAL AUDITOR HEATHER LOPEZ eventually responded to my request about whether I could appeal the conclusion in her report which contended that Marquette Books is subject to the university rules.

She said no.

I followed up with another e-mail that, among other things, asked her whether she would correct the errors in her report.

Again she said no.

Lopez's refusal to explain why my interpretation of the university rules was incorrect backed me into a corner. If I didn't file the form on Marquette Books, she and the university would probably use that to fire me.

So I e-mailed Austin and asked her what I needed to do to complete the documentation for Marquette Books.

She faxed the form that I needed to complete. It was cryptic, basically asking how many days a week one would perform outside work activities over the next year.

That was it? All of the fuss was over one oddly worded form? Why didn't they send me that form earlier?

The answer to that question was obvious.

They hoped I would refuse to complete the form, because then they might have the grounds to fire me.

Okay, maybe I was paranoid.

But paranoids have enemies, too!

I completed the form and sent it back.

Shortly after that, I ran into a Murrow faculty member who also had performed outside work activities. He was a consultant for private industry.

He said he didn't file the form, and he said he resented the university's intrusion into his private life. He said Austin had advised him to file the form, but she was not punishing him or intending to punish him for failing to do so.

"I think you are being singled out," he said.

No surprise there.

The faculty member, by the way, never did file the form.

Although I filed the form, it still wasn't clear whether the university could punish me for my involvement in Marquette Books. I mentioned this to one of my employment attorneys the following week.

"Why don't you just sell the company to your wife?" he said.

"But wouldn't I still have a vested interest in the company? My wife and I live in a community property state. And I still would have the problem of the past ownership — they might still punish me for something that happened several years ago."

"Not so," said the attorney. "It's possible to back-date the sale. It's all perfectly legal. People do it all the time. Moreover, you can exclude it from community property. We'll simply draw up a separate agreement and you'll have no financial interest in the company."

So that's what we did.

According to the law, I only owned Marquette Books for several days back in 2002. My wife was the real owner. This is one of the few times the law seemed to work in my favor.

On May 3, 2008, I e-mailed Austin and other university officials, informing them that I was relinquishing all ownership rights to Marquette Books and its related companies.

"Should I send them a copy of the paperwork?" I asked the attorney.

"Only if they ask for it. Why should you be nice to them after the way they have treated you? Besides, you can learn something from this. You'll see how interested they are in prosecuting you for your involvement in Marquette Books."

That wasn't the way a good Lutheran would approach it. He would have sent the paperwork to the other party out of courtesy.

But the attorney had a good point.

The university never did ask for the paperwork.

The Marquette Books issue turned out to be a paper tiger.

A month later Dean Lear would confirm this at a meeting to discuss the errors in my annual review. "I am satisfied that you are now in compliance with university rules," he said.

But the end of this issue wasn't going to stop other administrators from trying to force me to resign from WSU.

I decided it was time to go on the offensive.

On May 6, 2008, I sent a letter to President Floyd asking for access to numerous records and e-mails surrounding my case. I cited the state's freedom of information law as grounds for granting my request.

The records office on campus responded that it would take several months to assemble the records.

MY OPTIONS for appealing the errors in my annual reviews as well as in the internal audit were running out. As one attorney pointed out, the university hadn't punished me enough to justify filing a full-fledged lawsuit.

Yet it was clear that Austin and other administrators would continue to fabricate small things that might eventually build into a big case against me. The mobbing process was well underway.

"Have you tried talking with the university ombudsman?" one WSU administrator suggested shortly after I told him about Austin's review and the internal audit report.

According to the WSU website, the primary purpose of the ombudsman "is to protect the interests, rights, and privileges of students, staff, and faculty at all levels of university operations and programs."[5]

I wasn't too optimistic about the role that an ombudsman could play.

Several years earlier I had conducted some research on ombudsmen at newspapers and found that some news organizations have created ombudsman positions in an attempt to show the world that they can evaluate themselves objectively. Research shows, however, that they spend less time criticizing the newspaper than justifying to the public why journalists make the decisions they do."[6]

I suspected the same would be true for a university ombudsman — that he or she would identify more with the power structure than the aggrieved faculty member.

But it was worth a shot.

I called WSU ombudsman Ken Struckmeyer in late May or early June 2008. Struckmeyer was the professor who had criticized the process used to hire Elson Floyd.

Struckmeyer suggested I contact the Washington State attorney general's office about filing a complaint against the internal auditor. He assumed she worked for the state auditor.

But she didn't.

She was a WSU employee, so the state auditor's office refused to get involved. An attorney there also said my complaint was a personnel matter, which the state auditor does not investigate.

Another dead end.

I went back to Struckmeyer and told him what happened. I also told him that Dean Lear and Austin refused to meet with me if I tape-recorded the meeting.

"I wonder why they would refuse to do that," he said.

"Because they're afraid to be accountable," I responded.

Struckmeyer didn't react to that comment.

Instead, he suggested that I ask them whether they would be willing to allow him to sit in on a meeting. He would be a "neutral" observer.

That was a reasonable compromise.

Lear and Austin agreed to meet on June 30, 2008.

At the meeting, I presented a written report listing six major errors in the two annual reviews I received from Austin. I was most concerned about correcting the error that I had canceled classes, because that was the error duplicated in the internal audit.

Lear seemed a bit surprised to learn that I had not canceled classes. He then tried to justify Austin's error by saying that the "general feeling of the faculty" was that my behavior was inappropriate. He went on for another five minutes. I listened, patiently.

"I don't care what the faculty felt," I then responded, pointing my finger on the list of errors in my report. "The charge that I canceled classes is false, and I want it corrected. What I don't understand is how such a blatant error could have been made, because I changed my syllabus and instructed the teaching assistants to hold classes during dead week."

Austin then admitted that she never saw my syllabus.

"We weren't able to find a copy," she said.

"Why didn't you just ask me for a copy?"

She didn't respond.

"Your student evaluations also suggested that you had canceled classes," she said. "Many students say they like your class because you 'cancel classes on Fridays.'"

"That statement is inaccurate," I responded. "I conduct online quizzes or exams in my classes on some Fridays. The students love that because they don't have to walk over to the classroom. Some think that I'm 'canceling' class. But that's not true. We hold class in cyberspace. Why didn't you just ask me about those comments before accusing me of canceling classes?"

Austin looked shell-shocked. Her face was red. She didn't respond.

Struckmeyer then chimed in.

"So, Erich, you will be issuing a correction in Dave's annual review?"

"Yes, we will do that," Lear said.

"And you will send that correction to the internal auditor?"

"Yes," Lear said.

"And what about adjusting his annual review quantitative rating and level of compensation."

"I don't know that we can do that — "

I cut Lear off.

"I don't care about the compensation or the rating," I said. "I just want the record corrected. I'm most concerned about the internal audit. Lopez duplicated the error that I canceled classes. I'll be satisfied if that correction is made to the internal audit."

Lear added that he was also satisfied that I had addressed his concerns about Marquette Books.

"I am satisfied that you are now in compliance with university rules," he said.

"Well, I guess I didn't need to sell the company to my wife after all," I said, joking.

I was so relieved.

I shook hands with Struckmeyer.

When I returned home, I sent an e-mail to numerous administrators who had been involved in this dispute summarizing the results of the meeting.

I pointed out that one lesson to be learned from this is to always give the accused a chance to respond before issuing charges.

But my celebration was premature.

I DIDN'T SEE my revised annual review until two months later. I wasn't teaching summer session. I lived in Spokane and didn't get down to the university to get my mail.

When I did, I was stunned.

The paragraph which stated that I had deliberately violated Austin's directive was still there. The only thing changed was the word "canceled." Instead of accusing me of canceling classes, the review now stated that I had "failed to hold classes."

Of course, that statement was false.

I didn't "fail" to hold classes.

Every class session was conducted. Some were held online. University regulations clearly permit faculty to give quizzes or tests online. In fact, many of the classes taught through WSU statewide were and still are conducted completely online. The College of Business even offers a Master's of Business Administration completely through online courses.

I e-mailed Austin and other university administrators. I asked her to correct the annual review and strike all references to canceling or not holding classes.

She refused.

I e-mailed ombudsman Ken Struckmeyer, who suggested that I file another complaint with the Faculty Status Committee.

I was suspicious. Why didn't he take the matter to the president of the university? Something else was going on.

Were university administrators hiding something?

Chapter 37 Endnotes

1. Auditors' codes of conflict ban not only actual conflicts of interest but also perceived conflicts of interest.

2. Austin made a series of investigatory errors that led her to erroneously conclude I had canceled classes. The details are provided later.

3. I sent drafts of this book to every WSU official identified by name in the book, asking

them to correct errors or provide feedback. Their responses are provided at the end of this book and at <https://www.marquettebooks.com/response.html>.

4. Former Murrow Director Alex Tan sent me an e-mail saying he believed the internal audit charges were "petty" and "I believe you are being singled out."

5. For more details about the role and function of the Washington State University ombudsman, visit <http://www.wsu.edu/~ombuds>.

6. David Demers, "The *Spokesman-Review* Ombudsman: Watchdog or PR Man?" *The Local Planet Weekly* (July 25, 2002), p. 5.

Chapter 38

What Happened to the Golden Rule?

August 2008
Washington State University

In August 2008, WSU's office of records called and said some of the data I had requested under the state's FOIA laws was available for inspection.

On my drive down to Pullman, Sirius Radio's blues station played Stevie Ray Vaughn's "Crossfire," which was recorded in 1989 right after he became sober and a year before his unfortunate death in a helicopter crash.

Day by day, night after night
Blinded by the neon lights ...
Money's tight nothin' free
Won't somebody come and rescue me
I am stranded
Caught in the crossfire
Stranded ...
Save the strong lose the weak
Never turning the other cheek
Trust nobody don't be no fool
Whatever happened to the golden rule?[1]

The golden rule, also known as the ethic of reciprocity, is an ethical code which holds that one has a right to just treatment and also a responsibility to ensure justice for others.

Some scholars argue that the golden rule is the most important idea underlying the concept of human rights. The golden rule was certainly a major component of my Lutheran upbringing.

But the University of Wisconsin–River Falls never felt compelled to follow such a rule. Would WSU turn out to be the same?

I began looking at university records and e-mails surrounding my case.

Over the next six months I made several trips to the records office on campus, reviewing thousands of documents.

That's when I learned that Internal Auditor Heather Lopez's sister had initiated contact with and brought Lopez into the investigation. "Erica, I have asked my sister (Heather Lopez) for assistance."[2] Austin also sent Lopez's sister and other staff members to see if I was holding my classes, but oddly, they did not record the information in writing. I also learned that:

- Internal Auditor Lopez advised administrators that they could punish me if I failed to complete my sabbatical book and find a publisher.
- University administrators, including several attorneys, had exchanged hundreds of e-mails about the dispute for more than a year, but almost everything was redacted.
- Vice Provost of Faculty Affairs Frances McSweeney, Austin, and some of the faculty in the Murrow School assumed, incorrectly, that I was profiting from the use of Marquette books in my classes and that I had canceled classes in 2007.

At this point, I had only three options.

One was to go public with the internal auditor's conflict of interest.

The second was to make one last appeal to the administration.

Third, if neither of those strategies worked, then I would file a federal First Amendment lawsuit.

ON OCTOBER 14, 2008, I sent an e-mail to WSU President Elson Floyd, pointing out that my 2006 and 2007 annual reviews still contained six errors of commission and omission.[3]

I asked him to direct university administrators to fix the errors.

Floyd turned the matter over to interim provost Warwick Bayly, who didn't respond for several months. Not sure why it took so long. I was under no illusion that my complaint was a top priority with upper administration.

In fact, aside from the few administrators who were directly involved in this dispute (especially those whose reputations might be affected by the outcome), few people really cared, even if the issues directly affected them.

Most people are uncomfortable with conflict.

One of the biggest concerns of elites in any organization is social order and stability. Interpersonal or social conflicts within an organization can threaten the power of leaders or elites in the organization, because the disputes make the leaders look as if they don't have control.

A participant in a dispute perceives the issues to be very important, but their superiors more often than not do not care about the substantive nature of the dispute. They just want the problem to go away. They want order.

This doesn't mean that all conflict or disputes in an organization are inconsequential or unimportant. One could hypothesize that *the greater the number of individuals affected by an issue in a dispute, the more legitimacy elites will grant to the dispute*. But if the issue doesn't advance the interests of the elites, then they are likely to frame it in a way that reduces the potential of others to see a bigger, more substantive issue.

There was no question in my mind that Austin and other administrators were violating my First Amendment rights and were harassing me with no good reason. They knew that if the dispute were framed as a battle over free speech, they would have more difficulty defending themselves. So they framed the dispute as a case of professorial incompetence and thought they had evidence that I violated university rules or failed to perform my duties as a professor.

Although this "frame," as media scholars call it, is easy to peddle among other friends and administrators in an organization, not all administrators are easily co-opted. Some have the capacity to act professionally and render an "objective" decision in a case.

I always felt that my graduate school professors Simon Dinitz and Phillip J. Tichenor and my former editor Dick Carson had that ability.

I had heard good things about the WSU interim provost, but the sociologist in me predicted he would see the dispute as a case of incompetence rather than as a violation of civil liberties. McSweeney and Austin reported directly to him, and no doubt they had already had conversations with him about the case before I would meet with him.

But, again, maybe I would be proved wrong.

Bayly deserved a chance.

Chapter 38 Endnotes

1. "Crossfire" was written by Stevie Ray Vaughan's band members for their 1989 *In Step* album (Epic/Legacy), named after the 12 steps in Alcoholics Anonymous.
2. E-mail from Lopez's sister to Austin on August 9, 2006.
3. I excluded some of the smaller errors identified in the first annual review.

Chapter 39

Bayly's Kangaroo Court

February 18, 2009
Washington State University

By all accounts, Warwick Bayly was a man who had his head screwed on right.

He had been a professor of veterinary science at WSU for more than 20 years and had been named the first four-year Robert B. McEachern Distinguished Professor in Equine Medicine in 1995.

He also had served as the college's associate dean for continuing education and as interim chair of the department of veterinary clinical sciences. In 2001, he was promoted to dean of WSU's College of Veterinary Medicine on a near unanimous vote of the faculty in 2001.

"He's enthusiastic, a solid administrator, and has a strong background and experience in both research and academics," one WSU administrator said about Bayly in a WSU news release. "We are certain his leadership of the college will continue to advance WSU's place among other world class institutions. ... We are fortunate he's chosen to guide the nation's finest veterinary program at WSU."

Bayly grew up in Melbourne, Australia, where he earned a veterinary degree. He also earned a master's degree from The Ohio State University. He completed that in 1979, the year before I began working on my two master's degrees at Ohio State. He earned his doctorate from the University of Liège in Belgium.

Floyd appointed Bayly to the position of interim provost in fall 2007, replacing Robert Bates, the provost who had questioned why I had submitted my 7-Step Plan without going through Murrow channels.

Bayly served for one school year and then stepped down when the university gave the permanent position to University of Kentucky history professor Steven Hoch.

Hoch didn't last long.

On September 10, 2008, after two months on the job, Hoch chaired a budget meeting of top-level WSU officials (mostly vice presidents) when Floyd was out of town. The conversation upset many of those at the meeting.

There was some name-calling and Hoch alleged that one of the vice presidents "physically abused" him with a shove at the end of the meeting.

Three days later, Floyd asked Antoinette M. Ursich, senior assistant attorney general at Washington State University, to investigate.

Six days after that, she issued her report, which concluded that "Provost Hoch set the tone for the meeting, and the tone set was one of hostility towards and disrespect of colleagues" and that even though the vice president made "unprofessional comments," the "physical contact he had with Hoch was defensive, not offensive."[1]

Was the report designed to force Hoch to resign?

I don't know, but a time-honored practice in bureaucracies when an outsider stirs the pot is to appoint an investigator who you know will produce a report that reinforces the status quo. If the administration wanted to ensure an independent investigation, it should have hired a WSU outsider.

Hoch resigned as provost.

He returned to his position as a professor of history and was transferred to WSU's Tri-Cities campus, located about 140 miles to the west.

His contract stipulated that he would retain his provost salary, which, when converted from a 12-month administrative schedule to a nine-month teaching schedule, amounted to about $245,000 a year. That was about three to five times higher than most WSU professors earn.

Needless to say, Hoch's big salary spurred a flurry of news stories, commentaries and letters to the editor in local newspapers criticizing the university and the way it contracts with employees.[2]

But a contract is a contract.

In September 2008, Bayly once again put on the interim provost's hat.

A month later I e-mailed Floyd requesting that the errors in my annual reviews and the internal audit be corrected. Floyd responded immediately, asking Bayly to look into the case.

A month after that I also e-mailed Floyd, raising the issue of the internal auditor's conflict of interest.

I said I had no interest in seeing Lopez punished, but that I would like to file a conflict-of-interest complaint against her. I needed guidance on how to do that.

The state auditor's office already had refused to hear my case, saying it was a personnel matter. There were, to the best of my knowledge, no university rules governing how to file a conflict-of-interest complaint against a university employee.

Floyd turned the matter over to Ursich.

Several months passed with no response from either Bayly or Ursich.

Early in 2009 I e-mailed Floyd again, and he again asked both Bayly and Ursich to look into the matter.

Bayly responded that he would be willing to meet over the matter.

I asked if I could tape-record the meeting.

Through his administrative assistant, he refused to allow the tape recording.

However, he would allow ombudsman Ken Struckmeyer to attend the meeting.

"HELLO," I SAID to the receptionist. "I'm here for a meeting with Provost Bayly. I'm a few minutes early."

It was Wednesday, February 18, 2009.

"Yes, please take a seat," she said cordially but plainly not interested in small talk.

The scene reminded me of a time in high school, when I was sent to the vice principal's office to face "charges" that I had erased a friend's name from absentee lists after collecting them from classroom doors. The only difference this time was that I was innocent.

Five minutes later WSU Ombudsman Ken Struckmeyer arrived and began a jovial conversation with the receptionist. Struckmeyer also had friendly greetings with Bayly as we entered the meeting room, and with Frances McSweeney, the vice provost who had told me a year earlier that there was no rule prohibiting faculty from canceling classes but was nonetheless part of the group that was trying to punish me for allegedly doing that.

I was not informed in advance that she would be attending.

But her appearance suggested that McSweeney was the point person in the upper administration. I wished, then, that I had brought a friend, or, better yet, a stenographer.

Too late.

I handed everyone a copy of the list of errors in my two annual reviews and initiated the conversation.

"The reason I asked for this meeting," I said, "was to correct errors in my annual reviews and the internal audit, particularly the false allegation that I had canceled classes in 2007."

As I talked, I looked at Bayly for his reaction.

For the first minute or so he refused to look me in the eye. He stared at the documents on the table I had given him. I suspected that he probably had already made up his mind on the case. His body language completed the story.

"Listen," he said, interrupting me after a couple of minutes and sitting more upright in his chair. "As I understand it, your director [Erica Austin] already fixed the errors in your annual review. Isn't that correct, Ken?"

Struckmeyer was sitting on my left. He was fidgeting, and his face was redder than a radish.

He hesitated, an action that Bayly quickly interpreted as confirmation that the errors had been corrected.

Was Struckmeyer going to betray me?

"Ken," I intervened, "at the meeting on June 30 with Dean [Erich] Lear and Austin, Lear conceded that the accusation that I had canceled classes was false and that Austin would correct the error. But Austin failed to make that correction. You were there. You were the one to ask them to correct that error. Do you remember?"

"Yes, that is correct."

"What?" Bayly interjected. "Ken, are you sure that's what happened?"

"Yes, Lear agreed to correct the error."

Bayly's brow furrowed.

He apparently had not been fully informed of what happened at the meeting with Lear, Austin, Struckmeyer and me.

But Bayly wasn't ready to toss the noose onto the ground.

He tried, on two other occasions during the conversation, to get Struckmeyer to admit that the error was corrected or that the allegation that I had canceled classes was true. On both occasions, Struckmeyer stood behind my version of the story. That must have taken a lot of courage, because it was clear that Struckmeyer was on good terms with both McSweeney and Bayly.

McSweeney, meanwhile, looked like she had just seen a ghost.

Finally, after all this time, I thought, *the university is going to fess up and correct the errors.*

But Bayly switched topics.

"I don't think your performance here has been satisfactory," he said.

"Oh, really," I responded. "What makes you say that?"

"I've looked at your book [*History and Future of Mass Media*] and I don't see much theory in there." Austin had given me virtually no credit in my 2006 annual review for writing the book.

I was pleased to see Bayly emphasized theory as the primary component of a research program. As a media sociologist, I, too, argue that theory is the most important criterion. Fortunately, I had a copy of the book with me and I pushed it to Bayly's side of the table.

"My theory of corporate mass media is one of the most unique theories in the field," I said. "The last five chapters of the book focus heavily on my theoretical model."

"Well, I haven't read the whole thing, but it didn't look very significant to me."

"Were you aware, Provost Bayly, that in 2004 I ranked first or second on three measures of research productivity and scholarship among tenured faculty in the

Murrow School? I have written or edited 10 academic books, 20 first-author or sole-authored refereed articles, and more than 100 professional publications."

"Well, I hear your teaching isn't very good," he said, looking at McSweeney. "Isn't that true?"

Before McSweeney could respond, I said: "No, that's not true. My evaluations are at or above department and university averages. I get good evaluations and I love teaching."

McSweeney acknowledged that my teaching evaluations were good.

"Let's face it," Bayly said, "You really don't care much about your job, do you?"

Where the hell did that comment come from? Was Bayly really as smart and talented as people claimed?

McSweeney then chimed in that the administration was concerned that I was giving too many quizzes online. She implied that this was inappropriate.

I was caught off guard again.

Was this a new charge? No one has ever criticized me for giving too many online quizzes or exams in my classes.

"Fran, do you really want to go there?" I asked. "Hundreds of professors at the university conduct quizzes online and hold classes online. In fact, a substantial number of credit hours being offered at the university are offered exclusively online. If you indict me for conducting quizzes online, then you'll be indicting the entire university system."[3]

She didn't respond. She looked scared. I think she knew her reputation was now on trial here. Her case was falling apart.

But Bayly didn't see it that way. I represented a big threat to his authority.

"I don't see any merit to your complaint, and I'm not going to change your annual reviews. I'll speak with Dr. Lear and Dr. Austin and I'll send you my response."

Court was adjourned.

I gave Struckmeyer one of those shoulder-shrugging "I-can't-believe-this-happened" looks. His face had turned another, deeper shade of red. He turned his head away. As we got up to leave the room, Struckmeyer asked McSweeney if he could meet with her after the meeting.[4]

The following day I mailed a copy of my book to Bayly with a note attached: "My theory is summarized in seven major propositions on pages 3–5 in the introduction to the book. Yours to keep."

THE NEXT DAY Struckmeyer e-mailed me with questions about whether my quizzes or exams were conducted during class or at other times. I assumed the questions came from his meeting with McSweeney.

"Always during class," I responded, "except when we had problems with the Internet service. Then I gave the students more time. The reason I conducted the quizzes during class time is that it reduces cheating and I know all of the students are available at that time."

"And do you have records of this?" Struckmeyer asked.

"Yes. I have hard copies of all of the quizzes. They even have the time and date stamped on them."

It was easy to see where administrators were going with this.

If I had not conducted the quizzes during class time, they could accuse me of canceling classes (or Austin's favorite new phrase, "not holding them"). The administration was trying desperately to cover its ass.

Struckmeyer offered to write a report and give it to the administration. I declined, partly because I had talked with a Spokane attorney who'd had some dealings with Struckmeyer.

"He identifies with the power structure at the university," the attorney said.

A year later I met a WSU professor who also said Struckmeyer identified with the administration when she tried to appeal a poor annual review rating. Another WSU professor who heard about my case called me several weeks later and said administrators had also made factual errors in her annual review, and when she told Struckmeyer about the problem, he advised her "to transfer out of the department."

I couldn't say for sure whether Struckmeyer identified with the power structure when it came to my case. He never told me what he was thinking. And he did back up my version of events at the meeting with Austin and Lear on June 30 and in Bayly's "courtroom."

But Struckmeyer's decision to meet with McSweeney right after the meeting with Bayly troubled me. Over the past two years, Struckmeyer had never offered to meet in person with me to hear my side of the case. All of our contact, with the exception of his presence at two meetings, was through e-mail and one phone call.

Also, Struckmeyer had the authority to issue his own report directly to the president at any time. He didn't need my permission.

And, finally, the administrators had no problem with Struckmeyer sitting in on the meetings — perhaps they felt they could count on his friendship when it came time to take a side in the dispute.

My sixth sense told me that if I gave him permission to issue a report and it contained any negative comments about me, then the administration could use this against me.

I could hear them all saying: "Well, you gave the ombudsman permission to issue the report."

A WEEK OR SO after the meeting with Bayly, former Dean Lear sent an e-mail saying that the administration was no longer focusing on the issue of canceling classes. Instead, the problem now was that I conducted too many online quizzes or exams. I usually gave seven to 11 quizzes or exams per semester. Students perform better when the course content is broken up into smaller sections. But Lear implied that I should have spent more time lecturing or on other activities.

This comment seemed to support what McSweeney was saying at the provost meeting. Once again, I was dumbfounded.

"Is this a moving target?" I wrote in an e-mail to Lear.

"No, it isn't," he responded. He said the university administration has the authority to control the number of quizzes and other decisions affecting content in courses.

But if that was the case, then why did the administration wait so long to raise this issue?

About the same time I received an e-mail from Struckmeyer, who said he would not share with the administration any of the information I gave him. Then he added:

> I now believe I understand the whole situation and can speak to it in an informed manner and in a neutral position. The question appears to be: Can and should a faculty member give weekly quizzes in class and what is the format that is appropriate to give them? It is good that you have the records of quizzes, grades and grade books. Different departments and colleges would have different expectations on delivery of information and assessment of learning outcomes. I do understand that departments have different expectations. ... An interesting question is who sets the standard?[5]

I went online that evening and spent several hours researching state and federal law regarding the authority of university administrations to control the content in a class.

The case law basically suggested that universities can control things like the number of quizzes and books used for some classes, even though in practice most professors in most classes have a great deal of freedom to control the content and structure.

For a while I thought my goose was cooked.

And then it dawned on me: *Don't fight it. Simply grant WSU administrators the authority to control the number of online quizzes and ask them how many would be appropriate.*

"You watch," I told a friend. "I've just backed them into a corner. No administrator wants to get into micromanaging a professor's course in terms of the number of quizzes he or she can give."

I e-mailed McSweeney, Lear and Austin and asked them how many online quizzes I should give in a class.

Austin responded.

She said I could give as many as I wanted.

BAZINGA!

"It truly is an ivory tower of babel," I told one my best friends, who was a professor at another university.

"I can't believe what is happening at your university," he said. "It's crazy."

"You're a victim of workplace mobbing," another said.[6] "You've rocked the boat. You criticized administrators for incompetence, and your plan to improve the university has embarrassed them. The university doesn't appreciate libertarian First Amendment troublemakers like you. In the university, freedom of speech is a top-down value. Those at the top have more of it than those at the bottom."

"The ivory tower of administration has entered the babel zone," another one of my colleagues said one day, laughing.

But I wasn't laughing for long.

The response from Austin saying that I could conduct as many online quizzes as I wished was very revealing. It showed that there was confusion in the administration.

Bayly was perhaps the most confused and perhaps the most victimized.

The dispute apparently had been framed to him as a case of professorial incompetence, not one of administrative error.

He accepted the incompetence framing, even though he knew little about my professional and scholarly background.

One might blame him in part for conducting a kangaroo court, but most assuredly other administrators had misled him.

McSweeney flip-flopped on the issues.

At one point, she told me there were no hard-and-fast rules regarding the canceling of classes, and then she later turned around and supported efforts to punish me for allegedly canceling (or "not holding") classes. When that approach failed, she appeared to take Lear's position — that it was inappropriate for me to conduct so many quizzes in my classes. But that approach collapsed, too, when Austin told everyone that I could conduct as many online quizzes as I wished.

Very clearly these administrators were "not on the same page."

Austin's position is the most puzzling and difficult to explain.

On numerous occasions I offered to present evidence to her and other administrators showing that I did not cancel classes or fail to hold them in 2007, yet she continued to maintain that I was "not holding classes," even in her 2008 annual review of me, which I was about to receive.

In February 2009 I submitted my 2008 annual review.

I included the first three-fifths of what was to become my *Ivory Tower of Babel* book. The three previous professors in our department who had gone on sabbatical in recent years to write books never completed them. No one had tried to fire or punish them for that.

But I would not have that option, because the internal auditor had already implied in e-mails to various university administrators that the university could fire me if I failed to finish the *Ivory Tower* book.

"The university is cracking down on professors who go on sabbatical and fail to finish or make progress on their books," one administrator told me.

This suggested that I wasn't being singled out.

But none of the other professors on campus had been subject to a threat from the internal auditor. In that respect, my case was unique.

There was absolutely no question in my mind that Austin would fail to reward me for writing the *Ivory Tower of Babel*. Some of my friends at the time disagreed, saying the university wasn't dumb enough to subject itself again to allegations of violating the First Amendment rights of a professor. After all, they pointed out, my book contained some strong criticism of WSU officials.

They were wrong.

Austin gave me a 2.0 rating for the book (3.0 is meeting expectations) and an overall rating of 2.05, the lowest rating I ever received in an annual review. Her review stated that I should have published a refereed journal article. And she criticized my sabbatical book because it was "too interdisciplinary."

I won't burden you my entire response. But here's a brief response to the journal article and interdisciplinary criticisms.

> If Dr. Austin or the university didn't want me to write this book, then why did they approve the project? The university is sending a mixed message. Moreover, university administrators have been telling faculty for years that they should conduct more interdisciplinary research. Am I now being punished for doing just that?

Austin also criticized me for failing to "publish refereed scholarship in mainstream communication outlets as well." This comment supports Joanne Cantor's remark that professors are not rewarded for writing books and articles that try to influence the public policymaking process.[7]

My response to Austin:

> One of the reasons mainstream social scientists have so little impact on public policy is because they have trouble thinking "outside of the box." Refereed journal articles are important, especially for granting tenure ... , but refereed journal articles alone are not enough to solve social problems, as my book points out. Faculty must break out of the mold and produce some works that help non-academics and policymakers understand and solve social problems, AND administrators need to reward, not punish, faculty who engage in such endeavors (see my book for more details).

Austin also criticized me again for "failing to hold classes," even though two of her superiors (Lear and McSweeney) were no longer accusing me of canceling classes. Instead, they accused me of giving too many quizzes or exams in my classes.

My guess is that Austin was unaware of the events that took place during the meeting in Interim Provost Bayly's office. This is one of the weaknesses of bureaucratic systems (but a good thing for people fighting them): one part doesn't know what the other part is doing.

As I had done in the past, I responded that university rules require three hours of "organized activities" a week, and online quizzes or exams as well as lectures count as an organized activity.

She also criticized me for allegedly giving grades that were too high.

Jesus Christ, when is this going to stop?

I pointed out that in my media history class, only 10 percent of the students received an A- or A grade; 30 percent received a C or D. She apparently failed to look at the records I submitted.

To her credit, she corrected this error in a subsequent response to the provost's office. She raised my score 0.3 percentage points for teaching.

Wow!

But she refused to correct the error on "not holding classes." And she refused to give me service credit for editing and formatting the six open-access scholarly journals, even though now the work I did for Marquette Books could be counted as service because I had filed the requisite form.[8]

At dinner with friends one evening, I asked for their theories on why the university is refusing to correct the error about "not holding classes" in my annual reviews.

"Because they don't see any consequences to their actions," one psychiatrically trained social scientist said. "They have all the power."

Thus, in March 2009, the only apparent option I had left to get the errors corrected was a lawsuit.

Well, almost.

ON MARCH 31, 2009, Austin e-mailed me the results of a state auditor's report that had "indicted" a professor on another campus in Washington State who failed to hold classes.

The professor taught the course for three hours a week instead of five, as was required. The professor claimed that class was held online for the other two hours but was unable to produce evidence supporting that explanation.

I thanked Austin for the referral and added: "But the difference between that case and mine is that the professor failed to produce evidence that she had conducted classes online. That doesn't hold in my case — I have the evidence."

At the end of the e-mail, I added: "P.S. I'm still waiting to hear word on how to file a conflict of interest complaint against the internal auditor."

Five months had passed since I had asked President Floyd how I could file a conflict of interest claim against the internal auditor. He had referred the matter to the attorney general's office on campus.

But no one there responded.

Why was it taking so long?

But on April 3, three days after Austin e-mailed me, I received an e-mail from Floyd.

> I recently gave some thought to the disputes that you have brought to my attention and to the attention of Provost Bayly. I am not certain that we have yet satisfactorily resolved your concerns, or even that we have fully understood them. Consequently, I think it would be useful to hire an independent mediator who can help us explore and respond to them. I am willing to do this at University expense. Please let my assistant ... know if this is something you would like me to arrange.

My first reaction to Floyd's e-mail was bewilderment.

I had spent more than two years writing numerous e-mails and letters outlining the problem to various administrators.

Floyd's e-mail reinforced the idea that confusion prevailed in the administration.

My second reaction was one of delight. The e-mail was a sign that the university finally recognized that there was some merit to my complaint. Other friends, colleagues and attorneys I spoke to had reinforced this belief.

"They don't go to mediation unless they believe they have done something wrong," one said.

I sent an e-mail to Floyd saying that I wasn't eager to spend taxpayer monies on this dispute, but it certainly was much better and less costly than a full-blown lawsuit.

Chapter 39 Endnotes

1. Memo dated September 19, 2008, from Antoinette M. Ursich, senior assistant attorney general, to Elson S. Floyd, titled "Senior Staff Meeting – Incident Report," available online at <http://209.85.173.132/search?q=cache:oCV7MQuS_zwJ:www.wsunews.wsu.edu/Content/Images/news/report.pdf+provost+floyd+wsu+ pushing&cd=1&hl=en&ct=clnk&gl=us>.

2. Doug Clark, "For $245k, This Space Will Be Empty," Spokane *Spokesman-Review* (October 26, 2008), p. B1, and Dan Hansen, "WSU Dust-up Details Emerge: Most Witnesses Critical of Provost," Spokane *Spokesman-Review* (October 17, 2008), p. B1.

3. For $30,000, a student can earn a master's in Business Administration at WSU and never step on campus. The entire course is online.

4. At the end the meeting with Bayly, I had told Struckmeyer that I would probably re-file my complaint with the Faculty Status Committee, because that "appears to be the only option left." But I later changed my mind. It was unlikely that the committee would hear the case again, because the committee could subject itself to criticism for not hearing the case in the first place. There was nothing to be gained in obtaining another rejection from that committee.

5. E-mail from Ken Struckmeyer to David Demers dated February 24, 2009.

6. Some psychiatrists and sociologists define "workplace mobbing" as "ganging up" by others in a work environment to harass and intimidate an individual. In their book *Emotional Abuse in the American Workplace* (3rd ed., Civil Society Publishing: Ames, IA, 2005), Noa Davenport, Ruth Distler Schwartz, and Gail Pursell Elliott say mobbing is usually found in workplaces that have incapable or inattentive management and mobbing victims are usually "exceptional individuals who demonstrated intelligence, competence, creativity, integrity, accomplishment and dedication" (p. 21). My experience is that mobbing is top-down, not bottom up.

7. See Chapter 26 in this book for more details.

8. She made no mention in her review of my volunteer work for the open-access journals.

Chapter 40

Mediation Blues

Spring Semester 2009
Washington State University

In early 2009, the university created a search committee to hire a founding dean for the new Murrow College. I e-mailed President Elson Floyd and asked him whether a Ph.D. was a prerequisite for the position. He said it was not.

I e-mailed Floyd again and nominated a nationally recognized print journalist who had strong ties to journalism in the Pacific Northwest and to organizations that accredit journalism programs. He was the kind of candidate who could have repaired the poor relations between the Murrow program and the professional world. He also would have pursued accreditation for the professional mass communication programs. He didn't have a Ph.D., but he had a bachelor's degree from one of the best universities in the west.[1]

Three candidates were invited to campus. All had earned a Ph.D.

Interim Dean Erica Austin also applied for the position but was not among those invited to interview.

One colleague, who asked not to be identified, told me that Austin failed to get the support of some of the Murrow faculty members on the committee. Interestingly, on several occasions, Austin had defended the interests of some of those members. It reminded me of what happened to former Murrow Director Alex Tan: No amount of kindness can pacify your enemies.

But I suspect the main reason she failed to reach the final three was that administrators were looking for someone with more fundraising and real-world professional experience. As I noted in my 7-Step Plan, that's the kind of person universities are hiring to head up colleges of mass communication. Austin's strength was her research.

The university did give Austin a consolation award, however.

Administrators appointed her to a "director of research" position in Murrow program. As was the case with the appointment of the associate dean three years earlier, this appointment was made without a formal competitive search.

If other faculty were angry about the undemocratic decision, their voices were never heard in public. Everyone clapped when the announcement was made at a faculty meeting. The university also gave Austin a leadership award for her service as interim director/dean.

On May 20, 2009, the university announced that Lawrence Pintak, who was director of the Kamal Adham Center for Journalism Training and Research at The American University in Cairo, would become the founding dean of the Murrow College.

Pintak earned a Ph.D. degree in Muslim studies from the University of Wales. He had written two books about the Middle East and was finishing a third.

Gee, *will the university punish him, like it did me, for writing books instead of publishing refereed articles?*

According to a university news release,[2] Pintak was a veteran of more than 30 years in journalism on four continents.

I was impressed that the university decided to hire someone with a strong professional background. Many Murrow Ph.D. faculty would have preferred a traditional scholar and researcher. His only shortcoming was that Pintak did not have strong ties to mass media professionals in the Pacific Northwest, unlike the candidate I had nominated for the position.

MEANWHILE, the university hired William Mackey,[3] a Spokane attorney, to mediate our dispute at a rate of $300 an hour.

On paper, Mackey was about as mainstream as you can get when it comes to attorneys. He worked for a large law firm in Spokane, was a former attorney for a local government, and was described by several attorneys I spoke with as a "political conservative."

This alarmed me until I spoke with a liberal attorney friend of mine, who gave Mackey high marks for integrity.

On May 23, 2009, Mackey sent me a letter indicating that he would be mediating the dispute, which was scheduled for July 22. The process could begin as soon as the parties signed the "Agreement to Mediate."

The one-page document contained four points.

The first two and the last one were acceptable to me. The first said the mediator would not serve as an attorney for either party, and each of the parties would be responsible for whatever emerges from the mediation. The second point said either party could withdraw from the mediation process at any time. The fourth point said that the mediator could have private meetings with the parties and that the content of those meetings was confidential.

The third point was troubling, however.

It said that "the mediation process is confidential, including pre-session and post-session conversations and exchanges of information," and that none of the information is "subject to disclosure in any judicial or administrative proceeding." It added: "The only exception to this privilege is a written settlement agreement resulting from the mediation process."

What if the university refused to put the agreement in writing, or requested, as terms of the settlement, that the agreement be confidential? If this settlement were nonpublic, it couldn't help other WSU professors who might be victims of workplace mobbing. In addition, the public has a right to know how its tax money is being spent.

Mackey tried to convince me that the agreement would be made public, because WSU was a public institution.

But my experience told me that WSU administrators were not to be trusted.

I would not sign the agreement unless WSU agreed in advance that the final settlement would be released to the public. Everyone needed to be accountable.

About a week later, Mackey called and asked me to give a brief summary of my position in the dispute. I mentioned that I would have trouble signing the mediation agreement if the final results were not made public.

"The public has a right to know the details of this agreement as well as the costs," I said. "The university must be accountable for the errors it has made."

I tried to summarize the case as best I could, but after five minutes, he interrupted and said, "Why don't you come down to my office and we'll chat."

We met the following Monday.

His office was located in a high-rise building in downtown Spokane. He was one of three partners. He led me back to an office room, one of those rooms with all of the law books on the wall.

Do attorneys really use those books in this age of online legal resources, or is it just for show?

We briefly mentioned the weather — it was raining at the time — and we talked about some controversial attorneys in town. He had worked in government, and I was curious about his opinion of the attorneys. He defended them, saying they were doing the bidding of their clients.

"But don't attorneys have a responsibility to inform their clients when they are making bad decisions?" I asked.

He didn't disagree. He was adamant, however, that attorneys should not be judged by the actions of their clients.

I know that's how the profession defends itself.

But should attorneys continue to represent clients who violate the law or organizational rules or refuse to follow their advice? Where does one draw the ethical line?

I know how Ayn Rand would have viewed this situation. She would have called attorneys who refuse to draw an ethical line "second-handers" — as people who don't have the capacity to think on their own. Sociologist David Riesman would have called them "other-directed," as people who need the affirmation (and especially the money) of others.

Before I had time to process these thoughts, Mackey and I were deep into a discussion of the case. He then pointed out that both parties to a mediation must sign a nondisclosure agreement.

"I will promise to keep all aspects of the mediation process nonpublic except for two things," I said. "The final settlement agreement must be made public, and second, my list of demands must be public. Everything else will be nonpublic."

"You know, the university is afraid that you will quote them," he said.

"But they are public employees," I responded. "Most things they do are public record. If university administrators feel that the facts and truth are on their side, then what do they have to fear? The problem here, Bill, is a lack of accountability. This case would never have dragged on if administrators had allowed me to tape-record the meetings we had with Ombudsman Ken Struckmeyer. Your job, Bill, is to convince them that it is in their best interest to make the results of this mediation public."

I told Mackey about what happened when I was a professor at the University of Wisconsin–River Falls. Back then, my attorney and I were able to "frame" the news stories from our perspective, because the dispute was a personnel matter and privacy laws limited the amount of information that the university could release to the public.

The same holds in this case.

If I filed a lawsuit, the case would frame the Murrow College and WSU as free speech bullies. The university's reputation on free speech had already taken a number of hits, and the Murrow program's relationship with some parts of the mass communication professional community was also suffering from years of neglect. The last thing the Murrow program needed was to be on the receiving end of a free speech lawsuit.

Mackey disagreed with my assertion that the university would be unable to make public statements about my case, but he didn't elaborate, nor did that scare me.

Although the university would try to frame the dispute as one of incompetence, my publication and teaching records were too strong for that frame to hold up. Besides, my experience at the University of Wisconsin–River Falls also taught me that even if WSU attorneys gave administrators the power to say something, few would talk. No one would want to take the responsibility for the mistakes that were made.

Mackey knew his job wasn't to argue with me. He was supposed to be a neutral observer. He was just playing devil's advocate. He was testing the boundaries to determine whether he could get both parties to the negotiating table.

He agreed to do all he could to convince the university to modify the Agreement to Mediate. He told me that in the 2,000 mediations he had handled over the years, no one had ever refused to sign a mediation agreement. Most parties to a mediation agreement, especially those who win large cash settlements, do not want the results to be public, because "they don't want their neighbors to know they just got a huge settlement from a government bureaucracy," he said.

Vindication, not money, was the issue for me.

What I wanted was an apology, my record fixed, a promise that the university would set up an independent appeals process for annual reviews, my legal bills paid, and a commitment to eventually obtain accreditation for the mass communication programs. Of course, it was highly unlikely the university would agree to those demands. University attorneys would treat this case like all of the others where administrators are caught doing something wrong: They would offer a large sum of money and ask me to resign.

Since that kind of settlement didn't interest me, I figured I had nothing to lose by taking a position that the final settlement agreement be made public. In fact, if the university refused to sign the agreement, the university would look as if it were trying to hide something again. I wrote and posted to my website a news release predicting the university would reject my request to make the settlement agreement public.

On July 6, Mackey notified me that the mediation session for July 22 was canceled, because the university would not accept my terms for mediation. I e-mailed and thanked him for his efforts. He e-mailed back and wished me the best. I'm sure, though, as an attorney, he knew that I, as an individual fighting a large, powerful bureaucracy, would have a difficult time winning such a case.

But winning was never my most important objective.

Chapter 40 Endnotes

1. That candidate eventually landed an endowed chair at one of the best journalism programs in the United States — a nationally accredited program.

2. James Tinney, "Pintak Named Founding Dean of Murrow College," Washington State University New Service (Wednesday, May 20, 2009).

3. Not his real name.

Chapter 41

Time to Lawyer Up

Summer 2009
Washington State University

A First Amendment lawsuit was now my only option.

I realize that many people dislike people who file lawsuits. Plaintiffs and attorneys are often cast as greedy. Some are.

But as law professors point out, lawsuits are the civilized way to settle disputes. Compare that to earlier times, when disputes were often settled with a fistfight or a duel.

On July 11, 1804, Vice President Aaron Burr shot and killed former Secretary of State Alexander Hamilton, who called Burr a "profligate, a voluptuary in the extreme."[1] Hamilton's son also had been killed in a duel a few years earlier.

Doug Llewelyn, the court reporter in TV's *People's Court* in the 1980s, had it right when he said at the end of every show: "Don't take the law into your own hands: You take 'em to court."

My Lutheran elementary schoolteachers never taught me how to fight. "Turn the other cheek" was their motto. But they could have added: "And hire a good attorney."

I spent the rest of the summer of 2009 trying to find a good First Amendment attorney. I ran out of options in Spokane. The city was too small. So I expanded the search to Seattle.

The first four attorneys I contacted had done work with WSU, so they couldn't represent me.

Finally, I found one: Judith (Judy) Endejan at Graham & Dunn, a firm that employed more than 50 attorneys, but none had a relationship with WSU.

Judy once worked as a newspaper reporter in the Midwest. She understood my idealism. Former journalists rarely stop embracing free speech and the First Amendment.

She had received a 10 out of 10 rating by Avvo, a lawyer rating service, and she had received 11 other awards and honors, including "Best Lawyers in America"[2] recognition from Martindale-Hubbell.

From the University of Wisconsin she earned a journalism baccalaureate degree and a law degree, graduating summa cum laude, Order of the Coif.

Most importantly, she was an expert in First Amendment law.

I told her I had about $140,000 to pay for legal fees.

"Don't worry," she said. "We'll get back all of your attorney's fees."

That made me feel good, but I realized there are no guarantees when it comes to litigation.

MY SABBATICAL formally ended in summer 2009 and I started teaching again in August 2009.

Nothing much had changed in terms of the way people treated me. Many were uncomfortable in my presence.

One of the school's part-time receptionists was very friendly, but she appeared to be nervous. The sister of the internal auditor was evasive, not surprisingly. We had a polite greeting but it was clear neither of us would engage in any small talk from here on out. That made me sad, because we used to have a very collegial relationship.

Some faculty with whom I had been friends before the dispute deliberately avoided sitting next to me at the first faculty meeting.

I was persona non grata.[3]

The price of conviction.

But fall semester did include one pleasant surprise.

Former U.S. Congressman George R. Nethercutt Jr. called and asked whether Marquette Books would be interested in publishing a book he was writing.

Nethercutt, a Republican, was elected to Congress in 1994 after a grassroots election campaign in which he unseated Speaker of the House Tom Foley, a Democrat who had held Washington's 5th District office for 30 years.

Nethercutt, who retired from Congress after five terms, was now a political consultant and a philanthropist who was writing a civics book titled *In Tune with America: Our History in Song*.[4] The book traced the history of America through its famous songs.

Nethercutt was warm, friendly, charming, and very respectful to others — even to me, a progressive.

His book was a worthy project, very much in tune with the ideals of the Enlightenment. What impressed me was the objectivity and even-handedness of the text.

For example, Chapter 10 on the tumultuous 1960s and 1970s included P. F. Sloan's "The Eve of Destruction," which "becomes a theme song for the protest era and the list of complaints of students and activists," Nethercutt writes. Not many conservatives from that era have nice things to say about Vietnam War protestors.

The book was published 2010. Proceeds went to the Nethercutt Foundation, which promoted civics education to young people.

Although the book never made the *New York Times* best-seller list, it was a fun read and a unique contribution to the literature on American history.

MEANWHILE, I MET Lawrence Pintak, the new Murrow dean, in person at the first faculty meeting in late August 2009.

Several faculty had suggested creating a "certificate of journalism" program for citizen journalists and Pintak was promoting the idea. He was seeking some grant money to implement the program. I offered my support and sent a follow-up e-mail.

At the second faculty meeting, on September 2, 2009, Pintak presented his restructuring and hiring plan for the Murrow College. He said he would like, eventually, to seek accreditation for the mass communication programs and would like to develop professional master's degree programs.

Hurray!

He said the current structure of the graduate programs was "puzzling." He also would be creating outreach programs to the professional community and would be seeking grant money and donations. He said he would be traveling to the Seattle area for a weeklong series of meetings with possible donors and other officials.

Of course, I liked what he had to say. It looked like he was implementing some aspects of my 7-Step Plan, even though he wasn't familiar with it.

But many of the faculty at the meeting were not pleased.

After Pintak finished his presentation, he asked for questions or comments. No one spoke. You could have heard a mouse running in that room.

For three years, the faculty had restructured the Murrow program in their own image, and in one-half hour Pintak informed everyone that he planned to tear it down.

Pintak, though, appeared to unaware of what he had done.

I could hear the ghost of Machiavelli groaning in that room: "Be careful what you ask for — Be careful what you ask for — "

I, too, wanted to stand up and shout: "Welcome, colleagues, to the ivory tower of babel."

But, for once, I held my tongue.

A short time later faculty were asked to vote on some revised rules, which stated that only Ph.D. faculty could be "graduate faculty." In other words, professional faculty who had earned a master's degree but not a Ph.D. would not be allowed to serve as heads of master's committees.

"In light of Lawrence's proposed plans to create some professional master's degrees, isn't the language of these rules elitist?" I said. "Shouldn't we allow professional faculty to chair master's committees and advise graduate students? I don't think professional faculty should be treated as second-class citizens."

Several Ph.D. faculty, including two scholars sympathetic to neo-Marxist egalitarian doctrines, tried to defend the "elitist" rules.

I figured I would lose another battle. By now, I was used to it.

"But I think Dave has a point here," Pintak said.

That's all it took to win the day.

One elite endorsing a proposal.

After several minutes of wrangling about the wording of the new policy, faculty voted in favor of allowing professional faculty to chair graduate master's committees, albeit the measure did not pass unanimously.

It was the second time in a year that I had "won" a debate at a faculty meeting.

The other incident involved the hiring of a professional faculty member. I was a member of a five-member search committee that initially voted unanimously in favor of one candidate. When the recommendation went before the entire faculty, the director preferred the other candidate. When the vote was taken, every member on the search committee except me jumped ship and voted for the other candidate. When that candidate refused to accept the position, the committee members (and rest of the faculty) jumped back on board with me.

The incident illustrates the power of the collective over the individual. Most people, even professors, have a great fear of being isolated from others, especially administrators. I call it the "bureaucratic bandwagon effect."

At any rate, maybe my luck in the Murrow College was changing.

As I left the room, I made eye contact with one of the professional faculty who understood the power struggle being played out.

He smiled; I winked.

On the drive home, Sirius Radio's blues channel was playing Zakiya Hooker's "Hug U, Kiss U, Squeeze U."

I want to hug u, kiss u, squeeze you till my arms fall off ...
Did you know about that baby? I just love you so.

I E-MAILED PINTAK the following day and thanked him for his support. Several days later a colleague asked me what I thought of Pintak's plans for the program.

"How can I disagree?" I said. "He's implementing some aspects of my 7-Step Plan."

At the next faculty meeting, a proposal from Pintak to collapse the seven majors in our program into three (journalism, strategic communication and communication studies) was approved after one of the faculty pointed out that this change wouldn't have much effect on the structure of the Murrow College.

One faculty member turned to me and said: "Here we go again, for the umpteenth time, changing the program."

"Yeah, the sad part is that it creates cynicism among faculty," I said.

"Do ya think?" the faculty member sarcastically responded.

At another meeting, Pintak informed faculty that all new Ph.D. tenure-track hires would be required to seek grant money from the government or from private foundations to successfully obtain tenure in the Murrow program. The requirement would be written into each contract. Current faculty also would be expected to generate research money for the university to get maximum rewards at annual review time.

This announcement angered one tenure-track faculty member, who pointed out that the grant requirement was not part of his contract for obtaining tenure and that his research program did not lend itself well to obtaining grant monies. Grant-funded research generally focuses narrowly on the needs and problems of specific governmental agencies or private foundation goals, not on research that raises questions about their legitimacy, effectiveness or failure to enhance the ideals of the Enlightenment.

The faculty member was saying, in other words, that it was unfair to change the rules in the middle of the game.

He was right.

But Pintak showed no sympathy.

The marching orders, we all knew, were coming from the provost's office. Shared governance and democracy didn't apply here.[5]

None of this surprised me.

As state governments pulled back their funding of higher education in the 1990s and early 2000s, universities increasingly turned to grants and donations to generate more revenue. In mass communication programs, the emphasis on grants also goes hand-in-hand with the gradual transfer of power from the green-eyeshaders to the chi-squares.

But few faculty in the room that day understood the long-term social consequences of emphasizing grant-funded research: It meant a devaluation of research that challenges mainstream ideas, beliefs and institutions, and a potential devaluation of Enlightenment ideals that seek more democracy, due process and free speech protection for society.

Hence, the call for grant-funded research is an unwitting call for restraining scholarly criticism of dominant values and institutions — a form of social control so subtle that even those who do mainstream research usually cannot see the consequences.

Around the time of this faculty meeting, the local professional chapter of the Society of Professional Journalists invited Pintak to speak at an event in Moscow, Idaho, a 10-minute drive from Pullman.

Pintak talked about the problems facing journalism, including the declining number of journalists covering international news. He added that mass communication programs need to restructure their curriculums to help mass media industries deal with these problems.

The audience and I embraced most of his suggestions. As we were leaving the meeting, Pintak paid me a compliment for one of the comments I made at the meeting.

I remember thinking: *Maybe he won't be co-opted by the WSU administration.*

Meanwhile, a small controversy was brewing in the Murrow program. Word got out that Pintak had earned his Ph.D. through an online program.

That angered some Ph.D. faculty, who believed that online programs provided an inferior education. One member of the search committee told me that the committee itself was unaware that Pintak held an online Ph.D. Vice Provost Frances McSweeney's committee had not been thorough in its investigation.

But it didn't really matter. A Ph.D. was preferred but not required for the appointment, as President Elson Floyd had previously told me.

As usual, none of the faculty had the guts to go to the mat on this one. Administrators like that about faculty.

Chapter 41 Endnotes

1. Dueling was illegal in most states even in Hamilton's time, but the laws were often ignored. Burr was charged with murder but never tried.

2. Martindale-Hubbell Attorney Peer Ratings and Client Reviews, retrieved September 10, 2009, from <https://www.martindale.com/ratings-and-reviews>.

3. I also learned in 2007 that the graduate faculty were refusing to assign graduate students to me and several other faculty. Before 2005, the graduate director made tentative assignments, matching up students' interests to faculty areas of specialization. After he left office, the faculty would meet as a group to make the assignments. Faculty who didn't attend the meeting were shut out. I was accused of not taking on enough graduate students. However, those charges were blunted by the fact that I had been an adviser or committee member for 22 graduate students

in 11 years.

4. George R. Nethercutt Jr. with Tom M. McArthur, *In Tune with America: Our History in Song* (Spokane, WA: Marquette Books, 2010).

5. Contractually, though, the professor might have had a good case. Faculty contracts are binding documents, and changing the job requirements may have violated contract law.

Chapter 42

The Envy of Excellence

Fall Semester 2009
Washington State University

For more than two years I tried unsuccessfully to get WSU officials to correct errors in my annual reviews and an internal audit.

In the beginning, I thought the error about canceling classes would be corrected quickly because I had the physical evidence to dispute the allegations.

But, as the years passed, I realized that a simple resolution would not be forthcoming. As a media sociologist, I couldn't help but run a series of questions over and over in my mind — questions that related this dispute to bigger issues involving the impact of institutions in society:

> How could very bright people — administrators trained in scientific methods and one of its core principles, objectivity — engage in what can only be identified as irrational, illogical, nonobjective behavior? Why would they persist in trying to punish a faculty member who had followed university rules and the advice of high-ranking university officials? Why would they repeatedly fail to explain or justify their actions and, at the same time, fail to provide an explanation as to why my interpretations of the rules were wrong? Why would they ignore my evidence?

I found some of the answers in a book on workplace mobbing by Canadian sociologist Kenneth Westhues. *The Envy of Excellence: Administrative Mobbing of High-Achieving Professors*[1] focuses in particular on the case of one Canadian professor, Herbert Richardson, who, in Westhues's opinion, was wrongly mobbed.[2] Westhues writes:

> This book seeks to understand the process by which good and decent human beings square off in such a way that all the authorities, with public opinion following, are on one side, and one lone human being on the other side. How does it happen that a thousand accusing fingers all get pointed in one way, toward a target who is doing little harm and much good?[3]

The process that led to the dismissal of Richardson, who was a Protestant theologian teaching in a Catholic university, was a "form of savagery," according to Westhues.

> The process is not essential to academic or working life. It is wasteful. It brings out the worst in people. ... Less harm is done, I argue, by alleged goats among the sheep on university faculties, than by the search for goats and the rituals by which they are driven out. With good will and knowledge of how people behave in groups, our universities can and should function in more civilized, constructive ways.[4]

Westhues blames part of the problem on the fact that universities are not bound by rigorous legal rules and principles.

> Like courts, these in-house, quasi-judicial [academic] bodies can discredit and punish an accused person, destroy the person's life, but they are governed not by criminal law but only the newer, looser rules of administrative law. Proof beyond reasonable doubt is not required, just the weighing of probabilities. Charges need not be so specific as in criminal courts, nor rules of evidence so strict. Most of the professors and staff members sitting in judgment are unschooled in law. Procedures are informal, haphazard, entangled in campus politics, and free of the presumption of innocence of the accused. At worst, domestic tribunals function as kangaroo courts — better to say wallaby courts, the latter being a smaller marsupial.[5]

Although universities "are places where the 'law of reason' appears to reign supreme ... on most issues," Westhues writes that "in these same places, on exceptional occasions, people riot in complete exemption from that law."

> Academic knives are more polished and keen than those made of steel, and they are thrown with such grace that targets sometimes barely know they have been stabbed in the back until their campus lives are lost.

WESTHUES PLACES much of the blame for mobbing on "envy."

High-achieving professors are usually the victims.

This psychological theory fits well with explanations many of my friends and colleagues also gave me. I don't doubt that envy plays a big role.

But as a social structural theorist, I believe a more complete explanation must go beyond the confines of individual motivation.

Part of the reason the errors in my annual reviews were never corrected and why a mobbing atmosphere emerged at WSU can be attributed to the rules that guide the annual review process at WSU. The rules give administrators far more power than faculty and limit the ability of faculty to appeal their decisions. This was especially the case with the internal audit and my appeal to the dean.

Moreover, even when one can appeal, the "judge" usually has a conflict of interest. Higher-level administrators need the political support of the person who gave the review, so their independence is compromised.

The system also presumes that the higher-level administrator has a lot of knowledge about the performance of the faculty member. But administrators rarely do, nor do they have the resources to investigate each complaint. Although the higher-level administrator could support the lower-level administrator's decision, the safest approach is for the higher-level administrator to simply provide no rating at all, which the rules allow. This insulates higher-ups from responsibility. Then the lower-level administrator is forced to take responsibility.

That's what Dean Lear did in my case. He didn't formally endorse Austin's first two reviews, he simply refused to change them.

Because power in administrative structures is derived partly through loyalty and mutual support, obtaining an objective assessment is extremely difficult.

Clearly, a more objective, independent appeal process is needed, yet administrators will resist such changes, because that would seriously dilute their power and possibly increase appeals and criticism from faculty.

Under the current system at WSU, administrators enjoy a wide latitude of power over professors, because they know few will fight a bad review.

One dysfunctional side effect of not having a more independent review process, however, is illustrated by my case: The dispute may end up in litigation, consuming thousands of person-hours and university resources and going on for many years. Now the taxpayer is a victim.

In short, to reduce the problem of workplace mobbing, bureaucracies need to create rules that make the system more equitable and fair. They need to ensure more due process. This change is consistent with the ideals of the Enlightenment project and would serve as a check on the "envy factor."

WESTHUES WRITES that many victims of mobbing suffer from post-traumatic stress disorder and from physical health problems. Some commit suicide; some become nonfunctional.

But Richardson recovered quickly from the mobbing and continued to work in his multi-million-dollar publishing business.

"I was not humiliated," Richardson told Westhues. "It is the university that was humiliated ... They're the people who look silly."[6]

Westhues theorized that Richardson survived because his principles gave him strength.

"Richardson is a walking embodiment of inner-directedness," Westhues writes, citing Riesman's book, *The Lonely Crowd*.[7] "It [inner-directedness] is the quality that got him mobbed: stubborn determination to act on his principles and faith, regardless of public opinion or academic authority. It is also the quality that enabled him to survive the mobbing."[8]

Westhues was right.

Principles make all the difference.

Chapter 42 Endnotes

1. Kenneth Westhues, *The Envy of Excellence: Administrative Mobbing of High-Achieving Professors* (Lewiston, Canada: The Edwin Mellen Press, 2005).

2. News reports said Richardson was fired for losing his temper in class, for firing a graduate student, and for spending too much time working in a highly successful book publishing business he created. See "Professor fired over outside interest," *Times Higher Education* (October 28, 1994), retrieved August 20, 2009, from <www.timeshighereducation.co.uk/story.asp?storyCode=154569&sectioncode=26>.

3. Westhues, *The Envy of Excellence*, p. 5.

4. Ibid.

5. Ibid., p. 3

6. Ibid., p. 297.

7. David Riesman, *The Lonely Crowd: A Study of the Changing American Character*, in collaboration with Reuel Denney and Nathan Glazer (New Haven, CT: Yale University Press, 1950).

8. Westhues, *The Envy of Excellence*, p. 297.

Part VI

Secret Reports, Rulings & Lessons

Chapter 43

Demers v. Austin

October 28, 2009
Spokane, Washington

A front page story in the October 28, 2009, issue of *The Spokesman-Review* informed readers that fall colors on deciduous trees would be muted because of freezing temperatures two weeks earlier.

The story was a fitting metaphor for what was to come in my First Amendment lawsuit with Washington State University, which Judy Endejan filed electronically on this day in U.S. District Court in Spokane, Washington.

The case was initially assigned to Judge Lonny R. Suko, but he recused himself because he had earned a bachelor's degree from WSU. He presumably thought his affiliation with WSU might be seen by me or the public as a conflict of interest.

The case was reassigned to Judge Robert H. Whaley, a senior judge.

The complaint asserted that WSU administrators gave me low ratings in my annual reviews because they resented the contents of my (1) 7-Step Plan, which implied mismanagement of the Murrow program, and (2) *Ivory Tower of Babel* book, which, among other things, rebuked WSU and other research universities for failing to embrace free speech ideals and reward faculty for writing books and articles that seek to influence policymakers and the general public.

The complaint also accused WSU Internal Auditor Heather Lopez of violating ethical standards on conflict of interest.

I issued a four-page news release and distributed it via e-mail to several hundred local and national news media, pro-speech organizations, social scientists and colleagues. A portion of the release is reproduced below:

LAWSUIT ACCUSES WSU'S MURROW COLLEGE OF VIOLATING
JOURNALISM PROFESSOR'S FIRST AMENDMENT RIGHTS
University Auditor Also Accused of Conflict of Interest

SPOKANE, WA — A Washington State University journalism professor today filed a federal lawsuit against four administrators at his university who, he says, violated his First Amendment rights when they punished him for proposing a "7-Step Plan" to improve the quality of the unaccredited undergraduate mass communication programs in the Edward R. Murrow College of Communication.

Tenured associate professor David K. Demers filed the lawsuit in U.S. District Court in Spokane. The defendants are Erica Austin, former interim director and dean of the Murrow program; Warwick Bayly, interim provost and vice president; Erich Lear, former dean of the College of Liberal Arts; and Frances McSweeney, vice provost for faculty affairs. ...

"The pattern of actions taken by the defendants demonstrates a concerted effort to punish Dr. Demers for creating his 7-Step Plan and for criticizing the Murrow College administrators," the complaint states. [T]he complaint asserts that Austin falsely accused Demers of canceling classes in 2007 and 2008. One of those accusations was duplicated in a report issued by WSU Internal Auditor Heather Lopez, whose sister worked for Austin in the Murrow office. The complaint contends the auditor had a "patent conflict of interest."...

The lawsuit asks the court to expunge the annual reviews and the internal audit, make appropriate salary adjustments, pay reasonable attorney fees, and assess unspecified punitive damages. ...

The defendants, through their state-appointed attorney, Kathryn M. Battuello, denied the allegations.[1] The defendants would provide more details about their case a year later, when they filed a motion to have the case thrown out of court (details to come). The defendants did not issue a press release, but a university spokesman told local media that WSU would "vigorously" defend them against the lawsuit.

BRIEF STORIES about the filing of the lawsuit appeared in several news media, including the *Seattle Times*, the *Lewiston Tribune*, and the *Moscow-Pullman Daily News*.[2] The WSU *Daily Evergreen* and the *Spokesman-Review*, however, ignored the story.

I wasn't too surprised by the *Spokesman-Review* snub.

After all, I had, through the years, become an unwitting critic of the newspaper's management. I had criticized them for censoring citizen commentaries and letters to the editor and for their involvement in the River Park Square garage scandal. Another factor that may have contributed to the snub was the fact that Elizabeth Cowles, who managed the family's broadcasting stations, was a member of the WSU Board of Regents.[3]

But the *Evergreen* rebuff was puzzling.

Although student journalists most likely identified with the administrative power structure at WSU, even the most biased of editors could not fail to see that a federal lawsuit alleging that a journalism program director was violating the First Amendment rights of a faculty member was one helluva story.

Were WSU students getting proper instruction in their journalism classes?

One retired public relations colleague of mine shared an insightful perspective.

"First," he said, "they [student journalists] have to determine what might be their state of grace should they report the event. That likely will take a couple of days of careful eavesdropping on the conversations of their faculty advisers who likely will be just as carefully eavesdropping on degreed and titled scholars who hold the bully pulpits [in Pullman]. One thing about all those Ph.D. types, they forever test the winds of favor and, once satisfied their favored colleagues favor them, the bombs burst and the dawn comes early."

This public relations official must have read David Riesman's *The Lonely Crowd*.

I did ask one of the faculty advisers to the student newspaper why its editors didn't publish a story. The adviser said he did not know, but he agreed that the story was newsworthy. It's quite possible that one of the editors at the paper didn't like me. Most of them took classes from me. Sometimes it boils down to an individual bias.

To compensate for the shortage of information on campus, I wrote several letters to the editor and posted updates on the lawsuit to the WSU American Association of University Professors website. I was a member of the campus chapter.

As the months and years passed, I would occasionally issue news releases, which sometimes generated admonishing phone calls from the defendants' attorney to Judy.

"Tough shit," I responded. "If they (university officials) didn't want me to talk about the case, then they should have settled the dispute before I filed the lawsuit."

Controlling information about the lawsuit was one of the few power advantages I had over the WSU bureaucracy. Personnel and privacy laws prevented them from talking about some aspects of the case.

But those laws didn't apply to me.

My only constraint was the truth.

Truth is always a defense for libel.

THE LAWSUIT PRODUCED relatively little response from WSU students and faculty.

This did not surprise me, because the *Daily Evergreen* never published a story and I never talked about the lawsuit in class.

Of course, Murrow faculty were aware of the lawsuit. I had a few brief conversations with some of them. Some were sympathetic. But none would support the free speech principle in the lawsuit in public, not even the journalism professors. They no doubt felt they had a lot to lose and little to gain. It takes a great deal of courage to defend a principle when you have something big to lose.

Which brings me to another important lesson about activism.

People who are actively involved in principled disputes with bureaucracies often see their plight as an important matter to everyone else. But others do not, even when the matter involves issues that will personally or professionally affect them.

Having the constitutional right to criticize administrators and their policies — one of the key issues at stake in the lawsuit — may not have been perceived by most faculty as being much of a benefit. As Riesman and William H. Whyte had pointed out, most people who work in bureaucracies are compliant and seek praise and rewards from their bosses.

One might argue that Murrow print and broadcast journalism faculty presumably had a greater vested interest in First Amendment issues than other Murrow faculty. But not one of them publicly supported the idea that faculty should have the free speech right to criticize the administration and offer alternative plans for restructuring a program.

Even some WSU faculty associated with the American Association of University Professors, which is one of the strongest voices for free speech in higher education, were timid in their support.

"I have to be very careful about how I approach all this," said one AAUP member, who was worried that he would jeopardize his chances of being elected to an important position in Faculty Senate if he took a strong stand on the issue.

Power over principle.

Bureaucracies seem to be vulnerable to this proposition.

On one occasion I asked a WSU junior administrator whether he would defend a faculty member who was being falsely accused of violating university rules.

"Are you kidding?" the administrator said, laughing. "I have a family to support."

That administrator eventually became the head of an academic unit at a major university. This is the kind of person who succeeds in bureaucratic systems.

The WSU Faculty Senate, which presumably had a vested interest in supporting free speech on campus, also ignored the lawsuit, even when WSU administrators later argued in court that faculty do not deserve free speech protection when acting in their service-related (or "professional") roles, which included faculty participation on the Faculty Senate.

Yes — you read that right.

The Faculty Senate head-in-the-sand position can be explained in part by two other factors.

The first was a lack of leadership on issues involving academic freedom. One of the Senate presidents even denied me an opportunity to speak to the senators about the legal issues at stake, apparently unaware that Faculty Senate is a public body that legally cannot deny citizens or faculty the opportunity to address it.

The second factor, according to WSU AAUP members, was that the Faculty Senate leadership identified strongly with the administration on most issues. In 2006, the WSU Faculty Senate president supported the WSU regents' decision to hire President Elson Floyd without a formal interview process. Only one faculty member, the ombudsman, criticized the decision.

Co-optation is easy to achieve in most bureaucratic environments, especially those that are located in small towns and are geographically isolated. Pullman was a small town, which meant administrators and faculty often bumped into each other at the grocery store, church, restaurants and social events. Sociologists have pointed out for more than a century that small communities tend to inhibit dissent and conflict and reinforce consensus values and interpersonal cooperation.[4]

ALTHOUGH WSU INSIDERS may have been reluctant to speak out on the issues surrounding the lawsuit, this did not apply to observers outside of the university.

"You should drop this lawsuit," one expert on disputes between faculty and universities told me shortly after I filed the free speech lawsuit. "Your university will destroy you. They are too powerful. They will build a case against you that you can never beat. You can never win. It will cost you hundreds of thousands of dollars and you will end up bankrupt and bitter. I've seen it happen many times before. Life is too short."

"Do you really think anyone cares about your case?" said an attorney familiar with the lawsuit. "Do you really want to work at WSU? You should settle it while you can. Even if you win, you will lose. You will never get your money back. Life is too short."

Life is too short.

I heard that phrase a lot after the lawsuit was filed.

The speakers imply that whatever I'm fighting for is not worth the personal price that I will pay, either emotionally or in terms of cost and job security.

I respectfully disagree.

Life is too short not to stand up for what you believe in.

Complacency breeds regrets.

The only significant support I received with respect to the lawsuit came from friends and colleagues outside of the Murrow College and from nationally based free speech organizations.

Most of the colleagues were journalists-turned-professors who valued the fight for free speech in society.

This included one retired dean.

"This is an incredible situation," he said, "and one that has my deepest sympathy, and a good deal of empathy as well. I hope you win this case quickly and hands down. ... The 'mobbing' behavior is [a] new [concept] to me, but outrageous, and the faculty and other participants should be ashamed."

Chapter 43 Endnotes

1. "Defendants' Answer and Affirmative Defenses to Plaintiffs' Complaint for Violation of Civil and Constitutional Rights," *Demers v. Austin, et al.,* Case NO. CV-09-334-LRS, U.S. District Court, Eastern District of Washington, filed October 28, 2009.

2. Joel Mills, "Professor Files Lawsuit Against Four WSU Administrators," *Lewiston* (Idaho) *Tribune* (October 28, 2009), p. 1, and Sarah Mason, "WSU Professor to Sue Over Free speech Issues," *Moscow-Pullman Daily News* (October 28, 2009), p. 1.

3. She was a regent from 2003 to 2011. The Regents had to approve the university's decision to defend itself in the lawsuit. They also were updated on progress of the lawsuit through the years in closed session.

4. Émile Durkheim, *The Division of Labor in Society* (Glencoe, IL: Free Press, 1960), first published in 1893 as *De la Division du Travail Social,* and Ferdinand Tonnies, *Community and Society: Gemeinschaft und Gesellschaft,* translated and edited by Charles P. Loomis (Lansing, MI: The Michigan State University Press, 1957; first published in 1887).

Chapter 44

The State Auditor's 'Secret' Report

December 4, 2009
Spokane, Washington

Five weeks after my lawsuit was filed, I received another audit report from Provost Bayly, only this time the author was an auditor who worked at the University of Idaho.

The report duplicated all of the errors contained in Lopez's audit. Apparently WSU hired the UI auditor to write the report.

But why?

Why would they conduct another audit?

And why would the new auditor fail to contact me?

I initially didn't pay much attention to the report, because the lawsuit had been filed, and another negative report wouldn't change things.

But about two months later I would get the answers to my questions.

I was reviewing documents obtained from the university through discovery.

Among the hundreds of pages were two letters exchanged between President Elson Floyd and Washington State Auditor Brian Sonntag.

I called Judy, my attorney, immediately.

"Judy, Washington State Auditor Brian Sonntag investigated Internal Auditor Heather Lopez and concluded that she had a conflict of interest. But President [Elson] Floyd withheld that information. The internal audit is tainted. That's why his administration wanted to settle the case through mediation. And that's why the university hired the outside [Idaho] auditor — to produce another audit that would replace the tainted internal audit."

She was ecstatic.

Now it all made sense.

The university's case against me had fallen apart when Sonntag concluded that Lopez had a conflict of interest, and Floyd's administration was trying desperately to duct-tape it back together.

The events leading up to Sonntag's report began in fall of 2008, when I asked Floyd to give me instructions on how to file a conflict-of-interest complaint against Lopez.

Lopez's sister, who reported to Murrow Interim Dean Erica Austin, informed Austin that Lopez was the WSU internal auditor. Austin also had instructed Lopez's sister to monitor my classes on at least one occasion.

Floyd never gave me instructions on how to file a conflict-of-interest complaint against Lopez. But he and his administration obviously were worried about the potential conflict of interest.

On March 2, 2009, Floyd, without my knowledge, asked Washington State Auditor Brian Sonntag to investigate.

Dear Mr. Sonntag:
I am requesting your assistance in determining whether or not a conflict exists that would impair the independence of the Washington State University (WSU) director of Internal Audit in the performance of her duties.

In fall 2007 a complaint was received by the WSU Office of Internal Audit, initiating an investigation that was performed by the Director. The results of the investigation were posted in a report in April 2008. The subject of the complaint [Demers] has since claimed a conflict exists in the Director's participation in the audit due to the fact that the Director's sister works in the same department as the subject, and reports to the same supervisor. The subject also claims the Director's sister brought forward the complaint that initiated the investigation,[1] in an effort to make herself look good in the eyes of her supervisor, actions that would have influenced the objectivity of the Director in the performance of the investigation. ... [bracketed material added for clarity]

Sincerely, Elson S. Floyd, Ph.D., President

Sonntag investigated and concluded Lopez did, indeed, violate conflict of interest rules. He sent his reply to Floyd three weeks later, on March 23, 2009.

Dear Dr. Floyd:
Thank you for your letter asking us to review whether the independence of the University's Director of Audit was impaired during an investigation. After consulting Government Audit Standards, we concluded that a conflict of interest and impairment to independence did exist based on the facts you provided. ... Specifically, the Audit Director's investigation of her sister's co-worker was based on assertions from the sister. This relationship creates not only a personal impairment for the Director but also for all audit staff members who are under the Director's control and influence. ...

Sincerely, Brian Sonntag, Washington State Auditor

Floyd never gave me a copy of Sonntag's letter, because it undermined the administrative case against me.

Internal Auditor Heather Lopez tried to defend her actions in a letter she wrote to Floyd after receiving the results of Sonntag's investigation (another document obtained through discovery).

But she probably didn't need to.

Floyd never punished her.

Floyd's administration, realizing that it was in trouble, then tried to settle the case through mediation. But that failed when I demanded the settlement be made public.

Then Floyd's administration asked the auditor at the University of Idaho to issue a new audit report. The UI auditor never contacted me and duplicated the errors contained in the original audit.

On March 11, 2010, I issued a news release announcing the new evidence.

WSU's President Fails to Disclose State Auditor's Report; Breach of Ethics Alleged

PULLMAN — Washington State Auditor Brian Sonntag issued a report a year ago which concluded that Washington State University's director of internal audits had violated conflict of interest rules when she accused a WSU communication professor of canceling classes in violation of university rules. But WSU President Elson Floyd, who requested Sonntag's investigation, never informed the accused professor or the public.

"I don't know about criminal law, but withholding evidence that could exonerate a professor is unquestionably a serious breach of ethics and his due process rights," said David Demers, who was the target of the WSU's internal audit. "Floyd and other university officials continued to punish me even though they knew the audit was tainted. ..."

On June 10, 2010, Judy filed a motion to revise our original complaint. The additional revised material included this paragraph:

Unbeknownst to Dr. Demers, WSU President Elson Floyd was concerned about Dr. Demers' claim that the 2008 audit was tainted with a conflict of interest because the auditor was the sister of Dr. Austin's assistant. President Floyd asked Washington State Auditor Brian Sonntag on March 2, 2009 for his opinion on Dr. Demers' allegation that Dr. Demers' 2008 audit was tainted by a conflict of interest. Mr. Sonntag responded by letter dated March 23, 2009, advising President Floyd had he "concluded that a conflict of interest and impairment to independence did exist." None of the March 2009 correspondence between President Floyd and Mr. Sonntag was provided to Dr. Demers until the defendants made their initial disclosures in this litigation in February 2010.[2]

Nearly three years later I e-mailed Sonntag and asked him, among other things, whether state auditors have a responsibility under auditing codes of ethics to provide information to state employees when they are falsely accused of wrongdoing.[3]

He never responded.

Two months after that I also mailed him an early draft of this book, which included the story about the Sonntag letter and the statement that he (Sonntag) "failed to notify the target (me) of the (his) audit."

He responded on May 28, 2013: "Communicating directly with the head of a government agency (President Floyd) is in line with auditing standards. I think it is a misrepresentation to say we 'failed.' We took this seriously, as we did all of our work, and acted professionally."[4]

I responded: "You are correct: You and your agency acted professionally and legally. Yet, a great injustice has been done."[5]

So what did Floyd say when he was asked why he refused to give me a copy of Sonntag's investigation? His answer came in late September 2010, when he and five other administrators were deposed over a four-day period.

Chapter 44 Endnotes

1. University e-mails showed that Internal Auditor Heather Lopez's sister informed Murrow Director Erica Austin that Lopez was the university auditor. Austin thanked her for the information and subsequently made contact with Lopez. My conflict-of-interest complaint was based in part on the "halo effect," which means Lopez viewed Austin as being a very credible, unimpeachable source because of the relationship between Austin and her sister. That's why Lopez never asked me whether I had canceled classes in spring of 2007 — she assumed the information from Austin was accurate.

2. "First Amended Complaint for Violation of Civil and Constitutional Rights," *Demers v. Austin, et al.,* Case No. CV-09-334-RHW, filed June 15, 2010, U.S. District Court, Eastern District of Washington.

3. E-mail from David Demers to Brian Sonntag (January 1, 2013).

4. E-mail from Brian Sonntag to David Demers (May 28, 2013).

5. E-mail from David Demers to Brian Sonntag (May 30, 2013).

Chapter 45

The Damning Depositions

September 30, 2010
Washington State University

My attorney removed her reading glasses and stared briefly at WSU Vice Provost for Faculty Affairs Frances McSweeney, the deposed defendant sitting on the opposite side of the table.

"If an annual review accuses a professor of repeatedly canceling classes despite warnings that the level of cancellations was unacceptable, do you think the faculty member is entitled to find out specifically what classes were canceled?"[1]

During the early stages of discovery, my attorney and I learned that WSU administrators who accused me of canceling classes never kept a written record of the classes that they thought I was canceling. Without evidence of wrongdoing, that part of university's case against me would crumble. And my attorney, Judy Endejan, was trying to put that into the record.

"Surely the faculty member knows that," responded McSweeney, who was one the defendants in my free speech lawsuit.

"Well, how does the faculty know what particular classes are the subject of the criticism?" Judy asked.

"I would think they should ask," McSweeney responded.

"And if they ask, do you think they should be told by administration?"

"I don't know," McSweeney said. "I mean, in this particular case, Dr. Demers is doing the canceling of the classes. I believe he would know. By the way, let's rephrase that and not say 'canceling.' Let's say 'not holding the classes.' He knows that information."

"How do you know he knows that?"

The stenographer's hands paused as the vice provost, who also was a professor in the psychology department at Washington State University, leaned forward and pointed her index finger at me.

"He would certainly know whether he went to a class at a particular time," she said, raising her voice. "If he doesn't, he needs the help of somebody in my profession."

"Well, doctor, what would happen if no one told him that the conduct of online quizzes was unacceptable?"

That question angered McSweeney.

"He was told repeatedly," she said, raising her voice. "His violation of the rule in the academic regulations was considered to be out of line with the acceptable faculty standards, and he was told that repeatedly by many people."

The vice provost stared at me — the kind of stare that Johnny Miller gave me in third grade after I beat him in a game of tetherball and just before he slugged me. Thank goodness this time three feet of table served as a buffer.

But, despite the high drama, it turned out that McSweeney never needed to concede that the administration had no evidence that I canceled classes.

That's because three other administrators who also were deposed that week, including her boss, all said that conducting online quizzes or exams during class time was an acceptable university practice. In other words, I had violated no university rules.

The three administrators were Provost Warwick Bayly, former Liberal Arts Dean Erich Lear, and Murrow interim Dean Erica Austin.

My attorney changed topics. "You've testified here that you feel that Dr. Demers should not be here attending depositions in his litigation and that you view that to be a violation, I guess, of his teaching duties? Is that your —"

"Object to the form of the question," interjected the McSweeney's counsel, Kathryn Battuello, an assistant attorney general for the state of Washington. "Misstates her testimony."

"No," McSweeney said without hesitation. "Whether he's here or not is up to him. But if he is here, he should be taking leave without pay."

"Okay," Endejan said. "So, you do understand that Dr. Demers has alleged constitutional violations in his lawsuit?"

"Yes, I do."

"And you certainly wouldn't want to infringe upon his right to protect or vindicate those constitutional rights, would you?"

"I did not say he shouldn't be here. I'm just saying that we shouldn't be paying him to be here. We don't have to pay him to do this."

"Well, and if perchance Dr. Demers prevails, should the university be paying you for being here?"

"Absolutely, because it's part of my job. You're asking me questions about my knowledge about this —"

"To violate constitutional rights? Is that part of [your job] —"

"Object to the form of the question," Battuello interrupted again.

The deposition ended a few minutes later.

AS PROMISED, the university several weeks later docked my pay $500 for attending the vice provost's deposition and five others. But none of the defendants, who were working on university time as well, was docked.

I originally proposed that we do the depositions on weekends, when I wasn't teaching. But the defendants and their attorney didn't want to take time off on the weekends. That was their free time.

So the depositions were scheduled on a Monday through Thursday.

They obviously knew I was teaching, and I assumed they would not object if I had someone cover for me in my two classes.

So I informed Murrow Dean Lawrence Pintak via e-mail on the Sunday before the depositions that I had lined up educational videos for students in my Tuesday classes to watch. On Thursday, they would be taking online exams. I would be monitoring everything on my personal computer during the depositions, which were being conducted in the main administration building on campus.

"Please know that I am doing my best to accommodate university rules," I said in my e-mail to Pintak. "But I will need a 'yes' or 'no' no later than Monday afternoon on whether my plans for this week are acceptable to you and/or the university. If you say 'no,' I'll conduct classes in the classrooms on Tuesday. However, I will still give quizzes on Thursday, because Austin gave me permission to do that and [university rules][2] do not prohibit the giving of online quizzes or exams."

Pintak responded: "I am not in a position to begin evaluating your classes, quizzes/exams or pedagogy based on an arbitrary deadline. Such reviews are part of the annual review process. Nor am I prepared to get into a legalistic conversation about the definition of 'in-class' versus 'classroom' or evaluate/re-evaluate college policy on deadline. You have been a faculty member at WSU since 1996 and a tenured faculty member for the last eleven years. You should be thoroughly familiar with the teaching requirements and I trust you to meet the same."

In other words, Pintak was not going to tell me in advance whether the plans for my course during deposition week were in line with university rules.

Wow!

There was no longer any doubt about whose side Pintak was on.

Over the next two years, Pintak's administration would continue to give me lower than satisfactory evaluations.

And there was nothing I could do about it.

The wagons had completed a full circle.

Although U.S. courts have ruled that civil court litigants generally have a right to attend depositions without fear of punishment from the government, WSU administrators seemed to be saying that they could punish me for attending the depositions, and, furthermore, they would not provide me with advice to avoid that punishment.

Fortunately, on Monday, the first day of depositions and a day when I taught no classes, the problem was solved.

During his deposition, Provost Warwick Bayly said that showing films to cover a class for an important event, like depositions, or giving online quizzes is not a violation of university rules.

I'm beginning to like the guy from down under.

On Monday night, I e-mailed Pintak and an associate Murrow dean with this information.

"Please contact him [Bayly] if you have any questions," I said.

After McSweeney gave her deposition, one observer familiar with the events that had transpired said to me, "The vice provost hates you. She really hates you. This is personal for her. What did you do to her?"

"Nothing," I replied. "I don't even know her. I've only met her on a couple of occasions."

Did the vice provost hate me?

I didn't know.

But she certainly did not like what I stood for — a professor who challenged the competency of administrators and their policies. That's why I think McSweeney became angry during her deposition. Some administrators just can't stand it when their authority is challenged. Donald Trump is like that.

In contrast, none of the other five deposed defendants or witnesses showed signs of anger — except maybe WSU President Elson Floyd.

FLOYD WAS HIS usual charming self when he entered the room. He shook our hands. That Floyd charisma was there, at least for a few minutes. But I could tell he was nervous. His smile was strained.

He told everyone it was his first deposition.

As is typical, during the first part of the deposition the deposed gets to answer easy questions. They tend to get more difficult as the deposition progresses.

Near the end, Floyd admitted that he did not give me a copy of the letter from Sonntag, which concluded that a conflict of interest tainted the internal audit of me.

"Why didn't you give Dr. Demers a copy of the report?" my attorney, Judy, asked him.

Floyd was sweating. He no longer exhibited the characteristics of Morpheus, the inspirational leader and teacher that Laurence Fishbourne portrayed in *The Matrix*.

Floyd looked down at the table, and delivered the worst line of his career.

"Because the state auditor's report was minuscule," he said. "I had more important things to do."

Minuscule?

"You unethical bastard," I wanted to shout.

Instead, my attorney provided the closing line.

"This deposition is over," she shouted, slapping her hands on the documents in front of her.

Floyd looked shell-shocked, like he didn't understand what he had just said. The normally cool, calm administrative actor had just cast himself in a B movie with a lousy script.

He rose quickly from his seat and shook my hand but not Judy's. He was so flustered that he forgot to take his sport coat and had to return to the room.

Was the handshake snub deliberate or just an oversight?

Hard to say.

But Floyd's response was enlightening.

If he was telling the truth — that he failed to give me a copy of Sonntag's report because he had more important things to do — it meant that, to him, academic freedom and due process were not very important issues.

If he was lying, it meant he deliberately violated the administrative due process rights of a faculty member.

In either case, the failure to provide that document radically altered the outcome of the dispute. It meant the lawsuit would go on. It meant taxpayers now would have to fork out more than $1 million to defend the WSU administrators in a case with no evidence. It meant that Floyd could not be trusted to protect due process rights of faculty.

I distributed another news release to several hundred colleagues and news media across the United States.

WSU PRESIDENT FAILED TO GIVE STATE AUDIT TO ACCUSED PROFESSOR BECAUSE IT WAS 'MINUSCULE'

PULLMAN, Washington — Washington State University's president testified under oath Thursday that he never gave a professor accused of canceling classes a copy of a state auditor's report that discredited an investigation of the professor because the matter was "minuscule" — he had more important things to do. ...

Three other current and former administrators deposed Thursday conceded that Demers' practice of giving online tests did not violate university rules on class cancellations and one said that a scholarly book he published in

2007 [*History and Future of Mass Media*] satisfactorily meets standards for promotion. ... [bracketed material added]

The news release also pointed out that I was being targeted under an administrative policy that had already led to the forced resignations of "five to 10 faculty" during the last decade. McSweeney had provided that information during her deposition, and the policy of terminating tenured faculty violated AAUP guidelines.

The news release generated a flurry of e-mail responses, one from a sociology professor.

> Your president could not have defended himself as he did unless he regards a professor's good name and career as a mere trifle — unless, by extension, the actual work of the university, its mandated search for truth, is in his mind beside the point. The "more important things" on his agenda are probably things like the budget, major expenditures for new buildings, fundraising campaigns, the business of running a large organization. Against this background, what happens to one communications professor ... scarcely deserves ten seconds of the president's valuable time.

Another response came from Gary Rhoades, general secretary of the American Association of University Professors, who was concerned about the firings of tenured faculty: "Dear Dave, very interesting, and as you say, very troubling. I am copying two colleagues ... in our academic freedom, tenure, and governance department. They will respond to your inquiry as soon as possible."[3]

Two weeks later, Gregory F. Scholtz, associate secretary and director of the Department of Academic Freedom, Tenure, and Governance at AAUP, e-mailed:

> [U]nder AAUP-recommended governance standards, the primary responsibility for the formulation and implementation of dismissal policies belongs to the faculty. ... Did the faculty at WSU play a role in the formulation of this policy? Do other faculty members share your concern about it? And, if so, what have they done about it? *I should also point out that the AAUP does not endorse post-tenure review, which we believe can threaten academic freedom and tenure.* [emphasis added]

To justify the firing of the WSU faculty, the WSU administration was probably using an awkwardly worded clause in the faculty manual under the heading "Faculty Conduct Subject to University Discipline."

INCOMPETENCE OR SERIOUS OR REPEATED NEGLECT OF DUTY. Unless the act is serious or puts individuals and/or property at risk, employees will not be disciplined for inadequate work performance or neglect of duty *unless they have been given written notice of the areas in which the work is considered deficient, and an opportunity to improve their performance.* [emphasis added]

Although this section of the WSU Faculty Manual violates AAUP standards, as Scholtz pointed out, the only faculty on campus who seemed concerned about it were the dozen or so members of the local AAUP chapter.

Faculty Senate never investigated or commented on the matter.

And the names of the five to ten terminated faculty have never been released.

NOT SURPRISINGLY, no WSU group or state agency ever followed up on the allegations that President Floyd had violated the administrative due process rights of faculty members when he refused to provide me with a copy of Sonntag's letter.

That's the way it usually works in large bureaucracies.

To bring down a powerful figure like a university president, you have to have another powerful elite behind the effort.

Faculty Senate had that power.

But not one WSU senator openly criticized the president for his unethical behavior, or for the fact that WSU was terminating professors in violation of AAUP standards.

There was no doubt in my mind that WSU administrators had framed my lawsuit as a case of "incompetence" and the leadership of the WSU Faculty Senate had been sucked into that story line.

But four months later, the "incompetence frame" began fraying.

WSU administrators and their attorney decided they did not want to go to trial and fight the case out on its merits. I think they knew they had no case.

Instead, they asked the U.S. District Court judge to declare that WSU faculty do NOT deserve free speech rights when speaking in their service-related roles.

Big mistake.

This not only elevated the "free speech frame," it cast the defendants and the university administration as free speech bullies.

And, ironically, it reinforced my original claims that university administrators did not respect free speech rights of faculty.

"This is a very bizarre legal strategy," I told a colleague. "The administration is cutting off its nose to spite its face."

THE WSU DEFENDANTS and I both hired so-called expert witnesses to help their case.

I hired Kenneth Westhues, the sociologist mentioned earlier who was an expert on workplace mobbing at universities, to analyze the case.[4] He wrote:

> To judge by her vita, [Murrow Director Erica] Austin is above-average in the sense of having more than an average number of refereed articles to her credit. Demers is above-average in a different sense: not only having more than an average number of books to his credit, but having transcended, far more than most professors, a narrowly academic and professional definition of a professor's role. Demers is a culture critic in an era of academic specialists and ideologues. Excelling in this way tends to threaten colleagues and call forth animosity from them, especially when coupled, as in the Demers case, with undisguised disdain, even contempt for puffed-up ivory-tower professionals — "legends in their own minds," as he has called them.
>
> Demers is not only a bigger thinker than most professors, he is also bigger in practical engagement toward implementing the kind of scholarship he believes in. He is an activist, outspoken in support of the First Amendment of the U.S. Constitution, willing even to take his employer to court in defense of free expression. He is a reformer, appealing publicly to the Murrow alumni and the WSU administration for support of his "7-Step Plan," agitating for higher priority on "green-eyeshades" skills than on "chi-square" abstractions. He is an organizer, founding the Center for Global Media Studies ... and directing it for some years. He is an entrepreneur, founding and making a stupendous success (to judge by its website) of his publishing company, Marquette Books.
>
> In sum, Demers is a type of social-science professor who tends to get in steadily deeper trouble, the more success he enjoys in his work.

The defendants hired three expert witness administrators who would testify that my academic record was worthless and that I failed to do my job at WSU. Two of them were administrators from non-communication programs.

The third was one of the deans who visited WSU and rubber-stamped the Murrow College proposal created by President Elson Floyd. Her name was Jean Folkerts, whom I considered an amiable colleague at the time.

I was surprised to hear they had hired her, because years earlier she told me she wanted me to work for her when I interviewed for a position in the School of Media and Public Affairs at George Washington University, a program she directed. In addition, as editor of *Journalism & Mass Communication Quarterly* in the 1990s, she had accepted for publication eight refereed manuscripts I had submitted to the publication.

To undermine my academic record, she would have to devaluate the very journal that she edited for more than a decade and then explain why she wanted to hire me.

What's more, Folkerts's own academic publication record was far weaker than my own. She hadn't published a refereed manuscript in nearly two decades and, after 28 years as an academic, she had published only nine refereed journal articles and three books, two of which were textbooks and one an edited book. She had never published the more highly valued theoretical-monograph book.

In contrast, I had worked for 18 years and had 20 sole or first-authored articles or monographs, four theoretical books, six textbooks or edited books, seven book chapters, and more than 100 professional publications.

A further complication is that she had a conflict of interest, because she was one of the three visiting deans to whom I had sent a copy of the 7-Step Plan. I had asked her to support the plan and she refused. While at WSU, she probably was being hired to testify against me.

Folkerts charged about $300 an hour for her services. I had to pay half of the cost of her deposition, which alone was more than $12,000.

But it might have been worth it.

She was a better expert witness for me than for the defense.

THE DEFENDANTS' ATTORNEY, Kathryn M. Battuello, deposed me over two days in Seattle, a short time after the depositions at WSU.

Although Battuello only received a 6.5 out of 10 rating from Avvo,[5] she had an outstanding record when it came to trial-court experience and involvement in community organizations and issues.

She earned a bachelor's degree (summa cum laude) from the University of New Mexico in 1980, a J.D. degree from Duke University School of Law in 1983, and a master's of public health degree from the University of Washington in 2002. She worked for ten years as a litigation attorney and spent five years as a managing partner in a law firm that specialized in health-care issues.

Before joining the AG's office, Battuello was a faculty member in the health law concentration track at the University of Washington Law School. She had published articles and presented papers on a variety of topics, including genetic discrimination, medical malpractice, and other issues associated with genetics.

In 2008, she joined the Washington State Attorney General's Office.

But the most interesting thing about Battuello, to me, was that she and her husband had adopted a Chinese baby girl. We talked briefly about our experiences. Adaption was one thing we shared in common. To the best of my knowledge, the only thing.

Battuello was merciless during my deposition.

She grilled me with the intensity of a flamethrower.

Her goal was to impeach me, to discredit my reputation, to catch me in a lie or an unethical act, to show that I was a self-centered bastard who didn't care about teaching, research, the students or the Murrow program.

My goal, in contrast, was to educate her on the truth of what was happening at WSU — the history of free speech abuses at the university, the long-term structural problems in the Murrow program, the tainted WSU internal audit of me, President Elson Floyd's unethical decision to deny me access to the state auditor's conflict of interest investigation, the merits of the 7-Step Plan, the attempts to stifle free speech in the Murrow program, and the "kangaroo court justice" in Provost Bayly's office.

Of course, my attorney tried to impeach the deposed defendants and their witnesses too. And all of us deponents were being advised by legal experts to provide as little information as possible during the deposition. "Don't give the other side any ammunition."

That's the way the game is played.

And what about the truth?

Sure, the depositions shed some light on what was happening on both sides.

But, in hindsight, I'm not sure it was worth the $100,000 or so (my estimate) that it cost me and the taxpayers. The lesson I learned from the deposition stage is this: If you need the truth about a particular event or dispute, consider hiring an investigative journalist before an attorney.

At the end of the deposition, Battuello seemed confident she had obtained enough information to cremate me.

However, if she and the defendants were so confident that they could put my ashes into an urn, then why didn't they take the case to trial?

Chapter 45 Endnotes

1. Deposition of Frances K. McSweeney, September 30, 2010, recorded by Jeffory A. Wilson, court reporter and notary public in and for the state of Washington, in the case of *David K. Demers vs. Erica Austin, Erich Lear, Warwick M. Bayly and Frances McSweeney,* United States District Court for the Eastern District of Washington (Case No. CV-09-334-RHW), pp. 160-161, 166-167.

2. Oddly, Rule 27 (Credit Definition) says nothing about tests, quizzes or exams, but they obviously are part of time spent in class. The rule reads as follows: "Academic credit is a measure of the total minimum time commitment required of a typical student in a specific course. For the WSU semester system one semester credit is assigned for a minimum of 45 hours. The expected time commitment may include: 1) time spent in scheduled course activities organized by an instructor (lectures, discussions, workbooks, videotapes, laboratories, studios, fieldwork, etc.); 2) time spent in group activities related to course requirements; and 3) time spent in

reading, studying, problem solving, writing, and other preparations for the course. The minimum in-class time commitment, based on a 15-week semester and a traditional format, should follow these guidelines: 1) lecture—1 hour of lecture per week for each credit hour; 2) laboratory—3 hours of laboratory per week for each credit hour; 3) studio—2 hours of studio work per week for each credit hour; 4) ensemble—4 hours of ensemble work per week for each credit hour. The minimum time commitment for independent study is 3 hours of work per week for each credit hour. Courses taught in different time frames than the 15-week semester or in a different format need to define how the time commitment leads to the achievement of stated course goals. Achievement of course goals may require more than the minimum time commitment."

3. E-mail from Gary Rhoades to David Demers (October 3, 2010).

4. I paid Westhues $3,000 to do the analysis.

5. The relatively low rating was weighed down mostly by a low rating for "industry recognition." She received five out of five stars for "professional conduct" and 3.5 out of five stars for "experience." The rating was obtained in April 2015.

Chapter 46

A Motion to Dismiss

March 23, 2011
Washington State University

More than five months after the depositions, on March 23, 2011, the WSU defendants filed a motion for summary judgment, which meant they did not want to go to trial and were asking U.S. District Court Judge Robert H. Whaley to dismiss my lawsuit. In their memorandum, they argued that my claim should be dismissed because my 7-Step Plan did not deserve First Amendment protection.

> The First Amendment protects citizen speech commenting on a matter of public concern, as opposed to speech by an employee addressing matters within his job responsibilities.[1] ... Demers' alleged protected speech falls into two categories: 1) internal complaints about personnel decisions affecting Murrow School leadership; and 2) proposals for restructuring Murrow School, including distribution of the 7-Step Plan for achieving independent college status. Both categories reflect personal and/or personnel-related grievances from a disgruntled employee who is engaged in a workplace power struggle between "Com Studies" and "Mass Com" faculty.[2] As such, Demers' speech is not entitled to First Amendment Protection.
>
> ... Demers' second category of speech [7-Step Plan] ... fails to meet the public concern threshold. ... the mere fact that the topic is one in which the public might have an interest is not controlling.[3] The First Amendment does not require public universities to subject internal structural arrangements and administrative procedures to public scrutiny and debate.[4] ... Demers' speech regarding the 7-Step Plan, which emanated from an internal power struggle, was motivated by his self-interest; it is not constitutionally protected speech.
>
> Even if Demers can generate a factual issue regarding the public importance of his 7-Step Plan, he cannot establish that his proposals for restructuring [the] Murrow School reflect "citizen" speech. When public employees make statements pursuant to their official duties, they are not speaking as citizens for First Amendment purposes and the Constitution does not transform their speech into citizen speech.[5] [bracketed material added for clarification]

The defendants' legal arguments were predicated in large part on the 2006 U.S. Supreme Court decision in *Garcetti v. Ceballos*, which held that public employees do not have free speech rights when acting in their official duties.

In case you forgot, in this case a conservative majority of five justices — led by Justice Anthony M. Kennedy — ruled that an assistant prosecutor (Richard Ceballos) could be punished by his superiors (Los Angeles District Attorney Gilbert Garcetti, who is the father of LA Mayor Eric Garcetti) even after he reported that police had fabricated evidence to obtain a search warrant. Government employees, the majority opinion stated, have free speech rights only when they speak as citizens, not as employees.

In dissent, Justice David H. Souter wrote that he hoped the *Garcetti* ruling did not apply to public universities, "whose teachers necessarily speak and write 'pursuant to official duties.'"

Kennedy's majority opinion seemed to agree: "We need not ... decide whether the analysis we conduct today would apply in the same manner to a case involving speech related to scholarship or teaching."

But over the next four years, federal courts ignored these dicta and on seven separate occasions denied free speech rights to professors who criticized administrators for hiring too many adjunct faculty, made comments in support of a student during a disciplinary hearing, and raised questions about administrative distribution of grant monies.

Not one federal court after 2006 ruled in favor of a faculty member whose speech was uttered outside of the classroom or their scholarship.

The situation was so grave that, by early 2011, the American Association of University Professors was urging faculty "to defend their academic freedom ... not through the courts but through clear university policies."

Faculty at the University of Minnesota, University of Michigan and the University of Delaware did just that.

Minnesota's new policy gave faculty "the freedom, without institutional discipline or restraint, to ... speak or write on matters of public concern as well as on matters related to professional duties and the functioning of the university." At Delaware, faculty possess the "freedom to address the larger community with regard to any social, political, economic, or other interest" and to do so "without institutional discipline or restraint."[6]

Two weeks after WSU defendants filed their memorandum, the Fourth Circuit Court of Appeals ruled in *Adams v. Trustees of the University of North Carolina–Wilmington* (2011) that a professor who converted to Christianity and wrote a book critical of political correctness on campus had the right to speak without fear of retaliation.[7]

The title of his book was *Welcome to the Ivory Tower of Babel: Confessions of a Conservative College Professor*.

I had encountered Professor Michael S. Adams's book years earlier, after I decided to call my own book on social science *The Ivory Tower of Babel*. But I didn't realize until now that his book also was involved in a First Amendment controversy.

The headline in the *Chronicle of Higher Education* blared: "Appeals Court Hands Big Win to Advocates of Free Faculty Speech in Ruling on Pundit-Professor."[8]

"A ringing victory for academic freedom," added David A. French, senior counsel for the Alliance Defense Fund, a Christian organization that helped defend Adams.

But the Adams case did not expand or even deal with the issue of on-the-job service-related free speech rights for faculty. The court simply said that Adams's speech was protected because it was private speech, not related to his job as a criminologist. Therefore, his university could not deny him a promotion based on those writings, even though he had submitted them to the promotion committee.

The *Adams* case did not break new ground. It simply reinforced *Garcetti*, which refused to extend free speech rights to government employees.

Adams represented a two-edged sword for me.

On the one hand, it enhanced my chances of winning if my 7-Step Plan was defined as citizen speech. After all, I had formally submitted it as the publisher of Marquette Books, not as a professor.

If my plan was citizen speech, however, then my case would fail to address a more important question: Do faculty, while participating on administration-generated committees for the university, have a right to criticize administrators and their policies without fear of retaliation?

That question, to me, was far more important. The search for truth and knowledge cannot be complete without such protection.

But the WSU defendants opposed that idea.

In their memorandum, they wrote:

> The *Garcetti* court recognized that faculty expression related to academic scholarship or classroom instruction "could" implicate additional constitutional interests that are entitled to protection.[9] ... However, because the speech at issue is unrelated to Demers' academic teaching or scholarship responsibilities, any "academic freedom exception" does not apply.[10] *The teaching and scholarship exception does not apply to speech about internal organizational issues.* [emphasis added]

In other words, the WSU defendants were arguing that academic freedom does not apply to service-related or shared-governance speech, even though the WSU faculty manual specifically states:

> It is the policy of Washington State University to support and promote the rights of all individuals to express their view and opinions for or against actions or ideas in which they have an interest, to associate freely with others, and to assemble peacefully. The faculty has the right to dissent and protest.[11]

WSU's legal strategy was undercutting its entire policy on academic freedom. *What kind of crazy shit is this?*

The defendants also argued in their memorandum that even if they violated my First Amendment rights, they should not be held liable for civil damages, because the courts and legislatures have not established clear rules on statutory or constitutional rights.

The latter statement was true.

My case would finally provide some clarity.

ORAL ARGUMENTS WERE HEARD on May 12, 2011, before Judge Robert H. Whaley, a senior U.S. District Court judge for the Eastern District of Washington in Spokane.

On paper, Whaley was what we college students in the early 1970s called "an establishment man." But in fairness I need to point out that he did help some clients sue one of the nation's largest status quo corporations.

He was born in 1943. His father was an FBI agent. He earned a bachelor's degree from Princeton University in 1965 and a J.D. from Emory University School of Law in 1968. He joined the U.S. Marine Corps and became a trial attorney for the Land and Natural Resources Division of the United States Department of Justice from 1969 to 1971. He was an assistant U.S. Attorney for the Eastern District of Washington until 1972, when he returned to private practice in Spokane.

He and his law firm represented 12 independent gasoline dealers who sued Texaco for price discrimination. Texaco lost in the lower courts and the case went to the U.S. Supreme Court, which in 1990 also ruled in favor of independent gasoline dealers.[12]

From 1992 to 1995, Whaley was a Superior Court judge in Spokane County. In 1995, President Bill Clinton nominated Whaley to the U.S. District Court and the Senate confirmed the nomination.

The appointment from Clinton suggested that Whaley leaned more to the left than the right in terms of his politics.

But I had a bad feeling about this from the get-go. His face was stern, like a father ready to take his son out to the woodshed. He added to my discomfort when he grilled my attorney about some aspects of our case but did not reciprocate in kind when questioning Battuello, the defendants' attorney.

Courtroom impressions are often wrong.

Unfortunately, not here.

ON JUNE 2, 2011, Judge Whaley threw my case out of court.

Citing the *Garcetti* decision, Whaley wrote that "the First Amendment does not prohibit managerial discipline based on an employee's expressions made pursuant to official responsibilities."

These "expressions" included my speech about accreditation, whether the college should emphasize professional training or theoretical research, the restructuring of the college, and my 7-Step Plan. He also ruled that these speech expressions dealt with "internal matters at WSU" and "were not matters of public concern." He added:

> Even if the speech addressed matters of public concern, however, it is clear that Plaintiff was not speaking as a citizen when he initially presented the Plan to his fellow faculty members and to the university administration. He was writing and submitting his document as a member of the faculty. The scope of an employee's official duties include "those activities that an employee undertakes in a professional capacity to further the employer's objectives."[13] ... At WSU, faculty members' official duties are not limited to classroom instruction and research. *Faculty members are expected to participate in a wide range of academic, administrative and personnel functions in accordance with WSU's self-governance principle.* The writing and distributing of the Plan was the result of Plaintiff's job responsibilities. He initially distributed it internally as part of an ongoing faculty debate regarding the future of the journalism/communications studies department. [emphasis added]

The judge was wrong about how I distributed the plan. I gave it to numerous non-university sources, which the appeals court later acknowledged.

The judge was correct, though, that faculty members are expected to participate in "academic, administrative and personnel functions" under the university's principle of shared governance. Usually this involves work on various committees.

But if administrators don't like what faculty say on those committees, Whaley is saying that administrators can punish faculty.

What we have here is failure to communicate.

Also a Catch-22.

If faculty don't participate on those committees, then they can be punished. But if they participate and say things that the administration doesn't like, they can be punished.

What Judge Whaley and the WSU defendant administrators and their attorney didn't understand is that shared governance cannot exist without free speech protection for faculty.

Let me say that again: SHARED GOVERNANCE CANNOT EXIST WITHOUT FIRST AMENDMENT PROTECTION.

If universities continue to punish faculty for service-related speech and the courts back them up, then the logical conclusion is that shared governance eventually will cease to exist. Public universities will morph into the corporate (business) form of organization, in which power is highly centralized and the autonomy of individual faculty is diminished — the kind of world that George Orwell wrote about.[14]

The courts have yet to understand that the search for truth and knowledge cannot be divorced from structural and budgetary issues facing academic programs. They are interdependent.

And my *Ivory Tower of Babel* book? What did the judge say about that?

The book clearly fell into the category of scholarship, and, as such, probably would have garnered First Amendment protection.

Judy, though, never submitted a copy of the draft book as evidence to the court. She later pointed out that the book was included in my annual reviews, which was true. But Whaley wrote in his opinion:

> The actual work was not referenced in Plaintiff's Statement of Facts. It is Plaintiff's burden to establish that his speech was a matter of public concern. The Court is unable to make this determination without consulting the source. Consequently, the Court finds that Plaintiff has not met his burden of showing that the speech contained in *The Ivory Tower of Babel* was speech on a matter of public concern.

Would the book have made a difference in the judge's ruling?

Maybe.

Whaley could have dismissed all aspects of the case except for the book.

But I probably still would have appealed the 7-Step Plan aspect of the decision.

Judy believed, rightly so, that the plan, more than the book, initiated the penalizing action of university administrators.

In addition, had Judy and I not appealed the judge's ruling, the question of whether shared governance speech would be protected might never have been adjudicated.

Lastly, in his ruling, Whaley said the defendants were entitled to qualified immunity, which essentially meant I could not recover punitive damages even if the case went to trial. I didn't file the lawsuit to get rich. But I didn't want to go broke, either.

On June 4, 2011, I sent out a news release about Whaley's decision, the lead of which stated: "The First Amendment does not protect college professors who criticize the quality of university programs, even if they offer, as citizens, plans to improve the program and pledge to donate $100,000 of their own money to implement them, a U.S. district court judge has ruled."

Dick Carson, one of my former editors, reacted to the news: "Maybe I'm missing something here, but it sounds like the judge thinks the administrators can do no wrong under any circumstances and that employees better keep their mouths shut. Is that what the Framers had in mind for the First Amendment?"

By the way, this time the *Daily Evergreen*, WSU's student newspaper, did publish a story about the lawsuit this time. The headline was: "Lawsuit Against WSU Dismissed."[15]

WSU'S DECISION TO SEEK summary judgment rather than to fight the merits of the lawsuit at trial changed everything — FOR THE BETTER! That's because it fast-tracked the free speech issue. I never dreamed it would happen so quickly.

And university administrators, including President Elson Floyd, apparently didn't understand the consequences of their legal strategy.

They had cast themselves as free speech bullies — no, FREE SPEECH VILLAINS, that's more accurate.

The free speech villains were arguing that faculty do not deserve free speech rights when speaking in their service-related roles. And they were arguing a position that directly contradicted the WSU Faculty Manual,[16] which protected all "actions or ideas in which they [faculty] have an interest."

Thus, on principle, I had already won. I had argued that WSU administrators do not respect the free speech rights of faculty, and their legal strategy supported that position. But did President Elson Floyd and his four administrators really believe that faculty do not deserve free speech rights when speaking in their service roles?

I find it hard to believe they would deliberately take such a position.

Another, more plausible theory for WSU's bizarre legal strategy suggests Floyd gave the attorney general's office carte blanche over the case. And that agency's goal clearly was not to defend free speech principles, but to win.

There is one helluva lesson here.

When administrators cede control of a legal matter to attorneys or outsiders, they run the risk of losing control over the moral issues in a dispute. Bureaucracies are more susceptible to this problem because the lines of authority are not always clear.

Throughout the dispute, my administrative adversaries were often on different pages. They did not communicate clearly with each other. This produced confusion and contradictory responses. And even though every one of those administrators would no doubt support the principle of academic freedom, no one took the responsibility for ensuring that this principle would be protected when it came to a legal strategy.

My analysis may be wrong. But one thing is clearly right: WSU's legal strategy turned out to be its Achilles' heel.

Chapter 46 Endnotes

1. To support this statement, the defendants cite *Garcetti v. Ceballos*, 547 U.S. 410, 417, 126 S.Ct. 1951 (2006).

2. Footnotes from the memorandum are not produced here. They elaborate on the legal issues and contain citations for backing up the defendants' position.

3. *McCullough v. University of Arkansas*, 559 F.3d 855, 867 (8th Cir. 2009).

4. *Clinger v. New Mexico Highlands University*, 215 F.3d at 1167 (10th Cir. 1996), quoting *Bunger v. University of Oklahoma Board of Regents*, 95 F.3d 987, 992 (10th Cir. 1996).

5. *Garcetti*, 547 U.S. at 421-22.

6. Azhar Majeed, "Resolutions to Protect Academic Freedom of Faculty at UNC-Chapel Hill, University of Delaware," Foundation for Individual Rights in Education (November 19, 2010), retrieved May 28, 2015, from <https://www.thefire.org/resolutions-to-protect-academic-freedom-of-faculty-at-unc-chapel-hill-university-of-delaware>.

7. *Adams v. Trustees of the University of North Carolina–Wilmington*, 640 F.3d 550 (4th Cir. 2011).

8. Peter Schmidt, "Appeals Court Hands Big Win to Advocates of Free Faculty Speech in Ruling on Pundit-Professor," *The Chronicle of Higher Education* (April 6, 2011).

9. *Garcetti*, 547 U.S. at 425.

10. *Savage v. Gee*, 2010 WL 2301174 (S.D. Ohio 2010) and *Gorum v. Sessoms*, 561 F.3d at 179 (3rd Cir. 2009).

11. Washington State University Faculty Manual, 2010 edition, p. 16.

12. *Texaco, Inc. v. Hasbrouck*, 496 U.S. 543 (1990).

13. To back up this statement, the judge cites *Hong v. Grant*, 516 F.Supp.2d 1158, 1166 (C.D. Cal. 2007).

14. George Orwell, *1984* (London: Secker and Warburg, 1949).

15. Jillian Monda, "Lawsuit Against WSU Dismissed," *The Daily Evergreen* (June 13,

2011), p. 1. Interestingly, when I won the appeal two years later, the newspaper didn't publish a story. Was the pattern coincidence, or was the identification with the administration so strong that no student journalist wanted to write the story?

16. WSU Faculty Manual, 2010 edition.

Chapter 47

An Appeal and Complicit Professors

July 2011
Washington State University

Judy filed a notice of appeal with the Ninth Circuit Court of Appeals shortly after the District Court's decision. She wouldn't file the brief in the case for another seven months.

In the meantime, I began writing a commentary, titled "How Can Democracy Thrive If It Gags Its Own Public Employees?" The *Seattle Times* refused to publish it but the *Moscow-Pullman Daily News* accommodated. Here are the first couple of paragraphs:[1]

> Washington State University's Edward R. Murrow College of Communication has major structural and curricular flaws and the College needs to restructure and seek national accreditation for its programs.
>
> That opinion, which I have been expressing for more than a decade as a citizen and as a journalism professor in the Murrow College, is not protected by the First Amendment, according to a U.S. District Court judge in Spokane.
>
> Robert H. Whaley ruled last month that my speech is not protected because (1) the quality of education at the Murrow College is not a matter of public concern and (2) public employees do not have free speech rights, even if they reveal corruption, wrongdoing or incompetence in government. ...
>
> Is this America?
>
> I find myself asking that question a lot these days, especially when I am lecturing on constitutional law or the history of the First Amendment in my classes. Is America still committed to the Enlightenment ideals of democracy, free speech, accountability in government, and due process — ideals espoused by John Locke, Voltaire, Benjamin Franklin, Thomas Jefferson and others?
>
> A decade ago I knew the answer. Today I don't. ...

Taking the First Amendment high ground made me feel better, but it did little to improve my image in the Murrow College and the university as a whole during the 2011 calendar year.

I volunteered for or was a candidate for four department and university committees, including head of the journalism sequence, but was not appointed or elected to any of them.

The WSU Faculty Senate administration also refused to allow me to run for a position on the university-wide Graduate Committee, because it said my lawsuit would interfere with my ability to make decisions. That made no sense to me, but why fight that one?

I eventually was appointed to the campus library committee, which I volunteered to chair. This presumably was a position that would keep me marginalized in terms of university politics.

But I enjoyed working with and learning from the head librarian at WSU and the members of the committee, one of whom was a vocal critic of Floyd's policies.

I spent much of my summer editing the six open-access, free journals that Marquette Books was publishing. I also reviewed 14 scholarly articles for eight different journals in the field of mass communication.

The American Association of University Professors contacted me and said it would be filing an amici curiae brief in support of my lawsuit against the four WSU administrators. The Thomas Jefferson Center for the Protection of Free Expression also joined in.

In August 2011, the four defendants and I tried to mediate a solution to the dispute. Mediation was required under federal rules before a case could be heard before the Ninth Circuit Court of Appeals judges.

Mediation failed for reasons that I cannot disclose. All parties are prohibited from talking about it.

But I was not disappointed.

More than ever, I wanted the free speech issue to be adjudicated, win or lose.

The only problem was that I was running out of money.

By this time, I had spent more than $100,000 in legal fees and court costs. I still owed Graham & Dunn $150,000.

If I were unable to recover attorney fees from the lawsuit, I might have to file for bankruptcy.

In fall 2011, I asked the Faculty Senate leadership whether I could give a brief presentation to the senators about the implications of the administration's anti-free speech position.

The leadership refused my request.

When I pointed out that the Faculty Senate is a public body that cannot, under law, refuse one of its own "citizens" a right to speak before it, the leadership backed down — sort of. It couldn't fit me into its agenda for four months, so I declined.

Algora Publishing of New York City sent out for blind review a draft manuscript of my book, *The Ivory Tower of Babel: Why the Social Sciences Are Failing to Live Up to Their Promises.* Fortunately, the review was positive. Administrators were threatening to fire me if I was unable to get the book published. It was published in the fall.

Administrators sometimes sponsor department luncheons or after-hours get-togethers to celebrate when professors publish books.

But there would be no campus celebration for this bad-boy professor.

Instead, I dusted off my Three Dog Night record album and took my 11-year-old onto my living-room dance floor.

Celebrate, Celebrate, Dance to the Music
Celebrate, Celebrate, Dance to the Music
Celebrate, Celebrate, Dance to the Music

Okay, I can hear what you are thinking.
Three Dog who?

MEANWHILE, Judy was preparing the appeals brief. It was filed with the Ninth Circuit Court of Appeals on February 7, 2012.

Although I have always argued that professors have a right to criticize administrators on any topic related to university operations, Judy took the safe approach and, following *Garcetti* and other court rulings, argued more narrowly that my speech regarding the 7-Step Plan was protected because it came from Demers the citizen, not Demers the employee.

To be honest, Judy and I both believed that if my 7-Step Plan was classified as job-related speech, I would lose the lawsuit, per *Garcetti*.

"Dr. Demers spoke as a private citizen on a matter of public concern in the 7-Step Plan; namely, he sought to improve the quality of journalism education at a college named for a man long-associated with quality journalism — Edward R. Murrow," the opening brief argued.[2] "When the district court concluded that this topic was not a matter of public concern and that Dr. Demers' private speech was made in his 'official capacity' as a WSU professor, it committed reversible error."

To back up her argument, Judy cited *Adams v. Trustees of the University of North Carolina–Wilmington* — the Fourth Circuit Court of Appeals decision in which Professor Michael Adams's book about political correctness was found to be protected speech because it was citizen speech, unrelated to his job as a criminologist.[3]

Judy also argued that my *Ivory Tower of Babel* book was protected speech because it was related to scholarship.

The amici curiae brief from the American Association of University Professors and the Thomas Jefferson Center for the Protection of Free Expression employed a broader legal strategy, arguing that "affirming the district court's opinion will diminish open and honest debate in public universities."[4]

The amici brief acknowledged that the 7-Step Plan, unlike my book, did not fit neatly under either the teaching or scholarship exceptions carved out for protection by the federal courts. But the plan still deserves free speech protection, the brief argued, because "where an employee is hired to explore new and controversial topics, punishment for a researcher's ideas would defeat the purpose of his employment."[5]

This argument was similar to my own, which holds that it is illogical and ethically wrong to ask faculty for input on issues if administrators then punish them for the ideas they offer. The amici brief reasoned:

> In addition to sharing their viewpoints in the classroom and as a product of scholarly research, professors are encouraged to share their opinions on how the school runs, and what can be done to improve academic institutions. Most of Demers' speech relates to these topics, and the [U.S. District] court ... concluded that they were part of Demers' job duties. Because these statements, like in-classroom discussion, are part of the viewpoint-centered speech in which professors appropriately engage, they should fall under the academic exception to *Garcetti*.[6]

But the brief's strongest moral argument for protecting the 7-Step Plan, in my opinion, came at the end of a section that tried to explain why the federal district court erred in not extending First Amendment protection to the plan.

> Allowing Washington State University administrators to retaliate against Demers in this case would undermine the very purpose of Demers' job as a professor and a scholar. Challenging the status quo and speaking candidly about the world and the systems in it, as Demers has done here, are precisely the activities that courts have been careful to protect in academic settings even more so than in other settings. This is what allows professors to serve their most essential function — not just to teach students to memorize information, but to teach them how to think for themselves in order to better society.

On March 1, 2012, about a month after the appeals were filed, legal writer Peter Schmidt of the *Chronicle of Higher Education* published a story headlined "LEGAL

DISPUTE PITS WASHINGTON STATE U.'S JOURNALISM SCHOOL AGAINST FREE SPEECH GROUPS." Here are the first two paragraphs:

> Washington State University's college of journalism has found itself at odds with groups that advocate a First Amendment right to academic freedom after persuading a federal district court to adopt a limited view of the speech rights of faculty members at public colleges.
>
> The case is now pending before the U.S. Court of Appeals for the Ninth Circuit and expected to be heard in the fall. In a friend-of-the-court brief submitted to that court last month, the American Association of University Professors and the Thomas Jefferson Center for the Protection of Free Expression jointly warn the Ninth Circuit that a ruling upholding the district court's logic would set "a dangerous precedent" jeopardizing academic freedom and the sound governance of public higher-education institutions.[7]

On April 26, 2012, the WSU defendants filed their response to our initial brief:

> Indisputable facts establish that Demers' 7-Step Plan originated as an internal academic communication made by Demers as an employee of WSU on the structure of an academic department, a matter irrelevant to the public. The plan was not original research or scholarship, nor was it an example of controversial classroom teaching. It cannot serve as the basis for a First Amendment claim. ...[8]
>
> The 7-Step Plan emanated from an internal power struggle and was motivated by Demers' self-interest ... Demers' alleged protected speech reflects personal and/or personnel related grievances from a disgruntled employee who is engaged in a workplace power struggle between "Com Studies" and "Mass Com" faculty. As such, Demers' speech is not entitled to First Amendment Protection. ...[9]
>
> In short, despite Demers' efforts to characterize the 7-Step Plan as citizen speech presented by his alter-ego, the publisher of Marquette Books, the record is clear that his proposals for restructuring Murrow School are inextricably related to his discharge of faculty responsibilities and are therefore employee speech, not citizen speech.[10]

The defendants also argued that my claims regarding the *Ivory Tower of Babel* book should be dismissed because a copy of the book had not been submitted as evidence to the district court.

Oral arguments before a Ninth Circuit Court of Appeals panel of three judges was set for November 7, 2012.

By February 2012, most WSU faculty were aware of my free speech lawsuit and the administration argument that faculty do not deserve free speech rights when speaking in their service-related roles.

But why hadn't the WSU Faculty Senate "publicly gone on the record condemning the administration for its anti-free speech position?"

On April 8, 2012, I e-mailed and posed that question to Faculty Senate President David Ray Turnbull.[11]

He responded on April 19: "After consulting with a number of people, we have determined that it is not appropriate for us to take any position or become involved in a situation where there is a pending lawsuit."[12]

One WSU AAUP member familiar with the inner workings of politics at WSU said Turnbull probably consulted with administrators before generating that response.

I responded to Turnbull the following day:

"I didn't ask you take a position on the lawsuit. I asked you why the Faculty Senate has refused to criticize a university administration which is arguing in court that faculty do not, as employees, deserve the right to criticize the administration (in our service roles). You should know that if the appeals court rules in favor of the administration on this issue, all of you will lose the right to criticize the administration without fear of reprisal. Any protestations on the legal issues after that point will be too late."[13]

He did not respond.

In early May 2012, I wrote a letter to the editor to the WSU *Daily Evergreen* student newspaper explaining the anti-free speech arguments in the university's legal briefs and added:

> I am dumbfounded that WSU administrators and the Board of Regents could make such arguments while claiming they embrace the principle of shared governance, which presumes free speech protection. I am even more baffled by the lack of response from the Faculty Senate leadership, which is failing to protect faculty interests. Faculty Senate leaders apparently have forgotten philosopher John Stuart Mill's advice: "Bad men need nothing more to compass their ends, than that good men should look on and do nothing."

In fall 2012, I also asked the new Faculty Senate president, Robert E. Rosenman, why the Faculty Senate had not condemned the anti-free speech position of President Elson Floyd's administration.

He responded: "It is not the practice of this Faculty Senate Chair to respond to requests for information about our activities, including votes of record, which are publicly available."

THE 2011-2012 SCHOOL YEAR ended on an upbeat note — sort of.

In late April, the Murrow administration, after giving me five years of below average annual review ratings, gave me a passing grade on all three performance criteria: teaching, service and research (a 3.0 overall rating; the average department rating was 3.8).

I got the passing grade even though I was still giving online exams and quizzes in my classes. University administrators obviously were not on the same page when it came to that issue.

I wasn't much impressed with the rating, however.

Eighty percent of the faculty had been given higher scores, some of whom did not even publish anything during the past year.

I had spent more than a decade researching and writing *The Ivory Tower of Babel: Why the Social Sciences Are Failing to Live Up to Their Promises*. Other faculty who had published books in the previous five years had been given 4 or 5 ratings for scholarship/research.

But, at this point, I didn't really care much about annual reviews.

I decided to retire early, at the end of the year.

I was 59.

That decision was sparked in large part by the death of my high school and college buddy, Jerry. He suffered a heart attack. He was only 58.

There were a lot more things I wanted to do in life before I joined him. I especially wanted to do more writing that influenced the public policymaking process.

Don't get me wrong. I'm proud of my scholarly articles and books and believe theoretical research is extremely important in the social sciences.

But after writing a book about the relative lack of impact that social science research has on public policy and on solving social problems (the *Ivory Tower of Babel* book), it was difficult for me to see scholarly research as being something more than a ritual whose purpose was to boost the egos of the legends-in-our-own-minds tenure club.

In summer 2012, I sent a memo to administrators informing them that I would retire December 31.

ON NOVEMBER 7, 2012, the Ninth Circuit Court of Appeals heard the appeal (see Chapter 1). The Ninth Circuit Court of Appeals panel did not set a deadline for issuing its opinion in the case. Court guidelines advised that judicial panels can take anywhere from several months to one-and-a-half years to issue a ruling.

That gave me more time to work on this book and to begin preparations for our eventual move to Phoenix, Arizona.

Did I mention that?

I had wanted to move back to Phoenix for more than three decades. I lived and worked there for four years in the 1980s. I loved the warm weather and sunny blue skies. The big advantage of Phoenix is that life can be lived outdoors year-round.

Not that Spokane was a terrible place. The dry, sunny summers are wonderful. The winters are also much milder than in the Midwest, but they are too gray, too wet and too long for me.

Theresa, Lee Ann and I set the summer of 2014 as the date for the move.

That gave us enough time to sell our small vacation home in Surprise, Arizona, as well as our home in Spokane.

That schedule also gave Theresa enough time to complete 30 years of service to Eastern State Hospital, making her eligible for retirement benefits at 55.

And Lee Ann could start ninth grade at a high school in Phoenix.

So I had about a year and a half to find a bigger home in a Phoenix-area neighborhood served by a high-quality high school. I spent the next nine months working on this book, writing other articles about civil liberties and fixing up our Spokane house to get it ready for sale.

I also applied for an adjunct teaching position in the Walter Cronkite School of Journalism and Mass Communication at Arizona State University. I was grateful when the school offered me a position teaching one mass media law course in fall 2013. Faculty who sue universities are often blacklisted, even when they fight for good causes. It's possible ASU was not aware of my lawsuit.

At any rate, the part-time job would help defray the costs of searching for a new home in Phoenix.

I left in early August for the Grand Canyon state. I rented an apartment in Glendale, a suburb in metro Phoenix, and began teaching at ASU in late August.

The professional backgrounds of the faculty in the Cronkite School are impressive. They include print and broadcast editors and journalists from some of the nation's most impressive news organizations, including all of the major television networks, CNN, Fox, CNBC, *PBS NewsHour, Washington Post, Los Angeles Times, Minneapolis Star Tribune, Miami Herald, Houston Chronicle,* the Associated Press, *Forbes* magazine and *U.S. News & World Report.* The faculty have won Emmys and many news reporting awards, including a couple of Pulitzer Prizes.

The professional successes of the faculty are reflected in many of the Cronkite students. Year after year, the students have won more awards at the Broadcast Education Association's (BEA) Festival of Media Arts competition than any other school in the country — 14 total in the year before I taught there, twice as many as the second-place school. Cronkite students also have won more Hearst Awards and Society of Professional Journalists' Mark of Excellence Awards than any other school.

The Cronkite dean was Christopher Callahan, who earned a master's in public administration from Harvard University. He also served as the vice chair of the Accrediting Council on Education in Journalism and Mass Communications, the group that extends accreditation to journalism and mass communication programs. Of course, the print and broadcast programs at ASU were accredited.

I met with him on one occasion to talk about journalism education and the impact of *Demers v. Austin*.

Although the Cronkite program also includes a number of accomplished faculty scholars, the school as a whole does not rank very high nationally on measures of scholarly productivity. That was the only weakness in the program I could see, and that may be by design, as the administrative emphasis is on the professional programs, not the scholarly oriented graduate program.

The students in my law class were extremely inquisitive. They reminded me of the students at the University of Minnesota.

Chapter 47 Endnotes

1. David Demers, "HIS VIEW: Above All, Keep Your Mouth Shut," *Moscow-Pullman Daily News* (July 15, 2011), guest commentary.

2. Opening Brief of Appellant David K. Demers, *Demers v. Austin* et al. (Ninth Circuit Court of Appeals, Case No. 2:09-cv-00334-RHW), p. 21.

3. *Adams v. Trustees of the University of North Carolina–Wilmington* (640 F.3d 550; 4th Cir. 2011).

4. The authors of the *amici curiae* brief were Robert M. O'Neil and Kathi Wescott of the AAUP and J. Joshua Wheeler and Susan Kruth of the Thomas Jefferson Center.

5. *Amici Curiae* Brief of American Association of University Professors and the Thomas Jefferson Center for the Protection of Free Expression In Support of Appellant's Request for Reversal, filed February 14, 2012, in *Demers v. Austin*, Ninth Circuit Court of Appeals, p. 13.

6. Ibid., pp. 13-14.

7. Peter Schmidt, "Legal Dispute Pits Washington State U.'s Journalism School Against Free speech Groups," *The Chronicle of Higher Education* (March 1, 2012), retrieved April 22, 2015, from <http://chronicle.com/article/Legal-Dispute-Pits-Washington/130979>.

8. Appellees Responding Brief, *Demers v. Austin* (Ninth Circuit Court of Appeals, Case No. 2:09-cv-00334-RHW), pp. 32-33.

9. Ibid., p. 49.

10. Ibid., p. 54.

11. E-mail from David Demers to David Turnbull (April 8, 2012).
12. E-mail from David Turnbull to David Demers (April 19, 2012)
13. E-mail from David Demers to David Turnbull (April 20, 2012).

Chapter 48

The Enlightened Appeals Court

September 2013
Washington State University

At about 9:40 a.m. on September 5, 2013, just 20 minutes before my media law class was to begin in the Cronkite School, I received a phone call from Judy Endejan, my attorney.

"Dave," she said. "I've got some good and bad news."

"Okay, let me have it."

"We won on principle, but lost on money. The court ruled that the First Amendment protects your 7-Step Plan. I know you've said the money wasn't important. Are you okay?"

"I'm fine. That's wonderful," I said.

In fact, I was bursting with joy.

And I was shaking, something that I rarely do.

The dispute over my plan began eight years ago.

Eight long, difficult years.

But it was worth it.

When I entered the classroom a few minutes later, I apologized to the students, because I was still a bit shaken by the news.

I gave the students a nutshell version of the Ninth Circuit Court ruling.

They clapped.

I thanked them.

That evening I composed a news release.

APPEALS COURT RULING BOLSTERS PROFESSORS' FREE SPEECH RIGHTS

A U.S. District Court judge erred when he ruled that a Washington State University professor was not entitled to First Amendment protection when he developed a controversial plan for restructuring and improving a journalism program, the Ninth Circuit Court of Appeals ruled Wednesday.

"The decision is a great victory for those who cherish academic freedom, free speech ideals and shared governance," said David Demers, a former tenured WSU professor who created the plan to improve the quality of education in the Edward R. Murrow School of Communication.

"Professors should be able to criticize administrators and their policies and play an active role in the affairs of the university," added Demers. ... "The decision bolsters the idea that free speech protection for professors extends beyond their academic research programs and the classroom. It covers our service role, too."

Three days later *The State Press*, ASU's student newspaper, published a story about the lawsuit, under the headline ASU ADJUNCT PROFESSOR'S STRUGGLE FOR FIRST AMENDMENT RIGHTS TRIUMPHS IN COURT.

WSU's student newspaper, *The Daily Evergreen*, never published a story about the appeals court ruling.

OKAY, I ADMIT IT. I wrongly predicted the outcome of the Ninth Circuit Court ruling.

But not because I thought Chief Judge William A. Fletcher and his two colleagues were opponents of individualism and the Age of Enlightenment. In fact, all three have judicial records that would allow a reasonable person to classify them as defenders of liberty.

The reason I failed to predict the outcome of the case — as did all of the other attorneys and legal observers — is because I (we) failed to appreciate the significance of one word in the *Garcetti* decision.

I'll explain in a moment.

First, I want to point out, if I have not already made it clear, that judicial decisions are not simply a product of a rational legal process.[1] Although judges like to portray themselves as objective observers of facts and the law, research shows that their personal ideological beliefs and social ties to society often play a role in the way they decide cases.

One of the most important influences is party affiliation.

A 1999 study of more than 140 books, articles and papers between 1959 and 1998 found that political "party is a dependable yardstick for ideology: Democratic judges are more liberal on the bench than Republican ones."[2]

The study also found that the party relationship is stronger in federal courts than in state courts, explaining as much as half of the variance in decisions.

Two recent separate studies of the U.S. Supreme Court and appeals court judges reached the same conclusion.[3] Interestingly, one of those studies also found that, contrary to popular belief, liberal judges were no more likely to engage in judicial activism than conservative judges.[4] They both are willing to set precedent aside.

Before I give you the nitty gritty of the Ninth Circuit decision, I also want to give you some background of the judges in my case, to show you how party affiliation and their connections to the social world might have influenced their decision.

CHIEF JUDGE WILLIAM A. FLETCHER has strong social ties to ideologies that embrace individual rights and civil liberties.

His mother, Betty Binns Fletcher, was a Ninth Circuit Court of Appeals judge who was well-known for her progressive views and decisions.

Fletcher earned his law degree from Yale University, whose professors tend to be liberal. And Fletcher clerked, from 1976 to 1977, for U.S. Supreme Court Justice William J. Brennan Jr., who is often called the strongest proponent of individual rights ever to serve on the court.

Fletcher was appointed in 1998 to his federal judgeship by Democratic President Bill Clinton, his Rhodes scholar classmate at Oxford University. Fletcher was the Northern California director for Clinton's first campaign for president in 1992.

Fletcher's background as a law professor also likely influenced his decision in my case, in that he, no doubt, had a good understanding of the concept of shared governance and how universities function differently from major corporations and military organizations. Fletcher was a professor of law at UC Berkeley for 11 years and taught courses at Stanford University, the University of Michigan and the University of Cologne.

Like Fletcher, Ninth Circuit Judge Raymond C. Fisher also clerked for Supreme Court Justice William J. Brennan Jr. about a decade before Fletcher.

Fisher earned his law degree from Stanford Law School and later served as a special assistant to California Governor Jerry Brown, one of the most liberal governors in the state's history. Fisher also served as president of the Los Angeles Police Commission and was an associate attorney general in California before being appointed by Clinton to the Ninth Circuit.

Another background factor that may have influenced Fisher's decision in my case is that he was one of the appeals court judges who ruled in favor of free speech rights in the *Garcetti* case before it reached the U.S. Supreme Court.

Thus, even before hearing my case, Fisher was already on the record as supporting the right of government employees to criticize their employers, at least in cases where alleged government misconduct was the key issue. Fisher and two other

Ninth Circuit Appeals Court judges ruled in favor of Assistant District Attorney Richard Ceballos "because the law was clearly established that Ceballos's speech addressed a matter of public concern and that his interest in the speech [i.e., police misconduct] outweighed the public employer's interest in avoiding inefficiency and disruption."[5] [bracketed material added for clarity]

The conservative majority on the Supreme Court eventually would overturn the pro-Ceballos opinion. The *Garcetti* ruling is one of the most scorned decisions among advocates of civil liberties and freedom of speech. It has even been used to deny teachers free speech rights in the classroom.[6]

By the way, I called Ceballos in early 2015 to find out what had happened since his case. He was still working for the Los Angeles County District Attorney's office, though under a new DA. Ceballos said that, even though he lost the case, the new DA had instituted revised procedures to minimize police misconduct when it comes to obtaining search warrants.[7]

An activist need not always win lawsuits to generate good outcomes.

The third judge in my case, Gordon J. Quist, was a senior district federal court judge in Grand Rapids, Michigan, who had attended George Washington University Law School.

On paper, he was more conservative than Fletcher and Fisher, as he publicly had supported the Republican party before he became a judge. In the early 1990s, he donated several thousand dollars to Michigan-based Republican groups and candidates for office.[8]

Republican President George H. W. Bush appointed Quist to the federal bench in 1992.

But party affiliation doesn't always explain judicial temper.

The Associated Press reported that Quist had high regard for some judges who were appointed by Democratic presidents.[9] Quist also had issued a couple of free speech rulings that angered conservative groups.

One of those rulings ended Michigan's censorship of vanity license plates.

Quist wrote that a state law prohibiting plates "offensive to good taste and decency" was unconstitutionally over-broad and vague. Quist ordered the state to issue the vanity plate "WAR SUX" to a political activist, who was represented by the American Civil Liberties Union.

Quist also issued a ruling that allowed homeless sex offenders to stay overnight at shelters near schools in Grand Rapids, despite a state law prohibiting them from living within 1,000 feet of a school. He wrote that homeless people do not "reside" in emergency shelters if they go there only at night to sleep and have no guarantee of a place to stay.

No doubt that ruling did not sit well with parents and conservative groups.

There is no way to tell whether Quist would have supported the Ninth Circuit Court decision in *Ceballos v. Garcetti*.

But in my case even someone from the right side of the political aisle could easily agree that it was inappropriate to punish professors who offer plans to improve the quality of an academic unit. After all, criticism and feedback are necessary for making good decisions about academic programs. You don't need fancy legal thinking to come to that conclusion.

THERE WERE TWO RULINGS in the case. The first was issued September 4, 2013. Fletcher wrote the opinion and Fisher and Quist concurred.

The panel held that my 7-Step Plan was not citizen or private speech, but job-related speech. Like the district court, the panel ruling also extended qualified immunity to the defendant-administrators, because the Ninth Circuit had not yet provided guidance in cases like mine. That meant I could not obtain punitive damages even if I won my lawsuit at trial. I could recover actual damages, such as court costs and attorney's fees.

The appeals panel also ruled that the free speech issue pertaining to my *Ivory Tower* book was moot because it was not submitted into the record. No surprise there.

But, in my favor, the panel ruled that Garcetti did not apply to "teaching and writing on academic matters by teachers employed by the state," even when they are undertaken "pursuant to the official duties" of a teacher or professor. Instead, following the opinion expressed in the *amicus* brief prepared by AAUP and the Thomas Jefferson Center, the panel held that academic employee speech on such matters was protected under the Pickering balancing test. The court found that my 7-Step Plan was protected because it addressed a matter of public concern.

> [T]eaching and academic writing are at the core of the official duties of teachers and professors. Such teaching and writing are "a special concern of the First Amendment." ... We conclude that if applied to teaching and academic writing, Garcetti would directly conflict with the important First Amendment values previously articulated by the Supreme Court. ... The Supreme Court has repeatedly stressed the importance of protecting academic freedom under the First Amendment. ... We conclude that Garcetti does not — indeed, consistent with the First Amendment, cannot — apply to teaching and academic writing that are performed 'pursuant to the official duties' of a teacher and professor.[10]

The University filed a petition for panel rehearing and a petition for rehearing en banc, meaning they wanted all of the judges in the Ninth Circuit to render an opinion in the case. The university argued the Constitution does not protect employee grievances, implying that my 7-Step Plan was a grievance. They argued that none of the other federal courts since *Garcetti* had ever extended free speech protection to speech arising from "professional duties."

On this point, they were correct. The defendants' counsel derived the term "professional duties" from a 2006 Ninth Circuit Court of Appeals decision.[11] Service-related speech is another term for "professional" speech. I prefer the former term because it has a more restricted meaning than "professional" speech. Service is one of the three requirements of employment (the other two are teaching and research).

WHILE EVERYONE was waiting for the Appeals Court panel to rule on the *en banc* appeal, I turned my attention to finding ways to remind professors across the country that shared governance should not be taken for granted.

At Arizona State University, I called Thomas Schildgen, the president of the Faculty Senate in early October 2013, and asked if his organization was interested in sponsoring a panel or colloquium to discuss the implications of *Demers v. Austin* for faculty.

Let's talk over lunch, he said.

I met him and one of his colleagues at the University Club on ASU's Tempe campus.

Schildgen was very sympathetic, but he didn't believe the "time was right" to get the Senate involved. He did not elaborate, nor did I press him. I was used to having faculty senate leaders marginalize free speech matters.

Schildgen did refer me to two other groups of faculty that sponsor meetings, but they never responded.

I also tried to get the Cronkite School to sponsor a session.

But one faculty member told me that a top administrator in the program believed the *Demers v. Austin* "ruling wasn't very important."

I wanted to ask where they got that idea, but didn't.

What difference would it have made?

I RETURNED to my Glendale apartment and conducted a search of other federal free speech cases across the country after *Garcetti* and found seven other professors before me had fought the good fight and lost.[12]

It was time to write another press release — only this time, a commentary. I sent it to more than 500 scholars and academic and free speech organizations.

Shared Governance "Is Only One Court Decision Away from Annihilation," But Do Professors Really Care?

When I filed a federal free speech lawsuit in 2009 against four administrators at Washington State University (*Demers v. Austin*), where I was a tenured associate professor of communication, I did not expect a lot of support from anyone, including faculty.

Professors are, after all, suspicious by nature.

Many tend to view free speech lawsuits, even from their own kind, as a cover for personal grievances.

"Demers is a troublemaker," some said at WSU.

No surprise there.

But three years later — after a three-judge panel of the Ninth Circuit Court of Appeals rejected WSU's argument that professors do not deserve free speech rights when they speak in their service-related roles — I am puzzled by the lack of concern among faculty across the country for protecting shared governance, which is only one court decision away from annihilation.

Since the 2006 U.S. Supreme Court 5-4 decision in *Garcetti v. Ceballos*, the lower federal courts have ruled seven ... times that professors do not deserve free speech rights when they question or criticize administrators and their policies regarding budgets, resource allocation, curriculum and program development.

My lawsuit is the sole exception. ...

But if WSU succeeds on its *en banc* appeal to the Ninth Circuit (currently in progress), then administrators can go back to retaliating against faculty for anything — and I mean anything — they say when serving on committees or on faculty senates. Shared governance becomes controlled governance.

Yes, the stakes are extremely high. ...

Yet rank-and-file faculty and their leaders across the country cannot seem to get their head into the game.

For example, when I wanted to speak to the WSU Faculty Senate in 2011 about the importance of shared governance and academic freedom, the Senate chair at the time refused to allow me to appear before the Senate. ...

Over the last three years, I have sent more than two dozen informational e-mails to faculty at scores of universities across the country and had some letters-to-the-editor published in various newspapers, including the *Chronicle of Higher Education.* To date, though, not one faculty leader or Faculty Senate has publicly condemned WSU for its anti-free speech stance. ...

Surveys show that nine of 10 faculty believe "participation in shared governance is a worthwhile faculty responsibility" (see Research & Polling Inc., "Follow-up Survey: Shared Governance and Communication Issues, Faculty and Staff Survey," prepared for the University of New Mexico, May 2011).

But why, then, are faculty so reluctant to get into the game?

Some of the reluctance can be explained by fear. ... administrative co-optation ... [and] the "iron law of bureaucracy ..."

Whatever the reason for the lack of action, let there be no mistake.

There may never be another chance to save shared governance.

The time to get into the game is now.

One retired professor responded.

"You're right, Dave. Most faculty tend to identify with their administrations. In Ag and Engineering colleges, it's near 100%. Liberal Arts faculties are where we would most expect faculty to support shared governance — but even there I fear to predict what a good poll would find about their attitudes. My experience in faculty judicial processes in an arts college leads me to not be too surprised about the lack of support you're experiencing."

THE SECOND DEMERS RULING FROM THE NINTH CIRCUIT, which replaced the first one, was issued on January 29, 2014.

The court denied the petition for panel rehearing and the petition for rehearing *en banc*. In the original ruling, the court held that "teaching and writing on academic matters" by publicly employed teachers could be protected by the First Amendment because they are governed by *Pickering*, not by *Garcetti*. Fletcher wrote instead that *Garcetti* does not apply to "speech related to scholarship or teaching" and reaffirmed that "Garcetti does not — indeed, consistent with the First Amendment, cannot — apply to teaching and academic writing that are performed 'pursuant to the official duties' of a teacher and professor."

We conclude that The 7-Step Plan prepared by Demers in connection with his official duties as a faculty member of the Murrow School was "related to scholarship or teaching" within the meaning of *Garcetti*. See 547 U.S. at 425. The basic thrust of the Plan may be understood from its first paragraphs [condensed below]:

> The relationship between mass communication programs (e.g., journalism, broadcasting, public relations, advertising) and the academy in general has always been a rocky one. The first print journalism programs emerged in the early 1900s ... and were staffed largely with teachers who had professional backgrounds. ... As the years passed, increasing pressure was placed on journalism and other related programs (broadcasting, public relations, advertising) to "scholarize" their faculty — ... to hire faculty who had earned Ph.D. degrees in the social sciences and conduct research. ... Needless to say, this turn of events alienated many professionals and media-related businesses. ... The close relationship universities once had with the professional community was disappearing.

In Demers's view, the teaching of mass communications had lost a critical connection to the real world of professional communicators. His Plan, if implemented, would restore that connection and would, in his view, greatly improve the education of mass communications students at the Murrow School. It may in some cases be difficult to distinguish between what qualifies as speech "related to scholarship or teaching" within the meaning of *Garcetti*. But this is not such a case. The 7-Step Plan ... *was a proposal to implement a change at the Murrow School that, if implemented, would have substantially altered the nature of what was taught at the school, as well as the composition of the faculty that would teach it.* [emphasis added]

The court declared that academic employee speech is protected under the First Amendment by Pickering if it is a (1) matter of public concern, and (2) outweighs the interest of the state in promoting efficiency of service. The court ruled that the pamphlet did address a matter of "public concern" because it was broadly distributed and "contained serious suggestions about the future course of an important department of WSU."

Fletcher wrote that my plan did not focus on a personnel issue or an internal dispute, nor did it address the role of particular individuals in the Murrow School or voice personal complaints. Rather, the plan proposed changes to the direction and focus of the school.

> The manner in which the Plan was distributed reinforces the conclusion that it addressed matters of public concern. ... Here, Demers sent the Plan to the President and Provost of WSU, to members of the Murrow School's Professional Advisory Board, to other faculty members, to alumni, to friends, and to newspapers. He posted the Plan on his website, making it available to

the public. ... Demers's Plan contained serious suggestions about the future course of an important department of WSU, at a time when the Murrow School itself was debating some of those very suggestions.

I believe the single most important word in the panel's decision was "related."

This word was taken directly from the U.S. Supreme Court's majority decision in *Garcetti*: "We need not ... decide whether the analysis we conduct today would apply in the same manner to a case involving speech *related* to scholarship or teaching." [emphasis added]

The WSU defendants and their counsel had argued that the 7-Step Plan was not protected speech under *Garcetti* because it was not uttered in the classroom or in scholarship or research. They were arguing that the location of the speech — where it was uttered — was crucial.

The Ninth Circuit panel disagreed.

The issue isn't where the speech is uttered. The issue is whether it is "related" to scholarship or teaching.

One word made all the difference.

And that one word allowed the appeals panel to avoid accusations that it was engaging in judicial activism — that they were trying to create their own law. They were simply spouting back what two justices of the high court said.

In fact, Fletcher's opinion cited a host of court decisions to back up the idea that professors qualify for First Amendment protection when they speak on issues related to scholarship or teaching.

The opinion remanded the case back to the district court to determine (1) whether WSU had a "sufficient interest in controlling" the circulation of the plan, (2) whether the circulation was a substantial motivating factor in any adverse employment action, and (3) whether the university would have taken the action in the absence of protected speech.

But to recover my attorney's fees, I needed another $50,000 to $100,000 to take the case to trial. That's how much it would cost to bring in some witnesses and pay for other legal costs.

Unfortunately, I was broke. I had paid more than $100,000 to Graham and Dunn and I owed another $250,000. I was not able to find any free speech organizations to help with the costs.

I WAS FORCED to file for bankruptcy in January 2014, two weeks before the Appeals Court handed down its final decision.

Several lawyers had predicted this would happen.

So I won on principle but lost in the pocketbook.

I'd say that was fair exchange.

The lesson here is that you have to be prepared to lose almost everything if you want to stick to your principles.

Fortunately, I was able to keep my retirement funds, my Spokane house (as I continued to make payments on it), and my 9-year-old Volvo.

WSU did not appeal the decision.

Nine months later, on October 28, 2014, WSU and I settled the case out of court. As usual, I wrote another overly wordy news release, which was distributed on November 4, 2014.

WASHINGTON STATE UNIVERSITY PAYS PROFESSOR TO DROP FREE SPEECH LAWSUIT
WSU President Covers Up State Audit Report

Washington State University is paying former journalism professor David Demers $120,000 to drop his five-year-old federal free speech lawsuit against four WSU administrators.

"I am extremely pleased with the settlement," Demers said. "It sends a strong message to university administrators that those who intend to violate professors' free speech rights will be held accountable."

The settlement was reached after the Ninth Circuit Court of Appeals ruled late last year, and again in January, that Demers' "7-Step Plan" to improve the quality of the Edward R. Murrow School of Communication was speech protected under the First Amendment.

WSU President Elson Floyd's administration argued that professors do not deserve free speech rights when speaking in their "professional," or service-related, roles.

The appeals court rejected that argument. ...

All of the settlement funds are being used to pay Demers' legal fees, according to the agreement. ...

Legal bills of $350,000 in his case forced Demers to file bankruptcy in spring 2014. The U.S. Bankruptcy Court approved the settlement agreement on October 23.

Demers moved his family to Arizona in summer 2014.

The Murrow College is still not accredited.[13]

When all of the dust settled, Graham & Dunn earned about $180,000 from the case, about $2 of every $3 they billed (if you exclude the appeal).[14]

That came out to about $200 an hour.

The law firm gave Judy Endejan, my attorney and its former employee, a small bonus check for her role in the case. That was nice.

Just before the settlement, one of the lawyers at Graham & Dunn e-mailed and thanked me for agreeing to the settlement. He also acknowledged that the bankruptcy must have been difficult. I appreciated that.

I received nothing from the settlement, but that was okay.

The lawsuit cost me about $110,000, with most of that (about $85,000) going to the law firm and the rest to pay fees and expert witness costs.

I don't know how much the lawsuit cost the university and taxpayers. But it most likely was more than $1 million, because scores of different public officials, attorneys and employees were working on the case at various times over its eight-year history.

WSU PRESIDENT ELSON FLOYD never apologized for hiding the state audit report or for casting the university as a free speech villain. On June 20, 2015, he died of complications from colon cancer.

Some say it was bad luck.

I don't believe in luck.

Floyd wasn't punished for what he did. He was simply an unfortunate victim of some natural force that medical scientists have yet to fully understand.

Several news stories and editorials praised Floyd for his accomplishments.[15] None, however, pointed out that Floyd's administration almost killed shared governance and free speech rights for faculty. So I wrote this "letter to the editor" to the *Seattle Times*.

> The late WSU President Elson Floyd deserves accolades for many things he did in office. But he made some mistakes, too. His legacy includes a concerted attempt in the courts to eliminate free speech rights for faculty and shared governance. ... In *Demers v. Austin* (Ninth Circuit Court of Appeals, 2014), Floyd's administration argued that faculty do NOT deserve free speech rights when commenting on issues of public concern related to teaching and scholarship. Fortunately, the Ninth Circuit rejected this position. Floyd also threatened on one occasion to punish students who might engage in "uncivil" (impolite) speech, an administrative act that clearly violated students' free speech rights. Floyd's relative lack of concern about free speech on campus, which was evident during his deposition in the lawsuit, may stem in part from the fact that he never held a job as a faculty member and never published a scholarly paper. Let's hope the next WSU president is a teacher and an academic — not a corporate or managerial executive — who embraces the idea

that the First Amendment is a prerequisite in the search for truth and knowledge.

The *Times* refused to publish my letter.

Chapter 48 Endnotes

1. Richard A. Posner, "The Jurisprudence of Skepticism," *Michigan Law Review, 86*: 827+ (1988) and Dan Simon, "A Third View of the Black Box: Cognitive Coherence in Legal Decision-making," *University of Chicago Law Review, 71*: 511-586 (2004).

2. Daniel R. Pinello, "Linking Party to Judicial Ideology in American Courts: A Meta-Analysis," *The Justice System Journal, 20*(3): 219-254 (1999).

3. Frank H. Easterbrook, "Do Liberals and Conservatives Differ in Judicial Activism?" *University of Colorado Law Review, 73*: 1403-1416 (2002), and Corey Rayburn Yung, "Flexing Judicial Muscle: An Empirical Study of Judicial Activism in the Federal Courts," *Northwestern University Law Review, 105*(1): 1-60 (2011).

4. Easterbrook, "Do Liberals and Conservatives Differ in Judicial Activism?"

5. *Ceballos v. Garcetti*, 361 F.3d 1168, 1173 (9th Cir. 2004).

6. *Evans-Marshall v. Board of Education*, 624 F.3d (6th Cir. 2010).

7. Ceballos ran for DA in 2019 but withdrew when the Democratic Party endorsed another candidate. He was still working for the DA's office on November 13, 2020.

8. Some of Quist's donations are posted at <http://www.city-data.com/ elec2/elec-GRAND- HAVEN-MI.html>, retrieved May 2, 2015.

9. Kathy Barks Hoffman, "Federal Judge Richard Enslen to Go on Senior Status," Associated Press (June 1, 2005), retrieved May 2, 2015, from <www.freerepublic. com/focus/f-news/1414628/posts>.

10. *Demers v. Austin*, 729 F.3d 1011 (September 4, 2013).

11. The district court judge in my case wrote: "However, speech which 'owes its existence to an employee's professional responsibilities' is not protected by the First Amendment." Huppert, 574 F.3d at 704, quoting *Garcetti v. Ceballos*, 547 U.S. 410, 421 (2006)."

12. *Adams v. Trustees of the University of North Carolina –Wilmington* is not included in the list because the court ruled Professor Adams's speech was private speech.

13. The *Daily Evergreen*, WSU's student newspaper, did publish a story on the settlement.

14. Although the settlement earmarked $120,000 for Graham & Dunn, the law firm ended up with $98,801.60. The rest went to other four other creditors, three of whom were banks that provided funds that I used to help pay for the lawsuit. See Notice of Trustee's Final Report and Applications for Compensation and Deadline to Object, David K. Demers, Case No. 14-00125-FPC7-CF (June 1, 2015), United States Bankruptcy Court, Eastern District of Washington.

15. Katherine Long and Coral Garnick, "Elson Floyd, WSU's 'Visionary' President, Dies," *The Seattle Times* (June 20, 2015), and Editorial, "WSU President Elson Floyd Was State's Best Higher-Education Advocate: Elson Floyd Leaves a Remarkable Legacy, on and off the Palouse," *The Seattle Times* (June 22, 2015), retrieved June 27, 2015, from <http://www.seattletimes.com/opinion/editorials/wsu-president-elson-floyd-was-states-best-higher-education-advocate>.

Chapter 49

Impact of *Demers v. Austin*

July 5, 2018
Phoenix, Arizona

From a societal perspective, the single most important consequence of the Ninth Circuit Court of Appeals ruling in *Demers v. Austin* is the constitutional protection that it offers for service-related speech and shared governance in nine Western states. The ruling applies to public universities and K–12 school systems, as the court specifically referred to "teachers and professors."[1] Private schools generally are not covered.

The assumption underlying the Appeals Court ruling is that teaching and scholarship are impacted by the structure of the organization and its resources. And if those who do the teaching and scholarship have no say in how academic units are structured and how resources are distributed, then the academic search for and distribution of truth, knowledge and understanding of the world will be compromised.

"Had the Ninth Circuit ruled the other way," writes legal scholar and blogger Kenneth White, a former prosecutor, "then the state could fire professors at will if it didn't like, for instance, the stance that a history professor took about a historical event, or a political science professor took about a political dispute, or any professor took about an issue of academic governance on a committee."[2]

More broadly, had the ruling come down in favor of administrators, there is the possibility that they would have been given the authority to eliminate shared governance at their institutions. Now, they cannot administratively or legislatively eliminate that right.

Until *Demers v. Austin*, university governing boards and administrators presumably were under no legal obligation to provide shared governance to their faculty. They could, barring statutory or university rule restrictions, withdraw that authority at any time.

That's what happened at Idaho State University in 2011. Then-President Arthur C. Vailas disbanded the Faculty Senate, even though shared governance was part of the university rules.[3] Vailas then tried to push through a university constitution that completely ignored the principle of shared governance.

Although *Demers v. Austin* gives constitutional protection to the principle of shared governance, only a few of the attorneys, academics and legal scholars who have analyzed the case seem to understand this. In fact, some have even criticized the Ninth Circuit panel for engaging in what they claim is judicial activism.

The most prominent of these is an unsigned commentary published in the April 2014 issue of the *Harvard Law Review*, a legal journal controlled and edited by law students at Harvard University.[4] The commentary justifies its criticism of the ruling by appealing to the principles of traditionalism and judicial interference.

According to the *Review*, the Ninth Circuit decision in *Demers v. Austin* was misguided, because it (1) conflicts "with the trend toward greater deference to government employers in controlling workplace speech" and (2) "infringes upon institutional autonomy and introduces the excessive judicial interference expressly disfavored in Supreme Court tradition."[5]

The first argument is grounded in the principle of unbridled traditionalism. This is the notion that courts should always do as they have done before because that's the way things have always been done. The assumption is that social change leads to harmful conditions.

Tradition is not always bad.

It provides a basis for shared understanding and social action.

But traditionalism for traditionalism's sake is the bane of societies predicated upon alleviating injustice through truth and knowledge. No modern legal system can sustain itself through unbridled traditionalism.

Traditionalism fails to explain why giving more speech freedom to professors would lead to adverse effects.

The second major argument of the commentary contends that the Ninth Circuit ruling interferes with "institutional autonomy," because the ruling extends a constitutional protection to faculty that did not exist before.

Actually, the opposite argument can be made.

For more than three centuries, academia in America has given faculty a proactive role in university governance. Eliminating that role would actually interfere with a tradition.

In the *Garcetti v. Ceballos* decision, the five conservative justices who denied free speech protection to government employees did offer a logic, of sorts, for their ruling. They argued that government employers need a significant degree of control over their employees' words and actions, otherwise there would be "little chance for the efficient provision of public services."

This proposition holds weight if one assumes that corruption in government is itself efficient. But couldn't Ceballos reasonably argue that failure to punish police for falsifying affidavits likely would generate civil lawsuits from innocent victims, thereby creating even more inefficiencies in government services and risking big lawsuit judgments?

More important, the inefficiency proposition is simply not supported by the history of shared governance in American universities.[6] Many administrators even insist that service-related faculty speech deserves First Amendment protection.[7]

The *Harvard Law Review* commentary also claimed that "regulation of a professor's expression in the performance of administrative duties, as opposed to teaching or scholarly research, would not clearly interfere with the truth-seeking or marketplace-of-ideas values used to justify protecting the individual academic freedom of professors."

To support this statement, the commentary cites a paper by legal scholar David M. Rabban.[8] I carefully examined the article and was unable to identify the language in Rabban's paper that supports the statement that regulating service-related speech will not interfere with truth-seeking. To the contrary, Rabban makes it clear that professors should have First Amendment protection when they speak in their service-related roles.

"It makes no sense," Rabban writes, "to expect professors to engage in critical inquiry and simultaneously to allow punishment for its exercise,"[9] and "individual academic freedom should cover expression within a professor's scholarly expertise and intramural speech on matters of educational policy."[10]

In *Demers v. Austin*, the intramural, or service-related, speech was a 7-Step Plan that clearly focused on educational policy, because it sought to improve the quality of an academic unit, the Murrow mass communication programs.

Writing in response to the Ninth Circuit ruling, two university administrators on the East Coast also argued that even when faculty expression is deemed to be unhelpful or provocative, such speech is crucial to generating knowledge and understanding. University of Vermont President Thomas Sullivan and University of Delaware Vice President and General Counsel Lawrence White assert:

> As a legal principle and sound postulate of institutional governance, academic freedom should be deemed to protect the expression of faculty views even when they are deemed by some to be unhelpful or provocatively stated. This is especially compelling given the uniqueness of our universities as marketplaces of ideas where we seek to discover new knowledge and understanding and make it available to others.[11]

In response to the *Harvard Law Review* article, I wrote and submitted in November 2014 my own commentary to editors.[12]

The editors refused to publish it. No reason was given.[13]

THE VAST MAJORITY of commentaries that have been written about *Demers v. Austin*, were supportive of the ruling, however.

Los Angeles attorney and former prosecutor Kenneth White, writing before the *Demers* settlement agreement, said the Ninth Circuit ruling

> stands for the position that a professor's interest in free speech in the academic environment is uniquely important and entitled to the highest level of First Amendment protection. ... Some people are angered ... because they see it [special First Amendment protection for professors] as giving public employees superior rights to private employees. ... I submit that it's better to see the rule as a limit on state power, not a special right granted to public employees. State officials have a long history of attempting to increase their power by limiting the boon of state employment to people who support them. The state's power to police speech should be scrutinized with great skepticism and even hostility. What about David Demers? ... his prospects for winning [at trial in the District Court] are grim. ... the officials he sued are entitled to qualified immunity ... They couldn't let Demers profit. It wouldn't be civilized.[14]

In an article for *Engage* magazine, which is published by the conservative-leaning Federalist Society, Los Angeles First Amendment attorney Arthur Willner wrote: "The Ninth Circuit [in *Demers v. Austin*] ... strongly affirmed the First Amendment free speech rights of faculty employed at public colleges and universities. The opinion's robust language in support of free speech should be cause for celebration by both faculty and students on campuses, once famously regarded as the 'marketplace of ideas,' where these days a purported right not to be offended is thought to trump the First Amendment right to free expression."[15]

The Foundation for Individual Rights in Education noted on its website that "we are very pleased that the Ninth Circuit Court of Appeals has set this critically important precedent."[16]

Chicago-Kent College of Law professor Sheldon Nahmod wrote that "this decision overall is sound in its emphasis on the First Amendment protection of a college or university professor's teaching and scholarship."[17]

Robert O'Neil, former president of and professor of law at the University of Virginia, told *Inside Higher Education* via e-mail that the Appeals Court decision in *Demers* added to the view he shares that *Garcetti* should not be applied to higher education. The decision, he wrote, has "a level of certainty and conviction — a slightly sharper edge, if you will — which further narrows adverse inferences from *Garcetti*."[18]

City University of New York School of Law Professor Ruthann Robson wrote that "This is an important opinion recognizing academic freedom under the First Amendment. At a relatively brief 26 pages, it is nevertheless closely reasoned both doctrinally and in its application."[19]

Writing for *Law360*, an online subscription service owned by LexisNexis, legal analyst David Urban correctly points out that in the wake of *Demers v. Austin* "administrators possibly can be faced with personal responsibility for violation of civil rights if they are found to have improperly interfered with an instructor's ... speech. ... *Demers* makes faculty academic freedom rights as against their own employers a federal constitutional matter."[20]

Jayne Benz Chipman, an attorney in a California law firm, wrote that "the Ninth Circuit, in *Demers v. Austin*, ... has boldly gone — where other federal circuit courts have heretofore been reluctant to venture — in declaring that applying *Garcetti* to academic speech would conflict with the First Amendment. ... Other federal circuit courts that have had the chance to weigh in on the issue have been less boldly definitive. ... Only time will tell whether the Supreme Court provides clarity."[21]

Former university administrator Dean O. Smith wrote in his book *Understanding Authority in Higher Education* that "although Demers has not yet prevailed in court on the merits of the case, this [Ninth Circuit Court] decision was a major victory for advocates of the idea that college faculty members have speech rights beyond those offered other public employees."[22]

Michael Porter, an attorney in an Oregon law firm, wrote that "higher education lawyers and administrators have taken comfort in the Supreme Court's 2006 decision in *Garcetti v. Ceballos*. ... But that comfort came with an underlying anxiety — as though the decision were too good to be true. ... The Ninth Circuit [in *Demers v. Austin*] has taken much speech of faculty members outside its [*Garcetti's*] ambit."[23]

Attorneys and law firms that represent universities also recognize that *Demers v. Austin* circumscribes administrators when it comes to punishing faculty for their speech.

Sharon J. Ormond and Lisa R. Allred, two attorneys who work in a California law firm, wrote on the firm's website that "the *Demers* decision should not be read so broadly as to conclude that any teaching and academic speech by a teacher of faculty member addresses a matter of public concern. When teachers or professors speak or write on purely private matters or grievances ... , such speech will not be constitutionally protected. Still, before a public educational agency takes any adverse action against a teacher or faculty member, the agency should carefully consider the basis for the action and whether the action, if related to speech, can withstand constitutional scrutiny."[24]

A legal advisory issued by the Office of General Counsel for the University of California educational system noted that "the *Demers* decision is significant for the University because the court has signaled that academic employees are likely to have greater protection from adverse employment actions based on speech made in the course of their official duties than other public employees enjoy."[25]

Ronina E. Mummolo, a J.D. candidate at Cornell University, provides one of the more interesting analyses of *Demers v. Austin* and other free speech cases associated with educational institutions. She writes in the *Cornell Law Review* that the courts, when adjudicating First Amendment claims of teachers, should take into account "the cognitive and moral development of students" who are the recipients of the speech in question.[26]

She added, "Determining whether an educator's speech impairs the efficiency of the public service, being the school or university, requires assessing how the institution is achieving its goals in the classroom, which varies depending on the level of education and students' abilities."[27]

Matthew Jay Hertzog, director of educational technology at Methodist College, argues in a law journal that *Demers v. Austin* and other cases in the courts are establishing constitutional protection for academic freedom.

> With the decisions of the lower courts in these cases being reversed by various U.S. Courts of Appeals (as seen in *Adams* and *Demers*), the constitutionally protected rights of academics for their academic speech and writing is being recognized as a First Amendment protection. As social and political events within higher education over the past several years have led university administrators to question the parameters of Constitutional protections and challenge the academic's right to freedom of speech, the U.S. legal system has remained firm in its interpretation of the law by protecting a professor's civil rights as well as those rights awarded to their academic speech and writings.[28]

The most comprehensive legal analysis of *Demers* to date has been written by Patrick Fackrell, a law student at the University of Idaho who as of this writing works for a law firm in Houston.[29]

> Courts have long recognized the importance of academic freedom. But until *Demers,* academic freedom has received few protections, if any. Academic freedom should function to provide individual university professors and faculty members with First Amendment protection when conducting the research, scholarship, and teaching that they were hired to perform. At the same time, academic freedom requires that the institution be able to impose legitimate limitations and direct the professors and faculty whom it hires. ... Though

Garcetti left uncertain whether its threshold official duties inquiry was intended to apply to academic speech in universities, the Ninth Circuit in *Demers* properly resolved that uncertainty and provided a welcome analytical framework for academic speech that protects the future of academic freedom and disinterested research, scholarship, and teaching.[30]

DEMERS V. AUSTIN IS having some major effects on policymaking at universities and was cited in testimony before a congressional committee that is considering whether to enact a law that protects academic freedom.

At the University of Oregon, where faculty in spring 2013 voted to unionize, the UO faculty committee supporting the expansion of free speech rights for faculty cited *Demers v. Austin* to back up its position that faculty deserved First Amendment protection when speaking in their service-related, or shared-governance, roles.[31]

> The university is governed by the faculty and the president. ... Institutional policies and practices are informed by consultation and advice from the faculty, staff, and students. Therefore, members of the university community have freedom to address, question, or criticize any matter of institutional policy, action, or administration, whether acting as individuals or as members of an agency of institutional governance.[32]

UO President Mike Gottfredson's administration initially rejected the faculty proposal. Gottfredson then tried to limit academic freedom to only speech uttered in the classroom or in scholarship. The administrative proposal also tried to require every faculty member to be civil when "discharging his or her duties."

One of Gottfredson's lieutenants in the fight against free speech rights for faculty was Tim Gleason, former dean of the University of Oregon's School of Journalism and Communication and now serving as UO's strategic communications consultant.

Yes, you read that right.

Another journalism dean fighting free speech rights.

And not just any dean, but one who is a professor of mass media law and ethics.

Gleason was one of the four deans who rubber-stamped Washington State University President Elson Floyd's proposal to convert the Murrow School into a College. At that time, Gleason also opposed the idea of seeking accreditation for the new Murrow College programs, which was a key element of my 7-Step Plan. Now I understand why Gleason never responded after I sent him a copy of the plan.

At any rate, Gleason and another administrator fought against UO faculty free speech rights for 18 months before Gottfredson capitulated in May 2014 and signed into effect a policy that provides strong protection for service-related speech.[33]

That action came after O'Neil, the former University of Virginia president, told *Inside Higher Education* that administrators and faculty at Oregon "need to make sure the adequate language currently reflects *Demers* [*v. Austin*]."[34]

Several months after Gottfredson signed the pro-speech policy, he resigned (many faculty say he was forced out) from his position as president. The University of Oregon Board of Trustees gave him a $970,000 severance package.[35]

But before he left, Gottfredson appointed Gleason to the position of university Faculty Athletics Representative for the NCAA, which pays more than $100,000 a year for a half-time appointment. The rest of Gleason's pay, about $150,000, comes from his job as a professor in the journalism program.[36]

The appointment angered some UO faculty who believed that Gleason had worked against their best interests.[37]

Meanwhile, Rick Levy, a law professor at the University of Kansas, also used *Demers* to challenge a controversial Board of Regents proposal that would have allowed administrators "to suspend, dismiss or terminate from employment any faculty or staff member who makes improper use of social media."[38]

The policy change was prompted by a controversial tweet from a University of Kansas journalism professor, who criticized the National Rifle Association after the mass shootings in 2013 that killed 13 people in the Washington, D.C., Navy Yard.

In response to the proposed policy change, Levy wrote a memorandum that, he said, reflected only his views.

> Two federal appellate courts have ruled that there is a higher education exception to the *Garcetti* rule. ... In the most recent of these decisions [*Demers v. Austin*], the court declared, "*Garcetti* does not — indeed, consistent with the First Amendment, cannot — apply to teaching and academic writing that are performed 'pursuant to the official duties' of a teacher and professor." ... [T]he principles of academic freedom would require protection from sanction for expressions in the areas of research, teaching, and shared governance, whether or not the First Amendment is interpreted to offer this protection.[39]

The Regents policy, which was enacted in 2014, says universities can terminate faculty, administrators and staff who post messages on social media that incite "imminent violence" or, when made pursuant to the employee's official duties, are "contrary to the best interests of the employer."

The former statement on "imminent violence" conforms to national free speech standards, because it punishes action, not speech per se. The latter clause on speech "contrary to the best interests of the employer," however, was opposed by the faculty and may violate the First Amendment.

The University of Kansas Faculty Senate, after a year of work, created in April 2015 a procedure for ensuring due process for those accused of violating the policy.

My interpretation of the social media policy is that comments posted about matters related to scholarship or teaching are fully protected, even if administrators believe the comments are "contrary to the best interests of the employer."

On June 2, 2015, Greg Lukianoff, president and chief executive officer of the Foundation for Individual Rights in Education, urged the Subcommittee on the Constitution and Civil Justice for the U.S. House of Representatives to enact a law that would protect freedom of expression at public colleges and universities in the United States.[40]

A law is needed, he said, because the courts have handed down mixed rulings on the issue of speech on campus. He cited *Demers v. Austin* and other cases to back this up.

"By leaving unanswered the question of whether an academic freedom exception applies to public employee speech doctrine following *Garcetti*, the Supreme Court's decision threatens academic freedom and free speech," he testified. "Congress should statutorily protect academic freedom by making clear that there is an exception to *Garcetti* for academics."

Lukianoff proposed several draft bills. One of them borrowed directly from the language of the Ninth Circuit Court ruling in *Demers* and would amend a section of the Higher Education Act of 1964:

> No publicly operated institution of higher education ... shall take adverse personnel action, or maintain a policy that allows it to take adverse personnel action, against a faculty member in retaliation for expression related to scholarship, academic research, or teaching ... *or within the context of the faculty member's activities as an employee of the institution of higher education, related to matters of public concern, including matters related to professional duties, the functioning of the institution of higher education, and the institution's positions and policies.* [41] [emphasis added]

Chapter 49 Endnotes

1. "Although *Demers* evaluated the speech of a public university professor and despite earlier Ninth Circuit case law applying *Garcetti* to teacher speech, the Ninth Circuit's discussion

in *Demers* did not appear to foreclose its application to K–12 schoolteachers," pp. 273-274 in Amanda Harmon Cooley, "Controlling Students and Teachers: The Increasing Constriction of Constitutional Rights in Public Education," *Baylor Law Review, 66*(2): 235-294 (2014).

2. Ken White, "Ninth Circuit Clarifies First Amendment Rights of Public University Professors," *Popehat* (September 5, 2013), retrieved May 25, 2015 from <http://popehat.com/2013/09/05/ninth-circuit-clarifies-first-amendment-rights-of-public-university-professors>. Popehat is a legal blog.

3. Jimmy Hancock, "State Board of Education Suspends ISU's Faculty Senate," *Idaho State Journal* (February 17, 2011), retrieved December 4, 2011, from <www.idahostatejournal.com/news/online/state-board-of-education-suspends-isu-s-faculty-senate/article_39b418ec-3adc-11e0-8724-001cc4c03286.html>.

4. Unsigned commentary, "Ninth Circuit Finds Garcetti Official Duty Rule Inapplicable to Professional Speech in Public-University Context," *Harvard Law Review, 127*(6): 1823-1830 (April 18, 2014).

5. Ibid., p. 1820.

6. For brief history, see David Demers, "Harvard Law Review Commentary Fails to Justify Its Anti-Free speech Stance: Ninth Circuit Ruling in *Demers v. Austin* Implicitly Protects Shared Governance," available at <http://www.marquettebooks.com/harvardcommentary.html>.

7. Thomas Sullivan and Lawrence White, "For Faculty Free Speech, the Tide Is Turning," *The Chronicle of Higher Education* (September 30, 2013), available online at <http://chronicle.com/article/For-Faculty-Freespeech-the/141951>. Sullivan is president of the University of Vermont and White is vice president and general counsel at the University of Delaware.

8. The citation is David M. Rabban, "A Functional Analysis of 'Individual' and 'Institutional' Academic Freedom Under the First Amendment," *Law & Contemporary Problems,* 53(3): 227-301 (Summer 1990), p. 243. However, I could not find any discussion on page 243 or nearby pages that supported the HLR commentary's citation.

9. Ibid., p. 242.

10. Ibid., p. 300.

11. Sullivan and White, "For Faculty Free Speech, the Tide Is Turning."

12. Demers, "Harvard Law Review Commentary Fails to Justify Its Anti-Free speech Stance," available at <http://www.marquettebooks.com/harvardcommentary.html>.

13. But the editors did remark: "It is rare and always exciting to hear from someone who has been personally involved in a case discussed by one of our pieces."

14. White, "Ninth Circuit Clarifies First Amendment Rights of Public University Professors."

15. Arthur Willner, "Ninth Circuit Upholds Professor's First Amendment Claim in *Demers v. Austin,*" *Engage* 15(1): 40-41 (July 29, 2014). *Engage* is published by the Federalist Society, but it takes no position on the content of Willner's article. Willner is a partner at Gladstone Michel Weisberg Willner & Sloane in Los Angeles.

16. Susan Kruth, "Washington State U. Agrees to Pay $120,000 to Professor in First Amendment Retaliation Suit," Foundation for Individual Rights in Education (published online, November 5, 2014), retrieved May 26, 2015, from <https://www.thefire.org/washington-state-u-agrees-pay-120000-professor- first-amendment-retaliation-suit>.

17. Nahmod's remarks are posted at <http://nahmodlaw.com/2013/09/16/ new-university-academic-freedom-decision-from-ninth-circuit-demers-v-austin>.

18. Scott Jaschik, "Protecting Academic Freedom," *Inside Higher Education* (February 13, 2014), retrieved May 25, 2015, from <https://www.insidehighered.com/news/2014/02/13/court-ruling-takes-stand-faculty-free speech>.

19. Ruthann Robson, "Ninth Circuit Opinion Protects Academic Freedom Under First Amendment," *Constitutional Law Prof Blog* (September 7, 2013), retrieved May 25, 2015, from <http://lawprofessors.typepad.com/conlaw/2013/09/ninth-circuit-opinion-protects-academic-freedom-.html>.

20. David Urban, "First Amendment Employment Issues To Watch In 2014: Academic Freedom," *Law360* (February 12, 2014), retrieved May 26, 2015, from <http://www.law360.com/articles/503562/5-first-amendment-employment-issues-to-watch-in-2014>.

21. Jayne Benz Chipman, "Ninth Circuit Finds That The Garcetti 'Official Duties' Rule Does Not Apply To Public University Employee Academic Speech," Hirschfeld, Kraemer LLP law firm (posted at *The California Workplace Advisor* on November 22, 2013), retrieved May 26, 2015, from <http://blog.hkemploymentlaw.com/index.php/ninth-circuit-finds-that-the-garcetti-official-duties-rule-does-not-apply-to-public-university-employee-academic-speech>.

22. Dean O. Smith, *Understanding Authority in Higher Education* (Lanham, MD: Rowman & Littlefield, 2015), p. 114.

23. Michael Porter, "The Supreme Court Limits Garcetti," Miller Nash LLP attorneys (Posted on June 19, 2014 by Higher Education Council), retrieved May 26, 2015, from <http://elahighereducationcouncilreport.com/2014/06/19/the-supreme-court-limits-garcetti>.

24. Sharon J. Ormond and Lisa R. Allred, "Court Rules that Teaching and Academic Writing Pursuant to Official Duties Can Enjoy First Amendment Protection," posted at the website for Atkinson, Andelson, Loya, Ruud & Romo law firm (September 6, 2013), retrieved May 26, 2015, from <http://aalrr.com/publications/Alerts/QP/court_rules_that_teaching_and_academic_writing_pursuant_to_official_du>.

25. Legal Advisory, "Ninth Circuit Holds that Academic Employees' Speech Pursuant to Their Official Duties May be Protected by the First Amendment," Office of General Counsel for the University of California (March 3, 2014), retrieved May 26, 2015, from <http://ucop.edu/general-counsel/_files/legal-advisory/legaladv_140303.pdf>.

26. Rosina E. Mummolo, "The First Amendment in the Public School Classroom: a Cognitive Theory Approach," *Cornell Law Review*, 100(1): 243-267 (November 2014), retrieved May 26, 2015, from <http://cornelllawreview.org/files/2014/11/100CLR243.pdf>. The author made an error on page 244 when summarizing the *Demers v. Austin* case. She wrote: "Although the court ultimately found that the *appellant*, Demers, *did not assert a viable First Amendment retaliation claim*, it applied the more flexible balancing test that is not endorsed by all sister circuits." [emphasis added] The Ninth Circuit did NOT rule on the question of whether Demers had a viable First Amendment retaliation claim; rather, it remanded that issue back to the District Court for trial.

27. Ibid., p. 267.

28. Matthew Jay Hertzog, "The Misapplication of *Garcetti* in Higher Education," *Brigham Young University Education and Law Journal*, 2015(1): 203-225 (Spring 2015), pp. 223-224.

29. Pat Fackrell, "*Demers v. Austin:* The Ninth Circuit Resolves the Public Employee Speech Doctrine's Uncertain Application to Academic Speech," *Idaho Law Review*, 51(2): 513-546 (2015).

30. Ibid., p. 546.

31. Academic Freedom Work Group, "Rationale for Policy on Academic Freedom and Draft Academic Freedom Policy," unpublished memo to University of Oregon President Michael Gottfredson and University Senate (January 7, 2014), p. 2, retrieved May 26, 2015, from <http://senate.uoregon.edu/sites/senate.uoregon.edu/files/Academic%20Freedom%20rationale%20memo%20and%20proposal,%20January%202014.pdf>.

32. Ibid., p. 5.

33. Betsy Hammon, "University of Oregon President Michael Gottfredson Signs Academic

Freedom Policy Faculty Say Is Among Strongest in Nation," *The Oregonian* (May 28, 2014), retrieved May 26, 2015, from <http://www.oregonlive.com/education/index.ssf/2014/05/university_of_oregon_president_12.html>.

34. Colleen Flaherty, "Requiring Civility," *Inside Higher Education* (September 12, 2013), retrieved May 26, 2015, from <https://www.insidehighered.com/news 2013/09/12/oregon-professors-object-contract-language-divorcing-academic- freedom-free speech>.

35. Don Kahle, "One UO President Was Fired, One Simply Quit? Yeah, Right," *The* (Eugene, OR) *Register-Guard* (August 15, 2014), p. A9, retrieved May 26, 2015, from <http://projects.registerguard.com/rg/opinion/32011301-78/one-uo-president- was-fired-one-simply-quit-yeah-right.html.csp>.

36. Office of Institutional Research, "Unclassified Employees with a Record of Employment During the 10/1/2014 to 12/31/2014 Period," retrieved April 10, 2015, from <http://ir.uoregon.edu/sites/ir.uoregon.edu/files/Unclassified 100114to123114.pdf>.

37. Some of the critical comments are posted at the UOMatters.com website. See, e.g., <http://uomatters.com/2015/05/mike-gottfredsons-last-act-was-appoint-tim- gleason-as-far-so-hows-he-doing-on-representing-the-faculty.html#more-14862> and <http://uomatters.com/2014/ 05/gottfredson-pads-resume-with-credit-for-academic- freedom-after-getting-tim-gleason-and-randy-geller-to-fight-it-for-18-month.html>.

38. Richard E. Levy, "Recent Developments in the Law: Social Media and the Free Speech Rights of Public Employees," University of Kansas School of Law (unpublished report, May 30, 2014), retrieved May 26, 2015, from <https://law.ku.edu/sites/law.ku.edu/files/docs/recent-developments/(9)LevySocialMediaCLE2014.pdf>.

39. Ibid., p. 25.

40. Written Testimony of Greg Lukianoff, President and Chief Executive Officer, Foundation for Individual Rights in Education, Before the United States House of Representatives Committee on the Judiciary, Subcommittee on the Constitution and Civil Justice, June 2, 2015, Hearing on First Amendment Protections on Public College and University Campuses, retrieved June 6, 2015, from http://docs.house.gov/meetings/JU/JU10/20150602/103548/HHRG-114-JU10-Wstate-LukianoffG- 20150602.pdf>.

41. Ibid., p. 29.

Chapter 50

Lessons of a Quixotic Professor

November 2018
Phoenix, Arizona

After the Ninth Circuit Court of Appeals handed down its decision in *Demers v. Austin* in 2014, I assumed WSU administrators had learned a lesson about the importance of respecting free speech rights of faculty.

After all, their actions likely cost the taxpayers more than $1 million and consumed thousands of unproductive work hours among scores of state and university officials. Several administrators acted badly throughout the whole affair, producing numerous reports with errors and refusing to correct them.

I figured sociologist Michel Crozier had to be wrong about bureaucracies.[1] They have to learn from their mistakes when the consequences are high. If they didn't, how could they survive?

Well, I was wrong.

WSU administrators violated the First Amendment rights of another professor within two years of the *Demers* ruling, and elements of this new case were even more sinister than mine.

It began in 2012, just before my Ninth Circuit Appeals Court hearing.

The state of Washington hired WSU Professor Robert Wielgus, a nationally recognized wildlife researcher who was an expert on bears and mountain lions, to calculate a population model for Washington State's wolf-recovery plan. Wolves had been reintroduced in 1995 and were thriving, but ranchers were concerned about attacks on their cows and sheep.

The agency was pleased with Wielgus's research, and he was selected to oversee a multimillion-dollar research project. The state legislature funded it for at least four years, and the project would attempt to understand and solve the alleged wolf-predation problem.

Within a few years, Wielgus became one of the nation's premier experts on the predatory behavior of wolves in cattle country. His research found that killing wolves actually led to more cattle and sheep deaths, not less, because it destabilized the structure of wolf packs and produced more mating and offspring the following year.

These findings angered the ranchers, because they wanted permission to kill more wolves. They were so angry, in fact, that they persuaded Washington State lawmakers to cut Wielgus's funding and remove him as head of the wolf program. State lawmakers also secretly threatened to cut funding for WSU's new medical school in Spokane — the same medical school named after former president Elson Floyd, the guy who covered up the tainted audit of me.

So what did WSU administrators do?

You guessed it.

They refused to defend Wielgus's free speech rights and even issued news releases falsely accusing him of wrongdoing. Here's an example of one published in the August 31, 1996, issue of the WSU *Daily Evergreen* newspaper.

> WSU released a statement on Wednesday disavowing comments made by a WSU researcher regarding the killings of wolves ... , publicly accusing him of "inaccurate and inappropriate" statements.[2]

But wolf dung hit the fan when *The Seattle Times* obtained e-mails which confirmed that WSU administrators were trying to squelch Wielgus in order to obtain funding for the medical school.[3]

"Highly ranked senators have said that the medical school and wolves are linked," Dan Coyne, a lobbyist for WSU, wrote to a colleague in one of those e-mails. If the controversy isn't resolved, "there won't be a new medical school." His colleague and a WSU official also confirmed that the med school would not be funded.

Wielgus told the *New York Times* that university administrators made his life miserable.[4] As they did with me, they sent Wielgus dereliction of duty notices. Administrators also falsely accused Wielgus of fiscal misappropriation, illegal use of state resources, illegal political lobbying, and scientific misconduct, according to Change.org.[5]

Wielgus also told the *Times* that, at one point, Ron Mittelhammer, who was dean of the College of Agriculture at the time, ordered him not to speak to the public about wolves without coordinating with the university — a prior restraint action that, if true, clearly violated the ruling in *Demers v. Austin.*

Even WSU President Kirk Schulz failed to stop the assault on Wielgus's free speech rights. At one point, Schulz informed Mittelhammer that he was concerned WSU might be branded with an "anti-ranching sentiment." In an e-mail to Mittelhammer, Schulz said, "I feel that they (ranchers) need an internal champion or person that they can work with."[6]

Fortunately, Wielgus filed a free speech lawsuit early in 2018. The Public Employees for Environmental Responsibility helped defend him.

"Most people believe academic freedom exists, particularly for tenured professors," said Jeff Ruch, executive director of PEER. "But PEER is here to tell you that is not the case if there is any pushback. ... Rob published in very prestigious journals. You would think they (WSU officials) would be proud of him and have his back. Instead they had a knife in his back."

In a prepared statement, Wielgus lamented the closing of his world-famous laboratory at WSU. "This comes after years of political pressure from ranching interests and political interference by high-ranking state politicians."

In May 2018, WSU agreed to pay Wielgus $300,000 to drop the lawsuit. As part of the settlement, he resigned from his position at the university. But it should have been the other way around. Some administrators should have resigned. But none were ever publicly disciplined.

OKAY, CROZIER won this one. But bureaucracies, I still assert, are capable of correcting their problems. They just need two things.

First, they need to understand a basic proposition of human behavior: The greater the funding or resources involved, the greater the probability of bad behavior. Bureaucracies are more likely to lose their moral legs when the stakes are high. This proposition is not unique to bureaucracies. In fact, it's the logic behind the often-cited phrase, "Everyone has a price."

Second, to correct bad behavior, bureaucracies need to dole out consequences. You don't need a Ph.D. to figure this one out.

Talk to a parent who has read the social science literature on parenting.

You make it well-known to your children (everyone in the organization) that if they engage in illegal or unethical behavior, they will be given a time-out (or jail time, a pink slip, a demotion, or loss of wages and benefits).

If you don't create consequences for bad behavior, you are going to continue to get bad behavior. And anti-free speech behavior is the kind that can be deterred, because it is highly instrumental in nature, meaning offenders have lots of time to think about the consequences of what they are doing. They aren't doing it in the heat of passion.

To the best of my knowledge, no administrator involved in my dispute was ever given a time-out for engaging in bad behavior. Would discipline have reduced the chances that two years later the university would become another case history supporting Crozier's theory?

We'll never know.

To the best of my knowledge, the university never punished any administrators in the Wielgus case.

Okay, put on your theory caps.

If WSU has another *Demers* or *Wielgus*, what do you think will be the chances that it will engage in bad behavior again?

Good answer.

So the first and second lessons about bureaucracies that I want to hammer home in this chapter are:

1. If there are no consequences for bad behavior, bureaucratic actors will keep engaging in that behavior.

2. Never overestimate the moral principles of adversaries when they have something big to gain or lose. Money and economic resources are powerful mechanisms for co-opting bureaucracies as well as individuals.

And here are 38 additional lessons I've learned through my experiences as a journalist, market researcher and professor, grouped under six headings: Bureaucracies, Principles, Activism, Social Control and Social Change, Journalism, and Democracy and The Enlightenment.

BUREAUCRACIES

3. Bureaucracies tend to be more concerned about social control than moral principles. That's partly because conflict threatens administrators' job security.

4. Public bureaucracies have a great deal of power and, thus, are able to insulate themselves from public accountability.

5. When administrators cede control of a legal matter to attorneys or outsiders, they risk losing control over the moral issues in a dispute. Bureaucracies are more susceptible to this problem because multiple actors often fail to communicate with each other.

6. Although bureaucracies require cooperation and consensus from their members to achieve their goals, bureaucracies also contain more competition and conflict than their smaller counterparts (entrepreneurial organizations), because of the Quadratic Theory of Social Conflict (see Chapter 30).

7. When confronted with inconsistent behavior or illogical actions, bureaucratic elites rarely correct such problems. Even in the face of hard facts, elites in bureaucracies will actively work to marginalize those who draw attention to their shortcomings.

8. Larger bureaucracies, as a rule, tolerate conflict and disagreements more than their smaller counterparts, partly because they have more formal mechanisms (e.g., grievance boards) for controlling such conflict. But even big universities lack proper appeals processes to eliminate such conflict.

Principles

9. Principles fortify you, intellectually and emotionally.
10. Idealism changes the world. Realism maintains it.
11. Idealism is a necessarily but not sufficient element of guided change.
12. The vast majority of people are realists. Make friends with idealists.
13. Loyalty trumps principles, especially when principles and codes of ethics are weak or nonexistent.
14. Complacency breeds regrets. Get off the sidelines when an important principle or idea is on the line.
15. Always give the accused a chance to respond before issuing charges. Your reputation depends upon it.
16. Elites in bureaucratic organizations often use rules to punish recalcitrant members, but elites often break the rules when it suits their interests. They are able to do this because there are few options, other than a lawsuit, for holding them accountable.
17. People seek security (or stability and predictability) in their lives more than freedom. Money and climbing the social ladder mean more to most people than acting ethically or doing the right thing. The former are visible signs of success. The latter are not.

Activism

18. "Throw stones" at powerful institutions when they hurt people or deny them rights. Do the right thing.
19. When you seek to change the world, expect to be misinterpreted. People are suspicious and often envious of people who have good motives.
20. If you want to fight for your principles, be prepared to lose almost everything except your dignity.
21. Never assume leaders or followers in American organizations embrace civil liberties like freedom of expression, due process, democracy and individualism. Pay attention to their actions, not their words.
22. Never assume your organizational colleagues, friends or even relatives will support you in a dispute over civil liberties or some other issue. Most are more concerned about themselves than the abstract principles you champion.
23. Success is not a necessary condition for learning.

24. As Machiavelli pointed out, no amount of kindness can appease your adversaries. But don't be unkind. Don't turn into your adversary.

25. Remember, elites prefer to control you with fear, not love. Never assume an adversary loves you.

26. People who are actively involved in principled disputes with bureaucracies often see their plight as an important matter to everyone else. But others do not, even when the issue personally or professionally affects them.

27. Pick and choose your battles — ones with a principle worth defending.

28. Do not blame others who do not support you in a principled cause. There are many motivations for not joining a cause. But do not praise their behavior. Tyrants love people who stand on the sidelines.

29. If you find yourself in a jam, hire an attorney as soon as possible. They can help you navigate administrative and legal matters.

SOCIAL CONTROL AND SOCIAL CHANGE

30. Competition and conflict are more likely to produce meaningful social change than cooperation and consensus.

31. Social control and security are almost always more important to administrators than civil liberties and freedom.

32. Institutions that value competition and conflict are better equipped to adapt to a changing world.

JOURNALISM

33. Do not trust news organizations to champion your cause, because they tend to identify with powerful elites and institutions. But be honest with journalists, as they can be more effective than depositions in finding the truth.

34. The perceived credibility of news sources and their ties to community organizations play a powerful role in shaping what and how news is covered.

35. The greater the power of a news source, the greater the probability of getting news coverage and, in general, the more favorable news coverage.

36. Don't wait for news organizations to cover your activism and frame your case. Create and distribute your own messages.

DEMOCRACY AND THE ENLIGHTENMENT

37. Despite the concept of shared governance, decision-making at universities does not depend solely or principally on democratic processes. University bureaucracies are far more autocratic than democratic.

38. Conservatism represents the biggest threat to liberty and Enlightenment ideals. That's because conservatives value traditionalism over reason and because conservatism reinforces the ideology of American business.

39. People who have a strong need for personal security have less commitment to Enlightenment ideals such as liberty and individual freedom. The need for personal security increases as people get married, have children, go into debt, and climb the social and economic ladders.

40. The Enlightenment is an unfinished project. The essay in the appendix explores this lesson in depth.

EIGHT YEARS HAVE PASSED since the Ninth Circuit handed down its landmark decision in *Demers v. Austin*. A lot has changed at WSU and in my life.

As I recommended in the 7-Step Plan, the Murrow College eliminated the communication studies sequence — a program that consumed a fourth of the entire college's budget for just 5 percent of the majors. All seven communication studies faculty took jobs at other universities or have left the college. The two programs that remain are Journalism & Media Production and Strategic Communication.

The college also employs twice as many faculty (about 50) as when it was a school, and the number of staff is about ten times bigger. However, the mass communication programs still are not nationally accredited, which was the single most important recommendation of the 7-Step Plan.

WSU president Elson Floyd died of cancer in 2015.

Provost Warwick Bayly stepped down from his administrative position in 2013 and continues to teach and conduct research in the College of Veterinary Medicine.

Vice Provost Francis McSweeney retired in 2017.

Dean Erich Lear died of cancer in 2015.

Erica Austin continues to teach and conduct research in the Murrow program.

Lawrence Pintak's contract as dean was not renewed, but he remains on the faculty of the Murrow College.

Many people think I hold ill will toward these individuals, who were my adversaries at WSU.

Not true.

My wrath is directed instead at the bureaucracy in which they worked — a system that allowed and even encouraged unethical and inappropriate behavior. It failed to (1) protect the free speech rights of faculty; (2) reward faculty who defended free speech and other Enlightenment ideals; (3) provide an independent administrative appeals mechanism for aggrieved employees; (4) place a higher value on principles than resources; (5) employ democratic processes in hiring and termination decisions; and (6) be accountable to employees and taxpayers.

The structure of social systems has a tremendous influence over the choices and decisions that individual social actors make. There is no question in my mind that had WSU's bureaucracy accommodated the suggestions above, especially an independent appeals process, there would never have been a *Demers v. Austin*.

Structure matters.

And if American institutions don't do more to defend and promote Enlightenment ideals through structural change, then the American dream will die (see essay on page 393).

MY DAUGHTER, LEE ANN, graduated valedictorian of her high school class of 304. She received a full ride scholarship from the University of Arizona and earned her bachelor's degree in spring 2021, one year early, with a degree in statistics and sociology. I am so proud of her.

Theresa returned to Washington State to be closer to her family. She continues to work in an institution that helps severely mentally ill patients. She is very kind and loving to the residents.

Our dog Homer (a gray, white and black Maltese mix) has acclimated well to life in the desert. Lots of dogs to bark at and things to sniff.

Judy Endejan, my attorney, opened up her own law practice in Mukilteo, Washington (near Seattle).

In October 2017, I presented in Dallas a paper summarizing my legal case to participants at the first annual convention of the Foundation for Individual Rights in Education, which funded my trip.[7] I met a half-dozen other faculty who had been targeted by their universities. I appreciated the support FIRE has given me over the years.

I've been fixing up my Phoenix house for several years now. The work never ends, but I enjoy it. Marquette Books is still plugging along. A couple of its textbooks are still selling, and I've added a several biographies and a business book. I ghostwrote a couple of books for a real estate executive who helps others become financially independent.

Several years ago I began writing a dystopian novel that carries on the Enlightenment theme to young people. My goal is to prevent reactionary political groups from degrading civil liberties and free speech in America.

I still believe one person can make a difference.

Quixotic, I know.

Chapter 50 Endnotes

1. Michel Crozier, *The Bureaucratic Phenomenon* (Chicago: The University of Chicago Press, 1964), p. 187.

2. Jack Pappin and Cody Cottier, "WSU Disavows Researcher's Comments on Wolf Killings," *The Daily Evergreen* (August 31, 2016), retrieved November 19, 2020, from <https://dailyevergreen.com/7566/news/wsu-disavows-researchers-comments-on-wolf-killings>.

3. Lynda V. Mapes, "A WSU Wolf Researcher Takes the Payment to Go Away in the Settlement of a Lawsuit over Academic Freedom," *The Seattle Times* (May 14, 2018), retrieved November 19, 2020, from <https://www.seattletimes.com/seattle-news/wolf-researcher-gets-300000-to-settle-wsu-lawsuit>.

4. Christopher Solomon, "Who's Afraid of the Big Bad Wolf Scientist?" *The New York Times* (July 5, 2018), retrieved November 19, 2018, from <https://www.nytimes.com/2018/07/05/magazine/whos-afraid-of-the-big-bad-wolf-scientist.html?auth=login-email&login=email>.

5. "The Public Requests WSU Reinstate Dr. Robert Wielgus 100%," Change.org (undated), retrieved November 21, 2020, from <https://www.change.org/p/governor-inslee-the-public-request-you-reinstate-dr-robert-wielgus-to-100>.

6. Lynda V. Mapes, "A War Over Words: Outspoken Researcher Says His University and Lawmakers Silenced and Punished Him," *The Seattle Times* (August 10, 2017), retrieved November 26, 2020, from <https://projects.seattletimes.com/2017/wsu-wolf-researcher-wielgus>.

7. David Demers, "The Enemy Within: Why Faculty Themselves Are Often the Greatest Threat to Academic Freedom," unpublished paper presented to the 2017 annual convention of the Foundation for Individual Rights in Education (October 5-8, 2017). A free copy is available at <www.marquettebooks.com/firepaper.html>.

Appendix
Essay: Future of the Enlightenment in America

The Ninth Circuit ruling in *Demers v. Austin* is one step forward for the Enlightenment, as it transfers a small bit of power from administrators to faculty in nine Western states, who now have constitutional protection for out-of-classroom speech on issues of public concern related to scholarship or teaching.

The ruling joins a much larger body of evidence that Harvard University psychology professor Steven Pinker has compiled in his 2018 book, *Enlightenment Now*. He argues that Enlightenment ideals have led to scientific and humanistic advances that have dramatically improved the human condition.

> The story of human progress is truly heroic. It is glorious. It is uplifting. It is even, I daresay, spiritual. ... We live longer, suffer less, learn more, get smarter, and enjoy more small pleasures and rich experiences. Fewer of us are killed, assaulted, enslaved, oppressed, or exploited by the others. From a few oases, the territories with peace and prosperity are growing, and could someday encompass the globe. Much suffering remains, and tremendous peril. But ideas on how to reduce them have been voiced, and an infinite number of others are yet to be conceived.[1]

To be sure, dramatic strides have been made in the medical and natural sciences. Many diseases and ailments have been cured or ameliorated. Technology and inventions have increased the efficiency of production and eased the labor burdens of everyday life. The civil rights movement also has had many successes since the 1960s, as the Rev. Jesse Jackson pointed out in Chapter 24. The women's movement, too, has scored many legislative and legal victories, and the U.S. Supreme Court declared that the 14th Amendment protects same-sex marriage.[2]

Some scholars believe Pinker's optimism is overstated, however.

They point out that progress also is harming personal relationships.

"The very same economic and social forces (such as a global free market) that have fueled the progress that Pinker charts have also made it harder to maintain a network of local attachments," writes Alison Gopnik, a professor of psychology and philosophy at the University of California at Berkeley. She adds:

> Pinker's book doesn't include one notably pessimistic set of graphs: those that chart the signs that local relationships are threatened — even the most-basic relationships, between partners and between parents and children. Since 1960, the marriage rate in the U.S. has declined substantially, particularly for lower-income and less-educated people, and the proportion of single-parent families among American households has risen. Meanwhile, the child poverty rate has remained high. And public-support systems for families, such as paid parental leave and universal subsidized child care, hardly exist in the U.S.[3]

Gopnik's argument that relationships are threatened is not new.

Even French Enlightenment philosopher Jean-Jacques Rousseau worried about the moral decay that accompanied reason, science and progress.[4] A century after Rousseau's death, French sociologist Émile Durkheim called this phenomenon "anomie" — a breakdown of moral values, standards, or guidance for individuals (sometimes called normlessness). Social change puts rules in flux and leads some people to feel disconnected from others and the community.

Enlightenment proponents like Pinker could counter that anomie is not an insurmountable problem. In fact, the social sciences emerged in large measure to find solutions to social problems like anomie, poverty and crime (see Chapter 9). Although the social sciences haven't always produced solutions, they have generated a lot of knowledge that is useful to the public policymaking process.

Yet, for this argument to work, Pinker and other optimists must show that social scientific research is actually having an impact on public policy — a questionable assumption.

In my 2011 book, *The Ivory Tower of Babel*, I document in extensive detail, drawing upon scores of studies and anecdotes from the middle of the twentieth century to the present,[5] that the social sciences have had relatively little impact on the public policymaking process. Party ideology and personal and special interests, not scientific knowledge, are the key drivers of policymaking. This generalization can even be extended to the natural and medical sciences when conservative political extremism takes center stage, as it did during the Donald Trump administration, when opposition to masking, social distancing and vaccination reached epidemic levels.[6]

Fans of the Enlightenment recognize that reform has its ups and downs. Even Pinker admits that the second decade of the 21st century "has seen the rise of political movements that depict their countries as being pulled into a hellish dystopia by malign factions that can be resisted only by a strong leader who wrenches the country backward to make it 'great again.'"[7]

Yet, even without despotic leaders, it's difficult to be overly optimistic when the poor and working and middle classes have seen virtually no gains in terms of political power and economic wealth in more than a half century. In fact, wealth is more highly concentrated in America today than at any time in its history.[8]

Pinker acknowledges that economic inequality is growing, but he justifies the trend, saying it's the price of economic growth. Many scholars would beg to differ, as wealth has always had a friend in laws and rules that tilt the playing field toward the elites who control legislative, judicial and administrative systems. This inequity can be illustrated with three of the most important contributors to economic inequality: heredity, the ratio of capital returns to economic growth, and education.

More than half of all wealth in America is inherited, according to economists.[9] In this respect, America might be better conceptualized as an advanced stage of feudalism, when birthright determined everyone's social and economic prospects. Of course, this form of economic inequality cannot be ameliorated without eliminating some of the privileges of birth, but to date conservatives have successfully prevented the introduction of social reforms that would produce any meaningful effects.

The second factor affecting inequality is the ratio of returns on capital to the rate of economic growth. When returns outpace growth, inequality is the result, according to French economist Thomas Piketty. But this relationship, just like birthright, is not a law of nature. Legislative policies and actions play a big role in the returns/growth equation. As Piketty puts it: "The resurgence of inequality after 1980 is due largely to the political shifts of the past several decades, especially in regard to taxation and finance. The history of inequality is shaped by the way economic, social, and political actors view what is just and what is not, as well as by the relative power of those actors and the collective choices that result."[10]

The third factor influencing economic inequality is access to education, which provides people with the resources they need to climb the economic ladder. But, as discussed in Chapter 3, the higher education system in America does not operate on a level playing field. Students from privileged socioeconomic backgrounds still have a much higher probability of attending more elite educational institutions, while students from less privileged backgrounds have a much higher probability of attending community colleges and smaller public baccalaureate institutions.

Increasing inequality is a significant social problem because it promotes political polarization and social unrest. Economist and *New York Times* columnist Paul

Krugman observes that "the basic story of political polarization over the past few decades is that, as a wealthy minority has pulled away economically from the rest of the country, it has pulled one major party along with it. ... Any policy that benefits lower- and middle-income Americans at the expense of the elite — like health reform, which guarantees insurance to all and pays for that guarantee in part with taxes on higher incomes — will face bitter Republican opposition."[11]

The irony is many ordinary citizens, who are most adversely affected by income inequality, also support conservative economic policies. To them, inequality stems not from lower tax rates or tax cuts for the wealthy but from open immigration policies, lazy or irresponsible people, and socialism. The Republican leadership also has been able to successfully convince its followers, without evidence, that election fraud was widespread in 2020.

But even with universal access to voting, ordinary citizens would continue to have relatively little political power. Voters in local, state and national elections select representatives only once every two, four or six years, and occasionally cast ballots on local or state referenda. Political leaders hold the power, and scientific research shows that they act largely on behalf of their corporate and wealthy campaign contributors,[12] enacting policies and laws that often contradict the will of the people, who want but have been unable to obtain reasonable gun control legislation, universal health care, and higher minimum wages.

Civil liberties and due process also are virtually nonexistent for people who work in the private sector and very highly circumscribed even for tenured faculty at public universities. The courts, more often than not, protect and extend the power of bureaucratic institutions and corporations over the individual, as University of Berkeley Law School Dean Erwin Chemerinsky has documented.[13]

These findings are old news to social scientists and to those who study the Enlightenment, the Bill of Rights and the American political system.

But they are far from obvious to many Americans.

Many, if not most, have never questioned or examined why American institutions and their leaders have not done more to protect and expand democracy, due process, freedom of expression, economic equity, and other rights and liberties. They live their lives in the dull compulsion of economic relationships (see Chapter 7).

If ordinary Americans had time to study these matters, they would learn that, throughout American history, political and economic elites generally have opposed extending civil liberties and power to subordinates and to the public at large[14] — and those elites have not hesitated to suspend such rights when violence breaks out or when they feel their power has been threatened.[15] Take, for instance, President Abraham Lincoln's decision during the Civil War to suspend the writ of habeas corpus, which meant the militia could arrest and detain civilians indefinitely, without trial. More than 13,000 civilians were denied access to the courts.[16] McCarthyism and the Patriot Act also trod on the civil liberties of some innocent Americans and groups.[17]

The historical evidence also shows that violence or threats of terrorism are not necessary conditions for suspending civil liberties. Donald Trump's decision to forcibly clear peaceful protestors from the Capitol for a photo-op at a church showed contempt for the rule of law and the rights to free speech and assembly.[18]

Managers and administrators of many American institutions often talk about the importance of freedom of expression, due process, democracy, accountability, objectivity, equality and individualism, as these ideals can be used to justify hierarchical power relationships. But they frequently fail to practice what they preach.[19] This proposition applies not just to private business or nonprofit organizations (which of course are under no legal obligation to comply with many of these ideals), but to universities, journalism organizations, governments and the courts as well — institutions that historically have been expected to embrace and protect those liberties. As I reported earlier in this book:

- despite well-articulated codes of ethics, many journalists or journalism organizations ignore (i.e., self-censor) stories or commentaries that would harm their publishers' interests or subject their newspaper to public criticism;
- police routinely deny access to or make it difficult for citizens to inspect public records;
- some state supreme courts (e.g., Minnesota) have carved out special legal protections that make police less accountable to the public than citizens themselves;
- governments and politicians often refuse to take action against powerful community leaders and developers, even when they deliberately violate laws and rules;
- university administrators, to avoid being accountable, often refuse requests from aggrieved faculty to record meetings and hide the results of settlement offers from public view, even though the public often foots the bill;
- and the courts often give government leaders immunity from damages, even when they do wrong, and have extended to them an overwhelming amount of power to terminate employees, even at institutions whose rules embrace academic freedom and due process.

The lack of commitment to Enlightenment ideals is particularly evident in the declining support for journalism programs at major universities. A healthy press is central to the Enlightenment project, and a healthy press needs the support of institutions of higher learning to provide highly qualified reporters and experts in mass communication theory and philosophy.

Yet administrators at a growing number of universities over the past five decades have declared that journalism is not central to the mission of their institutions. They have eliminated or curtailed many of those programs and replaced seasoned journalism instructors with doctoral graduates who often have little or no professional experience. At Columbia University, for example, the only Ivy League school with a journalism program, administrators announced in 2015 that it was cutting a half-dozen faculty positions and student enrollment, too.[20]

The number of journalism programs at U.S. universities peaked at 491 in 2011 and dropped to 427 by 2018. That's a 13 percent drop in seven years.[21] That drop may not sound like much, but some of the discontinued or downsized programs had been operating at some of the most prestigious universities in the country — programs that have served as models for other institutions of higher learning. They include the University of Michigan, The Ohio State University, the University of Washington, the University of Colorado and Emory University.

Nearly one in ten universities with journalism and mass communication programs are considering merging their schools with other departments. Mergers almost always lead to less prominence and financial commitment for programs.

The transition from the green eyeshades to the chi-squares was documented in Chapter 15. I am not arguing here that scholarly research is unimportant to journalism education or to the public policymaking process. A good journalism and mass communication program needs a balance of both professional and theoretical training as well as scholarly research.

But the pendulum at many universities continues to swing toward scholarization at the expense of fundamentals in reporting and editing and a supporting curriculum in the liberal arts, which provide the best training for a journalist. These changes harm the Enlightenment project.

Some critics might argue that the decline in daily metro newspaper journalism is responsible for the declines in journalism and mass communication programs. But this proposition fails to take into account that specialized knowledge has grown rapidly and it, too, depends heavily upon professionals who are skilled in journalism and digital reporting techniques. Organizational structures may change, but the demand for political, economic and social news and information increases, not decreases, as social systems differentiate and become more politically, socially and economically complex.[22]

University administrators are monetizing their institutions, which means downsizing or eliminating non-profit-generating units that historically have played key roles in defending and promoting Enlightenment ideals. The most vulnerable disciplines are housed in the humanities, social sciences, and the library sciences. This includes journalism, English, history, philosophy, sociology and foreign languages. Enrollments, degrees, and number of faculty and programs have declined in either actual or relative terms or both over the past two or three decades.[23]

Anti-Enlightenment movements have been surging in America since the 1980s, primarily because of the growth of conservative political movements. In the 1980s and 1990s, conservatives placed a high priority on stacking federal and state courts with their own, taking a long-term view. They blocked President Barack Obama's appointments to the judiciary and approved Trump's appointments in record number. Trump alone has appointed more than one-third of all federal judges. And these anti-Enlightenment trends are not going away just because Trump lost the 2020 election, as the January 6, 2021, insurrection in the Capitol demonstrated.

Power flows down and wealth flows up.

That is the political and economic history of America since the 1950s.[24]

SO IF CIVIL LIBERTIES and other Enlightenment ideals are not very important to many administrators and managers of American institutions, then what is?

Social control and personal security.

Conservatives have expropriated the Black Lives Matter and #MeToo movements for their own gain, warning citizens that chaos and violence is just around the corner. And it appears this exaggerated law-and-order campaign played a major role in securing votes in the 2020 election, despite Trump's loss.

Top managers of private and public bureaucratic organizations also believe the goals of their organization, as well as their own personal goals, cannot be achieved without significant control over subordinates or the public. In fact, Robert J. Bies and Thomas M. Tripp, two organizational theorists, point out that defenders of centralized power in organizations believe that even though punishments of underlings "may be harsh or even cruel, they are absolutely necessary and essential for creating high-performance organizations. In other words, the survival of the organization demands tyranny!"[25]

Giving underlings or the public too much authority is perceived as a threat to elite rule, rather than as a mechanism for empowering individual rights and for generating ideas that can help organizations and society achieve their goals and adapt to change. Decentralizing power within organizations also is seen as inefficient and, thus, as a threat to accomplishing organizational goals.

Possibly even more important to managers and administrators than social order is personal security. Many are focused on climbing the social ladder or protecting their current jobs or positions. They value money and power far more than freedom of speech or standing up for others in the organization who are being unfairly targeted for retribution.

Personal security also is important to underlings. This means it is relatively easy for organizations to co-opt subordinates. Financial and status rewards usually are highly effective in regulating individual behavior. Reprimands or termination are only used as last resorts.

As subordinates climb the organizational ladder, so does their expected commitment to organizational values. Although they often think they have more freedom as they are promoted, the reverse is often true (see Chapter 17). The expected commitment to organizational values ensnares them even more. They have less freedom and it becomes more and more difficult to separate the organization man or woman from the individual person.[26] Faculty, for example, are often puzzled by how much their colleagues change when they are promoted into management. Professors who once believed strongly that administrators should protect and extend academic freedom and due process rights quickly fall silent on those issues as more money, status and power narcotize the potential Enlightenment activist in them.

Increased commitment to organizational values explains in part why many individuals abandon some of their principles and beliefs when they are promoted into management. Increased commitment also explains why some administrators can get very angry at subordinates who challenge the status quo. I know this firsthand.

Five major reasons or conditions help explain why organizational elites, politicians, university administrators, and judges resist extending civil liberties and more power or authority to subordinates or the public: (1) political impotence of the social sciences, (2) ideology of American management theory, (3) conservatism, (4) prescriptive bureaucratic control, and (5) insufficient knowledge.

1. Political Impotence of the Social Sciences

The vast majority of social scientists at universities in the United States embrace civil liberties and the Enlightenment project, at least in principle.

Few, however, are doing anything about it.

Most subscribe to the idea that their role in the policymaking arena is to produce knowledge and policymakers, in turn, are supposed to use that knowledge to make better decisions.

But this classic model of policymaking just doesn't work well in the real world.

As I document in great detail in *The Ivory Tower of Babel*, politicians and policymakers place far more importance on ideology than on reason and science when making policy-related decisions.[27]

Many, if not most, policymakers crave power, money and status and seek to do things that will get them promoted or reelected or make them look good in the eyes of their political party peers and voters. Using science to make decisions doesn't always help them achieve those goals.

The structure of American democracy is also partly to blame when it comes to incorporating social scientific research into public policy. As noted in *Ivory Tower*:

> The American political system is based on the idea that the best form of government is one in which different political, social and economic groups and people vie or compete with each other for resources or power. Some of these social actors believe truth and knowledge should play a pivotal role in policymaking. Others disagree. Instead, their mission is to gain advantage for their organizations and themselves, sometimes at any cost. This includes citizens seeking elected office. Without the support of powerful special interest groups, they normally will have a difficult time winning an election.
>
> The American political system is not structured to maximize the use of truth and knowledge in decision making. Instead, as critical scholars have shown quite convincingly, it's structured largely to meet, first, the needs of powerful institutions and elites, and then, second, to serve (sometimes) the interests of other, usually less powerful, groups or individuals.
>
> This does not mean America's political system is wholly hegemonic or repressive. ... Nevertheless, it is difficult to ignore the fact that ideology and self-interest often, if not most of the time, trump knowledge in the public policy arena. And many policymakers will defend this philosophy on moral grounds; after all, that's how a democracy works.[28]

But much of the blame for the impotence of social scientific research falls to the social scientists themselves and to their universities, which have devalued the role of the social scientist as an activist for social justice. Research universities place a much higher value on theoretical than applied social science research, which is undertaken specifically to fix social problems or influence public policy. Few institutions provide significant rewards for such activity. Esoteric peer-reviewed journal articles are valued instead.[29]

There is nothing wrong with rewarding faculty for generating and publishing theoretical knowledge. However, the failure to reward faculty who seek to influence public policy clearly impedes the goal of trying to solve social problems and adversely affects the legitimacy of the social sciences as a whole.[30]

In addition, a decision to not get involved in the policymaking arena is itself a political act that has consequences for civil liberties, as I note in *Ivory Tower*:

> Many [social scientists] believe that if [they] get too involved in the political process, policymakers and the public will perceive their research as biased or subjective. However, humanist scholars are quick to point out — accurately so — that not getting involved in policymaking is, itself, a bias. Lack of involvement means laws and policies will be more likely to be enacted without the benefit of scientific knowledge, and this, in turn, means more support for the status quo and ideologies that support the powerful rather than ordinary citizens.
>
> In other words, a decision to not get involved in the political process is a moral decision, and it has consequences for the distribution of power in a society. Humanists also point out that if a social scientist believes that a particular policy may harm people or the public, then he or she has a moral obligation to fight against that harm. And although mainstream researchers fear that too much involvement in the political arena may delegitimize the social sciences, too little involvement (i.e., failure to fight against a known harm) could have the same outcome.[31]

In short, the failure of social scientists to be more activist is one of the major reasons why social inequities and injustice continue to plague the American social landscape.

2. Ideology of American Management Theory

Management theorists Jerald Greenberg and Russell Cropanzano argue that power or hierarchies of authority in American organizations are justified by a concept known as the "organizational imperative,"[32] which is predicated upon two propositions.

The first: "Whatever is good for the individual can only come from the modern organization."[33] The second: "Therefore, all behavior must enhance the health of such organizations."[34]

From these two propositions the theorists conclude that "the core assumptions of modern management theory are totalitarian."[35]

The adjective "totalitarian" might be a bit too strong.

Some organizations, including employee-owned companies and public universities, give subordinates more authority and autonomy than other organizations. Some scholars also argue that the modern organization is more democratic today than it has ever been. This includes the recent management trend toward holacracy, an organizational structure which transfers some power from a management hierarchy to individuals or teams that execute tasks autonomously, without a micromanaging boss.[36]

But decentralization of power is usually circumscribed and often temporary. Administrators and managers can always eliminate or curtail the conveyed authority, as the suspension of Faculty Senate at Idaho State University showed.

The strong arm of management is most visible when a subordinate offers ideas or engages in behavior that challenges the conventional wisdom or the competency of managers.

The organization, according to American management theory, has the right, even the duty, to punish the subordinate. Punitive action is justified because it is perceived as being part of the natural order of things.[37] This hierarchy of power is enshrined in the popular phrase, "Hey, this isn't a democracy," which managers as well as subordinates vocalize to defend the punishment.

The ideology of American management theory also takes for granted the idea that organizational goals cannot be achieved without a strong hierarchy of authority. A few must lead; the many must follow. This naturalizes power and inhibits criticism of repressive managerial practices.

The *Harvard Law Review* commentary that justified the U.S. Supreme Court decision in *Garcetti v. Ceballos* is a good example of how power is taken for granted. The commentary failed to provide a logical reason for its opposition to the Ninth Circuit Court decision in *Demers v. Austin*. Instead, it simply asserted that the *Demers* ruling "infringes upon institutional autonomy" — a claim which implies that upper management has a natural right to control subordinates.

The ideology of American management theory also includes the idea that the modern private business corporation is the most efficient and effective form of organization ever created and that all organizational forms would benefit if they would adopt its rules and methods. Proponents often argue that universities would benefit if they got rid of tenure and centralized power in a hierarchical management system. "Corporate universities" might very well generate more revenues and profits. But what about the moral and social costs?

The history of the American corporation is rife with examples of organizational misconduct and illegal or immoral actions that have hurt tens of millions of Americans, according to criminologists Marshall B. Clinard and Peter C. Yeager.

> Simultaneously with the rise of the great productive power of the corporations there has evolved an equally great potential for significant social harm. ... The multinationals have often exercised undue political influence. ... They have often significantly changed the earth's ecological environment and balance on a large scale. Their ethics and sense of social responsibility have been seriously questioned. ... The many serious illegal acts knowingly committed by corporations against consumers, their workers, their competitors, and even

against foreign nations often individually involve millions of dollars and collectively total in the billions each year. ... The illegal practices of the large corporations include false advertising claims, price fixing, marketing of untested and unsafe products, pollution of the environment, political bribery, foreign payoffs, disregard of safety regulations in the manufacture of cars and other consumer products, tax evasion, and falsification of records to hide illicit practices.[38]

Business professors Ralph Gomory and Richard Sylla also point out that the history of the American corporation is marked by a shift away from a stakeholder view of corporate interests and purposes to one dominated by profit and shareholder value maximization, and they "strongly question whether this shift has been beneficial to the country as a whole."

> The great American corporations today are doing well for their top managers and shareholders, but this does not mean that they are doing well for the country as a whole. The growing concentration of income and wealth threatens both the long-range productivity of the country, through extensive off-shoring, and its long-range internal stability, through a growing concentration of wealth that carries with it political as well as economic dominance. These issues and what to do about them deserve more thought from the economics profession and, indeed, from all Americans.[39]

Despite these issues and problems, the ideology of American management theory is deeply imbedded in the American business psyche and, as such, represents a formidable obstacle to activists who seek to expand civil liberties in American institutions.

3. Conservatism

The ideology of conservatism reinforces the ideology of American management theory and also represents, in my opinion, the single biggest threat to democracy and the American dream.

Conservatives are far less likely than liberals to embrace democracy and civil liberties. This proposition is supported by poll data,[40] including my own research,[41] which is based on a secondary analysis of 40,000 American adults and 40 different questions.[42] The key finding: *Liberals are 39 percent more likely to embrace civil liberties than conservatives.*

When all of the 40 measures are summed, liberals offered responses in support of civil liberties 61 percent of the time, versus only 44 percent for conservatives.

Graphic 1 - Overall Civil Liberty Index by Political Ideology
(Data from General Social Survey 1972-2006) N=42,096

Liberal	Moderate	Conservative
60.7	49.2	43.7

Self-reported Political Ideology

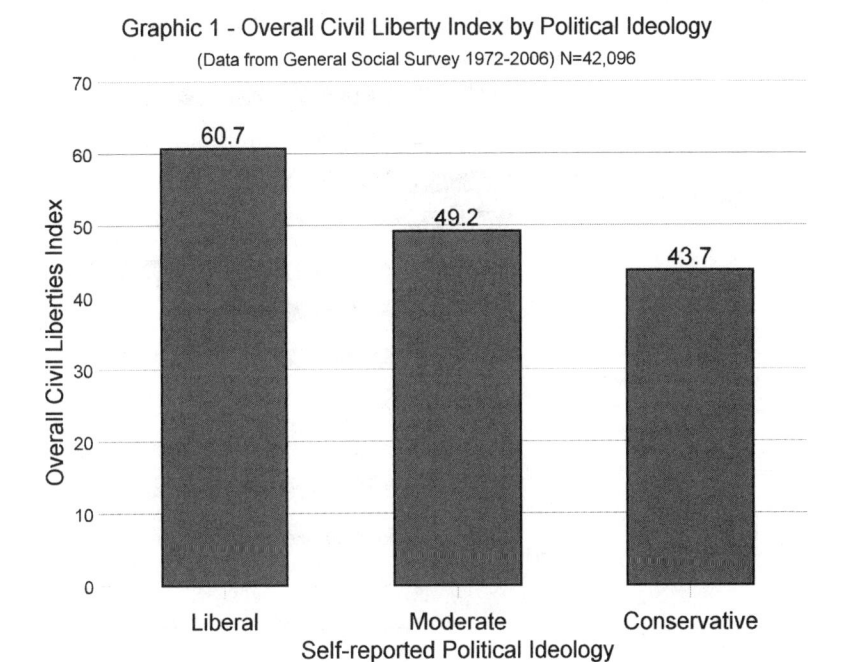

Moderates scored in-between, with 49 percent (see Graphic 1).

The biggest difference between liberals and conservatives emerged on a question that asked respondents how they felt about people protesting government. Fifty-eight percent of liberals said they had favorable or extremely favorable opinions toward protestors, versus 36 percent for conservatives and 46 percent for moderates (see Graphic 2 on next page).

Liberals also were more likely than conservatives to tolerate (a) nonmainstream teachers, such as socialists (60% v. 36%); (b) nonmainstream materials, such as anti-religious publications (75% v. 58%); (c) mass media who publish sensitive government data (44% v. 28%); and (d) nonmainstream speakers, such as homosexuals and communists (75% v. 61%). Liberals also were more intolerant of government surveillance or control of citizens and criminals, albeit the difference was slight (53% v. 46%).

"Whenever conservative elites and liberal ordinary citizens diverge, it is usually the liberal citizens who are more likely to protect individual rights," writes political scientist Paul M. Sniderman and his colleagues. "To give one example: fewer than one in every ten conservative elites believes that refusing to hire a professor because of his unusual political beliefs is unjustifiable; by contrast, one out of every two in the general public who are strong liberals reject such a political test as unjustifiable."[43]

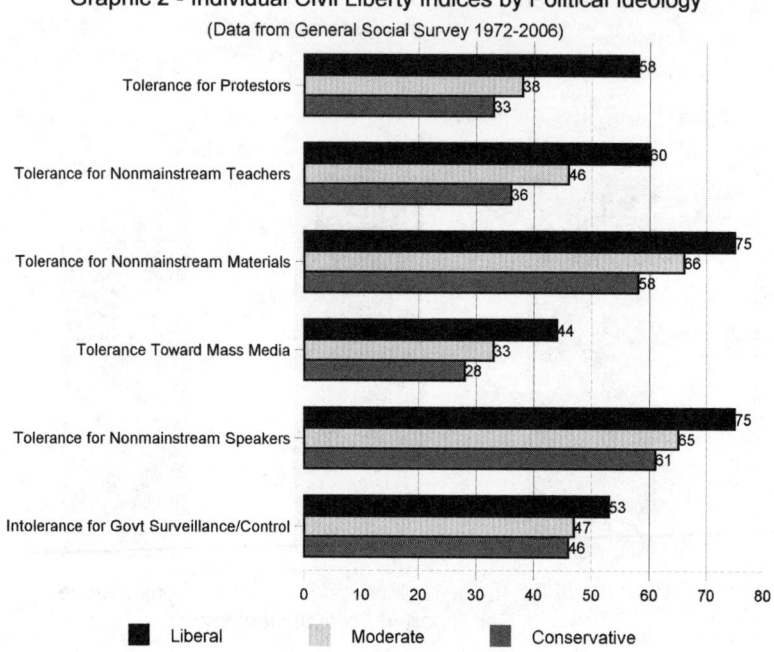

Graphic 2 - Individual Civil Liberty Indices by Political Ideology
(Data from General Social Survey 1972-2006)

Category	Liberal	Moderate	Conservative
Tolerance for Protestors	58	38	33
Tolerance for Nonmainstream Teachers	60	46	36
Tolerance for Nonmainstream Materials	75	66	58
Tolerance Toward Mass Media	44	33	28
Tolerance for Nonmainstream Speakers	75	65	61
Intolerance for Govt Surveillance/Control	53	47	46

Conservatives devalue civil liberties and scientific research because they value tradition and social order over reason and social change. Empowering individuals through civil liberties threatens conservative values and privileges, especially wealth and power, because empowerment enhances the prospects for social change.

One of the most prominent examples is global warming.

None of the Republican candidates running for president in 2016 and 2020 called for legislation to control and limit greenhouse gases that contribute to global warming.[44] They believe any action that threatens the profits and viability of American business must be discarded, even if 97 percent of the world's scientists agree that global warming is primarily caused by industrial pollution.[45]

Progressive social change is unnecessary, according to conservatives, because social problems stem more from a lack of individual initiative than from historical or structural conditions or problems, such as slavery, hereditary privilege, unequal access to education, discrimination and racism.

The conservative motto is "pull yourself up by your bootstraps." That's a lot easier to do when you are born into a family that shops for shoes at Nordstrom's as opposed to one that shops at Walmart.

In many areas of the country, conservatives in government and the judicial system are actively working to curtail civil liberties. The most notable recent example is the attempt in 2021 by Republican state legislators to enact more than 360 laws making it harder for the poor and racial minorities to vote. Conservative politicians and their appointees also tried to eliminate tenure, shared governance and academic freedom at Idaho State University and in the University of Wisconsin system. The U.S. Supreme Court decision in *Garcetti v. Ceballos*, which eliminated the right of most government employees to criticize governmental officials for incompetence or criminal behavior, was crafted by the five conservative members of the court.

Law professor Erwin Chemerinsky even argues that the U.S. Supreme Court historically has been far more likely to uphold government abuses of power than to stop them.[46] He points out that all of the high courts have been deferential to the power structure, but the conservative courts (especially those led by William H. Rehnquist and John G. Roberts Jr.) have done even greater harm to the principles of democracy, equality and freedom.[47]

But even if these attempts to eliminate or curtail civil liberties fail, conservatives are likely to continue to comprise the vast majority of top-level managers in American institutions. That's because American businesses thrive on a conservative political philosophy that uses the concept of a free-market to justify occupational and income differentials between social classes.

The historical seeds of contemporary conservatism were planted by Irish statesman Edmund Burke, who believed that ordinary people want to be ruled and that property ownership serves as the basis for controlling people.[48] Property ownership and class differences are natural, he argued, not the result of power struggles between groups.

Although some conservative libertarian groups claim they embrace civil liberties more than liberals, their philosophies are almost always predicated on the idea that government is the only major organizational entity in society that has the power to limit liberties and social justice.[49] This ignores the fact that large private corporations and businesses also represent a threat to liberty, sometimes even more than government, as the 124-plus deaths caused by General Motors' ignition problems demonstrate.[50] The libertarian philosophy also fails to recognize that government also has played a key role in protecting liberties and social justice.

The history of capitalism in America also demonstrates quite convincingly that the marketplace often is incapable of providing checks and balances that might protect or expand civil liberties. The two most prominent examples are the robber baron era of the late 1800s[51] and the current rapidly widening gap in income between the rich and the poor.[52]

A dedicated proponent of civil liberties sees any large-scale organization as a potential threat to liberty, even though organizational size does not guarantee that threat. Culture also matters. In other words, if those at the top of the organization make a commitment to protect and expand civil liberties and democracy, then the impact of organizational size can be tamed. This is why my research showed that large-scale corporate news media have a greater capacity to enhance the Enlightenment than entrepreneurial media as well as other institutions in general (see next section). Most mainstream journalism organizations have a strong commitment to finding facts and generating truth and knowledge, despite right-wing assertions to the contrary.

4. Prescriptive Bureaucratic Control

In the 1950s, sociologists and social commentators argued that the growth of bureaucratic organizations posed a significant threat to civil liberties, individualism and other ideals of the Enlightenment. This proposition applies to those who work within the organization as well as the public at large.

But bureaucracies are not inherently evil.

They also have the capacity to enhance civil liberties and the Enlightenment. In fact, modern representative democracies in the world today could not exist without bureaucratic organization. Voter registration processes and voting systems, for example, depend upon bureaucratically structured organizations to register voters, create ballots, administer the election and analyze the results.

Political debates and processes also depend upon voices from large-scale public and private bureaucratic organizations, which are engaged in a competitive struggle for limited resources. This struggle can be viewed as part of the democratic process, albeit some critics have argued that federal court rulings giving corporations First Amendment rights when it comes to spending money in election campaigns can produce just the opposite effect.[53]

Outside the government, many bureaucratic institutions also play a supporting role in democracy. News organizations are, of course, the first that come to my mind. They provide information, knowledge and opinions that organizations, elites and ordinary people use to solve problems at work or in life, or to criticize social institutions, including media themselves.

Moreover, news organizations, according to my research, generally do their jobs better as they acquire the characteristics of the corporate or bureaucratic form of organization. In fact, my studies have shown that bureaucratic news organizations produce more content — in absolute as well as relative terms — that is critical of the status quo than their entrepreneurial counterparts.[54] That's because bureaucratic news organizations are themselves products of larger, more complex social systems that have a wider variety of groups competing for limited resources (i.e., more social conflict).

My research also showed that bureaucratic news organizations (1) place more emphasis on product quality, (2) hire more talented reporters and employees, (3) are more likely to launch extensive investigations of incompetent, illegal or unethical activities in society, and (4) place more emphasis on professional codes of ethics. Professional codes also serve as a check, at least to some degree, on greedy owners or publishers.

Universities, as bureaucratic organizations, also produce knowledge — both technical and social — that can help democratically organized systems solve their social problems. Medical research at those institutions has produced pharmaceuticals and medical devices that have saved millions of lives, and social science research has revealed that structural inequalities are detrimental to the goals of democracy, even if political elites often ignore those findings.[55]

Although bureaucracies need compliant workers or members to achieve their goals, they also can tolerate more social conflict than their entrepreneurial counterparts, because social interaction increases at a faster pace as more individuals and groups are added to the organization. In response to the increased conflict, bureaucratic organizations often create more grievance boards and procedures for resolving such conflict.[56] This can be interpreted as enhancing due process and democratic processes, albeit most of the power still rests with management.

Large, bureaucratically structured universities — including the University of Minnesota, the University of Michigan and the University of Oregon — also were the first, after *Garcetti v. Ceballos*, to expand contractual free speech protection to faculty. Administrators at most large universities are more likely than those at smaller schools to recognize the beneficial aspects of giving a wide berth to free expression on campus.

And the courts, despite a spotty record on civil liberties, deserve credit for helping to legitimize the civil rights movement in the 1950s and for extending free speech protection to students and faculty and to student newspapers on campus.

In sum, bureaucratic organizations are not always in opposition to civil liberties.

But they can inhibit civil liberties.

Let's look at some of the ways.

As noted earlier, bureaucracies frequently monopolize information to the detriment of an open society. Police control over crime news is a good example.

Bureaucracies often resist change, especially when the call for action comes from outside sources, such as social movements and activists. The Veteran's Administration history of problems comes to mind here.

Bureaucratic hierarchies increase social distance and reduce understanding between those at the bottom of the hierarchy and those at the top. Each level of management above those at the bottom also reminds those at the bottom of how little power, influence and autonomy they have.

Bureaucracies also can de-skill work and increase feelings of alienation. That's because they are characterized by a complex division of labor and seek to reduce complex jobs into simple discrete tasks that anyone — or a machine — can do.[57]

Of course, as the 1950s-era sociologists argued, bureaucracies need compliant workers to achieve their goals. But compliancy is not unique to bureaucracies. All organizations, even dyads, such as married couples, need individuals who can cooperate to achieve goals.

But bureaucracies differ from other types of organizations in terms of how that cooperation is achieved.

In traditional or small entrepreneurial organizations, social control is achieved mainly through simple rules, often unwritten, that usually prohibit certain kinds of behavior. A married couple, for example, might agree to follow the Ten Commandments. Those rules prohibit, or *proscribe*, certain kinds of behaviors, such as lust or infidelity.

But bureaucracies are characterized by formal, written rules that not only proscribe, but also increasingly *prescribe*. In other words, they not only tell subordinates what they can't do, they also tell them what they must do!

A good example was the Murrow dean's statement at a faculty meeting that all Ph.D. hires henceforth would be required to obtain grant monies to obtain tenure. Grant-getting was now being written right into faculty contracts.

Of course, some tenure-track faculty were upset upon hearing this news. Telling somebody what they must do intrudes on the autonomy of the individual more than telling them what they cannot do. That's because the former requires the individual to act, while the latter does not.

Folks over age 40 remember a time when wearing a seat belt in an automobile was optional. Now every state except New Hampshire requires drivers and passengers to wear seat belts, and all states require them for juveniles. Seat belt laws were created not only to save lives, but also to reduce insurance payouts to accident victims. Insurance companies heavily lobbied state legislatures and the federal government to pass such laws, because it saved them and their investors money.[58]

Yes, the profit motive can lead to positive outcomes for individuals (if you assume, for the moment, that the loss in freedom stemming from mandatory seat belt laws is less important than the reduction in injuries and deaths from accidents).

In recent years, faculty at many universities have complained that administrators have been increasing their workload. I remember a time when staff, not faculty, used to input grades into the university's computer system and when faculty did not have to help raise donations for the university.

In sum, the main reason why bureaucracies represent such a threat to civil liberties and freedom is that they create more rules that prescribe. Bureaucracies are rule-driven — rule crazy, say some sociologists. They constantly attempt to reduce uncertainty and improve efficiency of the organization through the creation of more and more rules.

But, as every sociologist knows, rules often get in the way of the goals of the organization. The increased emphasis on grant-getting at WSU, for example, means that, by default, the institution is devaluing research that seeks to discover and understand political, economic and social inequities in American society, because public and private grant-givers do not give money to professors who strongly criticize their systems of authority.

This, in turn, means another step backward for the Enlightenment.

5. Insufficient Knowledge

Although most Americans have some knowledge of the Bill of Rights and the U.S. Constitution, few have an extensive knowledge of either or their origins.

In the abstract, most Americans embrace freedom of speech, assembly and religion, due process, liberty, individualism, reason and scientific progress. But they often fail to comprehend how organizations in everyday life can deprive them and others of these ideals. They are, in other words, unable to connect their abstract ideas about civil liberties to the real world in which they live.

This lack of awareness is evident in public opinion polls, where many respondents say in response to one question that they support freedom of speech but then, to a separate question, deny the right of a communist or fascist to speak in their community.

Most also are oblivious to the fact that contemporary society subtly controls many aspects of their lives, and some of those controls are malicious.

Do well in school and college, and the system will reward you with a well-paying job. Do well in the job, and your boss will promote you and give you a raise. Serve the bureaucracy well, and when you retire you will have good health insurance and a comfortable income.

But criticize your boss or your governmental organization for unethical or illegal behavior, and all rewards are off the table. You will be fired, and you have no power to stop it.

If you are a tenured professor and work for a university in the West, you have a few more protections under *Demers v. Austin*. The university may have to mob you to get rid of you. And only then — when you are fired or mobbed — do you realize how much power organizations have to control your life.

Although governmental officials, journalists, judges and scholars tend to be more knowledgeable about civil liberties, my experience is that many of them also have problems seeing how the structure of an organization can adversely affect those ideals.

Take, for instance, the lack of an independent appeals process for dealing with errors in annual reviews at WSU. The administrators I dealt with actually believed that they could render objective judgments on errors. They were oblivious to their conflicts of interest. Unfortunately, the lack of a structural mechanism for ensuring due process for annual reviews left me with no other option but a lawsuit, which ended up costing all parties, including taxpayers, more than $1 million.

Outside of the academy, hereditary privilege is another good example of how the structure of society can adversely impact civil liberties. Great inequalities in wealth in America continue to exist in part not because of merit or hard work, but because of pedigree. Children born into wealthy families inherit that wealth, which gives them a big advantage over children born into poor or middle class families.

Despite this unfairness, wealthy elites have been able to restrict passage of estate tax laws that could have helped level the playing field. These elites have successfully justified the inequity by invoking the Fourth Amendment right to property. But this right fails to account for the fact that much, if not most, of accumulated wealth in history stems more from privilege and power struggles than from individual effort.

Learning about the Enlightenment does not guarantee support for free speech rights or civil liberties, of course. Remember the Spokane publisher who declared that his newspaper would refuse to publish letters to the editor written by extreme right-wing groups (see Chapter 28)?

And greater knowledge doesn't mean judges will not hand down rulings opposing civil liberties or that attorneys will not give advice to governmental and university officials on how to restrict those liberties to their subordinates or the public.

But better knowledge and awareness of the Enlightenment, I submit, can help reduce some of the manipulation by special interest groups who are opposed to Enlightenment ideals. A better knowledge of academic freedom and the concept of civility, for example, might have prevented University of Illinois administrators from revoking, after pressure from Jewish donors, a job offer in 2015 to a professor who had posted highly critical comments about Israel.[59]

But the trend in higher education appears to be working in the opposite direction. University administrators are increasingly being drawn not from the ranks of faculty or from the humanities or social sciences, but from the private business sector. Political Scientist Benjamin Ginsberg drew attention to this problem more than a decade ago,[60] and the American Council on Education provided empirical proof: nearly a third of all university presidents have never held a teaching position at a university.[61] A more recent study found that 40 percent of the presidents at public land-grant universities never held a tenured or tenure track position.[62] The upshot is that many university presidents are more focused on raising money than on the needs and concerns of faculty, students and staff.

Of course, some administrators might even argue that the modern university needs to be run like a private corporation — that the Enlightenment is, itself, an anachronism. But English professor emeritus Paul Brians wisely advised his students at Washington State University that the Enlightenment is no less relevant today than it was three centuries ago.

> Today the Enlightenment is often viewed as a historical anomaly, a brief moment when a number of thinkers infatuated with reason vainly supposed that the perfect society could be built on common sense and tolerance. ... Religious thinkers repeatedly proclaim the Enlightenment dead, Marxists denounce it for promoting the ideals and power of the bourgeoisie at the expense of the working classes, postcolonial critics reject its ... notions as universal truths, and poststructuralists reject its entire concept of rational thought.
>
> Yet in many ways, the Enlightenment has never been more alive. The notions of human rights it developed are powerfully attractive to oppressed peoples everywhere, who appeal to the same notion of natural law that so inspired Voltaire and Jefferson. Wherever religious conflicts erupt, mutual religious tolerance is counseled as a solution. Rousseau's notions of self-rule are ideals so universal that the worst tyrant has to disguise his tyrannies by claiming to be acting on their [the public's] behalf. ... If our world seems little closer to perfection than that of 18th-century France, that is partly due to our failure to appreciate gains we take for granted.[63] [bracketed material added for clarity]

PROTECTING AND EXTENDING civil liberties in America, especially democracy and economic equity, will not be easy because of the political impotence of the social sciences, the ideology of American management theory, conservatism, prescriptive bureaucratic controls and insufficient knowledge. But the alternative — social unrest and possibility violence — presents even more problems.

The failure of the courts, government, universities and journalism organizations to more aggressively promote the Enlightenment means the American dream is turning into the American nightmare. Our most treasured institutions have lost their way. To get back on the path to freedom, they should try walking in the shoes of Edward R. Murrow, who represents the quintessential model of the ideal Enlightenment journalist and man (see Chapter 23).

Let there be no mistake: The original dream of America was to decentralize economic and political power, not to concentrate it into the hands of wealthy elites and politicians. It's time for these institutions and government to step up their game. America needs Enlightenment now, not a century from now, and there is no good excuse for not taking action.

When America's founding fathers created the Constitution and Bill of Rights, they didn't argue that the documents should limit the ability of the people to expand democratic rights and other civil liberties. We know this because of two reasons.

First, the founding fathers drew heavily on the writings of Englishman John Locke, Frenchman Voltaire and other philosophers of the Age of Enlightenment, all of whom viewed democracy and freedom as processes, not static states or conditions. Second, the Ninth Amendment to the Bill of Rights itself acknowledges that the Constitution "shall not be construed to deny or disparage [other rights] retained by the people."

So where do we begin?

The first step, I suggest, is to raise awareness of the problem. Change cannot occur if social actors cannot articulate the problem.

High schools need to spend more time teaching students about the origins of the Constitution and Bill of Rights and about the ideas of the Enlightenment philosophers. College students also need to take at least one course that expands upon the content covered in high school courses.

To further increase awareness, civil liberties activists should frame their pro-freedom messages to the public and policymakers in a way that draws more attention to the other four impediments to the Enlightenment mentioned above.

Of these, conservatism should be given the highest priority, for two reasons.

First, news coverage is essential for increasing awareness, and there is a greater chance of getting coverage by focusing on the adverse impact that conservatism has on civil liberties. News media are drawn to controversial political debates, especially those between various political factions or organizations. In contrast, journalists eschew discussions about the impact of management practices or bureaucratic structure because they are too complex.

Second, the fallacious claim that conservative groups are more supportive of civil liberties is masking and hindering efforts to build support for the Enlightenment project. If liberals or independents believe that conservatives control the civil liberties high ground, they may withdraw their activism from that battle, rather than trying to claim the high ground for themselves (which is what they need to do).

Civil liberties activists also need to draw attention to the fact, which is absent in conservative ideological debates, that private businesses and corporations have as much or even more potential as big government to do harm to liberty and freedom. A so-called free market does not necessarily produce a freer people.

Civil liberties and democracy can be protected only if there is a strong cultural commitment to those ideals in society and in its organizations.

In terms of structural political change, the power of the referendum should be extended to the national level. Many states give citizens the right to vote on issues of public concern. Why can't we do the same on a national level? There is no technological or political reason why the power of the referendum cannot be extended to national elections.

An even more radical approach would call for replacing the House of Representatives with the "House of the People," which would allow voters themselves to vote directly on all legislation. The Senate, President and Supreme Court would serve as a checks and balances on the people's house.

Taking action now is especially urgent, because there are no guarantees that the Enlightenment project will survive in a world beset with so many problems.

What will happen to civil liberties, for example, when some of the world's natural resources are exhausted and shortages of goods or services emerge?

What if terrorism or the number of groups whose intent is to kill innocent people continues to grow? Or somebody sets off The Bomb?

Will America and other information-based nations still embrace liberty, freedom, due process and democracy as ideals? Or will they eliminate them in the name of security?

I am not overly optimistic about the future of the Enlightenment project.

But I am not overly pessimistic.

I am sure only of one thing: that the Enlightenment as a guiding philosophy for human rights and dignity will not survive if activists and American institutions stop doing their job.

You, the reader, are free to create your own path, whether you choose to associate with an organization or become, like me, an independent activist.

But if you choose the latter, there is one piece of advice that you must take to heart: You must strongly believe in what you doing. You must have a clear set of principles. You must have them because they will keep you focused on your journey and also will help protect you emotionally from adversaries and regrets.

Be prepared, though, to face a hostile world — a world that has yet to fully embrace activists and the ideals of the Age of Enlightenment.

Appendix Endnotes

1. Steven Pinker, *Enlightenment Now: The Case for Reason, Science, Humanism, and Progress* (New York: Viking, 2018), p. 452-453.

2. *Obergefell v. Hodges,* 576 U.S. 644 (2015).

3. Alison Gopnik, "When Truth and Reason Are No Longer Enough: In His New Book, Steven Pinker Is Curiously Blind to the Power and Benefits of Small-town Values," *The Atlantic* (April 2018), retrieved November 17, 2020, from <https://www.theatlantic.com/magazine/archive/2018/04/steven-pinker-enlightenment-now/554054>.

4. Aaron R. Hanlon, "Steven Pinker's New Book on the Enlightenment Is a Huge Hit. Too Bad It Gets the Enlightenment Wrong," Vox.com (May 17, 2018), retrieved November 17, 2020, from <https://www.vox.com/the-big-idea/2018/5/17/17362548/pinker-enlightenment-now-two-cultures-rationality-war-debate>.

5. David Demers, *The Ivory Tower of Babel: Why the Social Sciences Are Failing to Live Up to Their Promises* (New York: Algora Publishing, 2011).

6. Robert Costa, "'Unjustifiable Hysteria': Republican Recalcitrance about the Virus Persists even as GOP Faces Growing Turmoil," *The Washington Post* (October 6, 2020) retrieved November 21, 2020, from <https://www.washingtonpost.com/politics/trump-coronavrius-republicans-election/2020/10/05/fdc570ea-071a-11eb-a166-dc429b380d10_story.html>.

7. Pinker, *Enlightenment Now*, p. 5.

8. Telford Taylor, "Income Inequality in America Is the Highest It's Been since Census Started Tracking It, Data Shows," *The Washington Post* (September 26, 2019), retrieved March 30, 2021, from <https://www.washingtonpost.com/business/2019/09/26/income-inequality-america-highest-its-been-since-census-started-tracking-it-data-show>, and Thomas Piketty, *Capital in the Twenty-First Century*, translated by Arthur Goldhammer (Cambridge, MA: The Belknap Press of Harvard University Press, 2014).

9. Facundoal Varedo, Bertrand Garbinti and Thomas Piketty, "On the Share of Inheritance in Aggregate Wealth: Europe and the USA, 1900–2010," *Economica*, *84*: 239–260 (2017), retrieved March 3, 2021, from <http://www.piketty.pse.ens.fr/files/AlvaredoGarbintiPiketty2017.pdf>.

10. Piketty, *Capital in the Twenty-First Century*, p. 20.

11. Paul Krugman, "Pollution and Politics," *The New York Times* (November 27, 2014), retrieved April 1, 2021, from <https://www.nytimes.com/2014/11/28/opinion/paul-krugman-pollution-and-politics.html>.

12. C. Wright Mills, *The Power Elite* (New York: Oxford University Press, 1959), and Michael Parenti, *Democracy for the Few* (New York: St. Martin's Press, 1974).

13. Erwin Chemerinsky, *The Case Against the Supreme Court* (New York: Viking, 2014).

14. See, e.g., Mary Beth Norton, David M. Katzman, Paul D. Escott, Howard P. Chudocoff, Thomas G. Paterson, and William M. Tuttle Jr., *A People and a Nation: A History of the United States* (Boston: Houghton Mifflin Company, 1982), and Carl Boggs, *The End of Politics: Corporate Power and the Decline of the Public Sphere* (New York: The Guilford Press, 2000).

15. Michael Feldberg, *The Turbulent Era: Riot and Disorder in Jacksonian America* (New York: Oxford University Press, 1980), pp. 23 and 32.

16. Justin Ewers, "Revoking Civil Liberties: Lincoln's Constitutional Dilemma," *U.S. News & World Report* (February 10, 2009), retrieved March 3, 2015, from <http://www.usnews.com/news/history/articles/2009/02/10/revoking-civil-liberties-lincolns-constitutional-dilemma>.

17. For evidence about the adverse impact of the Patriot Act, see Susan Schmidt, "Patriot Act Misunderstood, Senators Say; Complaints about Civil Liberties Go Beyond Legislation's Reach, Some Insist," *The Washington Post* (October 22, 2003), p. A4, which reports that 200 cities and three states have passed resolutions asserting the Patriot Act tramples on civil liberties.

18. Tom Gjelten, "Peaceful Protesters Tear-Gassed To Clear Way For Trump Church Photo-Op," National Public Radio (June 1, 2020), retrieved April 12, 2021, from

<https://www.npr.org/2020/06/01/867532070/trumps-unannounced-church-visit-angers-church-officials>.

19. Elite Democratic Theory and research shows that political elites embrace civil liberties more than ordinary citizens. But this doesn't mean they practice what they preach. See Paul M. Sniderman, Joseph F. Fletcher, Peter H. Russell and Philip E. Tetlock, *The Clash of Rights: Liberty, Equality, and Legitimacy in Pluralist Democracy* (New Haven, CT: Yale University Press, 1996).

20. John Lauerman, "Columbia Will Shrink Journalism School as Media Woes Mount," *Bloomberg Business* (March 11, 2015), retrieved June 20, 2015, from <www.bloomberg.com/news/articles/2015-03-11/columbia-will-shrink-journalism-school-as-media-woes-mount>.

21. See R. Glenn Cummins, Melissa R. Gotlieb and Bryan McLaughlin, "2018 Survey of Journalism and Mass Communication Enrollments," ASJMC Insights (Columbia, SC: The Association of Schools of Journalism and Mass Communication, 2019), retrieved November 13, 2020, from <http://www.asjmc.org/publications/ insights/autumn2019.pdf>; Lee B. Becker and Gerald M. Kosicki, "1996 Annual Survey of Journalism and Mass Communication Enrollments," The Ohio State University (1998), and Lee B. Becker, Tudor Vlad and Holly Anne Simpson, "2013 Annual Survey of Journalism and Mass Communication Enrollments," James M. Cox Jr. Center for International Mass Communication Training and Research at the Grady College of Journalism & Mass Communication, University of Georgia (2015). The latter reports and others are available online at <http://www.grady.uga.edu/annualsurveys/Enrollment_Survey>.

22. David Demers, *The History and Future of Mass Media: An Integrated Perspective* (Cresskill, NJ: Hampton Press, 2007).

23. Alex Berezow, "Humanities Enrollment Is in Free Fall," *American Council on Science and Health* (July 31, 2018), retrieved October 21, 2020, from <https://www.acsh.org/news/2018/07/31/humanities-enrollment-free-fall-13243>; James S. House, "The Culminating Crisis of American Sociology and Its Role in Social Science and Public Policy: An Autobiographical, Multimethod, Reflexive Perspective," *The Annual Review of Sociology*, 45: 1-26 (2019), retrieved November 2, 2020, from <https://www.annualreviews.org/doi/pdf/10.1146/annurev-soc-073117-041052>; and Andrew Albanese, "Are Public Libraries in Decline? In The Freckle Report 2020, Tim Coates offers a sobering, data-driven view of the state of public libraries in the U.S. and the U.K.," Publishers Weekly (April 3, 2020), retrieved November 2, 2020, from <https://www.publishersweekly.com/pw/by-topic/industry-news/libraries/article/82925-are-public-libraries-in-decline.html>.

24. Mills, *The Power Elite*, and Parenti, *Democracy for the Few*.

25. See Robert J. Bies and Thomas M. Tripp, "Two Faces of the Powerless: Coping with Tyranny in Organizations," pp. 203-220 in Roderick M. Kramer and Margaret A. Neale, *Power and Influence in Organizations* (Thousand Oaks, CA: Sage, 1998), p. 216.

26. This paragraph draws heavily from the work of William G. Scott and David K. Hart, *Organizational Values in America* (New Brunswick, NJ: Transaction Publishers, 1989), see Chapter 5.

27. Demers, *The Ivory Tower of Babel*.

28. Ibid., pp. 232-233.

29. The hard sciences are a different story, whose research is often incorporated into technology or used to improve the quality of products and goods.

30. Demers, *The Ivory Tower of Babel*, p. 230.

31. Ibid.

32. For this content, the author's cite William G. Scott and David K. Hart, *Organizational America: Can Individual Freedom Survive Within the Security It Promises?* (Boston, Houghton

Mifflin, 1979), p. 43.

33. Ibid.

34. Jerald Greenberg and Russell Cropanzano, *Advances in Organizational Justice* (Stanford, CA: Stanford University Press, 2001), p. 111.

35. Ibid.

36. Brian J. Robertson, *Holacracy: The New Management System for a Rapidly Changing World* (New York: Henry Holt and Company, 2015).

37. Critical management studies presents a more formal, more highly critical view of the ideology of American management. For a review of the field, see Paul S. Adler, Linda C. Forbes and Hugh Willmont, "Critical Management Studies: Premises, Practices, Problems and Prospects," pp. 119-180 in J. Walsh and A. Brief (editors), *Academy of Management Annals*, Volume 1 (New York: Routledge, 2008), retrieved June 14, 2015, from <http://www-bcf.usc.edu/~padler/research/CMS- AAM-1.pdf>.

38. Marshall B. Clinard and Peter C. Yeager, *Corporate Crime* (New York: The Free Press, 1980), p. ix.

39. Ralph Gomory and Richard Sylla, "The American Corporation" *Dædalus* (Spring 2013) <https://www.amacad.org/content/publications/pubContent.aspx?d=1053>.

40. Tim Pelzer, "Canada Conservatives Push to Curb Civil Liberties," *People's World* (March 11, 2015), retrieved June 9, 2015, from <http://peoplesworld.org/canada-conservatives-push-to-curb-civil-liberties>; and Sam Reimer and Jerry Z. Park, "Tolerant (In)civility? A Longitudinal Analysis of White Conservative Protestants' Willingness to Grant Civil Liberties," *Journal for the Scientific Study of Religion, 40*(4): 735-745 (December 2001).

41. David Demers, "Liberals Embrace Civil Liberties More than Conservatives," Unpublished Paper (October 10, 2016), retrieved July 21, 2020, from <www.marquettebooks.com/liberties.html>.

42. The findings are derived from national polls conducted in various years from 1972 to 2006 by the National Opinion Research Center at the University of Chicago. My secondary secondary analysis included more than 40,000 respondents interviewed in the General Social Survey. Respondents were asked to indicate on a seven-point scale whether they thought of themselves as a liberal or conservative. Fourteen percent identified themselves as "extremely liberal" or "liberal." Eighteen percent identified themselves as "extremely conservative" or "conservative." The remaining 68 percent — who identified themselves as "moderate" or "slightly liberal" or "slightly conservative" — were classified as moderates.

43. Sniderman, et al., *The Clash of Rights*, p. 47.

44. For the Republican presidential candidate information, see Paul Waldman, "Where the 2016 GOP Contenders Stand on Climate Change," *The Washington Post* (May 12, 2014), retrieved June 11, 2015, from <http://www.washingtonpost.com/blogs/plum-line/wp/2014/05/12/where-the-2016-gop-contenders-stand- on-climate-change>.

45. For documentation, see the National Aeronautics and Space Administration website at <http://climate.nasa.gov/scientific-consensus>.

46. Chemerinsky, *The Case Against the Supreme Court*.

47. Ibid., see Chapters 5-7.

48. Andrew Heywood, *Political Ideologies: An Introduction*, 3rd edition (London: Palgrave Macmillan, 2003), p. 74.

49. A good example of this circumscribed view of liberty and the relationship between social action and social structure is the right-wing Young Americans for Liberty, which argue that "government is the negation of liberty" and "voluntary action is the only ethical behavior." There is no mention of corporate power or the impact that history and social structure have on individual action. Source: <www.yaliberty.org>.

50. Chris Isidore, "Death Toll for GM Ignition Switch: 124," CNN (December 10, 2015), retrieved November 21, 2020, from <https://money.cnn.com/2015/12/10/news/companies/gm-recall-ignition-switch-death-toll/index.html>.

51. Matthew Josephson, *The Robber Barons* (New York: Mariner [Harcourt] Books, 1962; originally published in 1934).

52. Noam Scheiber and Dalia Sussman, "Inequality Troubles Americans Across Party Lines, Times/CBS Poll Finds," *The New York Times* (June 3, 2015), retrieved June 11, 2015, from <http://www.nytimes.com/2015/06/04/business/inequality-a-major-issue-for-americans-times-cbs-poll-finds.html?ref=topics&_r=0>.

53. *Citizens United v. Federal Election Commission*, 558 U.S. 310 (2010). The court held that the First Amendment prohibits the government from restricting independent political expenditures by a nonprofit corporation. The protection has been extended to for-profit corporations as well.

54. See, e.g., David Pearce Demers, *Menace of the Corporate Newspaper: Fact or Fiction?* (Ames: Iowa State University Press, 1996).

55. Demers, *The Ivory Tower of Babel*.

56. This is not to say that every conflict is addressed by a review board. WSU had no formal system of appeals for errors in annual reviews. As such, a lawsuit was my only option.

57. Demers, *History and Future of Mass Media*.

58. See, for example, Press Release, "Senators Warner and Clinton Introduce Legislation to Enact National Primary Enforcement Seat Belt Law: Coalitions of Highway Safety and Medical Groups Lend Support," Advocates for Highway and Auto Safety (December 9, 2003), retrieved June 18, 2015, from <http://www.saferoads.org/national-primary-enforcement-seat-belt-law>.

59. Scott Jaschik, "Out of a Job," *Inside Higher Education* (August 6, 2014), retrieved June 15, 2015, from <https://www.insidehighered.com/news/2014/08/06/u-illinois-apparently-revokes-job-offer-controversial-scholar>.

60. Benjamin Ginsberg, *The Fall of the Faculty: The Rise of the All-Administrative University and Why It Matters* (New York: Oxford University Press, 2011).

61. "Only 16 percent of presidents said their internal constituencies — campus administrators, faculty, staff, students — were the majority of their focus in 2011, a sharp decline from the 59 percent reported in 2006. A growing amount of time is spent with legislators, policymakers, and the university's governing board, presidents reported." Source: Chris Dunker, "University Presidents Coming from a More Diverse Background," *Lincoln Journal Star* (June 15, 2014).

62. Scott C. Beardsley, *Higher Calling: The Rise of Nontraditional Leaders in Academia* (Charlottesville: University of Virginia Press (2017).

63. Paul Brians, "The Enlightenment," Syllabus for Humanities 303 (Spring 2007), retrieved June 15, 2015, from <http://public.wsu.edu/~brians/hum_303/enlightenment.html>.

Acknowledgments

Many friends, relatives, colleagues, and former teachers, students and employers played an active or indirect role in the production of this book. But I, alone, take full responsibility for its contents.

I am most grateful to Lee Ann, my daughter, for her love and support; to Hector, my father, who taught me not to accept authority at face value; to Dick Carson, who nurtured my early career as a newspaper reporter, edited earlier drafts of this manuscript, and taught me that integrity is no less important than the truth; and to Liz Prouty, my book editor, who saved me from many embarrassing blunders and did so with a good sense of humor.

I also thank, in alphabetical order:

- The late Ridge Anderson, my first newspaper editor, who instilled in me an appreciation for politics in small organizations and communities;
- Kristina Bialaszewski, a former undergraduate student at CMU, who dug out the story from Central Michigan University Life on the anti-war protest in 1972;
- The late Hazel Dicken-Garcia, one of the members of my Ph.D. committee, who provided intellectual, emotional and financial support for this project;
- The late Simon Dinitz, one of my criminology professors, who pointed out that failing to solve a problem is far less important than failing to do your best;
- Judy Endejan, my attorney, who believed my free-speech case was worthy of a good fight and showed that it was;
- Igor Klyukanov, my good friend and professor of communication studies at Eastern Washington University, who gave valuable counsel about many of the experiences in this book and shared my belief that protecting civil liberties is a worthy cause;
- Karen Lindholdt, a friend and attorney, who provided advice about how to navigate the law in the real world;

- Paul Lindholdt, a dedicated English professor and friend, who critiqued early drafts of this book;
- The late Richard Lundman, one of my criminology professors, whose enthusiasm for research helped set me on a course of scholarship;
- Sue Nichols, my former undergraduate journalism professor, who edited drafts of this book, taught me how to report and write like a journalist, and infused in me a deep appreciation for the profession of journalism and its ideals;
- Trudy Patterson, for her love and support and for her help in restructuring this book to provide greater clarity to the major issues;
- Mona Pearce, who stood by me during the controversy at the University of Wisconsin–River Falls and continues to be a good friend;
- David Perlmutter, dean of the College of Media & Communication at Texas Tech University, who was the best devil's advocate a writer could have;
- Patrice Peterson, a friend and former student who offered kind words of support at a hearing and edited portions of this manuscript;
- The late Jan Polek, who encouraged me to write this book for policymakers and the public, not just for scholars and students, and steadfastly believed that the pursuit of justice was no less important than justice itself;
- Gary Rhoades, past general secretary of the American Association of University Professors, for listening to my concerns, for promoting the cause of academic freedom, and for writing the insightful foreword to this book;
- Dan Robison, who helped me manage Marquette Books and delivered a good sense of humor through it all;
- John Schulz, former dean of the College of Communication at Boston University, who provided much-appreciated support and advice through the lawsuit years;
- Joseph E. Scott, my criminology master's thesis adviser, who taught me the importance of constitutional law and civil liberties;
- Galina Sinekopova, my dear friend and professor of communication studies at Eastern Washington University, whose honest critiques helped moderate my views of organizations and activism;
- Theresa Stimson, who provided unwavering support and good advice during the ordeal at WSU;
- Alex Tan, my former boss and director of the Edward R. Murrow School of Communication, who supported research projects to educate not just academics but policymakers and the public as well;
- Phillip J. Tichenor, my Ph.D. adviser, an astute observer of social processes who taught me how to think like a sociologist;

- Carolyn Walker, a reviewer for *Writer's Digest*, who critiqued and copyedited an early version of this book;
- Kenneth Westhues, a professor emeritus of sociology at the University of Waterloo, Canada, who provided constructive feedback about the free-speech dispute at Washington State University and often predicted well in advance many of the events that unfolded.

I am indebted to the American Association of University Professors and the Thomas Jefferson Center for the Protection of Free Expression for coauthoring an amici curiae brief, submitted to the Ninth Circuit U.S. Court of Appeals 2012, in support of First Amendment rights for faculty; to the Foundation for Individual Rights in Education (TheFIRE.org) provided news coverage of the lawsuit as well as financial support so that I could attend and present a paper at its convention in Dallas in 2017; to the Frankenmuth James E. Wickson Library, which provided free access to *Frankenmuth News* archives; and to Kevin Anderson & Associates, which edited a portion of this manuscript and offered encouragement.

I also thank the thousands of students who took my classes through the years. I hope they learned as much from me as I from them.

David Demers
May 2021

Index

3rd Faction, 92
60 Minutes, 114-116, 121, 165
7-Step Plan, x, xii, xxiii, 3, 5-8, 252, 254, 255, 259, 262, 266-268, 276, 288, 300, 307, 309, 318, 319, 335-337, 339, 341, 343, 344, 350-352, 358, 362-367, 373, 377, 389

A

ABC, 23, 215
academic freedom, xiii-xviii, xxiii, 2, 16, 33, 34, 37, 72, 231-233, 238, 257, 258, 266, 272, 321, 332, 333, 340-342, 346, 352, 358, 362, 364, 373-382, 385, 391, 397, 400, 407, 412, 421
Accrediting Council on Education in Journalism and Mass Communication (ACEJMC), 23, 24, 41, 111, 113, 196, 356
Ackerman, Kenneth D., 77, 80
Adams, Michael (Mike), xix, xxiii, 241, 244
Age of Enlightenment (see "Enlightenment")
Alexander, Jeffrey, 200, 209
Algora Publishing, 350, 436
Alliance Defense Fund, 341
Allred, Lisa R., 375, 381
American Academy of Political and Social Science, 141
American Association of University Professors (AAUP), i, xii-xvii, 34, 41, 44, 231, 232, 238, 257, 320-334, 340, 349-353, 356, 362, 421-422
American Bar Association (ABA), 42
American Civil Liberties Union (ACLU), 152, 155, 176, 361
American Council on Education, xv, 113, 412
American dream, 390- 404, 413
American University in Cairo, 216, 301
Anderson, Ridge, 97, 98, 420
Anfinson, Mark, 141
applied Enlightenment, 67
Aristotle, 63, 69
Arizona State University (ASU), ii, 12, 172, 198, 355, 356, 359, 363
Associated Press (AP), 9, 16, 61, 70, 78, 82, 96, 97, 102, 108, 114, 120, 123, 127, 128, 148, 151, 153, 168-170, 175, 191-193, 208, 213, 217, 220, 225, 230, 247, 270, 287, 292, 295, 303, 324, 343, 350, 355, 361, 363, 385, 395, 407, 408
Association for Education in Journalism and Mass Communication (AEJMC), 181, 190, 204, 212
Atlanta Constitution, 153
Atlantic, The (formerly *Atlantic Monthly*), 35, 94, 106, 111
Austin, Erica Weintraub, vi, x-xiv, xix-xxi, 5, 6, 99, 135, 190, 197, 231, 243, 244, 249-252, 255, 256, 258, 259, 261-267, 273, 274, 277-283, 286, 287, 291-293, 295-298, 300, 301, 318, 319, 325, 327-330, 335, 350-352, 356, 362-364, 369, 371-377, 379, 383, 384, 389, 390, 393, 403, 411

B

Bagdikian, Ben H., 94, 106, 111, 112
Ball State University, 215
Bartholow, Bruce D., 205
Bates, Robert, 254, 288
Battle of Pine Creek, 171
Battle of Tohotonimme, 171
Battuello, Kathryn M., 5-7, 319, 329, 336, 337, 343
Bavarian Inn, 55, 56
Bayh, Birch, 78
Bayly, Warwick, 286-295, 298, 319, 324, 328, 329, 331, 389
BBC, 180
Becker, Lee B., vii, 117, 215, 398
Bell, Steve, 215
Benson, Renaldo, 85
Berenger, Ralph, 216
Bernstein, Carl, 82, 89, 173
Bies, Robert J., 399
biology, 16, 96, 183, 200
Bird, Donald, vii, 89, 90
Blethen, Frank, 189, 255
Boston University, 215, 421
Brandeis, Louis, 77
Brauer, Carl, 138
Brians, Paul, 247, 413

Bunger v. University of Oklahoma Board of Regents, 346
bureaucracy(ies), i, vi, xiii, xvi, xix-xxii, 33, 49, 58, 91, 100, 126, 137, 149-153, 158, 160, 162-164, 181, 184, 193, 227, 232, 242, 289, 304, 314, 320, 321, 334, 346, 365, 383, 385-390, 408-411
Burke, Edmund, 407
Bush, George H. W., 225, 361
Bush, George W., 74
Butler University, 179

C

Callahan, Christopher, 356
Cambodia, 246
Canada, i, xxiv, 74, 129, 215, 240, 422
Candide, 11, 13, 63, 67
Cantor, Joanne, 204, 205, 207
capital, 91, 108, 275, 395
Capital in the Twenty-First Century, 416
capital punishment, 115
capitalism, xii, xv, xviii, 56, 86, 127, 130, 137, 139, 151, 155, 180, 407
Carson, Richard (Dick) W., 100, 104, 106, 221, 287, 345, 420
Carter, Jimmy, 82
Catholic(s), 55, 56, 313
Catholicism, 56
Cayuse (Native Americans), 171
CBS, 114, 115, 121, 175-177, 179, 180, 182, 185, 419
Ceballos, Richard, 257, 340, 361
Center for Global Media Studies, 139, 208, 211, 215, 217, 225, 335
Central Michigan Life, 79, 93
Central Michigan University, 66, 68, 73, 76, 83, 88, 91, 95, 96, 420
Cervantes, xiii, xvii, xx, 40, 44
Chaffee, Steven, 181, 190, 207
Charles, Ray, 18
Chemerinsky, Erwin, 272, 275, 396, 407, 416, 418
Chile, 203
Chipman, Jayne Benz, 375
Chomsky, Noam, ix, 131, 134, 138
Chronicle of Higher Education, The, 12, 13, 139, 210, 237, 244, 341, 346, 351, 364, 365, 380
City University of New York, 375
civil liberties, xiv, xx, xxii, ii, 5, 9, 10, 65, 90, 92, 110, 136, 152, 165, 176, 179-181, 184, 185, 287, 355, 360, 361, 387, 388, 390, 396, 397, 399-401, 404, 406-409, 411-415, 420, 421
class consciousness, 64, 81
classic model of policymaking, 400

Clinard, Marshall B., 403, 418
Clinger v. New Mexico Highlands University, 346
Clinton, Bill, 6, 74, 342, 360
CNBC, 355
CNN, 355, 407
collegiality, 40-44, 48-50, 159, 165
Columbia Journalism Review, 105, 111
Columbia University, 158, 198, 398
Coming of Age in Samoa, 95
communication scholars, xxii, 189, 200, 204, 205
communism, 78, 89, 176
communists, 19, 78, 88, 89, 173, 175, 176, 405
Comte, Auguste, 69, 71, 72
Congress, vi, 78, 306, 379
Congressional Research Service, 42
conservatives, 115, 202, 307, 370, 389, 395, 399, 404-407, 414, 418
constitutional protection, vi, xix, xxi, xxiii, 3, 371, 372, 376, 393
Constitution, U.S., 64, 188, 269, 339, 363, 414
Cooke, Alistair, 177
Cooper, Gary, 34, 56
Cornell University, 208, 376
Corporate Crime, 404
corporations, xxiii, 11, 74, 85, 102, 123-125, 128, 152, 153, 180, 181, 205, 342, 360, 396, 403, 404, 407, 408, 414, 419
Coser, Lewis, 69
Covid-19, xxiii, 241
Cowles (family), 220-222, 319
Cowles, Elizabeth A. (Betsy), 221, 319
Cowles, (William) Stacey, 221, 222
Craig, Robert L., 136
crime, 11, 15, 18, 65, 68, 69, 77, 92, 97, 99, 104, 109, 113-119, 143, 190, 193, 204, 231, 394, 404, 409
Cronkite School (see Walter Cronkite School)
Crooks, Gary, 249
Cropanzano, Russell, 402, 418

D

Daily Evergreen, The, 12, 187, 319, 320, 345, 353, 359, 384
Daniels, Jeff, 69
DeFleur, Margaret, 215
DeFleur, Melvin, 215
Delta College, 61, 62, 68
Demerath, Peter, 201
Demers v. Austin, vi, x-xiv, xviii-xxiii, 8, 197, 238, 245, 260, 264, 268, 318, 323, 327, 356, 363, 364, 369, 371-381, 383, 384, 389, 390, 393, 403, 411
Demers v. City of Minneapolis, 143

democracy, x, xx, xxi, xxiv, 10, 31, 56, 63, 64, 74, 77, 78, 83, 84, 90, 110, 130, 131, 142, 151, 153, 158, 179, 184, 192, 244, 249, 309, 310, 348, 386-388, 396, 397, 399, 401, 403, 404, 407-409, 413-415
Democracy for the Few, 396, 399
Democrat, 82, 306
Democratic Party, 65, 152, 361
Department of Social Services, Michigan, 98, 99
Descartes, René, 63
Dewey, John, 34, 70, 83, 86
Dickens, Charles, 84
Dictionary of Mass Communication & Media Research, 226, 227, 260
Dinitz, Simon, vii, 114-117, 119-122, 268, 287, 420
discourse ethics, 130, 133
division of labor, 11, 13, 151, 154, 323, 410
Division of Labor in Society, 11, 13, 323
dominant ideology, 59
Donohue, George A., vii, 118, 139, 140
Dow Chemical Company, 10, 101, 102, 105
Du Bois, W. E. B., 207
dull compulsion of economic relationships, 54, 81, 396
Dunwoody, Sharon, vii, 191
Durkheim, Émile, 11, 13, 134, 323, 394

E

Eastern Washington University, 249, 420, 421
economics, 29, 63, 124, 184, 201, 202, 404
economists, 395
Edgerton, Gary R., 179
Edward R. Murrow College of Communication, 3, 5, 6, 12, 180, 182, 261, 268, 300, 301, 303, 307-309, 318-322, 335, 348, 368, 377, 389
Edward R. Murrow: An American Original, 173, 175
Edward R. Murrow School of Communication, 173, 181, 254, 261, 359, 368, 421
Einstein, Albert, 77
Eisenhower, Dwight, 176
elite democratic theory, 397
Ellul, Jacques, 10
Emory University, 342, 398
Endejan, Judith (Judy), 4, 305, 318, 328, 329, 358, 369, 390, 420
Engebretson, Mark, 10, 139, 144-147, 154
England, 61, 62, 135, 215
Enlightenment Now, xxii, 393, 415, 416
Enlightenment, The Age of (Enlightenment Project), i, vi, ix, xi, xiii, xiv, xx-xxii, 2, 61-67, 76, 79, 82, 83, 90, 96, 98, 105, 110-113, 116, 118, 120, 124, 127, 130, 135, 136, 141, 145, 149,
153, 168, 170, 179, 181, 184, 188, 191, 193, 200, 208, 306, 309, 310, 314, 348, 359, 386, 388-390, 393-400, 408, 411-415
ethic of objectivity, 97, 178, 185

F

Faculty Status Committee (FSC), 263, 283, 292
Family Circle, 205
Federal Bureau of Investigation (FBI), 77, 90, 212, 221, 342
First Amendment, i, ii, xiii, xvi, xxi, 3, 8, 10, 12, 19, 22, 25, 33, 37, 42, 44, 46, 49, 90, 117, 121, 156, 159, 164, 165, 188, 216, 233, 257, 268, 269, 271, 275, 286, 287, 295, 296, 305, 306, 318, 320, 321, 335, 339-345, 348, 351, 352, 358, 359, 362, 365-370, 373-383, 419, 422, 433
Fishburne, Laurence, 266
Fisher, Raymond C., 360-362
Fletcher, Betty Binns, 360
Fletcher, William A., 6, 7, 359-362, 365-367
Floyd, Elson S., 194, 195, 248, 249, 254, 256, 265-267, 269, 271, 280, 281, 286, 288, 289, 298-300, 310, 322, 324-327, 331, 332, 334, 335, 345, 346, 369, 384, 389
Floyd, George, 10
Flyvbjerg, Bent, 202
Folkerts, Jean, 267, 335, 336
Ford, Gerald, 82
Formaini, Robert, 202
Fortune, 73, 124, 182
Foundation for Individual Rights in Education (FIRE), 244, 270, 346, 374, 379, 380, 382, 390, 391, 422
Four Tops, 85
Fourth Circuit Court of Appeals, 340, 350
France, 63, 215, 413
Frankenmuth, 54, 55, 57, 62, 68, 97, 422
Frankenmuth News, 422
Frankfurter, Felix, 77
Franklin, Benjamin, 64, 348
freedom, vi, xiii-xix, ii, 10, 16, 29, 33, 34, 37, 63, 65, 69, 78, 90, 95, 118, 125, 127, 128, 140, 151, 153, 163, 179, 181, 184, 188, 190, 192, 231-233, 235, 257, 258, 266, 270, 272, 277, 280, 294, 295, 321, 332, 333, 340-342, 346, 352, 358, 361, 362, 364, 372-379, 384, 385, 387-390, 396, 397, 399, 400, 402, 407, 410-415, 421
Freeman, Derek, 96
French, David A., 270, 341
From Max Weber, 149-151

G

Gandy, Oscar, 191
Garcetti v. Ceballos, xiii, xv, xvi, xviii, xxiv, 8, 257, 258, 260, 340, 341, 346, 350, 351, 359-367, 3700372, 374-379, 380, 381, 403, 407, 409
Gaye, Marvin, 85
Gee, E. Gordon, 110
George Washington University, 194, 335, 361
Gerbner, George, 190
German Social Democratic Party, 152
Germany, 54, 126, 151, 179
Gerson, Jeffrey, 15-18, 20, 21, 30
Gillman, Howard, 272, 275
Gillmor, Donald, 130, 157
Ginsberg, Benjamin, xvi, xviii, 412, 419
Gitlin, Todd, 130, 132, 135, 138
Glaberson, William, 161
Glasser, Theodore L., 131, 204-206
Gleason, Tim, 268, 377, 378
Global Media News, 139, 215
Gorum v. Sessoms, 346
Gottfredson, Mike, 377, 378
Gould, Jack, 177
Graham & Dunn (law firm), 4, 305, 349, 368, 369
Great Britain, 62, 64
Great Society program, 66
Greenberg, Jerald, 402
Guardian Weekly, 177
Gulf of Tonkin, 91

H

Habermas, Jürgen, 130, 131, 132
Hamilton, Alexander, 305
Harvard Law Review, 372, 373, 380, 403
Harvard University, xxii, 83, 96, 172, 204, 356, 372, 393, 395
Hated Ideas and the American Civil War Press, 157
Hayden, Tom, 77
Heider, Fritz, 117, 118, 121, 124, 125
Herman, Edward S., 135
Hertzog, Matthew Jay, 376
High Noon, 34, 56
Hillard, Jan, 32
historians, xxii, 88, 175, 180, 207
history, i, iv, vi, xiv, xix-xxi, 9, 20, 33, 39, 55, 61, 64, 68, 71, 76, 77, 82, 83, 91, 95, 97, 101, 106, 112, 115, 116, 119, 138, 143, 152, 171, 172, 176-178, 183, 189, 194, 199-201, 205, 207, 232, 235, 247, 254, 260, 262, 269, 273, 274, 288, 289, 297, 306, 307, 337, 348, 360, 369, 371, 373, 374, 385, 395-399, 403, 404, 407, 409, 410, 412

History and Future of Mass Media, iv, 152, 178, 199, 232, 260, 262, 273, 274, 398, 410
Hoch, Steven, 288, 289
holacracy, 402
Homer, 390
Hong v. Grant, xxiii, 346
Hoover, J. Edgar, 77, 78
House of Representatives, 148, 379, 415
Houston Chronicle, 355
humanities, xxi, 65, 69, 112, 172, 201, 399, 412, 413
Hume, David, 62
Huron Daily Tribune, 98, 100, 101, 104

I

I. F. Stone's Weekly, 91, 173, 177
Idaho State Journal, 380
ideology, 72, 137, 157, 178, 200, 202, 206, 209, 359, 389, 394, 400-404, 413, 418
Illinois Supreme Court, 170
independents, 414
industrialization, 63, 65, 69
Inside Higher Education, 24, 374, 378, 380-382, 419
Institute of Pacific Relations, 176
internal audit, x, 276, 278, 280-282, 289, 290, 312, 314, 319, 324-326, 331, 337
Internal Audit Office, WSU, 276
Internal Revenue Service (IRS), 116, 221
International Communication Association (ICA), 199, 209
Iowa State University, 94, 133, 155, 161, 165, 436
iron cage, 151, 155, 158
Italy, 157
Ivory Tower of Babel, iv, x, xxi, xxiv, 72, 106, 122, 155, 208, 210, 211, 229, 295, 296, 307, 318, 341, 344, 350-352, 354, 394, 400, 416, 417, 419

J

Jackson, The Rev. Jesse, 190, 204, 207, 393
Jasper, Debra, 111
Jefferson, Thomas, 64, 67, 348, 349, 351, 352, 356, 362, 413, 422
Jesus, 50, 297
John Glenn School of Public Affairs, 111
Jordan, Isamu, 187, 191
journalism, vi, ix, xiv, xx, xxi, 3, 5, 7, 10, 12, 17, 19-22, 25, 26, 28, 30, 31, 33, 34, 41, 44, 46-49, 51, 82, 89-91, 93-97, 100, 101, 104-106, 108-112, 117, 123, 129, 140, 141, 144, 157, 159-161, 163, 164, 173, 177-184, 188-190, 196, 197, 199, 204, 206, 207, 212,

221, 227, 255, 262, 267, 268, 276, 300, 301, 306, 309, 310, 318, 320, 321, 335, 343, 348-350, 352, 355, 356, 358, 366, 368, 377, 378, 386, 388, 389, 397-399, 408, 413, 421
Journalism & Mass Communication Quarterly, 184, 267, 335
journalists, vi, xx, xxii, 10, 16, 25, 27, 32, 39, 42, 57, 65, 89, 90, 97, 104, 105, 108-112, 115, 153, 160, 173, 175, 177, 178, 182, 187, 192, 193, 197, 199, 222, 225, 234, 281, 305, 307, 310, 319, 322, 355, 388, 397, 412, 414

K

Kant, Immanuel, 66
Keillor, Garrison, 129
Kennedy, Anthony M., xvi, 340
Kennedy, George, 60
Kennedy, John F., 180
Kent State University, 17, 75
Kiplinger Letter, 108
Kiplinger Program, 106, 108, 111
Klyukanov, Igor, 420
Krugman, Paul, 396, 416
Kuhn, Thomas S., 200, 209

L

Lasch, Christopher, 88
Laux, John, 141, 144
Law360, 375
Lear, Erich, 182, 195, 236, 243, 255, 319, 328, 329, 389
Learning to Hate Americans, 215
Leary, Timothy, 172
Levy, Rick, 378
Lewiston (Idaho) *Morning Tribune*, 243, 319
liberalism, 179
liberty, 19, 64, 75, 110, 118, 359, 389, 397, 407, 411, 414, 415
Lillie Suburban Newspapers, 147
Lindholdt, Karen, 420
Lindholdt, Paul, 421
Lippman, Walter, 83, 84, 86
Lipton, Douglas, 115
Llewelyn, Doug, 305
lliberal(s), 90, 109, 135, 178, 184, 190, 192, 193, 224, 301, 359, 360, 398, 404-407, 414, 418
Local Planet Weekly, The, 214, 222, 281
Locke, John, 62, 64, 67, 348, 414
London, 54, 135, 152, 179, 344, 407
Lonely Crowd, 127, 128, 315, 320
Lopez, Heather, 265, 266, 272-274, 276-279, 282, 286, 289, 318, 319, 324-326

Los Angeles Times, 74, 355
Louisiana State University, 198, 276
Lukianoff, Greg, 270, 379, 382
Lundman, Richard, vii, 112, 117, 119, 120, 421
Lutheran(s), vi, ix, xiv, xx, 51, 54-57, 59, 64, 79, 104-106, 156, 168, 216, 261, 280, 285, 305

M

MacDougall, Curt, 112
Machiavelli, 196, 198, 235, 242, 245, 307, 388
MacKinnon, Catharine, 85
Madison, James, 64
mainstream researchers, 402
mainstream social scientists, 124, 137, 138, 297
Man of La Mancha, xvii
Manufacturing Consent, 134, 135
Marcet, Marco, vii
Marcuse, Herbert, 126, 132
Marquette Books, 208, 215, 216, 226, 249, 254, 265, 272, 276-282, 297, 306, 335, 341, 349, 352, 390, 421
Martin, Steve (professor), xix
Martinson, Robert, 114-117, 120
Marx, Karl, 18, 45, 64, 67, 86, 89, 94, 135, 137-139, 184, 186, 308, 413
Marxism, 89, 135
Marxist, 135, 137, 308
mass communication, xiv, xxii, 5, 12, 17, 20, 21, 76, 110, 111, 113, 117, 119, 129, 130, 134-136, 150, 153, 157, 159, 160, 175, 178, 181-184, 189, 190, 196, 199, 200, 202, 204, 207, 208, 212, 215, 217, 225-227, 244, 250, 251, 254, 255, 260, 262, 265, 267, 268, 271, 273, 276, 300, 303, 304, 307, 309, 310, 319, 335, 349, 355, 356, 366, 373, 389, 398
mass media, iv, xx, 3, 5, 12, 37, 76, 89, 110, 117, 126-128, 130, 131, 134, 135, 137, 152, 153, 158, 178, 184, 189, 190, 199, 205, 207, 208, 215, 217, 232, 234, 244, 260, 262, 273, 274, 291, 301, 310, 333, 355, 377, 398, 405, 410
Mass Communication & Society, 436
mathematics, 20, 26, 172, 182, 200
McCain, John, 88
McCall, George J., 66
McCarthy, Joseph R., 130, 173, 175-179
McCarthyism, 90, 175, 177, 397
McCullough v. University of Arkansas, 346
McLeod, Jack, 181
McSweeney, Frances, 231, 232, 251, 252, 257, 265, 286, 287, 290-295, 297, 319, 328, 329, 331, 333, 389
Mead, Margaret, 95-97
media violence, 205, 207

medical sciences, 200, 394
Merrill, John C., 136, 216
Merton, Robert K., 152
Miami Herald, 355
Michels, Robert, 151, 155, 158
Michigan State Police, 103
Midland (Michigan), 10, 101
Midland Daily News, 101-103, 106, 158
Midland Police Department, 103
Miller, Jerome G., 114
Mills, C. Wright, i, xiv, xx, 149, 396
Milwaukee Sentinel, 30
Minneapolis Civil Rights Commission, 145
Minneapolis police, x, 10, 140, 141, 143, 144, 149-151, 158, 192
Minneapolis Star Tribune, 140, 355
Minnesota Court of Appeals, 142, 144, 149
Minnesota Department of Revenue, 158
Minnesota Supreme Court, 10, 142-144
Mittelhammer, Ron, 384
Montesquieu, 62, 64
Mortimer, Jeylan T., vii
Moscow-Pullman Daily News, 169, 188, 319, 348
movies, 56, 57, 65, 128, 157, 205
Mummolo, Ronina, 376
murder, x, 19, 100, 117, 168, 170, 193, 305
Murrow, Edward R., viii, xii, 3, 12, 173, 175, 177, 178, 180, 181, 254, 255, 261, 265, 319, 348, 350, 359, 368, 413, 421
Murrow programs, 195, 267

N

Nashville Tennessean, 153
National Cancer Institute, 204
National Guard, 74, 76, 170
National Rifle Association, 378
Native Americans (of the Palouse), 129, 171
natural science(s), 69, 183, 202, 393
NCAA, 42, 45, 378
Nelson, Willlie, 50
Nethercutt, George, 436
New York Herald Tribune, 177
New York Times, The, 78-80, 153, 161, 162, 165, 177, 178, 225, 307, 384, 391, 395, 396, 407, 416, 419
Newman, Paul, 48, 57
Newspaper Research Journal, 184
newspapers, 12, 27, 42, 97, 98, 109, 142, 147, 152, 153, 158, 160, 161, 163, 184, 188, 199, 281, 289, 364, 366, 409, 436
Newsweek, 177
Newton, Isaac, 62

Nichols, Suzanne (Sue), vii, 28, 90, 93, 97, 100, 421
Ninth Circuit Court of Appeals, xiii, xix, xxi, 3, 6, 12, 348-352, 355, 358-365, 367-369, 371-377, 379, 383, 389, 393, 403, 422
Nixon Administration, 83
Nixon, Richard, 73, 76
norms, 41, 69, 127, 207, 270
Northwestern University, 198, 359
Nothing Works, 114

O

Oakland University, 95, 96, 100
Obama, Barack, 135, 399
Obergefell v. Hodges, 415
objectivity, 97, 178, 185, 306, 312, 325, 397 (also see "ethic of objectivity")
Oedipus the King, 235
Oh, Cheol H., 202
Ohio State University, The 106, 108-111, 113, 114, 116, 117, 119, 123, 173, 189, 190, 204, 215, 268, 288, 398, 436
Olien, Clarice N., 139, 140
Olympia, 171, 172
Ormond, Sharon J., 375
Orwell, George, 344
Overseas Press Club, 177
Oxford University, 360

P

Pacific Northwest Newspaper Association, 183
Paine, Thomas, 64
Palmer, Ted, 115
palouse, x, 167, 168, 170, 171, 230, 369
Palus (Native Americans), 170, 171
Parenti, Michael, 396
Fackrell, Pat, 376
PBS Newshour, 355
Pearce, Mona, 22, 37, 38, 48, 129, 143, 147, 156, 162, 164, 168, 421
Pentagon Papers, 78
Perlmutter, David, 421
Persico, Joseph E., 173-175, 178, 179, 185, 186
Peterson, Patrice, 36, 46, 421
Pew Research Center, 31, 105
Pezeshki, Charles, 248
Pickering v. Board of Education of Township High School District, 205, Will County, 258, 260, 362, 365, 366
Piketty, Thomas, 395, 416
Pintak, Lawrence, 301, 307-310, 330, 331
Pioneer Press Dispatch, 16, 17
Plato, 83, 244

political parties, 77, 130, 151
political science, 15, 17, 31, 32, 61, 83, 131, 183, 190, 196, 201, 202, 266, 371
political scientists, xxii
Porter, Michael, 375
positivism, 69
poverty, 65, 77, 84, 109, 204, 394

power, xiv, xix, xxi, ii, 5, 12, 19, 27, 31, 33, 38, 43, 48, 49, 57, 62, 64, 65, 77, 79, 83, 97, 98, 100, 111, 112, 125-127, 134, 135, 142, 148-151, 153, 158, 175, 178, 193, 195, 196, 199, 225, 231, 233-236, 242, 263, 265, 267, 273, 281, 286, 293, 298, 304, 308, 309, 314, 319-321, 334, 339, 344, 352, 374, 386, 388, 393-397, 399-403, 406, 407, 409-415
Pratt, Edwin, 193
press, the, ii, 10, 65, 78, 83, 92, 135, 158, 160, 188, 193, 445
Princeton University, 342
Principles of Sociology, 69
Pritchard, Charles L., 225
professionalization, xvi
Prometheus, 39
Protestant(s), 125-128, 313
psychologists, 9, 181
public discourse, 131
public policymaking, xxi, xxii, 152, 200, 203, 297, 354, 394, 398
public sphere, 396
Publishers Weekly, xxiv, 417
Pullman (Washington), 162, 168-171, 175, 188, 192, 193, 212, 213, 230-232, 246, 248, 285, 310, 319, 322, 326, 332, 348
Pullman Police Department, 168, 192
punishment, 39, 115, 117, 235, 242, 256, 257, 276, 330, 331, 351, 373, 403
quantitative research, 110, 112, 124

Q

Quill, 160, 163, 164, 165
Quist, Gordon J., 361, 362

R

Rabban, David M., 373, 380
radio, 9, 22, 73, 129, 144, 180, 221, 397
Rand, Ayn, 38, 44, 126, 127, 132, 138, 303
Rawlins, Lane, 246, 254, 255, 270
Reagan, Joey, 262, 271, 273
reason, viii, ii, 10, 29, 30, 49, 50, 62-64, 78, 97, 118, 135, 137, 144, 150, 175, 197, 202, 203, 235, 244, 247, 263, 281, 287, 290, 293, 300, 313, 314, 319, 359, 365, 372, 373, 389, 393, 394, 396, 400, 403, 406, 411, 413, 415
recidivism, 115
Reckless, Walter C., 120
Redford, Robert, 82
rehabilitation, 114-117
Reichert, Peggy, 139
representative democracy, xx, 31, 78
Republican Party, 361
Republican(s), 15, 65, 127, 173, 175, 176, 306, 359, 361, 394, 396, 406, 407, 445
Rhoades, Gary D., i, ix, xii, xv, xviii, 333, 421
Rich, Robert F., 202, 204, 206, 209-211
Richardson, Herbert, 312
Riesman, David, 127, 128, 132, 151, 153, 184, 303, 315, 320, 321
Robber Barons, 69, 407
Rochester, 95-97
Rochester Clarion, 95
Rockefeller, John D., 173
Rockefeller III, John D., 77
Rogers, Jim, 144
role of social science, 203
Roosevelt, Eleanor, 77
Rosenman, Robert E., 353
Ross, Edward A., viii, 69-72
Roth, Edward, vii
Russian Revolution, 152

S

Sadid, Habib, xix, xxiii
Sadid v. Idaho State University, xxiii
SAT, 20, 43, 79, 110, 172, 263
Savage v. Gee, 346
Schmidt, Peter, 13, 346, 351, 352, 356
Schmidt, Rudolph, vii
Scholtz, Gregory F., 333
Schulte, Henry, vii, 109, 173
Schulz, John, 421
Schulz, Kirk, 384
Scott, Joseph E., 117, 119-121, 421
Scottsdale, Arizona, 123
Seattle, 3, 4, 9, 11, 170-172, 183, 188, 189, 193, 207, 222, 225, 247, 255, 277, 305, 307, 319, 336, 348, 369, 384
Seattle Times, 172, 189, 222, 255, 319, 348, 369, 384
security, xv, 15, 82, 83, 90, 118, 123, 125, 160, 225, 322, 386-389, 399, 400, 402, 415
Seguin, Peter, 30
Senate, iv, xiii, xvi, 31, 32, 77, 92, 93, 248, 321, 322, 334, 342, 349, 353, 354, 363-365, 371, 377, 379, 403, 415

Shaw, George Bernard, viii, 243
Shaw, Kenneth, 16
Simon, Paul, 190
Sinclair, Upton, 173
Sinekopova, Galina, 421
Smith, Adam, 62, 81
Smith, Dean O., 375, 381
social liberalism, 136
social movements, xvi, 135, 207, 409
social psychologists, 181
social sciences, iv, xxi, 65, 71, 96, 113, 120, 125, 131, 152, 201-204, 208, 350, 354, 366, 394, 399-402, 412, 413, 436
social structure, 152, 247, 407
Society for Collegiate Journalists, 436
Society of Professional Journalists (SPJ), 25, 26, 29-34, 37, 42, 160, 310
Sociological Imagination, ix, xiv, xx, 68
sociologists, xxii, 54, 68-71, 114, 151, 158, 202, 295, 322, 408, 410, 411
sociology, i, vi, xx, xxi, 66, 68-71, 88, 89, 98, 117, 119, 123, 127, 130, 131, 140, 149, 150, 152, 158, 183, 190, 200-203, 208, 240, 251, 333, 390, 399, 422, 436
Sonntag, Brian, 324-327, 331
Sophocles, 235
Souter, David H., 340
Southern Illinois University, 190
Spokesman-Review, 12, 172, 187, 213, 220-223, 231, 248, 249, 270, 281, 289, 318, 319
St. Lorenz Lutheran School, 55
St. Paul Pioneer Press Dispatch, 16, 17
Stanford, Jane Eliza Lathrop, 70
Stanford University, 20, 69, 70, 72, 128, 140, 159, 190, 204, 360, 402
State Board of Equalization Study, 147
State Department, 102, 175, 176, 230, 231
State Press, The, 359
Steele, Norma, 109
Steely Dan, 18
Steptoe, Lt. Col. Edward J., 171
Stewart, Jimmy, 56
Stimson, William, 174
Stone, I. F. (Izzy), 5, 8, 12, 90, 91, 92, 94, 173
Struckmeyer, Ken, 248, 281-283, 290-294, 303
Student Press Law Center, 29, 160, 187, 191
Student Voice, 27, 29, 32, 33, 160
Students for a Democratic Society (SDS), 77, 78, 130, 131
subjectivity, 178
Suko, Lonny R., 318
Sullivan, Thomas, 373
Sumner, William Graham, 70
survey research, 124

T

Tallman, John, 26, 47
Tan, Alex, 190, 226, 232, 236, 242, 243, 252, 259, 262, 268, 278, 300, 421
Tanick, Marshall, 158-164
Tarbell, Ida, 173
technology, 10, 110, 112, 134, 182, 200, 376, 393, 401
television, 56, 115, 124, 169, 170, 175, 177, 180, 205, 355
Terminiello v. City of Chicago, 94
Terrell, W. Glenn, 247
Texaco, Inc. v. Hasbrouck, 346
Texas v. Johnson, 15, 22
The American Institute of Stress, 9
The Case Against the Supreme Court, 416, 418
The Envy of Excellence, x, 244, 312, 315
The Fall of the Faculty, xviii, 419
The Fountainhead, 38, 44, 126, 128, 132, 274
The Great Gatsby, 56
The Ivory Tower of Babel, iv, xxi, 71, 96, 120, 152, 202, 204, 208, 296, 307, 341, 344, 350, 352, 354, 394, 400, 401, 409
The Lonely Crowd, 127, 132, 315, 320
The Man in the Grey Flannel Suit, 126
The Media Essays, 13, 224, 227
The Menace of the Corporate Newspaper, iv, 94, 155, 161, 165, 436
The Organization Man, 125, 126, 131, 400
The Power Elite, 416, 417
The Prince, 198, 242, 245
The Public Interest, 115, 120
The Republic, 83, 86
The Social Contract, 66
The Structure of Scientific Revolutions, 209
The Theory of Social and Economic Organization, 44, 154
The Theory of Communicative Action, 130, 132
The Theory of the Leisure Class, 56, 60
The Whole World Is Watching, 130, 132, 138-139
Thibodeau, Gary, 16, 18, 26, 27, 29, 31, 32, 50
Thomas Jefferson Center for the Protection of Free Expression, 349, 351, 352, 356, 362, 422
Tichenor, Phillip J., vii, 79, 139, 140, 150, 158, 163, 287, 421
Times Higher Education, 315
Toledo Blade, 142, 145
Tripp, Thomas M., 399, 417
Truman, Harry S., 78
Trump, Donald, 74, 75, 83, 207, 209, 331, 394, 397, 399, 416
truth, ix, 11, 55, 64, 84, 89, 96, 98, 101, 114, 116, 153, 158, 178, 179, 184, 200, 232, 250, 272,

273, 303, 320, 332, 333, 337, 341, 344, 370-373, 388, 394, 401, 408, 420
Turnbull, David Ray, 353, 357
Turner, Brian S., 59
Twin Cities Reader, 10, 143-145, 147-149

U

U.S. District Court, 8, 165, 318, 319, 323, 327, 334, 339, 342, 345, 348, 358
U.S. government, 77, 124, 180, 206
U.S. House of Representatives, 379
U.S. News & World Report, 23, 77, 355, 416
U.S. Senate, 92
U.S. Supreme Court, xiii, 4, 5, 15, 19, 20, 22, 23, 27, 90, 110, 121, 145, 257, 340, 342, 359, 360, 364, 367, 393, 403, 407
United Kingdom (UK), 42, 202, 312
United States, vi, xvi, xix-21, 25, 55, 66, 68, 76, 77, 84, 88, 100, 115, 123, 135, 152, 171, 180, 182, 184, 195, 207, 214-216, 225, 250, 265, 267, 300, 328, 332, 342, 368, 379, 396, 400
University of Arizona, i, xii, xvii, 214, 390
University of California system, 376
University of California, Santa Barbara, 207
University of California at Berkeley, 198, 394
University of California, Irvine, xix
University of Chicago, 418
University of Delaware, 340, 373
University of Florida, 198
University of Georgia, 215, 398
University of Idaho, 170, 172, 324, 326, 376
University of Illinois, 198, 202, 412
University of Kansas, 378, 379
University of Michigan, 23, 121, 340, 360, 398, 409
University of Minnesota, 17, 121, 129, 131, 134, 139, 140, 155, 118, 153, 156, 159, 183, 197, 198, 201, 201, 203, 340, 356, 409, 436
University of Missouri, 198, 248, 265, 266
University of New Mexico, 336, 365
University of North Carolina–Wilmington, xix, 241, 340, 350
University of North Carolina at Chapel Hill, 266
University of Oregon Board of Trustees, 378
University of Oregon, 268, 377, 378, 381, 409
University of Pennsylvania, 135, 191
University of Texas, 99, 135, 190
University of Virginia, 374, 378, 413
University of Washington, 172, 189, 255, 336, 398
University of Wisconsin–Madison, 191, 204
University of Wisconsin–River Falls (UW-RF), ix, xiv, 1, 15-23, 25, 28, 29, 31-33, 35, 40, 41, 44,
46, 47, 49, 154, 156, 158, 160, 164, 165, 183, 188, 196, 197, 222, 223, 272, 285, 303, 421
Urban, David, 375
urbanization, 63, 65
Ursich, Antoinette M., 289

V

Vailas, Arthur C., 371
values, xiv, xx, xxi, 17, 69, 75, 79, 90, 124, 127, 128, 147, 148, 153, 158, 178, 179, 222, 270, 310, 322, 362, 373, 394, 400, 406
Variety, 20, 25, 177, 252, 336, 408
Veblen, Thorstein, 56
Vietnam War, 58, 59, 63, 65-68, 74, 75, 79, 88, 89, 101, 106, 128, 130, 134, 135, 307
violence on television, 205
Viswanath, K., 131, 204, 205
Voice of America, 176
Voltaire, 11, 13, 61-64, 66, 67, 348, 413, 414

W

Wackman, Dan, 159
Walker, Carolyn, ii, 422
Walla Walla (Native Americans), 171
Wallace, Mike, 115
Walter Cronkite School of Journalism and Mass Communication, 12, 182, 355, 358, 363
war, 4, 15, 57-59, 63-66, 68, 73-79, 88, 89, 101, 126, 128, 130, 134, 135, 152, 157, 172, 179, 202, 216, 246, 247, 307, 344, 384, 394, 396, 420
Ward, Frank Lester, 69, 71, 72
Wartella, Ellen, 191
Washington Post, The, 20, 80, 82, 89, 93, 111, 120, 355, 416, 418
Washington state Department of Ecology, 230
Washington state Human Rights Commission, 247
Washington State Democratic Central Committee, 247
Washington State University (WSU), vi, xii, xiii, xv, xvi, xix, xx, 3, 5, 10, 12, 137, 153, 162, 163, 165, 168, 170-173, 175, 180-183, 185, 187-189, 192-197, 216, 217, 225, 226, 230-233, 236, 237, 240, 243, 246-249, 252, 254-256, 258, 259, 261-263, 265-273, 277, 278, 280, 281, 283, 285-290, 292, 293, 295, 296, 300-305, 310, 312, 314, 318-332, 324-326, 328, 330-337, 339-345, 348, 349-353, 358, 359, 364-369, 377, 383-386, 389, 409, 411-413, 421, 422
Wayne, John, 56
Wealth of Nations, 81

Weather Underground Organization, 77
Weber, George H., 67
Weber, Max, 41, 44, 134, 149-151, 154, 155, 158
Weisman, Steven R., 225
Weiss, Carol, 209, 210
Weizmann, Chaim, 77
Welcome to the Ivory Tower, 341
Wershba, Joseph, 177
Westhues, Kenneth, i, xxiv, 240, 241, 244, 273, 312-315, 335, 338, 422
Whaley, Robert H., 318, 339, 342-345, 348
White, Lawrence, 373, 380
Whitney v. California, 23, 223
Whyte, William Foote, 208, 211
Whyte Jr., William H., 124-128, 131, 132, 151, 153, 184, 211, 321
Wicklein, John, 113
Wielgus, Robert, 383, 384,
Wilson, William Julius, 172

Willis, Margaret Y., vii
Wills, Frank, 82, 83
Wilson, Sloan, 126, 132
Winona Research, 123, 125, 128, 129
Wisconsin Attorney General, 26
Wolfe, Tom, 88, 94
Woodward, Bob, 82, 86, 89, 173
workplace mobbing, i, vi, x, xvi, xix-xxi, 2, 240, 241, 244, 267, 273, 295, 299, 302, 312-315, 335
World War II, 4, 57, 58, 126, 172, 179, 202
Wright, Col. George, 171
WSU Board of Regents, 246, 248, 319
WSU Faculty Senate, xiii, 321, 322, 334, 349, 353, 364

Z

Zehnder Sr., William, 54, 55
Zeus, 39

Responses from Officials Mentioned in the Book

ALL INDIVIDUALS named and associated with controversies identified in this book were provided with drafts of this manuscript and were invited to provide criticisms and comments. Their responses are printed verbatim at the end of this book and at <www.MarquetteBooks.com/response.html>. Pseudonyms are used for some individuals. Real names are used for public officials and public figures.

Verbatim response from Ron Mittelhammer, former dean of the College of Agriculture (e-mailed March 29, 2021)

> Thank you for providing me with the opportunity to observe how you referred to me in your upcoming book. Regarding the following quote from your book:
>
>> "Wielgus told the [New York] Times that, at one point, Ron Mittelhammer, who was dean of the College of Agriculture at the time, ordered him not to speak to the public about wolves without coordinating with the university."
>
> What is true about that statement is that Wielgus did tell the Times that I "ordered him not to speak to the public about wolves without coordinating with the university." What is patently false about that statement? I never ordered him to do anything of the kind. I am well aware of the First Amendment to the U.S. Constitution.
>
> He chose to interpret our interactions in the light he did, but it misrepresented my interactions with him. I will give you the short version, focusing on the two principal germane issues. First of all, I told him that there is such a thing as freedom of speech for citizens of the United States, and speaking as a private citizen, he can say anything that the law allows. As you well know, David, that is a very widely scoped right in our country. But I also said that he should be careful not to implicate WSU in any purely personal opinions or conjectures that were not solidly scientifically supported by his WSU research program. I simply asked

for him to differentiate the two sources of messaging and make explicit that he was speaking or writing purely as a private citizen when called for.

Secondly, regarding me allegedly ordering him not to speak to the public without coordinating with the university first, what that really entailed was an offer from the College to provide him with communication advice and resources that he might use to help ensure that communications issues by him were not inadvertently misinterpreted. Wielgus himself was complaining that his statements and messages were sometimes being misinterpreted by some, and in order to help mitigate that problem, he was offered communications assistance. He, in fact, voluntarily availed himself of that offer/service on a number of occasions. But he was never ordered to do so.

I hope that provides you with some additional perspective on these issues. Even my short version above is likely too much detail for you to incorporate wholly in your book, and it likely doesn't support the narrative in that section of your book. But that is what really happened, and I hope in some form you provide some additional context. Thank you.

Verbatim response to Mittelhammer's comment from Robert Wielgus, former WSU professor whose research on wolves angered state and WSU officials (e-mailed March 29, 2021)

What BS. Both my graduate students and myself were told not to speak to the press or even publish scientific papers without WSU consent. When I wrote 12 drafts with WSU consent of my annual report and press release, the dean okayed the report. After release of the WSU sanctioned report, he condemned it and me in public at the WDFW WAG [Washington Department of Fish and Wildlife/Wolf Advisory Group] meeting with state representative Joel Kretz (Republican, Wacounda). Then they charged me with illegal political lobbying (contact with WA representatives) and use of state resources (e-mail) to submit my report to the WA legislature and WDFW WAG. He is a liar and was a shill for WA representative Joel Kretz.

About the Author

David Demers worked as a newspaper reporter, market research analyst, and journalism and mass media sociology professor for four decades before embarking on a full-time writing career.

He is author or editor of 17 books, including *The Ivory Tower of Babel: Why the Social Sciences Are Failing to Live Up to Their Promises* (New York: Algora, 2011); *History and Future of Mass Media: An Integrated Perspective* (Cresskill, NJ: Hampton Press, 2007); and *The Menace of the Corporate Newspaper: Fact or Fiction?* (Ames: Iowa State University Press, 1996).

In the 1970s, he earned a bachelor's degree in journalism from Central Michigan University and worked for three different newspapers in Michigan, earning two statewide first-place awards for investigative reporting. During the 1980s, he earned master's degrees in journalism and sociology from The Ohio State University and was senior research analyst for a national marketing research company in Phoenix, Arizona.

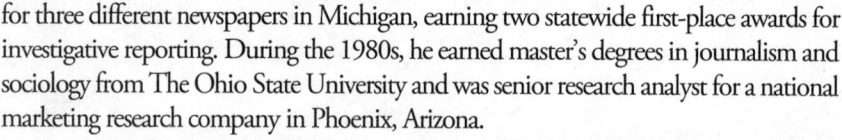

In 1992, he earned a Ph.D. in mass communication from the University of Minnesota. From the late 1980s to 2013, he taught courses in mass media theory, media and society, news reporting, media history, criminology, and media and constitutional law at The Ohio State University, University of Wisconsin-River Falls, University of Minnesota, Washington State University and Arizona State University.

Demers's research specialties include organizational structure, social systems theory, and mass media law. His research on corporate media structure has earned five national scholarly paper awards. In 2010, the Society for Collegiate Journalists honored Demers with the Louis Ingelhart Freedom of Expression Award, which is given to individuals who contribute to freedom of expression at the risk of personal and/or professional cost.

He is founding editor of *Mass Communication & Society* and also founded and directed the nonprofit Center for Global Media Studies and Marquette Books LLC, a private company that has published more than 150 academic and trade titles. Demers has served as a consultant to public and private companies and individuals, including former Congressman George Nethercutt. He lives in Phoenix and is writing a dystopian novel that carries the Enlightenment themes in this book to a youthful audience.